LIFE-WRITINGS BY BRITISH WOMEN, 1660–1815

LIFE-WRITINGS
BY BRITISH WOMEN
1660–1850

AN ANTHOLOGY

Edited by Carolyn A. Barros and Johanna M. Smith

Northeastern University Press
BOSTON

Northeastern University Press

Library of Congress Cataloging-in-Publication Date

Life-writings by British women, 1660–1815 : an anthology /
ed., Carolyn A. Barros and Johanna M. Smith.

p.   cm.

Includes bibliographical references.

ISBN 1-55553-432-5 (cloth : alk. paper)—

ISBN 1-55553-431-7 (pbk. : alk. paper)

1. English prose literature—Women authors. 2. English prose
literature—Early modern, 1500–1700. 3. English prose literature—
18th century. 4. English prose literature—19th century. 5. Women—
Great Britian—Biography. 6. Women authors, English—Biography.
7. Autobiography—Women authors. I. Barros, Carolyn A.
II. Smith, Johanna M.

PR1286.W6 L54   2000

828'.08—dc21   99-086617

Designed by Ann Twombly. Composed in Bembo by
Binghamton Valley Composition, Binghamton, New York.
Printed and bound by Edwards Brothers, Inc.,
Lillington, North Carolina. The paper is
EB Natural, an acid-free stock.

MANUFACTURED IN THE UNITED STATES OF AMERICA

04   03   02   01   00   5   4   3   2   1

Contents

Illustrations

Editors' Note

We hope this book will meet a number of needs. We included a wide range of texts, in part to facilitate a number of classroom uses: courses in eighteenth-century literature, in women's writing, in early modern history, in autobiography. Although we arranged the selections chronologically, they could of course have been arranged in a number of other ways and according to a number of thematics. The opening Introduction suggests some of these thematics, and it also includes both historical and generic information about the lives and life-writing of British women in the long eighteenth century. Each headnote is specific to its author and text, but we also meant the heatnotes to be used in conjunction with the Introduction, so that each author and text is situated historically and generically.

Except where noted, all selections were taken from the first extant edition of the text. We have modernized the long s and silently corrected obvious typographical errors but otherwise retained original spelling and punctuation. By and large, the explanatory footnotes were provided by the volume editors; footnotes written by an author are indicated by the author's name in brackets.

LIFE-WRITINGS BY BRITISH WOMEN, 1660–1815

Introduction

Women's Lives and Life-Writing in the Long Eighteenth Century

WOMEN'S LIVES

The term "women's lives" might seem straightforward enough, but it teeters on the brink of two assumptions which feminist theory has called into question: that "women" is an inclusive term and that "lives" is an unproblematic one. While "women" seems to take in all humans meeting a particular set of biological criteria, this very inclusiveness may function to elide cultural differences between women—differences of sexuality, ethnicity, class, or occupation—which may be at least as defining for some women as gender is for others. The word "women" may also occlude the historical specificity of women's material conditions, the specific ways in which some women at some times have been oppressed or empowered, and particularly the ways in which some women at some times have themselves been oppressors.

The term "lives" might seem a way to correct these occlusions, for it indicates a focus on the real experiences of real women. To some extent this is true: certainly it would be instructive to compare the lives of such privileged women as Lady Fanshawe and Lady Mary Wortley Montagu with those of their servants. But it is difficult to make such comparisons because we are far less likely to have records of servants' experiences than of ladies'. Furthermore, textual records cannot provide direct access to experience. In other words, "experience" is a "category that mediates between the raw material data of a life and its cultural construction as subjectivity" (Donaldson 137), and often that mediation occurs in a text. Hence we can know the real experiences of real women only through the filter of a textual record, and a partial record at that.

If all these caveats are kept in mind, the texts in this book can tell us much about "women's lives" during the long eighteenth century, for they were written in a variety of forms for a variety of reasons. They range from autobiographies traditionally conceived (for example, a full record of a life or a linear narrative of development or change) through letters, journals, travel narratives, apologies (for specific acts or general conduct), appeals (for funds, justice, and so on), testimonies (generally of spiritual conversion), and adventures (for example, in cross-dressing). This diversity signals the rich mix of women's experiences, class and occupational position, and gendered status in Britain between the restoration of the Stuart monarchy in 1660 and the end of the Napoleonic Wars in 1815.

These years constitute the period known as the long eighteenth century. Like all such periodizations, this one is somewhat arbitrary, and to understand the significance of its opening point, the Restoration, we need to begin somewhat earlier, with the religious and political tumult of the 1640s and 1650s. When Charles I came to the throne in 1625, he was a beneficiary of the ideology of divine right, the belief that a king had been appointed and anointed by God to rule. This political principle had religious and social ramifications: religious, because the king of England was also head of the national or established Church of England; and social, because the hierarchy of government served as a model for the hierarchies of master and servant, employer and employee, husband and wife, parent—especially father—and child. It would be difficult to overestimate, then, the impact of events in the 1640s and 1650s; in Christopher Hill's phrase, the world turned upside down. The civil war between Royalists and Puritan Parliamentarians began in 1641 with the rebellion of Catholics in Ireland against Protestant rule; it concluded in 1649 when the victorious Parliamentarians beheaded King Charles, abolished the House of Lords as well as the monarchy, and disestablished the established church. In the 1650s, under Oliver Cromwell and then his son, Richard, England was a commonwealth rather than a divine-right monarchy.

Although the world turned right side up with the restoration of the monarchy, the aristocracy, and the established church in 1660, the consequences of the previous twenty years' upheaval were immense, and many of them appear in the lives and texts of the women in this anthology. One of the most important effects was the proliferation of dissenting theologies and religious practices. "Dissenters" was the blanket term for all those who separated themselves in some way from the community of the Church of England, but they were by no means united themselves. Among the sects were Fifth Monarchists, Presbyterians, Baptists of various stripes, Congregationalists, Quakers, Diggers and Levellers and Ranters, independents and separatists and seekers.

Two of these groups in particular demonstrate the dislocation of authority relations that continued even after the Restoration. The first, mentioned in passing in Margaret Fell Fox's *Relation*, is the Fifth Monarchists.

They believed that the execution of Charles I had concluded the first four empires of earthly government and presaged the fifth monarchy, "the literal descent and direct rule of King Jesus" (Ormsby-Lennon 73); hence they opposed the restoration of earthly government in the person of King Charles II. More broadly, the Fifth Monarchists represent opposition to the principle of divine-right monarchy, an opposition that affected the other authority relations for which monarchy had been the paradigm.

Here a second group of Dissenters—the Quakers—becomes especially significant. In keeping with the egalitarianism signaled by their name, the Society of Friends, they refused the social and legal signs of subordination: they addressed all individuals with the familiar "thee" and "thou" rather than the formal and respectful "you"; instead of arcane or learned language, they spoke in what they called plain language; crucially, they refused to swear political oaths of loyalty and allegiance and the judicial oaths that attested the truth of legal testimony. If these were spiritual practices—the refusal of worldly standards of honor, distinction, and truth—they were also political and social practices, for they resisted the class stratification on which English society still, albeit somewhat shakily, rested. Such practices had material consequences, for women as well as men. Women in the book trade were prosecuted for printing and selling radical texts; while most of these texts were written by men, women were important in "material production and circulation" (Bell 192) and indeed were at greater risk than the often anonymous authors. Nor is it coincidental that a period in which women recovered their earlier authority as religious teachers, leaders, and prophets also saw a "new wave of witchcraft persecution" (Stuard 10). Persecution of every sort is a recurring thematic in the spiritual autobiographies and conversion narratives represented in this book. Mary Pennington was only one of many who lost property in legal actions "because we could not swear" (41). Margaret Fell Fox was only one of many imprisoned under laws, such as the Quaker Act of 1662 and the Conventicle Act of 1664, which penalized those who refused the oath of allegiance and held or attended religious meetings. Although Mary Churchman was not herself imprisoned, her *Memoirs* records other material effects of persecution. Like Churchman's, Agnes Beaumont's text shows that dissenting women might be persecuted in the domestic as well as the public realm.

The domestic struggles of these women demonstrate the impact of religious dissent on relations of class and gender. This impact was uneven, because hierarchical relations of class and gender interpenetrated but were variously weighted. As women of property, for example, Fell Fox and

Pennington had class advantages that included the "fair degree of autonomy" allowed women (Trevett). As wives, they seem to have benefited from the Quaker ideal of companionate marriage, and Fell Fox was further valorized as one of the "mothers in Israel," women who combined religious and administrative activities with "more conventional" domestic duties (Mack, "Gender" 54). If the Quaker ideal of marriage was antithetical to the property-based standard for marriage among the upper orders, however, it was not irreconcilable with a gender ideology of women's subordination. The consequent potential for conflict between spiritual equality and "practical equality" (Wilcox 31) is particularly evident in the narratives of Churchman and Beaumont. Daughters of prosperous men, both had the advantages of class, but they were also disadvantaged by a domestic hierarchy in which a daughter was subject to, and economically dependent on, her father. Churchman's and Beaumont's narratives record struggles and negotiations with their fathers, actual resistance as well as "writing contra-dictions" (Spargo 173). As these texts thus indicate the contradictory nature of "pious rebellion" (Camden 6), they also suggest how gender hierarchies had been affected but not dismantled by decades of civil war and religious dissent.

Certainly the Restoration delivered at least some of the hoped-for political and social stability. Although Lady Fanshawe's *Memoirs* begins with the years of civil war in which she and her husband were Royalists on the run, it concludes with a description of the years Sir Richard Fanshawe served as the restored monarch's ambassador to the court of Madrid. Written for her son as a memorial of a much-loved husband, Lady Fanshawe's text shows the stability in gendered relations that a happy marriage might provide. Yet the fact that it took three years for the widowed Lady Fanshawe to pry compensation for her husband's services out of Charles II indicates the financial difficulties that destabilized his government. Religious controversies also continued throughout the Restoration period: Fell Fox's several audiences with Charles on behalf of persecuted Quakers is one indication, and another is Churchman's complaint that his reign was "bringing in Popery [at] a great pace" (66). Similar and widespread suspicions of Stuart Catholicism fueled first a panic in 1678 over the alleged Popish Plot against the government, and then repeated efforts to exclude Charles's Catholic brother, James, from the succession. This Exclusion Crisis is a particularly striking instance of how problematic the analogy between king/state and father/family could be: the crisis came about because, despite having (as John Dryden's poem "Absolom and Achitophel" cheekily put it) "scattered his maker's image throughout the land," Charles had not fathered a legitimate heir to the throne. At Charles's death in 1685, his brother succeeded to the throne as James II. Within three years, however, James's Declarations of Indulgence to Catholics and Dissenters had so alienated powerful factions in Parliament that several peers secretly invited William of Orange, husband of James's daughter, Mary, and a Protestant, to invade England.

William and Mary's accession to the throne in 1689 is known as the Glorious Revolution because it was a relatively peaceful transition, yet it inaugurated decades of war over European territories and colonial possessions. England warred with France from 1689 to 1697, and all but one year of Queen Anne's twelve-year reign (1702–1714) were given over to the War of the Spanish Succession. From the treaty which concluded that war in 1713, England gained the asiento, the monopoly right to supply slaves for the colonies in Spanish America. Until the abolition of the slave trade in 1807, England was thus one leg of the infamous golden triangle: a ship took trade goods from England to Africa, exchanged the goods for slaves and transported them to the West Indies, and then returned to England with the rum and sugar produced by slaves on the West Indian plantations. Although—indeed because—this trade was extremely lucrative, it also created difficulties in foreign as well as domestic policy. Since the so-called sugar colonies were "the most valuable possessions of any empire" (Black 68), the century's European warfare was matched if not exceeded by conflict in the colonies. Internal difficulties are encapsulated in the fate of the South Sea Company, set up in 1711 to manage the asiento. Frantic trade in company shares (by Lady Mary Wortley Montagu, among other ladies) produced the South Sea Bubble of unchecked speculation, and it burst in 1720. The results "realigned British foreign policy" (Carswell xii), and commentators saw other troubling ramifications for class and gender hierarchies. William Hogarth's print *South Sea Bubble* points up these fears of social disorder: an ape is dressed as a gentleman; a shoeblack and a nobleman sit side-by-side on a merry-go-round, as do a clergyman and a prostitute; and dozens of women line up to enter a building (crowned with cuckold's horns) in order to take part in "Raffling for Husbands and Lottery Fortunes."

The Irishwoman Christian Davies can serve as a figure for such dislocations of the century's early years in several ways. England's continuing efforts to subdue Ireland are suggested at the beginning of her *Life and Adventures*, with her recollections of her Royalist father. Although the Irish rebellion of 1641 was finally crushed with great ferocity by Cromwell, in 1689 another revolt again pitted Catholics (supporters of King James II) against Protestants (supporters of William of Orange). Christian Davies's father joined James's forces; they were defeated by William's army at the Battle of the Boyne in 1690, and this defeat began the process whereby Irish Catholics were systematically stripped of most of their civil rights. It is thus illustrative of Ireland's tangled relations with England that Christian Davies spent almost twenty years, first as a soldier and then as a cook, in the army of the Protestant William.

A second dislocation that Davies's narrative figures is the unsettling of gender identity suggested by her cross-dressing as a soldier. Such complication of gender roles was rare but not unheard of in the long eighteenth century. Like her contemporaries Hannah Snell (a soldier), Mary Ann Talbot (a sailor), Anne Bonney and Mary Read (both pirates), and later women such as Hester Hammerton (a sexton) and Mary East (also known as James Howe, the female husband), Davies wore men's clothes to assume a man's role. There were other reasons why a woman might cross-dress, some of them at odds with each other: when an actress wore men's clothes to play a "breeches" part onstage, for example, "the display of leg enhance[d] the sexual display of womanhood even as it pretend[ed] to mimic manhood" (Rogers 248); but when an actress traveled from town to town as Charlotte Charke did, she might wear men's clothes precisely to avoid "sexual display" and the consequent unwelcome male attention. Furthermore, although we have few records of eighteenth-century lesbian sexuality as outspoken as Anne Lister's early-nineteenth-century diaries, it is quite likely that some cross-dressing women were "female husbands" in more than name. What is noteworthy about Christian Davies's cross-dressing is the brio with which she combines gendered roles: wife and soldier, wooer of young girls and (repeatedly) object of sexual assault, mother and brawler. Davies's insouciance is even more striking when we know that women who "passed" as men might be prosecuted for fraud if they married. At the same time that Davies's various incarnations suggest a fluidity of gender, then, legal records indicate rather a felt need to fix boundaries and identities—to "establish, with increasing precision, the parameters of the factual" and to "counteract any discrepancy between appearance and truth" (Friedli 255). The Act of 1721 by which impersonation with intent to defraud became a felony may owe something to the South Sea Bubble, but it also suggests an unease with gendered as well as commercial "discrepancy between appearance and truth."

In some ways these instabilities of the early years of the century were settling by the 1750s. The 1701 Act of Settlement had vested succession to the throne in the house of Hanover, and the first two Hanoverians,

George I (1714–1727) and George II (1727–1760), weathered the risings of 1715 and 1745 in which Scotland, although joined to England by 1707's Act of Union, abetted the efforts by James Stuart (1715) and his son, Charles Edward (1745), to restore the Stuart succession. Further stabilizing was a period of peace from 1748 (the end of the War of the Austrian Succession) to 1756 (the beginning of the Seven Years War). The London theater, which in the 1720s and 1730s had been a vehicle for criticism of government policies, was also entering a peaceful period, having been effectively muzzled by the Licensing Act of 1737. (The nature of this peace is attested by the "remarkable resurgence of royal patronage" [G. Stone 188], for the first two Georges preferred pantomimes and farces to drama.)

Other elements of theater history indicate how women were faring under the Georges. At the Restoration, theaters closed by the Puritans had been reopened, and for the first time women's roles were played by actresses rather than by boys. Another of the Restoration's "most striking innovations" (Pearson 256) was the involvement of women of every class at every level of production, which continued into the eighteenth century. Lady Davenant managed the Duke's Company theater from 1668 to 1673, and it was not uncommon for ladies to hold shares in theater companies. From Aphra Behn in the 1670s to Hannah Cowley in the 1780s, women playwrights were active and successful, and there were charwomen, candlewomen, dressers, box-keepers, orange sellers, and prostitutes working in theaters nightly. Although the Licensing Act of 1737 bore hard on some women—like Charlotte Charke, many either stopped writing plays or left London for the less restrictive provincial theaters—other women remained influential. Prologues and epilogues routinely appealed to female as well as male audience members for their support; ladies requested performances of plays they approved and were "largely responsible" (Pearson 40) for the upsurge in productions of Shakespeare and Shakespeare-influenced plays. While most actresses could expect lower status and pay than actors, some achieved the success and celebrity that George Anne Bellamy records in her *Apology*.

But Bellamy's success was double-edged in a way that suggests how working women in the 1750s had to negotiate toward independence in public as well as private authority relations. Although Bellamy's *Apology* records fewer material hardships than does Charke's *Narrative*, for instance, it does show that actresses suffered from the perception, common since the Restoration, that equated them (and women playwrights) with prostitutes—all public women selling their talents. Another example of working women's trials is the changing status of women employed in "that traditional female activity, sewing" (Prior, "Women" 110). Into the 1670s, making clothes was a male employment; this included women's clothes, because the boning that shaped a dress was sewn into it, and this procedure required training restricted to male apprentices. Women entered the trade around 1676 with the fashion for the mantua, a loose outer garment that required little stitching and no fitting, and for a time they competed successfully with the male guilds. By the mid-eighteenth century, however, practitioners of this women-only profession were widely regarded as "convenients," or go-betweens for prostitutes and their clients. Other, more respectable employment had opened to women by the 1750s, and although the vast majority of working women were servants in households and on farms, some achieved a measure of financial independence by completing apprenticeships or, like Jane Elizabeth Moore, by working in the family business.

In assessing levels of independence, it is important to distinguish among the positions of wives, of widows and single women, and of daughters. According to Blackstone's legal *Commentaries* of 1753, a wife was *feme covert*, or "under the protection and influence of her husband" (qtd. in B. Hill 196); hence she had no legal existence apart from her husband. Yet a wife might be wholly responsible for some areas of agricultural production, for instance, a farm's dairy; or she might be partner in all but name with a husband's shoemaking or bookselling or printing shop; or she might, like Hannah Robertson, support an ailing husband. Widows who inherited a husband's property or succeeded to his business, and single women who were legally *feme sole* and thus entitled to own property and trade independently (B. Hill 221), might achieve economic security or at least, like Robertson after her husband's death, scrape by. A daughter, on the other hand, was economically dependent on a father and thus doubly subject to his authority. An heiress, or a particularly determined daughter like Catherine Jemmat, might escape her dependence by marrying. Jane Elizabeth Moore, for example, negotiated her father into dowering her with the "daughter's share" (1:297) she felt she had earned as his business manager. But Jemmat's marriage was not happy, and Moore's *Memoirs* shows that her relations with her father remained conflicted; in this connection, her fascination with "Miss Blandy the horrid parricide" (1:91, 2:103) is perhaps suggestive.

The case of Mary Blandy indicates another kind of daughterly negotiation, and it indicates too some changes from Christian Davies's time in the legal (and gendered) definition of fact. Blandy was convicted of poisoning her father and hanged on 6 April 1752. Her case became a cause célèbre in part because of the threat her actions posed to paternal authority. Some thought was given to charging her with petty treason, for she was living with and dependent on her father, and her "crime against the familial patriarch thus constituted a 'petticoat' version of a crime against the King and his State" (Heinzelman 318). It is understandable, then, that the prosecutor of her case urged the Oxford undergraduates attending the trial to learn from it "the dreadful consequences of disobedience to parents," educators, governors, magistrates, and "all others who are put in authority" (qtd. in Roughead 76). Blandy's trial is also important in legal history as the first to use circumstantial evidence in its modern legal sense, and here it demonstrates changes from earlier ways of establishing "the parameters of the factual" (Friedli 255). By the midcentury some distinctions were being made between legal narratives—"objective, factually based, and enabled by logic and rules"—and literary narratives, by contrast subjective, imaginative, and "enabled by emotion and image" (Heinzelman 310). Blandy's case, however, shows the instability of these distinctions. If circumstantial evidence counts as evidence precisely according to "its capacity to be narrativized" (Heinzelman 323), then it is no less liable to fictionalization or falsification than Blandy's account. And her version of the evidence was also subject to gendered expectations, for women were "suspect, as women, in their capacity to authorize faithful representations of reality" (Heinzelman 309).

The question of "fact or fiction?" raised by Blandy's *Account* further complicates the problem with which this introduction began: if what can be known of women's lives in the long eighteenth century is necessarily limited by an incomplete textual record, it is additionally limited if the texts available might be fictional rather than factual. Davies's *Life and Adventures*, for example, was once thought to be the work of novelist Daniel Defoe, and theater historians have questioned, even dismissed, the data recorded in Bellamy's *Apology*. The problem becomes particularly acute in the genre known as *mémoires scandaleuses*, which first appeared in the late 1740s and early 1750s. For contemporaries, these narratives were automatically suspect because written by (or as if by) sexually transgressive women; for modern scholars, they are suspect because they follow many of the same narrative patterns, such as seduction and betrayal, found in novels of the period. If these textual and generic uncertainties are reformulated as cultural problematics, however, the question "fact or fiction?" is no longer a stumbling block but rather a starting point. That is, if the scandalous memoirist's choices of narrative patterns and conventions are read as negotiations with her assumed audience, then her text can be read as the author's effort to maneuver within her status as "public woman." In this way the memoirs become historically specific "sites of converging and competing discourses that display ideologies of gendered character" for our examination and analysis (Nussbaum, *Autobiographical* 179).

A spate of scandalous memoirs appeared in the 1780s and 1790s, including those by George Anne Bellamy, Ann Sheldon, Elizabeth Gooch, and Margaret Coghlan excerpted in this anthology. These later texts demonstrate "converging and competing discourses" of class as well as gender, for the previous two decades had seen great changes in economic, political, and social status markers. Although its onset is notoriously difficult to date, the Industrial Revolution is said by some historians to have begun with the improvements in banking, iron production, machinery, and transportation that occurred in the 1760s and 1770s. Herself a merchant in the newly important oil industry, Jane Elizabeth Moore provides an index of this revolution in the third volume of her *Memoirs*, a treatise on industry that ranges from improvements in agriculture and inland navigation to changes in coinage and debt law. Her relentless titled-name-dropping indicates another set of changes, the shifts in class status that link her otherwise highly respectable text with the scandalous memoirs. The newly powerful moneymen and industrialists might be dismissed as nouveaux riches by some among the aristocracy and landed interests, but business contacts and, crucially, intermarriage between the classes meant some increase in status. Politically the new men began to achieve influence, as their interests in expanding trade coincided with those of government factions pursuing an aggressively acquisitive colonial policy. A broader political change in the 1760s was the new importance of public opinion. If the Fifth Monarchists had proved relatively easy to suppress in the 1660s, in the 1760s it proved far more difficult to control widespread dissatisfaction with a parliament seen as nonrepresentative and corrupt, a king seen as tyrannical and inept, and a foreign policy that, despite some successes in Europe and India, had by 1781 lost the North American colonies.

England's defeat in the American War of Independence led to the constitutional crisis of revolving-door ministries which features in Mary Tonkin's *Facts*, and one of its main figures, Charles James Fox, also appears in Bellamy's and Coghlan's scandalous memoirs. This last fact, coupled with the veritable roll call of the ruling class in Sheldon's scandalous memoir, Phillippina Hill's *Apology*, and Mary Robinson's *Memoirs*, is indicative of more than one kind of scandal. That is, if courtesans like Coghlan and Sheldon are sexually scandalous in transgressing increasingly rigid norms of the chaste and domestic woman, there is class and political scandal in these texts' portraits of ruling-class men at least as engaged by gambling, fornicating, and frolicking as by governing. In this way, women's scandalous memoirs may point to the parliamentary reform movements of the 1770s and 1780s and to the revolutionary politics of the 1790s. Coghlan's *Memoirs* is illustrative: completed after her death with additions criticizing the British ruling class and subtly threatening it with the fate of French aristocrats, the book was published in 1794 during the revolutionary Terror in France.

England had declared war on the French Republic in 1793, and fighting continued off and on until Napoleon's final defeat at Waterloo in 1815. Like the century's previous wars, this one was fought not only in Europe but also in and over colonial possessions. Among the richest pickings were India and the West Indies, and by the 1790s women as well as men were integral to colonial rule in these areas. To see how this came about, it is necessary to begin with the early histories of colonial India and Jamaica.

The East India Company, founded in 1599 and granted a royal charter in 1600, was a small group of venture capitalists interested in profiting from the India trade. Some of its shareholders were ladies, and between 1675 and 1691 the number of these shareholders doubled, in part perhaps because stock was one of the few forms of property that married women could legally retain as personal estate (Carswell 8). Single ladies too might become involved in the India trade, often as commodities themselves: East India Company merchants looking to raise their families' status might offer large dowries to attract poor but titled sons-in-law. After Robert Clive defeated the French-backed nawab, or ruler, of Arcot in 1751 and the nawab of Bengal at Plassey in 1757, the English presence in India extended from trade to include administration, a change that affected women's roles in colonial rule. India now became a land of opportunity for younger sons hoping to make a fortune in trade or at least a subsistence in military, legal, or other administrative work, and they were often accompanied or joined by their wives. Jemima Kindersley's *Letters* records her journey to join her husband, a colonel of the Bengal artillery, in 1765; Eliza Fay was on her way to India in 1779 with her lawyer husband when they were captured by the buccaneer Haidar Ali, one of the most persistent opponents of English rule in India. Fay's journal of her captivity shows that wives as well as husbands might suffer the fallout of England's colonial policy in India.

But women might also help shore up that policy in various ways. Lady Mary Wortley Montagu's *Turkish Embassy Letters*, written when her husband was England's ambassador to Turkey, is one of many women's travel narratives that introduced British readers to areas of the East in which England had foreign policy interests. Lady Craven baldly states her desire to see "a colony of honest English families" (177) in Greece, "establishing a fair and free trade," teaching "industry and honesty" to the Greeks, and "waking the indolent Turk from his gilded slumbers" (178). As this language indicates, women's travel narratives (like the Oriental tales that became fashionable in the mid-eighteenth century) might display what Edward Said has termed Orientalism, by representing the East in a particular way: as the Other, the not-us, less a place in its own right than a construct, a locus of values and traits in binary or polar opposition to an equally constructed set of Western values and traits. Of course, women travelers' Orients might differ from those of men; where men travelers focused on the harem in a fantasy of sexually available women, for instance, Lady Mary Wortley Montagu's description of the Turkish women's bagnio specifically repudiates this version of Orientalism. Yet other descriptions in her *Letters* are no less insistent than men's on sexualizing the Oriental woman, and in women's texts as well as men's a particular version of the East—degenerate, effeminate, superstitious, despotic, and generally benighted—served colonial interests by presenting a field for the intervention of soi-disant civilization and enlightenment. For instance, Kindersley refers to the "wretched sufferers" (275) in the Black Hole of Calcutta, where more than one hundred English prisoners suffocated during the 1756 battle for the city; that this incident was "so much talked of in England" suggests the importance of representations of treacherous Orientals to a colonizing ideology. Fay's revulsion at suttee, the "horrible custom" (292) of widows immolating themselves on their husbands' funeral pyres, is particularly evocative of a colonial policy in which, to paraphrase Gayatri Spivak, white men and white women saved brown women from brown men: after the East India Act of 1784 transferred some of the East India Company's powers to a board of control whose president was a member of the cabinet and answerable to Parliament, one of the new administrators' first initiatives against traditional Hindu culture was interference in the laws governing suttee.

As in India, in the Jamaica of the eighteenth century women's lives were interwoven with the course of colonization. African women preceded English women in Jamaica, when the first slaves were brought by Spanish settlers in 1509 to what was still a Spanish colony. It was occupied by an English fleet in 1655 and officially ceded to England in 1670. The following year Margaret Fell Fox's husband, George, was urging West Indian Quakers to free their slaves, and in 1672 the Quaker missionary

Elizabeth Hooten arrived in Jamaica. Jane Hoskens's *Life* demonstrates that Quaker women were proselytizing in the West Indies well into the 1740s, and Quakers were also instrumental in the late-eighteenth-century campaign to abolish the slave trade.

Long before this movement of English philanthropists, however, there was much West Indian resistance to slavery and colonial rule, by women as well as men. Resistance began on the slave ships, with suicides and spontaneous rebellions, and it continued on the plantations. Women were considered especially refractory, as they refused to work, feigned illness, and developed such techniques as oversoaping the laundry or "losing" clothes (Bush 61). The communities of freed and runaway slaves known as Maroons warred with the colonizers throughout the eighteenth century, and women participated in such rebellions in various ways; during the 1720s and 1730s, for example, the Maroons were inspired by a woman, the "spiritual leader," "tactician and political adviser" Nanny (Bush 70). By 1801, when Sir George Nugent arrived in Jamaica with his wife, Maria, to assume the lieutenant governorship of the colony, English rule had outlasted the First Maroon War in the 1730s, the Coromanti rising in 1760, and the Second Maroon War in the 1790s. But Jamaica's House of Assembly, an elected body that represented the planters' interests, proved resistant to Lieutenant Governor Nugent's remit in the colony, and Lady Nugent's *Journal* records both his struggles with the Assembly and her role in smoothing them over.

Lady Nugent can thus serve as an example in late-eighteenth-century colonial administration of "the incorporated wife." This term is a specific instance of a general phenomenon, the process whereby a woman is "socially identified as the 'wife of' a particular kind of worker" (Callan 1). When the male worker is, as Lieutenant Governor Nugent was, himself "socially identified" with the colonial service, his wife may be incorporated into that service. Lady Nugent, for instance, copied her husband's official dispatches and made herself agreeable to ambassadors and Assembly members visiting her husband in his official capacity. But because the incorporated wife does not herself have an official capacity, she raises questions about "the nature of institutional boundaries" (Callan 1), and especially about the relation between public and private that so many eighteenth-century women had to negotiate. For Lady Nugent, the private was the domestic—first her tête-à-têtes with her husband and later their time alone with their children. But such a private sphere was "available to the incorporating institution" (Callan 9) and thus could have public uses, as when Lady Nugent used her pregnancy as an excuse not to receive official French visitors during a period of diplomatic stress. Furthermore, the incorporated wife's "nurturant and restorative functions" (Gartrell 168) should be seen as "material services" (Callan 20) that have "resource value" for the institution as well as the husband. Lady Nugent's love and care for her husband were certainly genuine, but such wifely services also proved useful for a colonial structure whose administrators suffered "job stress created by isolation, climate, maintaining domination over people of other cultures, and structural strains within the organization" (Gartrell 173).

Such strains became particularly severe in England's colonial structure after 1789. Certainly there were imperial successes: southern India came under full British control in 1799. But Lady Nugent's ruse to avoid French diplomats indicates on a small scale the stresses consequent on England's war with France being fought in the Caribbean as well as in Europe. Another structural strain came from the campaign to abolish the slave trade, which took formal shape in 1783 and bedeviled England's colonial administrators until achieving its goal with the Act for the Abolition of the Slave Trade in 1807. This campaign focused on Parliament but also mobilized extraparliamentary action such as petitions, boycotts of West Indian sugar, and antislavery verse. Like the reform movements of the 1760s and 1770s, then, the abolition movement shows the importance of public opinion. And because the public opinion against the slave trade included women, the woman abolitionist (like the incorporated wife) blurred the boundaries of the public/private divide. Seventeen eighty-seven saw the first newspaper appeal to women to support the abolitionist cause, "suggesting a recognition of women as a constituent of the public" (Midgley 20). When women subscribed to local abolition societies, they were recognized by others and by themselves as "members of the public" (Midgley 23). Rather than simply confronting "an established and fixed public sphere," then, women abolitionists were "constructing, reinforcing, utilising, negotiating, subverting or more rarely challenging the distinction between the private-domestic sphere and the public-political sphere" (Midgley 5).

The figure of the incorporated wife suggests the complexity of this dynamic. Mary Ann Parker was incorporated in England's colonial enterprise insofar as she provided both public and private support during her husband's mission of transporting supplies and a new lieutenant governor to the convict settlements in Australia. But she concludes her mainly sympathetic description of the aboriginals with a quotation from William Cowper's abolitionist poem "The Negro's Complaint," which suggests a potentially subversive refusal of other forms of colonizing.

Even more complicated is the position of Anna Maria Falconbridge vis-à-vis Sierra Leone, the settlement on the coast of West Africa founded by the abolitionist Sierra Leone Company. This settlement was in part a response to another strain on England's colonial structure, the arrival in England after the American War of Independence of thousands of black loyalists. Sierra Leone was to be a refuge for these free blacks, but it was also intended as a self-supporting commercial venture; the settlers were to grow crops and trade with England, thus providing an alternative to the African or slave-trade leg of the golden triangle. The free blacks who made up London's Black Society met to discuss the plan, which suggests that some went to Sierra Leone by choice, but there seems to have been some coercion as well. One historian terms the project "deportation" (Ramdin 17), and Anna Maria Falconbridge half-believed charges that the British government had tricked one hundred white prostitutes into marrying and accompanying the black emigrants. As this suggests, her relation to the Sierra Leone project was vexed. She traveled to and resided in the settlement with her abolitionist husband, Alexander, a commercial agent for the Sierra Leone Company. Nominally an incorporated wife, in fact she gradually distanced herself not only from her hard-drinking and bad-tempered husband but also from the company. For example, she appended to her *Narrative* the letters to the company directors in which she represented herself as an incorporated wife in order to claim compensation due Alexander, but the letters also align her with the black settlers from Nova Scotia disgruntled because the company had not made good on its promises of land. The *Narrative* itself indicates her disaffection from the company's abolitionist project: by 1793 she has decided that the slave trade is "consistent" with both morality and religion, and she argues that it tends to promote the happiness of Africans by transferring them from the "innate prejudices, ignorance, superstition, and savageness" (238) of their "murdering, despotic chieftains" (236) to "the cherishing hands of Christian masters." Like the Orientalism of earlier women's texts, this fantasy of a Christian slave trade demonstrates that women as well as men could be instrumental in representing and defending colonialist interests.

If women contributed to public opinion for and against the slave trade, they were also influential in defending and attacking not only the two events that closed the long eighteenth century, the French Revolution and the Napoleonic Wars, but also the disruptive new forms of feminism. Lady Craven's *Letters* includes a mixture of defense and attack: she travels to Russia in part because of her admiration for Empress Catherine's "most magnificent and god-like acts" promoting women's education (308); but this feminist strain is undercut by her criticism of the French Revolution's "*she* freemasons" (26) and "*she* philosophers." Perhaps the best-known "she philosopher" of 1790s England was Mary Wollstonecraft. Notorious first for her defense of the French Revolution in *Vindication of the Rights of Men* (1790) and then for the *Vindication of the Rights of Woman* (1792), in these texts Wollstonecraft makes a revolutionary critique of both class and gender hierarchies.

Wollstonecraft's travel writing indicates another area of revolutionary feminism in the 1790s, for her *Letters* rewrites a conservative and masculinist language of aesthetics. This aesthetic assumed ideologies of class and of gender. The ideal of the picturesque, which dominated painting and writing about nature for much of the eighteenth century, was achieved by arranging the natural world and its inhabitants into an aesthetically pleasing picture. In this aesthetic, part of the pleasure was the organizing and distancing power of the spectator, a power available only to a class with the wealth and leisure to spectate. The ideal of the sublime, an enjoyment of pleasure via terror attainable only by those of the most cultivated taste, was gendered masculine, while the lesser category of the beautiful was gendered feminine. Furthermore, achieving the sublime conferred "empowerment, transport, and the self's strong sense of authority," properties regarded as "abnormal or deviant" in a woman (Yaeger 192, 210). In this aesthetics, Wollstonecraft's *Letters* might seem a merely beautiful or feminine text, in the sense that it records such gentler emotions as maternal love in addition to a sensibility so attractive that William Godwin, later her husband, said the book "would make a man fall in love with its author" (qtd. in J. Moore 145). But the text also has moments of a sublimity that does not empower, moments that undermine the masculine sublime and by extension the class and gender hierarchies on which it rested. If Ann Radcliffe's *Journey* is more conservative in its aesthetic language of the picturesque and the sublime, it is akin to Wollstonecraft's writings in its persistent critique of the Napoleonic Wars that were ravaging Europe. Thus both women's writings reflected but also shaped the revolutionary mood of the 1790s.

To conclude this review of eighteenth-century women's lives, Mary Eleanor Bowes's *Confessions* and Mary Stockdale's "To the Reader" can suggest post-Restoration changes in the opportunities and legal status of married and single women. The legal status of marriage itself had changed greatly, moving away from the earlier forms—contract marriage, clandestine marriage, and customary union—to the form dictated by Hardwicke's Marriage Act of 1753. From the thirteenth century into the seventeenth, contract marriage had been legally binding as long as the parties were over the age of consent and performed a verbal contract by exchanging vows in the present tense (I take thee . . .) before two witnesses. A contract in the future tense (I shall take thee . . .), however, was legally binding only if followed by sexual consummation, and a conditional contract (I take thee if my father or friends consent) was not binding at all. Clandestine marriages were binding if they were performed by a clergyman according to the Church of England rites laid down in the Book of Common Prayer. To add to the confusion, many people, especially the poor, simply joined in customary unions, which were not legal but had a certain force because they were recognized by the community. But most such nonofficial matings did not secure the all-important property arrangements, and all were liable to legitimate misunderstandings (both Robertson and Jemmat suffered when contracted marriages fell through) as well as abuse. Clandestine marriages became an especial problem, for London abounded in professional marrying shops and hence "an ever greater variety . . . of trickery, falsification, and perjury" (L. Stone 31).

By midcentury, legal and religious authorities as well as public opinion had exerted sufficient pressure to secure Hardwicke's Marriage Act, which mandated a single form of binding marriage and invalidated any marriage made by a minor without the written consent of parents or guardians. But this act applied only in England, so clandestine marriages continued to be legal in Scotland, as Mary Blandy learned to her cost. Nor did the act much affect the practices of the propertyless poor, and it had only limited success in protecting heiresses from adventurers. The Countess of Strathmore, a wealthy widow when she married Andrew Robinson Stoney, cannily protected her property by placing it in trusts. Within months, however, Stoney had broken them, and the results for Bowes—verbal and physical abuse, her husband's attempts to balk her divorce suit first by abducting her and then by publishing the *Confessions* without her consent, and the lengthy process of suits and appeals and countersuits she endured before being granted a divorce—demonstrate that even wealthy and titled women remained legally disadvantaged at the end of the long eighteenth century.

What of single women? Barbara Todd notes that Restoration comedies made the remarrying widow a figure of fun precisely because widows were in fact not remarrying, for in a patriarchal culture the independent widow was an "anomaly" (55). Far more anomalous from the Restoration on was the single woman, whether she achieved financial independence outside a family structure and thus undercut the economic foundations of that structure or failed to do so and became an economic liability to her father or brother or the state. A staple of midcentury scandalous memoirs was the courtesan in debt, and the earlier discussion of seamstresses and other working women shows that they, too, were often in financial straits. In that sense, Mary Stockdale seems a sign of better times: supported by her family through a series of illnesses, her poems published by her father's printing business, she is a far cry from the persecuted Dissenting daughters of the 1660s and from the many daughters forced by parents into unhappy marriages or by circumstances into prostitution. But the life of her contemporary Jane Austen—unmarried, living in genteel poverty with her mother and sister and dependent on her brothers, earning almost nothing from her novels—reminds us that not all single women of the gentry had Stockdale's advantages. And women of the laboring classes would be increasingly exploited in the boom-slump capitalism that characterized England's economy after the close of the Napoleonic Wars. If there were hopeful changes in women's lives over the long eighteenth century, then, there were discouraging continuities as well.

WOMEN'S LIFE-WRITING

Mary Blandy, in publishing the *Account of the Affair between her and Mr. Cranstoun,* wants the whole of what happened to her submitted to the "Judgment of the Public." Jane Elizabeth Moore, "[c]onscious of the presumption, [she] may be censured with, in uttering, (from a female pen) a treatise on the trades, manufactures, laws, and police of this country," recounts her endless "misfortunes" in the hope that others will escape similar evils and that she will become "a useful member of society." Ann Radcliffe, in telling of her 1794 journey through Holland and western Germany, records the "mutual observations" of both her husband and herself. *We* serves in the stead of *me* as "a design to attract attention by extraordinary novelty." Christian Davies describes what happened to her as she disguised herself as Christopher Welsh, foot soldier and dragoon under King William and the duke of Marlborough, to go in search of her missing husband. At its most basic, autobiographical discourse may be defined as someone telling someone else "something happened to me" (Barros vii). For our purposes, this definition must be extended to give it more specificity and flexibility in terms of current feminist theory, eighteenth-century studies, and poststructuralist critiques. An extended definition is intended to avoid the extremes of both idealist and poststructuralist views of autobiography in which "the body has been eclipsed in dualistic and idealistic theories of meaning, aiming at a view from 'everywhere' or erased in poststructuralist theories seeking a 'view from nowhere' " (Fleckenstein 281). The idealist would universalize the someone telling, the someone told, and the "something happened" to every woman everywhere; the poststructuralist would collapse the someone telling and the someone else into the told. For this study, however, autobiographical discourse is defined as the textual account of an actual someone in an actual time and place persuading some situated others of one's view of what happened.

"Autograph" and "autogynography" (Stanton), "autobiographics" (Gilmore), "female sociograph" (Stimpson), "grandmatologies" and "authorgraph" (Gilbert and Gubar), and "autography" (Perreault) are thoughtful attempts to clarify the relationship between the writer and the text. To encompass the many and various first-person accounts written by women—letters, diaries, travelogues, confessions, pleas, apologies, vindications, and scandalous memoirs—we have chosen the term now current in feminist studies, "life-writings." This is not to suggest that *real* autobiography has long been the domain of the masculine as argued by some feminist critics, or that any text that deviates from the traditional models of autobiography may not be identified as such, but rather that autobiography is continually being revisioned to account for versions that have been excluded because of the gender, class, or ethnicity of its authors and/or the forms in which they took up their telling. The term "life-writing," then, is both synonymous with and larger than autobiography, as it draws in and validates variant forms of first-person narratives.

"Life-writing" is an especially appropriate term for eighteenth-century British women's first-person accounts. Their male contemporaries had their professional accomplishments, military victories, economic successes, political careers, and literary writings to speak for them. Women's actual *lives*—as observed and reported by others—were all their contemporaries knew of them. (Exceptions were clearly the case with writers like Wollstonecraft, Robinson, and Montagu.) Their reputations depended on gossip, scandal sheets, cartoons, and caricatures, and they had a limited number of avenues for setting the record straight. Writing their lives served as one corrective for the misunderstandings of their actions, values, and beliefs that had been imposed by others. "Life-writing," then, is the term adopted for this text and will be used interchangeably with "autobiography" in its widest sense.

It is a simple matter to take the idealist or universalist position in reading women's autobiographies; women's narratives draw us into their authors' joys, successes, sufferings, and crises. In point of fact, this may be one of the reasons for autobiography's popularity. We identify with the "someone telling" as we remember our adventures in "dressing up" with Charlotte Charke or traveling to exotic places with Lady Mary Wortley Montagu. We identify with a wife's loss of her husband as we do with Lady Fanshawe or feel the anxiety at the loss of a lover with Mary Wollstonecraft and Mary Robinson. We reexperience our anger at being misunderstood, unheard, and unheeded with Agnes Beaumont. We are cheered by the spiritual and economic successes of Mary Pennington and relieved when Eliza Fay escapes from captivity. These personal readings are not an indication of failure on our part as readers, but instead they are places where we as readers begin—at points of connection or identification with the "someone telling" of the text. This being absent, we will set the book aside in favor of another.

The poststructuralist position insists that we may know the self only through (or as) some form of discourse. This critique is particularly relevant to the study of autobiography. The self of the text and its author are not to be thought of as one and the same. The textual self is a linguistic construct. (Friedrich Nietzsche, Jean-Paul Sartre, and Roland Barthes were among the earliest writers to construct their autobiographies on this premise.) In opposition to the idealist's eclipsed body, a common feature of the postmodern stance is that "the body is dead—or at least irrelevant, . . . an arbitrary abstraction or floating signifier somehow separable from the local, specific historical and concrete bodies marked by it" (Finn 72, 75). While some may see the autobiographical subject as ahistorical, a floating signifier, erased, dissected, murdered, or written out of existence, Anne Balsamo argues that "discourse is not entirely divorced from the material manifestations of the 'flesh and blood' entity" (23). For Teresa de Lauretis, the absent subject is doubly problematic for women: "If 'woman' is a fiction, a locus of pure difference and resistance to logocentric power, and if there are no women as such, then the very issue of women's oppression would appear to be obsolete and feminism itself would have no reason to exist" (10).[1] The female autobiographical subject, then, calls into question the universal female and problematizes the poststructuralist critique. "The autobiographical 'I' is not merely a textual construction, but the textual double of a woman in history who has been produced by the material differences in men and women's lives, and has selected, from the totality of her experiences, those which retrospectively appear to her to be the more significant" (Joannou 32). If we choose, then, to move beyond our initial and often naive position of identification—that an individual woman's autobiography speaks for all women everywhere—and if we refuse to be erased as bodied subjects, we must consider that the "someone telling" is of a particular race, gender, class, economic condition, and religion, situated in a particular place and time while negotiating a unique aspect of her culture. "Autobiography is the insertion of the self into historical narrative, a claim to be counted as significant in a particular time and place" (N. Walker 10). Sharing the long eighteenth century in British history, the life-writings collected here represent women of all classes, ideologies, positions of power, levels of education, and gendered status and provide vital insights into women's lives.

We must also consider that the "someone told" is historically and socially situated as well. An action that is seen as a minor infraction or social faux pas by today's readers might have serious consequences for eighteenth-century citizens. Her riding on the back of a horse with John Bunyan caused Agnes Beaumont's father to lock her out of the house. George Anne Bellamy suffered "cruel aspersions" for being an actress, noting "that every fool who happened to be possessed of a fortune, should think himself licensed to take liberties with me" (13). Hannah Robertson, the granddaughter of Charles II, was imprisoned for debt. Expelled from the family for riding on a horse behind a Protestant minister, treated as a whore for being an actress, or imprisoned for debt with no recourse to family wealth were hard facts of life that were understood by eighteenth-century readers. Yet the "someone told" had to be presented with narratives, pleas for vindication, letters, memoirs, and arguments that convinced them and others similarly situated, if women were to set the record straight. The "someone told" of Mary Pennington's narrative, as the subtitle indicates—*"from her Manuscript, left for her family"*—was her "dear children." Robbed of her estate by relatives when she became a Quaker, her testimony of conversion was published "for the general benefit [spiritual] of the present and succeeding generations"; her economic recovery stood as proof of God's blessings. Beyond her own family, then, her "dear children" might well include those whom she had helped to convert and those who were yet to be converted by her testimony.

Lady Fanshawe wrote to her son with instructions for living. The boy's father, Sir Richard Fanshawe, died when his son was only ten months old. Lady Fanshawe urged him to behave in the manner of his exemplary father. "Be innocent as a dove, but as wise as a serpent. . . . Hate idleness and curb all passions. . . . and be more pleased to do good than to receive good"; further, do not "omit your duty to your king and country." Lady Fanshawe also addressed all "you that read"; thus the published version, appearing over a hundred years later, finds its audience in the citizenry of George III's reign, a time when loyalty to king and country might be seen as a censure of the Prince of Wales, Charles James Fox, and Lord North.

Mary Stockdale's "To the Reader" was written to the intended readers of her poems that they might become acquainted with their author, because she herself had "uniformly felt a strong desire to become in some measure acquainted" with the authors of books she read (xiii). Her readers, she believed, were exactly like her. Stockdale constructed her intended readers out of her own desires.

Be it Mary Pennington, Lady Fanshawe, or Mary Stockdale, today's readers must identify the writer's intended audience and place the "someone told" within the contemporary cultural situation to make sense of the life-writing. While reading is constitutive, not every reading will suffice. "We can choose our interpretations, but we can't choose our range of choices" (Michaels 199–200), and our choices are limited by the values, beliefs, attitudes, and expectations of, in this case, eighteenth-century British language and culture. Moreover, the "disobedient reader," Nancy Walker's term for a reader who engages in a reading that "resists sexist and racist formulations remaining sufficiently referential to the original to make clear its point of origin" (3), relies on and assumes an informed, contextualized reading.

Negotiating Cultural Conflicts through Life-Writing

The female autobiographer must come into some kind of conflict with the culture and its values and laws, else there is no need to tell someone else "something happened to me." As noted earlier, eighteenth-century British women were entangled in a number of conflicts that, though they often affected women more severely than men, were disputes over which they had little, if any, control: European wars, battles with colonies, religious suppression, economic disasters, marriage and property laws. The initial conflict that had to be negotiated by the eighteenth-century British woman writer, however, had to do with writing itself. Women autobiographers were "caught in mimicking the dominant ideologies of themselves. . . . [They] positioned themselves all along the feminist and antifeminist spectrum from the discourse of inferiority to the assertion of equality. . . . They may assume a position that implies moral or spiritual superiority, they may speak their own denigration and collude in their subjugation, or they may attempt to disrupt the ideology of gender by disguising themselves as males" (Nussbaum, *Autobiographical* 133). Eighteenth-century British women—whether feminist or antifeminist, assertive, disruptive, or denigrated—took up their pens against great odds. The stigma of being a woman writer combined with their often powerless states, even when titled or wealthy, compromised their positions as authors of autobiography. "In the eighteenth and nineteenth centuries, in particular, the act of writing in itself appeared to lend women a self-assertiveness which seemed out of keeping with properly feminine aspirations" (Newton 7). That the majority of their life-writings remain in obscurity is one of the reasons for bringing them to this anthology.

Setting the record straight through the self-assertive act of writing was but one of the many complex spirtual, political, economic, and social conflicts that had to be negotiated by eighteenth-century British women. In terms of spiritual conflicts, Mary Churchman, when she joined the Dissenters, was turned out of her father's house. She would have fled to Holland to avoid harassment and arrest had her family not agreed to reconciliation. Margaret Fell Fox broke both the Quaker Act of 1662 and the Coventicle Act of 1664 when she held Quaker services in her home. She was not in conflict with her husband over the meetings, but she and her Quaker friends were beaten, robbed of their property, and imprisoned, and no amount of pleading before Charles II could stop the persecutions. In terms of political conflict, Royalists Lady Fanshawe and her husband were forced into exile during the civil war (1642–48) when Cromwell came to power. Their loyalty to the Crown put them at odds with Parliament, and they were not allowed to return to England until the Restoration in 1660. The English spy Mary Tonkin was at odds with her government when it refused to pay for her services during the war with the American colonies. When Charlotte Charke left the London theater over disputes with theater managers and became a strolling player in the provinces, she often found herself arrested as a vagrant and fined or imprisoned for failure to pay her debts. The Licensing Act of 1737 extended the laws against vagrants, beggars, rogues, and vagabonds to include traveling players, and Charke and others like her were its victims. Marriage and property laws allowed Elizabeth Gooch to be expelled from her estate by her husband, "her person deemed an incumbrance" once he had secured her property. Economic troubles plagued Jane Elizabeth Moore as well. Having managed her father's business in the leather trade, she was left out of his will when he died. Later, when her husband died, she was forced to take out a disastrous loan to pay his son's legacy. Travelers such as Lady Mary Wortley Montagu, Eliza Fay, Mary Wollstonecraft, Lady Nugent, and Anna Maria Falconbridge encountered cultures in which they were expected to negotiate cultural differences while retaining English values. Actresses such as Mary Robinson, George Anne Bellamy, and Phillippina Hill were treated with contempt by aristocratic women while being wooed by ruling-class men.

These female autobiographers, being both in time and in conflict with their times, elaborated "the relationship between individual consciousness and the social world" (Swindells 6) and established a "fittingness between narrative and being in the world" (Gunn 17) through the negotiation of "relationship and symbolic systems" (Lacan, qtd. in Graham, *Her Own Life* 19). The subgenres of life-writing they chose were limited by the range of genres available in the literary tradition. Yet for autobiography there were no ideal forms. "The genre itself testifies to the artificiality of all generic classifications and the repudiation of a model of genres as natural kinds. Thus autobiography is important as the most conspicuous example of a 'genre' which exposes the heterogeneity of all literary production" (Marcus, "Face" 14).

Eighteenth-century British women's life-writings make the "conspicuous example" even more conspicuous. The forms these writers appropriated were ones seemingly best suited to their purposes. Each of the thirty excerpts that follow is a unique instance of the forms of life-writing available to their authors. For purposes of discussion, we consider them under five major categories: family histories, conversion narratives, scandalous memoirs, defenses (apologies, appeals, vindications), and travel writing. These are merely working categories; as the women writers negotiate their conflicts with the culture, they subvert the forms and blur their already dim boundaries. Although readers may see these categories as limiting and prescriptive, they are intended as heuristic, as ways to expand the exploration of women's life-writing rather than restrict it.

Family Histories.   Attaching an autobiography to a family history has a tradition dating back at least to the Romans. Agrippina the Younger, wife of Claudius, sister of Caligula, and mother of Nero, wrote her memoirs when she was forty-four (59 A.D.) and folded them into those of her mother, Agrippina the Elder. Tacitus tell us that she "described her life and the fate of her family for posterity" (qtd. in Fantham 310–12). Lady Fanshawe's family history borrows on this tradition but attaches the history to a sort of "instructional manual" for her son. Written in 1676, the instructional aspects of the *Memoirs* shade into a family history embedded in a social/political history of court life during and after the Commonwealth. Lady Nugent's *Journal* is both travel journal and family history. The *Journal* documents the Nugents' travels to Jamaica, where her husband served as Lieutenant Governor and chief of the military and where insurrection in the colony broke out with regularity. In addition to articulating the cultural differences that had to be negotiated in Jamaica, Lady Nugent chronicled her children's growth and development, the happy moments and devastating losses she shared with her husband, and her charitable activities in England and Jamaica, collected, along with personal treasures, for her children's "future information."

Conversion Narratives. Six of the women in this collection chose one of the oldest and most familiar forms, the conversion narrative, to negotiate the religious conflicts they faced during the era of the Clarendon Code. The *Confessions* of Saint Augustine (354–430) is generally considered the model for this form of life-writing, and subsequent converts to Christianity followed the pattern of his conversion narrative: detailed descriptions of a sinful past, long and arduous struggle in the "lost" condition, miraculous conversion—accompanied by praise to God for his mercy—concluding with an account of the new life and ministry. But the authors of conversion narratives included in this volume would have been more familiar with Saint Paul's conversion on the Damascus road from reading their Bibles or with John Bunyan's *Grace Abounding to the Chief of Sinners* (1666). In Mary Pennington's case, her Quaker conversion narrative—with its attendant preconversion account of "recreations, foolish mirth, carding, dancing, singing, and jovial eatings and drinkings," her sufferings in the misery of her "lost" condition, and her ultimate victory in salvation as she "became obedient to the heavenly voice"—follows these earlier patterns (16–17, 25, 36). While Pennington's *Account* is in many ways typical, it is unique in its focus on economics and how she was able to restore financial stability to her family after suffering economic deprivation, loss of title, and property rights because of her conversion. She makes sure her readers understand that she was a faithful Christian *and* an astute manager. Likewise, Margaret Fell Fox's *Relation* recounts a meaningful conversion experience, but her focus is on the persecution and imprisonment she and other Quakers suffered and on her leadership role in holding the Friends together as she pleaded their cases to Charles II. Mary Churchman's *Memoirs* includes not only her own conversion but also the near deathbed conversion of her adamantly antidissenting father and her Anglican mother to Protestantism. Jane Hoskens's *Life* blurs the boundaries between conversion and travel narratives and subverts gender roles as she speaks mainly of her ministry, traveling through England, the colonies, and Barbados preaching the gospel. Agnes Beaumont's *singular Experience* is, as her title suggests, perhaps the most exceptional. In recording her conversion she relates how she is falsely accused of causing her father's death when he becomes enraged at her association with John Bunyan. In all these cases, eighteenth-century women blur the boundaries of the conversion narrative with accounts of politics, economics, and family history and subvert gender roles when they become spiritual leaders and preachers.

Scandalous Memoirs. Loss of reputation for eighteenth-century British women was no small matter. Publishing the fall from virtue was considered even more abhorrent; "fallen women" were expected to hide their shame rather than proclaim it. Seven women included here wrote scandalous memoirs, "the first significant public form of self-writing that women take up, other than the spiritual autobiography" (Nussbaum, *Autobiographical* 180). Scandalous memoirs would appear much like confessions or spiritual conversion narratives were it not for the fact that many of the women were not particularly sorrowful. By presenting their life-narratives to the public, they were defining themselves as subjects rather than objects and pointing to conditions in their cultures that contributed to their situations. While they may have at times portrayed themselves as victims, they were nonetheless vindicating themselves to themselves and others. Hannah Robertson and Mary Robinson were perhaps the most famous of the scandalous memoir writers, due to their associations with royalty. Robertson's *Life* details her royal lineage: her father was the illegitimate son of Charles II. After the death of her husband and heavily in debt, she wrote the *Life* in an effort to obtain a pension from the court. It is unlikely that she ever received it. Mary Robinson was, for a brief time, mistress to the Prince of Wales. She set the record of her life straight when she left her *Memoirs* to be published after her death. Volume three, republished from earlier articles, borders on revenge for the public's ill treatment when the prince abandoned her, containing as it does a series of anecdotes exposing the scandalous behavior of her contemporaries. Scandalous memoirs shared readership with novels of the seduced maiden and the licentious whore. Some claimed to read the memoirs as moral tales, while others satisfied their voyeuristic tendencies. Ann Sheldon hoped that presenting her history to the public would "in some measure relieve me from it" (4:247). But she also hoped to profit from the "public curiosity" regarding women of her "sort." In *Confessions,* Mary Eleanor Bowes, the Countess of Strathmore, recounts her numerous "misdeeds," ranging from walking with male friends in public to sexual indiscretions and attempted abortions. The *Con-*

fessions is unique in that her husband may have forced her to write it. He published and distributed the *Confessions* in pamphlet form in an effort to prevent her from divorcing him and recovering her estate. Catherine Jemmat's *Memoirs*, like Bowes's *Confessions,* reveals the consequences of bad marriage bargains. "Night after night have I laid my lordly master in his bed, intoxicated and insensible: Day after day have I received blows and bruises for my reward." Jemmat's *Memoirs* is notable in that, like Lady Mary Wortley Montagu's *Letters*, it contains poetry; in fact, one poem is by Lady Mary herself. In her *Memoirs*, Margaret Coghlan relates how, at the age of fourteen, she was married to John Coghlan in what she characterized as "honorable prostitution." With the failure of her marriage, she engaged in a series of affairs with a number of England's prominent and not so prominent citizens. The *Memoirs'* generic boundaries are blurred; volume two, which may have been completed by another writer, is remarkable in that it incorporates revolutionary political discourse into the narrative. Christian Davies's *Life and Adventures* serves as another instance of the blurring of genre designations. Because of her wide-ranging battle experiences, the *Life* could be read as a travel narrative. It also shares aspects of family history, as Davies folds the recollections of her Royalist father's soldiering in James II's army into her own autobiography. Davies's "scandals" center on the twenty years she served as Christopher Welsh, a foot soldier and dragoon in King William's army, and the *Life's* long popularity is attributable to these adventures. Even as she portrayed herself as behaving in unprecedented ways and filling nontraditional roles, Davies did not see herself as a victim, nor did she voice any regrets over her life. She maintained a sense of humor, often quite bawdy, and she challenged gender roles with the same courage and energy that she took into battle. Charlotte Charke's *Narrative* shares with Davies's the details of a life in "breeches" (see Charke xx). Like Sheldon and Robertson, she hoped to profit from the publication of her "farcical life" as Mr. Brown, since her father would not pay her to suppress it. Charke regretted being out of favor with her family, but she seemed to take pride in playing Mr. Brown and attracting readers to her "Adventures in Mens Cloaths." Scandalous life-writings reveal at least two important developments in autobiographical discourse: "scandalous women" had courageous voices and would be heard, and their self-assertive acts of writing often paid off in actual money, if not in restoration of reputation.

Defenses (Apologies, Appeals, Vindications). Each of the thirty life-writings here considered may be read as some form of defense or *apologia*, as eighteenth-century women brought their cases to the public (even posthumously) for disposition. The five women included under this heuristic category, however, were specifically concerned with justice due them or vindication of their actions. Isocrates (436–338 B.C.E.), the Athenian orator and teacher of rhetoric, was one of the first in Western history to employ autobiography as defense. Accused of disloyalty to the city, he presents a fictional court defense to prove his virtue and his care for Athens. It is unlikely that George Anne Bellamy, Phillippina Hill, Elizabeth Gooch, Mary Tonkin, or Mary Blandy read Isocrates; nor would they have been trained in legal discourse. Each testifying on her own behalf had as her only defense the life-narrative. Justice under these conditions was hard won, if won at all. George Anne Bellamy's *Apology* might also be read as a scandalous memoir since it, like Robinson's *Memoirs* and Charke's *Narrative,* detailed her life as an actress—that most tainted of women's professions. But her *Apology* was also a defense of women in the theater, "a vindication of those of the profession in which I was engaged" (Letter XXII). Written in the form of letters to a fictional recipient, Bellamy exposed the disrespect and mistreatment actresses were forced to endure. "I concluded by declaring that I thought a woman who preserved an unblemished reputation on the stage, to be infinitely more praiseworthy, than those who retained a good name, merely because they were secured by rank or fortune from the temptations actresses are exposed to" (XXII). The same disrespect was shown to Phillippina Hill. She was subjected to the whims of the Prince of Wales and his mistress, Mrs. Fitzherbert, humiliated by the prince's associates, and forced by their patronage to perform the "breeches" role of Scrub in *The Beaux' Stratagem.* Hill's *Apology* was written to make a public case for recovering from the prince the costs she incurred in producing the performance. Elizabeth Gooch's *Appeal* documents from Fleet Prison her destitute condition, "the dupe of treacherous lovers, false friends, and worthless acquaintance" (xx). Having lost her estates to her estranged husband and heavily in debt, the *Appeal* effected its intended purpose when her family paid her debts and she was released from prison. It is not known if Mary Tonkin was successful in her attempts to secure justice. *Facts. The Female Spy* was the pamphlet she addressed to Queen Charlotte, "laying at your Majesty's feet, the particulars of her extraordinary case" ("Dedication"). After repeated failures to obtain compensation for serving as an English spy, Tonkin published the *Facts,* in which she laid out her financial claims against the government. Mary Blandy's pleas failed completely. Her *Account of the Affair between her and Mr. Cranstoun,* published at her dying request, recorded the events leading to the charge of murdering her father. Though she maintained her innocence to the end, she was tried, convicted, and hanged. Her case remains a subject of current debate. In many instances life-writings as defense, apology, and appeal brought the conditions of women's lives to the attention of the public for adjudication and were influential in changing marriage and property laws and the rules of evidence.

Travel Writing. Travel letters or journals may well have been one of the earliest forms of first-person narratives. Around 430 B.C.E. Ion of Chios recorded his visits to Athens and the prominent Athenians he met there. "A few fragments of what might be called Ion's 'Travel Pictures' are extant, recollections of Pericles, Sophocles, and Kimon, and also of Aeschylus" (Misch 98). Travel writing became quite fashionable in late seventeenth- and eighteenth-century Britain. Writers of travel letters and journals developed their own sets of stylistic conceits and reader expectations. They usually took a didactic tone, outlined the geography, described the landscape, and defined the culture with emphasis on difference and novelty. British travel narratives had to be about an unusual, unfamiliar place and written from a nationalistic/critical stance rather than from the perspective of one interested in learning and appreciating different cultures. The citizen of the "unusual place" was treated as the outsider—the Other, while the English traveler served as point of reference for the civilized, educated "*man* of the world."

Lady Mary Wortley Montagu's *Letters* documents her travels to Turkey. Jemima Kindersley writes *Letters* from Tenerife, Brazil, the Cape of Good Hope, and her final destination, India. Eliza Fay also sends *Original Letters* from India. Jane Elizabeth Moore's *Genuine Memoirs* catalogs her journeys through Great Britain. Lady Craven writes *Letters* from Russia. Anna Maria Falconbridge's *Narrative* is of her two voyages to Sierra Leone. Ann Radcliffe's *Journey* takes her readers to Holland and Germany. Mary Wollstonecraft's *Letters* originates in Sweden, Norway, and Denmark. Mary Ann Parker's *Voyage*, the longest of the journeys, recounts her arduous journey to New South Wales. The full titles of these works leave no doubt that they are first-person accounts of women's travels and that the authors' destinations, like those of their male counterparts, are unusual, less-traveled places. Each of the travel writers, as well, constructed her view of the Other with British eyes. Yet as their writings reveal, each attempted in some way to negotiate cultural differences, some more successfully than others.

Lady Mary Wortley Montagu's Turkish letters are unique to travel writing in her determination to give a woman's view of the Orient. In doing so, she solved the problem of the male gaze, but even as she was admitted to the bagnio, dressed in Turkish costume, and adopted their methods of smallpox inoculation, Turkish women remained the exotic Other. Kindersley's travel letters display a keen sense of observation—she gives accounts of everything "worthy of notice"—but, like her male contemporaries, she seems unable to move beyond the superior stance of the colonial. "It must be acknowledged, that the religion of the *Hindoos* is now so overgrown with absurd and ridiculous ceremonies, that it is difficult to believe there has ever been any degree of common sense in it" (XXXIV). Eliza Fay's *Original Letters* is unusual in that it contains, along with general travel information, a captivity narrative in journal form. Captured by Sudder Khan, governor of Calicut, Fay painted vivid pictures of the evil captor, who, among other cruelties, refused fever medicine for a captive: "he, like the Pharisees in Scripture, refused to profane it by doing good—Should the woman die in the interim what cares he?" (23 November 1779). Like Kindersley's *Letters* and Fay's *Original Letters*, Lady Craven's *Letters* discloses the superior stance she took toward the cultures she encountered en route to Prussia. She derided French politics, Muslims, and foreign cities—their environs, cultures, and citizens.

The uniqueness of Jane Elizabeth Moore's *Genuine Memoirs* resides in its focus on the "Trade, Manufactures, Navigation, Laws and Police of this Kingdom, and the necessity of a Country Hospital." While her travels are limited to Great Britain, her travel narrative takes up issues that generally do not arise "from a female pen" (xxx). She contended that her long tenure at running the family business qualified her as an expert in these matters. Anna Maria Falconbridge's *Narrative* is unrivaled in chronicling a woman's views of the Sierra Leone Company. First sympathetic to the project's abolitionist ideals, she rejected them when many company policies and practices regarding the resettlement of ex-slaves became indefensible. Although Ann Radcliffe is famous for her Gothic novels, her *Journey* takes on the romantic qualities of late-eighteenth-century travel literature, incorporating her personal responses to the sites and cultures of Holland and Germany. Unprecedented in that Radcliffe's *Journey* shared coauthorship with her husband, it is also remarkable for its political and economic discourse and antiwar commentary. Mary Ann Parker's *Voyage round the World* takes a lighthearted tone when she recounts the arduous voyage to New South Wales. Like the Sierra Leone project in its experimental nature, New South Wales was a colony established for convicts. When Parker documents the situations there, however, the *Voyage* becomes politically reflective and displays a concern for needed reforms. Mary Wollstonecraft's

Letters shares romantic qualities with Radcliffe's *Journey*, but the Scandinavian letters go far beyond Radcliffe's personal responses. Wollstonecraft's letters "have long been recognized as a revelatory psychological document, but they are also a literary experiment, thematically unified and formally organized through a very personal version of associationism" (Myers, "Wollstonecraft" 166). The *Letters* is most remarkable, however, in that it sets new standards for travel literature as it provides readers with climatic and geographic explanations for Scandinavian character and material explanations for the lack of education and limited economic progress of the people. British women's travel narratives presented new information on other cultures and, particularly those of Montagu and Wollstonecraft, took to task " 'frivolous, superficial remarks' on pictures, buildings, and social occasions," "detached observations," and inaccurate information. "It is the reflective traveler's consciousness which most often makes connections and supplies unity; indeed, [as Wollstonecraft remarked,] 'the art of travel is only a branch of the art of thinking' " (Myers, "Wollstonecraft" 166–167).

The Preface.   This collection concludes with an unusual instance of women's life-writing, the preface. The preface was not considered a major strain of women's autobiographical discourse in the eighteenth century. A number of medieval women writers, however, prefaced their plays and poems with brief life-narratives. Hrotsvitha (935–1000), a playwright and nun of the Gandersheim order, chronicled her development from *ingeniolum*, a little genius, to *ingenum*, genius, in the prefaces to her double cycle of legends and plays (Dronke 64–65). Mary R. Stockdale's "To the Reader" harkens back to this tradition as she prefaced her collection of poems, *The Mirror of the Mind*, with a catalog of the sufferings of her young life. Making sure that her readers understood that she had received the tenderest care and financial support from her family, Stockdale explicated the way in which painful physical affliction shaped her poetry and how she hoped that her poetry would make "her fellow creatures" fall in love with virtue (xcv).

CR BD

The thirty women whose texts are included in this anthology are a varied group: ministers, actresses, businesswomen, authors, aristocrats, middle class, and servants. They address their concerns to audiences of sympathizers and scornful critics. Their life-writings, be they family history, conversion narrative, scandalous memoir, defense, travel narrative, or preface, are remarkable both in the astounding range of forms and in the courageous and determined way they give voice to women's lives.

Note

1. Kristie S. Fleckenstein draws the insights of Geraldine Finn, Anne Balsamo, and Teresa de Lauretis together for composition studies. They are particularly applicable to women's autobiography (282).

Ann, Lady Fanshawe

1625–1679

*Memoirs of Lady Fanshawe, Wife of the Right Hon. Sir Richard Fanshawe, Bart.
Ambassador from Charles the Second to the Court of Madrid in 1665. Written by
herself. To which are added, extracts from the Correspondence of Sir Richard Fanshawe.* London: Henry Colburn, 1829.

Ann Harrison was born in 1625, the fourth child of Sir John Harrison
and Margaret Fanshawe, his wife and first cousin. She was educated by
her mother in needlework, French, lute, virginals, singing, and dancing
but later felt that her "beloved recreation"—riding, running, "all active
pastimes"—had taken "too much" of her time (32). After her mother's
death in 1640, "as an offering to her memory" (33) Ann gave up her
"little childishnesses" and ran her father's house; they lived "in great plenty
and hospitality" (34) but without "lavishness" or "prodigality," as exemplified by the fact that her father never drank more than six glasses of wine
per day. The Harrison family's fortunes changed with the beginning of the
civil war in 1642; Ann's father was imprisoned by order of the Parliamentarians and deprived of his property. In 1643 he moved his family to Oxford. There Ann met Sir Richard Fanshawe, a cousin of her mother; she
was twenty years old and he thirty-six when they married in 1644. Having
little money and being Royalists on the run, they began married life as
"merchant adventurers" (38). Sir Richard became secretary to the Prince
of Wales and followed him into exile in 1645. For the next five years the
prince's court moved repeatedly—from Cornwall, to the Channel Isles, to
Paris, Holland, Ireland—and Lady Fanshawe was often separated from her
husband, since it was not "the fashion for honest women, except they had
business, to visit a man's Court" (54).

The *Memoirs* details a series of Lady Fanshawe's adventures both with
and without Sir Richard. She made several solitary journeys to England on
business for him, on one of which she was shipwrecked; during another
voyage, this time with her husband, she dressed in a cabin boy's clothes in
order to join him on deck, and when he recognized her he "snatched [her]

up in his arms, saying, 'Good God, that love can make this change!' " (93).
In 1651 Lady Fanshawe returned to England, while her husband joined
Charles II in Scotland as a chief adviser in the Royalist plan to invade England and overthrow Cromwell's Commonwealth. When the rising was
defeated, Sir Richard was arrested and imprisoned in London; Lady Fanshawe stood outside the prison every day at 4 A.M. to speak with him and
eventually obtained his release. In 1653 they settled in near Barnsley. Although Sir Richard was under a form of house arrest, they left this home
in grief after a favorite daughter, Ann, died in July 1654 of smallpox. Lady
Fanshawe wrote that "we both wished to have gone into the same grave
with her" (122). More moves and adventures followed, as well as births
and deaths of children. Over the course of her marriage Lady Fanshawe
bore six sons (only the last lived) and eight daughters, four of whom survived. With the restoration of the monarchy in 1660 the Fanshawes returned to England, and in 1661 Sir Richard was entrusted with several delicate diplomatic missions on which Lady Fanshawe accompanied him. He
was appointed ambassador to the Court of Madrid in January 1664 and by
December 1665 had successfully negotiated a commercial treaty with Spain;
for reasons that remain shadowy, he was then dismissed from his post, and
he died suddenly on 26 June 1666. Devastated, Lady Fanshawe had his
body embalmed and accompanied it across Europe to England; the *Memoirs*
ends at this point. Although Charles II condoled with Lady Fanshawe
about the loss of her husband, it was three years before she could wrest
back pay and reimbursements from the government. She died in 1679.

TEXT: The manuscript was written down under Lady Fanshawe's inspection in 1676
for the instruction of her son. It was copied in 1766 by her great-granddaughter,
copied again in 1786, and first published in 1829 with the 1786 manuscript as copy-
text. Before its publication, the *Memoirs* appears to have circulated in manuscript;
according to the 1829 preface by Lady Fanshawe's descendant Charles Robert Fanshawe, it was not only "frequently cited, but copiously quoted, in various popular
works" (v). In 1979 John Loftis edited Lady Fanshawe's *Memoirs* and published it
with Lady Anne Halkett's. The first selection (pp. 1–9 of the 1829 *Memoirs*), addressed
to Lady Fanshawe's son, touchingly demonstrates her loving relationship with her
husband; the second selection (pp. 179–197) covers the first months of the Fanshawes' sojourn in Spain.

☙ ❧

I HAVE THOUGHT IT GOOD to discourse to you, my most dear and
only son, the most remarkable actions and accidents of your family, as well

Ann, Lady Fanshawe, painting by an unknown artist, attributed to Cornelius Jonson. In a private Scottish collection, courtesy of the Scottish National Portrait Gallery.

as those more eminent ones of your father; and my life and necessity, not delight or revenge, hath made me insert some passages which will reflect on their owners, as the praises of others will be but just, which is my intent in this narrative. I would not have you be a stranger to it; because, by the example, you may imitate what is applicable to your condition in the world, and endeavour to avoid those misfortunes we have passed through, if God pleases.

Endeavour to be innocent as a dove, but as wise as a serpent; and let this lesson direct you most in the greatest extremes of fortune. Hate idleness, and curb all passions; be true in all words and actions; unnecessarily deliver not your opinion; but when you do, let it be just, well-considered, and plain. Be charitable in all thought, word, and deed, and ever ready to forgive injuries done to yourself, and be more pleased to do good than to receive good.

Be civil and obliging to all, dutiful where God and nature command you; but friend to one, and that friendship keep sacred, as the greatest tie upon earth, and be sure to ground it upon virtue; for no other is either happy or lasting.

Endeavour always to be content in that estate of life which it hath pleased God to call you to, and think it a great fault not to employ your time, either for the good of your soul, or improvement of your understanding, health, or estate; and as these are the most pleasant pastimes, so it will make you a cheerful old age, which is as necessary for you to design, as to make provision to support the infirmities which decay of strength brings: and it was never seen that a vicious youth terminated in a contented, cheerful old age, but perished out of countenance. Ever keep the best qualified persons company, out of whom you will find advantage, and reserve some hours daily to examine yourself and fortune; for if you embark yourself in perpetual conversation or recreation, you will certainly shipwreck your mind and fortune. Remember the proverb—such as his company is, such is the man, and have glorious actions before your eyes, and think what shall be your portion in Heaven, as well as what you desire on earth.

Manage your fortune prudently, and forget not that you must give God an account hereafter, and upon all occasions.

Remember your father, whose true image, though I can never draw to the life, unless God will grant me that blessing in you; yet, because you were but ten months and ten days old when God took him out of this world, I will, for your advantage, show you him with all truth, and without partiality.

He was of the highest size of men, strong, and of the best proportion; his complexion sanguine, his skin exceedingly fair, his hair dark brown and very curling, but not very long; his eyes grey and penetrating, his nose high, his countenance gracious and wise, his motion good, his speech clear and distinct. He never used exercise but walking, and that generally with some book in his hand, which oftentimes was poetry, in which he spent his idle hours; sometimes he would ride out to take the air, but his most delight was, to go only with me in a coach some miles, and there discourse of those things which then most pleased him, of what nature soever.

He was very obliging to all, and forward to serve his master, his country, and friend; cheerful in his conversation; his discourse ever pleasant, mixed with the sayings of wise men, and their histories repeated as occasion offered, yet so reserved that he never showed the thought of his heart, in its greatest sense, but to myself only; and this, I thank God, with all my soul for, that he never discovered his trouble to me, but went from me with perfect cheerfulness and content; nor revealed he his joys and hopes, but would say, that they were doubled by putting them in my breast. I never heard him hold disputation[1] in my life, but often he would speak against it, saying, it was an uncharitable custom, which never turned to the advantage of either party. He would never be drawn to the fashion of any party, saying, he found it sufficient honestly to perform that employment he was in: he loved and used cheerfulness in all his actions, and professed his religion in his life and conversation. He was a true Protestant of the Church of England, so born, so brought up, and so died; his conversation was so honest that I never heard him speak a word in my life that tended to God's dishonour, or encouragement of any kind of debauche[r]y or sin. He was ever much esteemed by his two masters, Charles the First and Charles the Second, both for great parts and honesty, as for his conversation, in which they took great delight, he being so free from passion, that made him beloved of all that knew him, nor did I ever see him moved but with his master's concerns, in which he would hotly pursue his interest through the greatest difficulties.

He was the tenderest father imaginable, the carefullest and most generous master I ever knew; he loved hospitality, and would often say, it was wholly essential for the constitution of England: he loved and kept order with the greatest decency possible; and though he would say I managed his domestics wholly, yet I ever governed them and myself by his commands; in the managing of which, I thank God, I found his approbation and content.

Now you will expect that I should say something that may remain of us jointly, which I will do though it makes my eyes gush out with tears, and cuts me to the soul to remember, and in part express the joys I was blessed with in him. Glory be to God, we never had but one mind throughout our lives. Our souls were wrapt up in each others; our aims and designs one, our loves one, and our resentments one. We so studied one the other, that we knew each others mind by our looks. Whatever was real happiness, God gave it me in him; but to commend my better half, which I want sufficient expression for, methinks is to commend myself, and so may bear a censure; but might it be permitted I could dwell eternally on his praise most justly; but thus without offence I do, and so you may imitate him in his patience, his prudence, his chastity, his charity, his generosity, his perfect resignation to God's will, and praise God for him as long as you live here, and with him hereafter in the Kingdom of Heaven. Amen.

January 15th [1664], I took my leave of the King and Queen, who, with great kindness, wished me a good voyage to Spain. Then I waited on the Queen-mother[2] at Somerset House: her Majesty sent for me into her bed-chamber, and after some discourse I took my leave of her Majesty. Afterwards I waited on their Royal Highnesses, who received me with more than ordinary kindness, and after an hour and a half's discourse with me, saluted[3] me and gave me leave to depart.

On Tuesday, January 19th, my husband carried the speaker, Sir Edward Turner's eldest son, and my brother Turner, to the King at Whitehall, who conferred the honour of knighthood on them both, my husband particularly recommending my brother Turner to his Majesty's grace and honour.

On the 20th of January my husband took his leave of his Majesty and all the Royal Family, receiving the despatches and their commands for Spain, from which hour to our going out of town, day and night, our house was full of kindred and friends taking leave of us; and on Thursday the 21st, 1664, in the morning, at eight o'clock, did rendezvous at Dorset House, in Salisbury Court, in that half of the house which Sir Thomas Fanshawe[4] then lived in, who entertained us with a very good breakfast and banquet. The company that came thither was very great, as was likewise that which accompanied us out of town. Thus, with many coaches of our family and friends, we took our journey at ten of the clock towards Portsmouth.

The company of our family[5] was my husband, myself, and four daughters; Mr. Bertie, son to the Earl of Lindsey, Lord Great Chamberlain of England; Mr. Newport, second son to the Lord Baron Newport; Sir Benjamin Wright, Baronet; Sir Andrew King; Sir Edward Turner, Knight, son to the Speaker of the Commons' House of Parliament; and Mr. Francis Godolphin, son to Sir Francis Godolphin, Knight of the Bath. The most part of them went by water.

We lay the first night at Guildford, the second at Petersfield, the third at Portsmouth, where we staid till the 31st of the same month, being very civilly used there by the Mayor and his brethren, who made my husband a freeman of the town, as their custom is to persons of quality that pass that way;[6] and likewise we received many favours from the Lieutenant Governor, Sir Philip Honywood, with the rest of the commanders of that garrison. As I said before, we went on board the 31st, being Sunday, the Admiral of the Fleet then setting out, Sir John Lawson, Chief Commander, in his Majesty's ship called the Resolution; there was Captain Bartley, Commander of the Bristol frigate, Captain Utbert, Commander of the Phœnix, Captain Ferne, Commander of the Portsmouth, Captain Moon, Commander of the York, and Sir John Lawson's ketch, commanded by Captain King.

Thus, at ten o'clock, we set sail with a good wind, which carried us as far as Torbay, and then failed us: there we lay till Monday the 15th of February, at nine o'clock at night, at which, it pleasing God to give us a prosperous wind, we set sail, and on the 23rd of February, our stile,[7] we cast anchor in Cadiz road, in Spain.

So soon as it was known that we were there, the English Consul with the English merchants all came on board to welcome us to Spain; and presently after came the Lieutenant-Governor from the Governor for the time being, Don Diego de Ibara, to give us joy of our arrival, and to ask leave of my husband to visit him, which Don Diego did within two hours after the Lieutenant's return. The next morning, *stilo novo*, came in a Levant wind, which blew the fleet so forcibly, that we could not possibly land until Monday, the 7th of March, at 10 o'clock in the morning. Then came the Governor, Don Deigo de Ibara, aboard, accompanied by most of the persons of quality of that town, with many boats for the conveyance of our family, and a very rich barge covered with crimsom damask fringed with gold, and Persia carpets under foot. So soon as it was day we set sail to go nearer the shore. We were first saluted by all the ships in the road, and then by all the King of Spain's forts, which salutation we returned again with our guns.

My husband received the Governor upon deck, and carried him into the round-house, who, so soon as he was there, told my husband, that contrary to the usage of the King of Spain, his Majesty had commanded that his ships and forts should first salute the King of England's Ambassador, and that his Majesty had commanded that both in that place of Cadiz and in all others to the Court of Madrid, my husband and all his retinue should be entertained upon the King's account, in as full and ample manner both as to persons and conveyance of our goods and persons, as if his Majesty were there in person. My husband and self and children went in the barge, the rest in other barges provided for that purpose.

At our setting off, Sir John Lawson saluted us with very many guns, and as we went near the shore the cannon saluted us in great numbers. When we landed we were carried on shore in a rich chair supported by eight men: we were welcomed by many volleys of shot, and all the persons of quality of that town by the seaside, among whom was the Governor, did conduct my husband with all his train. There were infinite numbers of people, who with the soldiery did show us all the respect and welcome imaginable. I was received by his Excellency Don Milcha de la Cueva, the Duke of Albuquerque's brother, and the Governor of the garrison, who both led me four or five paces to a rich sedan, which carried me to the coach where the Governor's lady was, who came out immediately to salute me, and whom, after some compliments, I took into the coach with me and my children.

When we came to the house where we were to lodge, we were nobly treated, and the Governor's wife did me the honour to sup with me. That afternoon the Duke of Albuquerque came to visit my husband, and afterwards me, with his brother Don Milcha de la Cueva. As soon as the Duke was seated and covered,[8] he said, "Madam, I am Don Juan de la Cueva, Duke of Albuquerque, Viceroy of Milan, of his Majesty's privy council, General of the galleys, twice Grandee, the first Gentleman of his Majesty's bed-chamber, and a near kinsman to his Catholic Majesty, whom God long preserve:" and then rising up and making me a low reverence with his hat off, said, "These with my family and life, I lay at your Excellency's feet."

They were accompanied by a very great train of gentlemen. At his going away, he told me his Lady would suddenly [i.e., soon] visit me. We had a guard constantly waited on us, and sentries at the gate below and at the stairs' head above. We were visited by all the persons of quality in that town. Our house was richly furnished, both my husband's quarter and mine; the worst chamber and bed in my apartment being furnished with damask, in which my chamber-maid lay; and throughout all the chambers the floors were covered with Persia carpets. The richness of the gilt and silver plate, which we had in great abundance, as we had likewise of all sorts of very fine household linen, was fit only for the entertainment of so great a Prince as his Majesty, our Master, in the representation of whose person my husband received this great entertainment; yet, I assure you, notwithstanding this temptation, that your father and myself both wished ourselves in a retired country life in England, as more agreeable to both our inclinations.

I must not forget here, the ceremony the Governor used to my husband. After supper, the Governor brought the keys of the town to my husband, saying, "Whilst your Excellency is here, I am no Governor of this town, and therefore desire your Excellency, from me, your servant, to receive these keys, and to begin and give the word to the garrison." This night my husband, with all the demonstrations of sense of so great an honour, returned his Catholic Majesty, by him, his humble thanks, refusing the keys, and wishing the Governor much prosperity with them, who so well deserved that honour the King had given him. Then the Governor pressed my husband again for the word, which my husband gave, and was this: "Long live his Catholic Majesty!" Then the Governor took his leave, and his Lady of me, whom I accompanied to the stairs' head.

The next day we were visited by the Mayor and all the Burgesses of the town: on the same day, Saturday the 8th, the Governor's Lady sent me a very noble present of India plate and other commodities thereof. In the afternoon the Duchess of Albuquerque sent a gentleman to me to know if with conveniency her Excellency might visit me the next day, as the custom of the Court is.

On Sunday the 9th, her Excellency with her daughter, who was newly married to her uncle Don Milcha de la Cueva, visited me. I met them at the stairs' head, and at her Excellency's going, there parted with her. Her Excellency had on, besides other very rich jewels, as I guess, about two thousand pearls, the roundest, the whitest, and the biggest that ever I saw in my life.

On Thursday the 13th, the English Consul with all the merchants brought us a present of two silver basins and ewers, with a hundred weight[9] of chocolate, with crimson taffeta clothes, laced with silver laces, and voiders,[10] which were made in the Indies, as were also the basins and ewers.

This afternoon I went to pay my visit to the Duchess of Albuquerque. When I came to take coach, the soldiers stood to their arms, and the Lieutenant that held the colours displaying them, which is never done to any one but to kings, or such as represent their persons, I stood still all the while, then at the lowering of the colours to the ground, they received for them a low courtesy [i.e., curtsy] from me, and for himself a bow; then taking coach with very many persons, both in coaches and on foot, I went to the Duke's palace, where I was again received by a guard of his Excellency's, with the same ceremony of the King's colours as before.

Then I was received by the Duke's brother and near a hundred persons of quality. I laid my hand upon the wrist of his Excellency's right hand; he putting his cloak thereupon, as the Spanish fashion is, went up the stairs, upon the top of which stood the Duchess and her daughter, who received me with great civility, putting me into every door and all my children till we came to sit down in her Excellency's chamber, where she placed me on her right hand, upon cushions, as the fashion of this Court is, being very rich and laid upon Persia carpets.

At my return, the Duchess and her daughter went out before me, and at the door of her Excellency's chamber, I met the Duke, who with his brother and the rest of the gentlemen that did accompany our gentlemen during our stay there, went down together before me. When I took my leave of the Duchess, in the same place where his Excellency received me, the Duke led me down to the coach in the same manner as his brother led me up the stairs, and having received the ceremony of the soldiers, I returned home to my lodgings, where after I had been an hour, Don Antonio de Pimentel, the Governor of Cadiz, who that day was newly come to town, after having been to visit my husband, came to visit me with great company, on the part of his Catholic Majesty, and afterwards upon his own score. He sent me a very rich present of perfumes, skins, gloves, and purses embroidered, with other nacks[11] of the same kind.

Sir John Lawson being now ready to depart from Cadiz, we presented him with a pair of flaggons, one hundred pounds, and a tun of Lusena wine, which cost us forty pounds, and a hundred and forty pieces-of-eight for his men. We sent Captain Ferne two hundred pieces-of-eight, and to his men forty pieces-of-eight, they being very careful of our goods, the most of which he brought. We sent Captain Bartley a hundred pieces-of-eight, and to his men twenty; he carried part of our horses, as did Captain Utbert, to whom we sent the like sum.

On the 19th of March, we took our leave of Cadiz, where we gave at our coming away, to persons that attended on us in several offices, two hundred and eighty pieces-of-eight. We were accompanied to the water-side in the same manner. We were received on shore with all points of formality, and having taken our leave, with many thanks and compliments to the Governor and Don Diego Ibara, his lady, and all the rest of those persons there, to whom we were as much beholden for their civility, we entered the King's barge, which was newly trimmed up for the purpose by the Duke of Medina Celi, and Puerta Sancta Maria. No person ever went in it before but the King. The Governor, Don Antonio de Pimentel, went with us in the barge, and many other barges were provided by him for all our train.

At our going we had many volleys of shot, afterwards many cannons, and as we went, the guns of all the ships in the harbour. When we were come over the bar, all the forts by St. Mary's port saluted us, and when we came to the shore-side, we found many thousand soldiers in arms, in very great order, with their commanders, and a bridge made on purpose for us, with great curiosity, so far into the river, that the end of the bridge touched the side of the barge. At the end of the bridge stood the Duke of Medina Celi and his son, the Duke of Alcala. During the time of our landing, we had infinite volleys of shot, presented with drums beating and trumpets sounding, and all the demonstration of hearty welcome imaginable.

The two dukes embraced my husband with great kindness, welcoming him to the place, and the Duke of Medina Celi led me to my coach, an honour that he had never done any but once, when he waited on your Queen[12] to help her on the like occasion. The Duke d'Alcala led my eldest daughter, and the younger led my second, and the Governor of Cadiz, Don Antonio de Pimentel, led the third. Mrs. Kestian carried Betty in her arms.

Thus I entered the Duchess of Alcala's coach, which conveyed me to my lodging, the ceremony of the King's colours being performed as at Cadiz. We passed through the streets, in which were an infinite number of people, to a house provided for us, the best of all the place, which was caused to be glazed[13] by the Duke on purpose for us. At our alighting out of the coaches, the Duke led me up into my apartment, with an infinite number of noblemen and gentlemen, his relations; there they took their leave of me, conducting my husband to his quarter, with whom they staid in visit about half an hour, and so returned to his house. After I had been there three hours, the Duchess of Alcala sent a gentleman to say her Excellency welcomed me to the place, and that, as soon as I was reposed after my long voyage, she would wait upon me: in like manner did the Marquis of Bayonne and his lady, and their son with his lady.

I must not pass by the description of the entertainment, which was vastly great, tables being plentifully covered every meal for above three hundred persons. The furniture was all as rich tapestry, embroideries of gold and silver upon velvet, cloth of tissue, both gold and silver, with rich Persia carpets on the floors: none could exceed them. Very delicate fine linen of all sorts, both for table and beds, never washed, but new, cut out of the piece, and all things thereunto belonging. The plate was vastly great and beautiful, nor for ornament were they fewer than the rest of the bravery [i.e., splendor], there being very fine cabinets, looking-glasses, tables, and chairs.

Notes

1. Apparently a reference to the formal exercise in which parties attack, defend, and sustain a question or thesis.

2. Henriette Marie, mother of King Charles II.

3. To salute is to give a ceremonial kiss of greeting or farewell.

4. A brother of Sir Richard.

5. "Family" connoted all members of a household, not simply blood relations.

6. A freeman has the freedoms, or privileges of citizenship, of the town; as Lady Fanshawe indicates, these freedoms were often conferred to honor an eminent person.

7. "Our stile" refers to the Julian, or Old Style, calendar, used in England until 1752; it was eleven days behind the Gregorian, or New Style, calendar used in continental Europe.

8. Replaced his hat, which he had removed at greeting as a gesture of respect.

9. Unit of weight equal to 100 pounds.

10. Receptacle into which something is emptied.

11. Trinkets (obs.); cf. modern knickknacks.

12. Catherine of Braganza, wife of King Charles II.

13. Covered with a thin coat of transparent paint to heighten the underlying color.

Mary Pennington

1616?–1682

Some Account of Circumstances in the Life of Mary Pennington, from her Manuscript, left for her family. London: Harvey and Darton, 1821.

Mary Proud was born in 1616 or 1625, the only child of Sir John Proud and Anne Fagge Proud. Her father died in battle when she was three years old, and her mother died soon thereafter; thenceforth she appears to have been cared for by various relatives and family friends. She took little notice of scripture until the age of eight, a delay she chalks up to the "loose Protestants" (1) with whom she lived, whose laxity included celebrating Christmas and attending only one church service on Sundays. Some time later Mary went to live in the household of Sir Edwin Partridge, which included his widowed sister Katherine Springett and her three children. Receiving a "more religious" upbringing (2), Mary became "very serious" (4) about religion, indeed "deeply exercised" about the nature of true prayer. Unsurprisingly, she came into conflict with relatives and friends, "vain persons" all (10), and rejected the various matches they proposed. In 1641 or 1642 she married Katherine Springett's son, Sir William, who shared Mary's strict beliefs; they tore out of their Bibles psalms by poets and several forms of prayer that did not meet with their approval, and they were among the first of their class to object to the "superstitious customs" (70) of baptism. Mary's mother-in-law appears to have been a formidable woman as well: famous for her skill with medicinal herbs, she sometimes had as many as twenty patients in a morning, and she trained Mary as an oculist and manufacturer of patent medicines. After Sir William died in 1643 or 1644, Mary was "a by-word and a hissing" (13) for continuing in her refusal to have their daughter, Gulielma, baptized (Gulielma eventually married William Penn, the founder of what is now Pennsylvania). Mary grieved deeply for her husband, and later she exchanged religious devotions for "foolish mirth" (16–17), "jovial eatings and drinkings," and the like.

"Wearied in seeking and not finding" (25), she married Isaac Pennington in 1654, to be "a companion to him" (26). Although she had decided to be "without a religion, until the Lord taught me one" (27), within a few years both of the Penningtons were devout members of the Society of Friends, better known as Quakers. Indeed, Isaac became an important defender of the plain language favored by the Quakers. He was imprisoned for his beliefs six times between 1661 and 1671, while the *Account* indicates the social ostracism and financial losses both suffered under such anti-Quaker persecution. As the *Account* also indicates, however, Mary contrived to hold on to a portion of her property and took a recognizably secular satisfaction in managing it. Isaac died in 1679, and Mary contracted a serious fever the following year; at that point she appears to have begun to put her worldly and spiritual affairs in order, although her death did not occur until 1682.

TEXT: Mary Pennington's *Account*, published in 1821, combines two texts: *A brief account of some of my exercises from childhood*, and a letter to her grandson Springet Penn, intended for him after her death. *A brief account* was begun some time before 1668, then laid aside to be shown after her death. In 1672, however, she wrote it out "for the use of my children, and some few particular friends" (36), and she updated it in 1680 and again in 1681. It was first published in 1797; another edition appeared in 1911, and that edition was reprinted in 1992. The letter to Springet Penn is primarily concerned with the life of his grandfather, her first husband. The excerpt (pp. 40–60 of the *Account*) is the updates of 1680 and 1681; it covers both Pennington's care of her estate and a review of her spiritual condition, a conjunction which is quite characteristic.

I SHALL NOW PROCEED to make an addition to the foregoing narrative.[1] After my dear husband and I had received the truth of God's faithful servants, to the light and grace in the heart, we became obedient to the heavenly voice, receiving the truth in the love of it, and took up the cross to the customs, language, friendships, titles, and honours of this world; and endured, patiently, despisings, reproaches, cruel mockings, and scornings, from relations, acquaintances, and neighbours; those of our own rank, and those below us, nay, even our own servants. To every class we were a by-word: they would wag the head at us, accounting us fools, mad, and bewitched. As such, they stoned, abused, and imprisoned us, at several towns and meetings where we went. This not being enough to prove us, and work for us a far more exceeding weight of glory, it pleased the Lord to try us by the loss of our estate, which was wrongfully withheld from

Lady Springett, later Mary Pennington, by an unknown artist presumably
during the period of her marriage to Sir William Springett, 1642–1644.
Courtesy of Pennsbury Manor, Pennsylvania Historical and
Museum Commission.

us, by our relations sueing us unrighteously. Our own tenants withheld what the law gave, and put us into the Court of Chancery,[2] because we could not swear.[3] Our relations also taking that advantage, we were put out of our dwelling-house, in an injurious, unrighteous manner. Thus we were stripped of my husband's estate, and a great part of mine.

After this, we were tossed up and down from place to place, to our great weariness and charge. We had no place to abide in, near our former habitation at Chalfont, where our meetings used to be held; yet were we pressed in our spirits to stay amongst the gathered flock, if a place could be found any way convenient, though but ordinarily decent. We sought within the compass of four or five miles, but could find none; yet we had such a sense that was our proper place, that we had not freedom to settle any where else. So we boarded at Waltham Abbey, for the sake of having our children accommodated at a school there, and desired our friends to enquire after, or provide a place for us, at a Friend's house, to winter in, hoping to be provided with a house against the ensuing summer.

All the time we were seeking for a place, we never entertained a thought of buying one to settle ourselves in; not choosing to be cumbered with either house or land by purchase, as we both desired a disentangled state. I, seeing no provision likely to be made for us in this country, near Friends, told my husband, that, if we must leave them, I should choose to go to my own estate in Kent; which proposal he did not approve of, objecting against the badness of the air, and dirtiness of the place.

I was now greatly perplexed about what to do: my husband's objections, together with my own extreme unwillingness to leave those people whom we had been instrumental in gathering to the truth, and who had known our unjust sufferings respecting our estate, and many others of our trials, and had compassionated us: (we had suffered together, and had been comforted together:) I say, these considerations, and to be obliged to go, and not to go to my own estate, was cause of sore exercise [i.e., worry] to me. How irksome was it to think of going among strangers! The people in our neighbourhood knew of our former affluence, and now pitied us for being so stripped; and did not expect great things of us, suitable to our rank in the world; but wondered how it was that we could still support a degree of decency in our way of living, and were able to pay every one their own. We contentedly submitted to mean things, and so remained honourable before them.

Whilst I was thus distressed, and we had nearly concluded on going to Waltham Abbey, R. T.[4] came to see us, and much bewailed our going out of the country, and having no place near them to return to. At length he asked why we did not buy some little place near them? I replied, that our circumstances would not admit of it; for we had not one hundred pounds, beside rents becoming due; and, that to do that, we must sell some of my estate. He said he had an uncle, that had a little place that he would sell for about thirty pounds a year, that stood about a mile from the meeting-house, in a healthy situation; that there was a house on it, which might be trimmed up, and made habitable for a little expense. My husband was not there when mention was made of this place. Soon after T. B.[5] came in: I told him of the proposal made by R. T. He encouraged the thing, saying, he had heard there were some rooms in the house that might serve. That night Thomas Elwood[6] came out of Kent, and told me he had much to do to come back without selling my farm at Westbeer.

I laid all these things together, and said: "I think our best way is to sell Westbeer, and purchase this place which R. T. has mentioned; and, with the overplus of the money, put the house in a condition to receive us." For I now saw no other method for our remaining in the country. Next day I took Anne Bull[7] with me, and went on foot to Woodside, to John Humphrey's[8] house, to view it and its situation. We came in by Hill's Lane, through the orchard. The house appeared in such a ruinous condition, so unlikely to be fitted up, that I did not go into it; and we gave over all thoughts about it, till we were disappointed of a house at Beacon's-field, which my husband was in treaty about. Upon this we were pressed to go and see the house, which T. E. H. B.[9] and I did. Whilst I went about the house, they viewed the grounds. In less than half an hour I had the whole thing clearly in my mind, what to pull down, and what to add; and thought it might be done with the overplus money of the sale of Westbeer, that being valued at fifty pounds a year, and this at thirty. I was quite reconciled to the thing, and willing to treat about it. The day we went to see it, we walked to Chalfont, and took my son Penn's[10] coach thither, desiring him to make enquiry respecting the title, &c. and let us know at Waltham; which he did, and sent us word that the title was clear, but that it was judged fifty pounds too dear.

After reading this information, my mind was much retired to the Lord, desiring that if this was the place we ought to settle in, he would be pleased to order it for us. Seeing we had now lost all but my estate, and had no other provision for ourselves or children, and were so tossed about, without having any dwelling-place, I requested my husband to give me leave to engage for it; for my mind was quite easy so to do. I told him he should not be troubled about the building; that should be my care, (he being very averse to building.) At length he, considering that the estate was mine, that he had lost all his own, and had been the innocent cause of bringing great sufferings upon me, he willingly consented that I should use my own mind about it; adding, that it was, and ever should be his delight, to gratify me in every respect. So I sent to desire my friends to conclude for it; saying, I did not mind fifty pounds, if they thought it would answer for us in other respects. The bargain was concluded. I often prayed, with tears, that I might be kept free from entanglements and cumber, and that it might prove such a habitation as would manifest that the Lord was again restoring us, and had regard unto us. I went cheerfully and industriously about the business of making alterations, entreating the Lord that I might go through it in his fear, keeping my mind from cumber or darkness. Every difficulty seemed to vanish, and I went on to plant, and make provision for the building; but I was put out of my own way by surveyors, who were for raising from the ground a new part. My husband falling in with it, I would not contend about it; though it brought great trouble upon me, for I could not see my way about the business as before; nor could I see the end of it, it being far beyond my own proposal; and I thought I could not compass it, on account of the great charge. I took no pleasure in doing any thing about it: I fell ill, and could not look after it. Great was my exercise: one while fearing the Lord did not approve of our undertaking, and another while that I did wrong in consenting to it. I would often say: "Lord, thou knowest I did not seek great things for myself: I desired not a fine habitation." As I intended doing it, it would have been very ordinary. When I first consented to the addition, the very great expense was not discerned by me. The Lord knew my earnest prayers, close exercise, and honest intent.

After a while I felt freedom to go on, and was freed from care or disquiet. The building was wholly managed by me, with great ease and cheerfulness. Part of the old house undesignedly fell down. I was most remarkably preserved from being hurt thereby, yet the loss was a little trial to me; but after that all things went on well, and whenever I had occasion to pay money, I never wanted it. Having contracted our family greatly; the rents coming in; and having sold some old houses, bark,[11] and several other things, instead of pain, I had now pleasure in laying out my money. Indeed, my mind was so daily to the Lord in this affair, and I was so constantly provided with money, that I often thought, and sometimes said, that if I had lived when building houses for the service of the Lord was accepted and blessed, I could not have had a sweeter, stiller, and pleasanter time. I set all things in order in the morning, before I went to meeting, and so left them till my return; rarely finding them rise up in my mind when going to, coming from, or whilst sitting in meeting: so my mind was mercifully kept in a sweet, savoury frame.

My chief care about my business in hand, was, by my own eye, to prevent any waste; which was done without any disquiet, fretting, or anger. I lay down sweetly, and rested pleasantly, and awoke under a grateful sense of the Lord's goodness to me. The labour of my body kept it healthy, and my mind was easy. In less than four years the building was completed, except the wash-house part. I could have compassed it in much less time, but then I should have been straitened for money: my doing it by degrees, made it steal on undiscerned, in point of expense; the whole of which amounted, in planting, building, &c. to but about one hundred pounds. During this expensive time, we did not omit being helpful, by giving or lending to such as were in distress.

And now the Lord has seen good to make me a widow, and leave me in a desolate condition, by depriving me of my dear companion;[12] yet, through his mercy, I am quite disentangled, and in a very easy state as to outward things. I have often desired the Lord to make way so for me, as that I might continually wait upon him, without distraction or the cumber of outward things. I most thankfully, and gratefully, and humbly, under a deep sense of the Lord's kind and gracious dealing with me, receive the disposal of my lands from his hands. Through his kindness I have cleared off [a] great part of the mortgage that was upon them, and paid most of my bond debts; and can now very easily manage the land in my hands. And in this 4th month, 1680, I have made my will, and disposed of my estate, which is clear of any considerable debt. I have left a handsome provision for T. P. M. P.[13] and enough for my younger children, to put them out to trades or decent callings; and also provision for the payment of my legacies and debts. I call my children's a handsome provision, considering it is all out of my own inheritance, having nothing of their father's to provide for them with.

And now I am mourning for the loss of my dear, worthy companion, and exercised with the great sickness and weakness of my children; but my outward situation and habitation is to my heart's content. I have no great family to cumber me, am private, and have leisure to apply my heart unto wisdom, in the numbering of my days to be but few; holding myself in readiness to bid farewell to all transitory things. In reference to my outward affairs, having set my house in order, I am waiting, sensible of the approach of death; having no desire after life, enjoying the satisfaction that I shall leave my children in an orderly way, and having less need of me, than when things were less contracted and settled. I feel that death is a king of terrors, and know that my strength to triumph over him, must be given me by the Lord, at the very season when the trying time cometh. My sight to-day of things beyond the grave, will be insufficient in that hour, to keep me from the sting of death when he comes. It is the Lord alone will then be able to stand by me, and help me to resist the evil one, who is very busy when the tabernacle is dissolving: his work being at an end "when the earthen vessel is broken."[14] O Lord, what quiet, safety, or ease is there in any state but that wherein we feel thy living power. All desirable things are in this; and nothing but sorrow, amazement, anguish, distress, grief, perplexity, woe, and misery, and what not, out of it. O let me be helped by thy power, and in it walk with thee, in thy pure fear; and then I matter not how low, how unseen I am in this world, nor how little friendship, or any pleasant thing I have in it. I have found thy power to be sufficient for every good word and work, when stripped of every pleasant picture, or acceptable, or other helpful thing. O Lord, thou knowest what I have yet to go through in this world; but my hope is in thy mercy, to guide and support. Aided by thee, I need not be doubtful or concerned about what is to come upon me.

Thus far I wrote before I went to Edmonton which was in the sixth Month, 1680. It appeared as if I was to go thither, on purpose to put all the foregoing things in practice, and to be proved by the Lord according to what I have before written; and to be exercised by him in all the things that were in my view when I set my house in order, and that I was to return no more. In about a week after my arrival, it pleased the Lord to visit me with a violent burning fever. It was the sorest bodily affliction I had ever experienced since I was born: indeed, it was very tedious and trying to me, insomuch that I made my moan in these doleful words: "distress! distress!" finding these words comprehended all my feelings, which were sickness, uneasiness, want of rest, lowness of spirits, &c. besides ill accommodations in the house, it being at a school. I was greatly disturbed, and but a little attendance was to be had.

All these things made it very heavy upon me; far from my own house, where I might have needed nothing. All this was attended with many aggravations. My two youngest children lay sick in the same room, one of them in the same bed with me; my elder children many miles from me, ignorant of my melancholy situation, now most desperate; my physician and others about me believing I could never recover. In all this illness I had scarcely one quarter of an hour wherein I should have been able to do any thing about my outward affairs, if I had then had it to do; but such was the eminent kindness and mercy of the Lord to me, that he put it into my heart to consider that it may be, I might never return home again, as he did into the heart of my dear husband. So I had nothing to do in this sickness, but to suffer patiently, waiting upon the Lord; and, if it had been his will, to lie down this body without distraction about outward concerns.

These memorable, merciful dealings of the Lord with me, I now recount, the 3d day of the 9th Mo. 1681, in an humble sense of his mercy, being still in bed, unrecovered of the forementioned illness, it being eight months since. And now it is in my heart, in the holy fear of the most High, to declare to you, my dear children, of what great service it was to me in my illness, to have nothing to do but to die, if it had been his holy will: for the Lord was pleased to assure me of his favour, and that I should not go down to the pit with the wicked, but should have a mansion, according to his good pleasure, in his holy habitation. This assurance left me in a quiet state, out of the feelings of the sting of death, not having the least desire to live. Though I did not witness any great measure of triumph or joy, yet I could say: "Lord, it is enough: I am quiet and still, and have not a thought about any thing that is to be done in preparation for my going hence. Though thou afflictest, thou makest me content both night and day."

In about fourteen days my fever was abated, and in about a month I came from Edmonton to London, favoured with some degree of strength. After having been absent about seven weeks, the Lord brought me home again to my own house. That very night I was smitten with a distemper, from which I remain weak and low in body to this day; on which morning, it springs to my mind to express something of the dealings of the Lord with me in my present sickness and exercises.

On the 27th of the 4th Mo. in the morning, as I was waiting upon the Lord with some of my family, I found an inclination to mention the continuation of my illness to this day, which, from the time of my being visited, is near a year; in all which time, such was the goodness of the Lord to me, that as it was said of Job, "In all this he sinned not, nor charged God foolishly," so I may say, (through the power of his might,) in all this time I have been a stranger to a murmuring, complaining mind; but this hath been my constant language: "It is well I have no very grievous thing to undergo," except some severe fits of the stone,[15] which have been full of anguish and misery. And the Lord has graciously stopped my desires after every pleasant thing, that I have not been at all uneasy at my long confinement, for the most part to my bed; and to this present day to my chamber, where I have very little comfort from sleep, or pleasantness from food, or any thing of that kind. Yet I have not found in my heart to ask of the Lord to be restored to my former health and strength, that I might have the pleasure of natural sleep, and eating my food with acceptation to my palate, or be able to attend to my outward affairs, or go abroad in the air to view the beautiful creation; but all I have desired respecting my house of clay is, that the Lord would be mercifully pleased to make my future fits of my distemper less severe than the former ones were; in which I have cried earnestly to the Lord for help, or that he would be pleased to direct me to some outward means that would lessen my anguish. Except in these violent fits, I have not asked any thing of the Lord concerning life or health, but have rather felt pleasantness from being debarred from those things which are acceptable to the senses; because thereby I have been drawn nearer to the Lord, and have waited upon him with much less distraction than when in my health. I have many times said, within myself: "Oh! this is sweet and easy. He makes my bed in my sickness, and withholds my eyes from sleeping, to converse with him."

Death hath many times been presented to me, which I have rather embraced than shrunk from; for the most part finding a kind of yielding up in my spirit to die, like as it is said: "He yielded up the ghost." Even before I came to be settled in the truth, I entertained an awful sense of death, and was in subjection to the fear of it. But now that fear of death, and the state of death is removed; but there remaineth still a deep sense of the passage from time to eternity, how strait, hard, and difficult it is; and even many times to those on whom the second death hath no power, yet subjected to such feelings as were our dear Lord's and Saviour's, when in agony he cried out: "My God! my God! why hast thou forsaken me!"

Another striking instance is that of my certainly blessed husband, whose mind was constantly with the Lord in his last illness; yet, when the last breath was breathing out, his groans were dreadful. I may call them roarings, as it seemed to be, through the disquiet of his soul at that moment. Indeed, this hard passage of his hath so deeply affected me, that I have often since said: "If it be thus with the green tree, how will it be with me, who am to him but as a dry tree."

Notes

1. The record of Pennington's life to 1668.
2. Next to the House of Lords, the highest court in England.
3. In obedience to Christ's injunction to "swear not at all," Quakers refused to take oaths of any sort.
4. Probably Ralph Trumper, a Quaker known to Isaac.
5. Not identified.
6. Tutor to Isaac and Mary's children.

7. One of Mary's servants.
8. Probably Ralph Trumper's uncle.
9. Not identified.
10. Mary's son-in-law, William Penn.
11. Perhaps the portion of tree bark used for tanning.
12. Mary's husband Isaac died in 1679.
13. The Penningtons' eldest son and daughter.
14. The reference is to Revelations 2:27.
15. Kidney stones.

Margaret Fell Fox

1614–1702

A Relation of Margaret Fell, Her Birth, Life, Testimony, and Sufferings for the Lord's Everlasting Truth in her Generation. In *A Brief Collection of Remarkable Passages and Occurrences Relating to the Birth, Education, Life, Conversion, Travels, Services, and Deep Sufferings of that Ancient, Eminent, and Faithful Servant of the Lord Margaret Fell.* London: J. Sowle, 1710.

The bare bones of Margaret Fell Fox's life are discernible in her *Relation*: born in 1614, married Thomas Fell in 1631, bore nine children during this twenty-six-year mariage, converted to the Society of Friends in 1652, widowed in 1658, took the first of nine journeys to London on Quaker business in 1660, imprisoned repeatedly for her religious beliefs from 1664 on, and married George Fox in 1669. Widowed a second time in 1691, she remained a Quaker activist until her death in 1702. It is fitting that the last incident she records is a letter of 1690 to the Women's Meeting in London, for Fell Fox initiated this element of the Friends' organization, and she is best known for such innovations. Indeed, she was perhaps the first "mother in Israel," the Friends' term for what Phyllis Mack has called the "archetypal female Quaker" ("Gender" 55). Such a woman combined "ecstatic prayer and public evangelizing" with "more conventional" (Mack, "Gender" 54) as well as domestic activities; Fell Fox, for instance, ran her first husband's estate of Swarthmore Hall during his long absences and raised their eight surviving children while supervising the Friends' "growing missionary network" (Dailey 61). "Mothers in Israel" tended to have wealth, property, and "a relatively privileged class position" (Mack, "Gender" 55), and the confidence with which Fell Fox took on so many tasks testifies in part to the class position she defines at the beginning of *Relation*: daughter to a gentleman of "ancient name" and "considerable estate," wife of an influential Member of Parliament and magistrate, and owner of substantial property in her own right.

Even a "mother in Israel," however, might find it difficult to negotiate her gender role. On the one hand, Quakers were far more open to women than many radical religious groups, and Fell Fox was both architect and beneficiary of this policy: her tract *Womens Speaking Justified* (1666) publicized the Friends' belief that women as well as men could "receive, and express, the Word" (Stuard 13); the Women's Meetings she advocated set priorities that were then extended to the whole Society of Friends; she and other Quaker women settled religious questions in ways that were "favorable to women's participation and leadership" (Stuard 15); her *Relation* shows that she converted without her husband's approval and that she felt entitled to confront male leaders, up to and including the king. But if the seventeenth century established such "a tradition of female independence in religious matters" (Wilcox 140), it also saw a "new wave of witchcraft persecution" (Stuard 10), so neither Fell Fox's entitlement nor women's leadership should be exaggerated. The language of the *Relation* negotiates a conflict between the "mystical autonomy" Quaker women could expect and a "traditional prescription" (Dailey 60) of wifely subordination, but it also demonstrates that this conflict was as inherent in Quakerism as in other dissenting religions. Despite the Friends' egalitarian rhetoric and practice, for instance, the separate Women's Meetings "encoded gender specific roles within a traditional patriarchal context" (Dailey 67), and "mothers in Israel" such as Fell Fox "continued and greatly amplified" women's customary roles (Mack, "Gender" 56). By the same token, of course, it was women who held the movement together in its early years, through the kinds of activities detailed in the *Relation*—not only the less conventional activities, such as bearing testimony to King Charles II on his deathbed, but the more customary, such as maintaining the networks of "dear friends" with whom the *Relation* concludes.

TEXT: Margaret Fell Fox wrote the *Relation* in 1690; it was first published in 1710, in the *Brief Collection* with several of her other writings. The text is reprinted in full.

☙ ❧

I WAS BORN IN THE YEAR 1614. at *Marsh-Grange*, in the Parish of *Dalton*, in *Fournis* in *Lancashire*, of good and honest Parents, and of Honourable Repute in their Country. My Father's Name was *John Askew*, he was of an Ancient Family, of those esteem'd and call'd Gentlemen, who left a considerable Estate, which had been in his Name and Family for several Generations. He was a Pious Charitable Man, much valu'd in his Country, for his Moderation, and Patience, and was Bred after the best way and manner of Persons of his Rank in his Day. I was brought up and liv'd with my Father, until I was between Seventeen and Eighteen Years of Age, and then I was Married unto *Thomas Fell* of *Swarthmore*, who was a Barrister-at-Law of *Grays-Inn*; who afterwards was a Justice of the *Quorum* in his Country, a Member of Parliament, in several Parliaments; Vice-Chancellor of the County Palatine of *Lancaster*, Chancellor of the Dutchy-Court at *Westminster*, and one of the Judges that went the Circuit of *West-Chester*, and North-*Wales*.

He was much esteem'd in his Country, and valu'd and honour'd in his Day by all sorts of People, for his Justice, Wisdom, Moderation and Mercy; being a Terror to Evil-doers, and an Encourager of such as did well, and his many and great Services made his Death much lamented. We liv'd together twenty six Years, in which time, we had nine Children. He was a tender loving Husband to me, and a tender Father to his Children, and one that sought after God in the best way that was made known to him. I was about sixteen Years younger than he, and was one that sought after the best Things, being desirous to serve God, so as I might be accepted of him; and was Inquiring after the way of the Lord, and went often to hear the best Ministers that came into our Parts, whom we frequently entertain'd at our House; many of those that were accounted the most Serious and Godly Men, some of which, were then call'd *Lecturing-Ministers*, and had often Prayers and Religious Exercises in our Family. This I hop'd I did well in, but often fear'd I was short of the right way: And after this manner I was inquiring and seeking about twenty Years.

Then in the Year 1652. it pleas'd the Lord in his Infinite Mercy and Goodness to send *George Fox* into our Country, who declar'd unto us the Eternal Truth, as it is in Jesus; and by the Word and Power of the Eternal God, turn'd many from Darkness unto Light, and from the Power of Satan unto God; And when I and my Children, and a great part of our Servants were so convinc'd and converted unto God, at which time my Husband was not at Home, being gone to *London*. When he came Home, and found us the most part of the Family chang'd from our former Principle and Perswasion which he left us in, when he went from Home, he was much surpriz'd at our suddain change: For some envious People of our Neighbours, went and met him upon the Sands, as he was coming Home, and Inform'd him, that we had entertain'd such Men as had taken us off from going to Church, which he was very much concern'd at; so that when he came Home, he seem'd much troubled. And it so happen'd, that *Richard Farnsworth*,[1] and some other Friends[2] (that came into our Parts a little time after *G. Fox*) were then at our House when my Husband came

Home; and they Discours'd with him, and did perswade him to be still, and weigh things, before he did any thing hastily, and his Spirit was something calmed.

At Night *G. Fox* spoke so powerfully and convincingly, that the witness of God in his Conscience answer'd that he spake Truth; and he was then so far convinc'd in his Mind that it was Truth, that he willingly let us have a Meeting in his House the next first Day[3] after, which was the first Publick Meeting that was at *Swarthmore*; but he and his Men went to the Steeple-House (our Meetings being kept at *Swarthmore* about 38 Years, until a new Meeting-House was built by *G. Fox*'s Order and Cost [i.e., expense] near *Swarthmore-Hall*,) and so through the good power and word of God, the Truth encreas'd in the Countries all about us, and many came in, and were convinc'd, and we kept our Meetings peaceably every first Day at *Swarthmore-Hall*, the residue of the time of his Life. And he became a kind Friend to Friends, and to the practicers of Truth upon every occasion, as he had opportunity. For he being a Magistrate, was Instrumental to keep off much Persecution in this Country, and in other Places where he had any Power.

He Liv'd about six Years after I was convinc'd; in which time it pleas'd the Lord to visit him with Sickness, wherein he became more than usually loving and kind to our Friends call'd *Quakers*, having been a merciful Man to the Lord's People. I, and many other Friends were well satisfy'd the Lord in mercy receiv'd him to himself. It was in the beginning of the 8th Month, 1658. that he died, being about sixty Years of Age: He left one Son, and seven Daughters, all unpreferr'd; but left a good and competent Estate for them.

And in the Year 1660. King *Charles* the Second came into *England*,[4] and within two Weeks after, I was mov'd of the Lord to go to *London*, to speak to the King concerning the Truth, and the Sufferers for it, for there was then many hundreds of our Friends in Prison in the three Nations, of *England, Scotland*, and *Ireland*, which were put in by the former Powers. And I spake often with the King, and writ many Letters and Papers unto him, and many Books were given by our Friends to the Parliament, and great Service was done at that time.—And they were fully inform'd of our peaceable Principles and Practices. I staid at *London* at this time one Year and three Months, doing Service for the Lord, in visiting Friends Meetings, and giving Papers and Letters to the King and Council whenever there was occasion. And I writ and gave Papers and Letters to every one of the Family several times, *viz.* To the King, to the Duke of *York*, to the Duke of *Gloucester*, and to the Queen Mother, to the Princess of

Orange, and to the Queen of *Bohemia*. I was mov'd of the Lord to visit them all, and to write unto them, and to lay the Truth before them, and did give them many Books and Papers, and did lay our Principles and Doctrines before them, and desired that they would let us have Discourse with their Priests, Preachers, and Teachers, and if they could prove us Erroneous, then let them manifest it: But if our Principles and Doctrines be found according to the Doctrine of Christ, and the Apostles and Saints in the Primitive Times, then let us have our Liberty. But we could never get a Meeting of any sort of them to meet with our Friends—Nevertheless they were very quiet, and we had great Liberty, and had our Meetings very peaceably for the first half Year after the King came in, until the Fifth-Monarchy-Men raised an Insurrection and Tumult in the City of *London*,[5] and then all our Meetings were disturb'd, and Friends taken up; which if that had not been, we were inform'd the King had intended to have given us Liberty. For at that very time, there was an Order Sign'd by the King and Council for the Quaker's Liberty, and just when it should have gone to the Press, the Fifth-Monarchy-Men rose, and then our Friends were very hardly used, and taken up at their Meetings generally, even until many Prisons throughout the Nation was filled with them. And many a time did I go to the King about them; who promis'd me always they should be set at Liberty; and we had several in the Council were Friendly to us, and we gave many Papers to them; and with much adoe, and attendance in that time, about a quarter of a year after their first taking Friends to Prison, a General Proclamation from the King and Council was granted, for setting the Quakers at Liberty, that were taken up at that time; and in some time after the Proclamation came forth, and Friends were set at Liberty. Then I had freedom in Spirit to return Home to visit my Children and Family, which I had been from fifteen Months. And I staid at Home about nine Months, and then was moved of the Lord to go to *London* again, not knowing what might be the Matter or Business that I should go for. And when I came to *Warrington*, in my way to *London*, I met with an Act of Parliament, made against the Quakers for refusing Oaths.[6] And when I came to *London*, I heard the King was gone to meet the Queen,[7] and to be Married to her at *Hampton-Court*. At this time Friends Meetings at *London* were much troubled with Soldiers, pulling Friends out of their Meetings, and beating them with their Muskets and Swords; insomuch that several were wounded and bruised by them; many were cast into Prison, through which, many lost their Lives; and all this being done to a peaceable People, only for Worshipping God, as they in Conscience were perswaded. Then I went to the King, and Duke of *York* at *Hampton-Court*, and I wrote several Letters to them, and therein gave them to understand what desperate and dangerous work there was at *London*; and how the Soldiers came in with lighted Matches, and drawn Swords amongst Friends, when they were met together in the fear and dread of the Lord to worship him; and if they would not stop that cruel Persecution, it was very like[ly] that more Innocent Blood would be shed, and that would witness against their Actions, and lie upon them, and the Nation. And within some certain days after, they beat some Friends so cruelly at the *Bull-and-Mouth*, that two died thereof.

The King told me when I spake to him, and writ to him, that his Soldiers did not trouble us, nor should they, and said the City Soldiers were not his, and they would do as they pleas'd with them; but after a little time they were more Moderate, and the King promis'd me that he would set those at Liberty that were in Prison; and when he brought his Queen to *London*, he set them at Liberty. And then I came Home again, when I had staid about four Months in and about *London*. And in the 3d Month, 1663. I was mov'd of the Lord again to Travel into the Countries to visit Friends; and I travel'd through the Countries visiting Friends, till we came to *Bristol*, where we staid two Weeks, I, and some other Friends that were with me, and then we went into *Somersetshire, Devonshire*, and *Dorsetshire*, visiting Friends, and then came back to *Bristol*: From whence, we passed through the Nation into *Yorkshire*, to *York*, and into *Bishoprick* and *Northumberland*, visiting Meetings all along amongst Friends, and then went into *Westmoreland*, and so Home to *Swarthmore*.

This Journey, that I then went, and one of my Daughters, and some others that were with me, it was thought we Travelled about a Thousand Miles; and in our Journey we met with G. *Fox*, who came to *Swarthmore* with us, and stay'd about two Weeks; and then the Magistrates began to threaten: for G. F. went into *Westmoreland* and *Cumberland*, and had some meetings amongst Friends, and came again to *Swarthmore*; and they sent out Warrants for him, and took him, and committed him to *Lancaster-Castle*. About a Month after, the same Justices sent for me to *Alverstone*, where they were sitting, at a private Sessions; and when I came there, they asked me several Questions, and seem'd to be offended at me, for keeping a Meeting at my House, and said, They would tender me the Oath of Allegiance. I answer'd, They knew I could not Swear, and why should they send for me from my own House, where I was about my lawful Occasions, to ensnare me? What had I done? They said, If I would not keep a Meeting at my House, they would not tender me the Oath. I told them, I should not deny my Faith and Principles, for any thing they could do against me; and while it pleased the Lord to let me have a House, I would endeavour to worship him in it. So they caus'd the Oath to be read, and tender'd it unto me; and when I refused it, telling them, I could not take any Oath for Conscience sake, Christ Jesus having forbid it. Then they made a *Mittimus*,[8] and committed me Prisoner to *Lancaster*-Castle, and there *G. Fox* and I remained in Prison until the next Assizes;[9] and then they Indicted us upon the Statute for denying the Oath of Allegiance: For they tender'd it us both again at the Assizes; but they said to me, if I would not keep a Meeting at my House, I should be set at Liberty. But I answer'd the Judge, That I [would] rather choose a Prison for obeying of God, than my Liberty for obeying of Men, contrary to my Conscience. So we were called several times before them at that Assizes, and the Indictments were found against us. The next Assizes we came to Tryal, and *G. Fox's* Indictment was found to be dated wrong, both in the Day of the Month, and in the Year of the King's Reign, so that his Indictment was quash'd; but mine they would not allow the Errors that were found in it, to make it void, altho' there were several; so they passed Sentence of *Praemunire* upon me, which was, That I should be out of the King's Protection, and forfeit all my Estate, Real and Personal, to the King, and Imprisonment during Life.[10] But the great God of Heaven and Earth supported my Spirit under this severe Sentence, that I was not terrified; but gave this Answer to Judge *Turner*, who gave the Sentence, *Although I am out of the King's Protection, yet I am not out of the Protection of the Almighty God*; so there I remained in Prison Twenty Months, before I could get so much Favour of the Sheriff, as to go to my own House; which then I did for a little time, and returned to Prison again. And when I had been a Prisoner about Four Years, I was set at Liberty by an Order from the King and Council in 1668.

And then I was moved of the Lord again, to go and visit Friends; and the first that I went to visit were Friends in Prison; and I visited the most part of the Friends that were Prisoners in the *North* and *West* of *England*, and those in my way to *Bristol*; and after I had stay'd two Weeks there, I visited Friends in *Cornwall, Devonshire,* and *Somersetshire*; and then through all the Western Counties to *London*. And I stay'd in and about *London* about three Months, and then I went and visited Friends throughout all *Kent, Sussex,* and some part of *Surrey*; and then to *London* again, where I stay'd above two Months; and then I returned through the Countries, visiting Friends, until I came to *Bristol*, in 1669.

And then it was Eleven Years after my former Husband's Decease; and *G. Fox* being then returned from visiting Friends in *Ireland*. At *Bristol* he declared his Intentions of Marriage with me; and there was also our Marriage solemnized, in a publick Meeting of many Friends, who were our Witnesses.

And in some time after, I came homewards, and my Husband stay'd in the Countries visiting Friends. And soon after I came home, there came another Order to cast me into Prison again; and the sheriff of *Lancashire* sent his Bailiff, and pulled me out of my own House, and had me to Prison to *Lancaster*-Castle, where I continued a whole Year; and most part of that time I was sick and weakly. And after some time, my Husband endeavoured to get me out of Prison; and a Discharge at last was got, under the great Seal,[11] and so I was set at Liberty.

And then I was to go up to *London* again; for my Husband was intending for *America*, and he was full two Years away, before he came back into *England*; and then he arrived in *Bristol*, where I went to meet him; and we stay'd sometime in the Countries thereabout, and then came to *London*, and stay'd there several Months. And I was intending to return home into the North, and he came with me as far as the middle of the Nation. But before we parted, we went to a Meeting in *Worcestershire*; and after the Meeting was ended, and Friends mostly gone, he was taken Prisoner, together with my Son-in-Law *Thomas Lower*, by one *Parker*, a Justice, so called, and sent to *Worcester*-Jayl; the Account whereof is set forth in his Journal. And when I came home, with my Daughter *Rachel*, leaving him confin'd in Prison, where he became much weaken'd in Body, and his Health impair'd, by his long Confinements. Howbeit, after much endeavours used, he was Legally Discharged, and set at Liberty. We got him home to *Swarthmore*, where he had a long time of Weakness, before he Recovered. And when he had stay'd there about One and Twenty Months, he began his Journey towards *London* again, in 1677. although he was but weakly, and unable to ride well, but the Lord supported him. And when he had stay'd some time in London, then he went over into *Holland*, and travelled to *Hamburgh*, and into some part of *Germany*, and to several places in those Countries, and then returned to *London*; and then went to *Bristol* to visit Friends, and back again to *London*: And then, after a little time, came to *Swarthmore*, where he continu'd again above a Year. And then he began his Journey, and travelled through several Countries, visiting Friends, until he came to *London*.

And when my Husband was at *London*, it being a time of great Persecution by Informers,[12] the Justices in our Country were very severe, and much bent against me, because I kept a Meeting at my House, at *Swarthmore-Hall*: So they did not Fine the House as his, he being absent, but fined it as mine, as being the Widow of Judge *Fell*; and fined me 20*l.* for the House, and 20*l.* for speaking in the Meeting; and then fined me the second time 40*l.* for speaking; and also fined some other Friends for speaking, 20*l.* for the first time, and 40*l.* for the second time; and those that were not able, they fined others for them, and made great Spoil amongst Friends, by distraining and selling their Goods, sometimes for less than half the Value; they took Thirty Head of Cattle from me: Their Intentions were to ruine us, and to weary us out, and to enrich themselves; but the Lord prevented them.

So I was moved of the Lord to go to *London*, in the 70th Year of my Age [1684]; and the Word was in me, *That as I had gone to King* Charles, *when he first came into* England; *so I should go, and bear to him my last Testimony, and let him know, how they did abuse us, to enrich themselves.* And so I went up to *London*; and a Paper was drawn up, to give a true and certain Account, how they dealt with me, and other Friends. And it was upon my Mind, to go first to the Duke of *York*; and I writ a short Paper to him, to acquaint him, That as he had sometimes formerly spoke in my behalf to the King, my Request was, that he would now do the like for me; or Words to that effect. And I went with this Paper to *James's* House; and after long waiting, I got to speak to him. But some who were with him, let him know, that it was I that had been with him and his Brother, soon after they came into *England*. So I gave him my little Paper, and asked him, If he did remember me? He said, *I do remember you.* So then I desired him to speak to the King for us, for we were under great Sufferings, and our Persecutors were so severe upon us, that it look'd as if they intended to make a Prey upon us: And he said, He could not help us, but he would speak to the King. And the next Day, with much ado, I got to the King, and had my great Paper, which was the Relation of our Sufferings, to present to him; but he was so Rough and Angry, that he would not take my Paper; but I gave several Copies of it to his Nobles about him. And afterwards I went to Judge *Jefferies*, and told him of our Sufferings: For he had been in the North-Country with us, but a little before, and he told me we might speak to the King. I answer'd, it was very hard to get to the King; he said, give me a Paper, and I will speak to him; but said, Your Papers are too long, give me a short Paper, and I will speak to him. So I writ a little Paper from my self to him, to this effect;

King Charles, *Thou and thy Magistrates puts very great and cruel Sufferings upon us: But this I must say unto thee, If you make our Sufferings to Death it self, we shall not, nor dare not but confess Christ Jesus before Men, lest he should deny us before his Father which is in Heaven.*

There were some more Words in it, but this was the Substance. So *Jefferies* read it, and said, He would give it him; and we gave Papers to several of those that waited on him, and they gave us some Encouragement, that we should be helped: So we expected and waited for it. And about a Week or two after, in the beginning of the 12th Month, *Geo. Whitehead*[13] and I were going to one of the Lords, who had promised *George* before, that he would speak to the King for us: We went to his Lodgings early in the Morning, thinking to speak with him, before he went out; but his Servants told us, he was not within, being gone to the King, who was not well. Then we came forth into *White-Hall-Court* again; but all the Gates were shut, that we could not get forth. So we waited and walked up and down, and several came down from the King, and said, *He could not stand*; others said, *He could not speak*. Then, after some Hours waiting, we got through *Scotland-Yard*, and came away; and the King continued Sick and Ill until the Sixth Day after, and then he died. So this confirmed that Word, which God put into my Heart, That *I was sent to bear my last Testimony to the King.*

Then *James* Duke of *York* was proclaimed King; and about two Weeks after, I went to him, and gave him a Paper, wherein was writ to this effect:

King James, *I have waited here some Months, until this Change is come, and now I would return Home: But I cannot live peaceably there, except I have a Word from thee, to give a Check to my Persecutors.*

I spoke to him to the same purpose, that I had writ in my Paper. He said to me, *Go home, go home.* So after a few Weeks I went home.

And a little time after, *William Kerby*, a Justice, one of our greatest Persecutors, met with my Son-in-Law, *Daniel Abraham*, upon the Road, and said to him, Tell your Mother, that now the Government will be settled again, and if you keep Meetings, you must expect the same again. My Son answered him, We must keep Meetings, unless you take our Lives. Then *William Kerby* said, We will not take your Lives, but whilst you have any thing, we will take it. So I writ a Letter to King *James,* in which I said, *Thou bid'st me come home, and so I am; but as I said to thee, I could not live peaceably, so it is like to be*: And then I hinted in my Letter, *W.* Kirby's Discourse with my Son. And I desired of the King, *to let me have something from him, that I might live peaceably at my House.*

This Letter was deliver'd to him, and, as I heard, he carried it to the Council, and it was read; and that some of the Council said, She desires a Protection, that she may live Peaceably at her own House; and that some made answer, They could give no Protection to a particular ———. However (I do suppose) they gave our Persecutors a private Caution, for they troubled us no more; but, if that had not been, it's likely they had a mind to begin a new upon us. For, a little before the time of the Informers, they brought that Law upon us, concerning Twelve Pence a *Sunday*, so call'd; and they carry'd me, and my Son and Daughter *Abraham*, to *Lancaster*-Prison, and kept us there about three Weeks. And when they consider'd, that they could not Fine me, nor my House, when I was in Prison, then they let us go home; and soon after, they did fine us both for the House, and for Speaking, as is before hinted.

And thus have they troubled and persecuted us divers ways: But the Lord God Almighty hath preserved me, and us, till this Day; Glorious Praises be given to him for evermore.

And the Lord hath given me Strength and Ability, that I have been at *London* to see my dear Husband and Children, and Relations and Friends there, in 1690. being the Seventy Sixth Year of my Age: And I was very well Satisfied, Refreshed, and Comforted in my Journey, and found Friends in much Love; Praises be returned to the Unchangeable Lord God for ever. This being Nine times that I have been at *London*, upon the Lord's and his Truth's Account.

And after I returned Home, I writ this short *Epistle* following, to the Women's Meeting in *London*.

Dear Friends and Sisters,

In the Eternal Blessed Truth, into which we are begotten, and in which we stand, and are preserved, as we keep in it, and are guided by it: In this is my dear and unchangeable Love remember'd unto you all; acknowledging your dear, tender, and kind Love, when I was with you; in which my Heart was rejoyced, to feel the Ancient Love and Unity of the Eternal Spirit amongst you: And my soul was, and is refreshed in my Journey, in visiting of my dear Husband and Children, and you my dear Friends. And now I am returned to my own House and Family, where I find all well: Praised and Honoured be my Heavenly Father.

And, dear Friends, our Engagements are great unto the Lord, and he is Dear and Faithful unto us: And Blessed and Happy are all they, that are Dear and Faithful unto him. And those who keeps single and chaste unto him, they need not fear Evil Tidings, nor what Man can do: For he that hath all Power in Heaven and Earth in his Hand, he will surely keep his own Church and Family, those that worshippeth him, within the Measuring Line, that measures the Temple, and the Altar, and those that worships therein, they are kept safe, as in the Hallow of his Hand.

And so, dear Friends, my Heart and Soul was so much Comforted and

Refreshed amongst you, that I could not but signifie the Remembrance of my dear Love unto you: And also my Acknowledgment of your dear Love and Tenderness to my dear Husband; for which, I doubt not, but the Lord doth and will Reward you: Into whose Hand, and Arm, and Power, I commit you.

Swarthmore, *the 10th of*   *M. Fox*
  the 5th Month, 1690.

Notes

1. An eminent Quaker leader.

2. Members of the Society of Friends.

3. Sunday; in accordance with their commitment to "plain language," Quakers did not use the names of days or months.

4. In order to be restored to the throne.

5. The Fifth-Monarchy-Men were a politico-religious group who opposed the restoration of Charles II, believing that the beheading of King Charles I in 1649 had heralded the earthly rule of King Jesus, the last of the five great empires foretold by the Old Testament prophet Daniel (Dan. 2:44). In January 1661 a group of Fifth Monarchists, led by Thomas Venner, attempted the "Insurrection" to which Fell Fox refers; it failed.

6. Not until the Affirmation Act of 1696 were Quakers allowed to "make an affirmation" instead of an oath of allegiance.

7. Actually the queen-to-be, Catherine of Braganza.

8. Warrant issued by a justice of the peace to the keeper of a prison to detain someone in custody.

9. Session held periodically in a county to administer civil and criminal justice.

10. Standard punishment for the offence of praemunire, or denying the king's ecclesiastical supremacy.

11. The Great Seal authenticates documents of the highest authority or importance.

12. The persecution of Quakers, including the use of spies and informers, was particularly virulent in the early 1680s.

13. George Whitehead (1636?–1723), itinerant preacher and activist, had several audiences with Charles II, and by the end of the century his efforts had led to much improvement in the Quakers' legal position.

Jane Hoskens

1693/94–1760?

The Life of that Faithful Servant of Christ, Jane Hoskens, a Minister of the Gospel, among the People called Quakers. Manchester: John Harrison, [1837].

Born in London on 3 January 1693/94, Jane Fenn was raised as an Anglican by "religious parents" (3). She often slighted their counsel, instead delighting in music and frequenting "unprofitable company," until a serious illness at the age of sixteen determined her to dedicate her life to God's service. Although she soon forgot these vows, she was occasionally reminded of God's words during her illness—"if I restore thee, *go to Pennsylvania*" (4)—and finally asked her parents' permission to go to America; when it was refused, she was again diverted from her purpose. This pattern of oscillation continued until a friend introduced her to Robert Davis, who was going to Pennsylvania with his wife and daughters and agreed to pay Jane's passage; she and the Davises arrived in Philadelphia on 6 March 1712.

Within a year Jane had met a group of Quakers, and by 1715 she had joined the Society of Friends, although not without the backslidings that are so large a part of her narrative. For the next few years she worked as a maid, moving from place to place and always attending Quaker meetings but otherwise "pretty much retired from company" (18) to strengthen her "infant state of religion." In 1717 Jane felt a call to preach, but it was not until 1719 that she began to speak in meetings. In this year she took a position as housekeeper for the family of David Lloyd, who remained her spiritual mentor until his death in 1731. From 1722 to 1725 Jane accompanied Elizabeth Levis on a traveling ministry to Maryland, Virginia, North Carolina, Barbados, Rhode Island, and New England. She and Abigail Bowles covered 1,700 miles in a similar circuit in 1726, and from 1727 to 1730 she accompanied a group of Quakers traveling throughout Britain. Although she married Hoskens in 1738, Jane continued her traveling ministries; for the next eighteen years she attended Yearly Meetings and proselytized in the Americas from Long Island to Barbados. The last journey she records occurred in 1756, and she is thought to have died in 1760.

TEXT: Jane Hoskens's *Life* was first published in 1837, in the Friends' Library series of spiritual autobiographies. Little is known about its provenance beyond her statement that she wrote to "commemorate the tender dealings of a merciful God, in visiting my soul in the days of my youth" (3). The selection (pp. 6–18 of the *Life*) records Hoskens's first exposure to the Society of Friends and demonstrates at once the seriousness and the difficulties of her consequent spiritual state.

ↄ⃝ ℬↄ

AFTER I HAD BEEN in Philadelphia somewhat more than a quarter of a year, Robert Davis insisted I should sign indentures, binding myself a servant for four years, to a person who was an utter stranger to me, by which means he would have made considerable advantage to himself. But as this was contrary to our agreement before-mentioned, which I was willing to comply with to the utmost of my power, and as a remarkable uneasiness and deep exercise attended my mind, when I endeavoured to comply with his mercenary will, I thought it best to withstand him in it, let the consequence be what it would; whereupon he had recourse to the law, and by process[1] laid me under confinement. This was a trying circumstance. I was a poor young creature among strangers, and being far separated from my natural friends, they could not redress my grievances nor hear my complaints.

But the Lord heard my cries and raised me up many friends, who visited me in this situation and offered me money to pay Davis for my passage, according to contract, but I could not accept even of this kindness, because I was well assured Philadelphia was not to be the place of my settlement, though where I was to go was yet hid from me; however, as I endeavoured to wait, the Lord provided for me after this manner: The principals of four families living at Plymouth, who had several children, agreed to procure a sober young woman, as a school-mistress to instruct them in reading, &c. And on their applying to their friends in town, I was recommended for that service. When we saw each other, I perceived it my place to go with them; wherefore, on their paying Davis twelve pounds currency, being the whole of his demand against me, I bound myself to them by indenture, for the term of three years, and went cheerfully with them to the aforesaid place. And I have thought how wonderful it was, that though various scenes attended me, yet I was enabled to perform the service they had for me. The children learned very fast, which afforded comfort to me, and satisfaction to their parents; my love to them was great, and theirs equally so to me, so that all my commands were obeyed with pleasure, and when we met could tell one another of it with sincere regard and affection. They proved sober, religious, men and women.

I served my time faithfully, and never had cause to repent it; the people with whom I lived, were those called Quakers, and as I had not been among any of that denomination before, I had desires in my mind to be acquainted with their principles, and manner of worship, and having liberty, was very ready to go to their meetings, though at first only as a spy; but after I had been some time among them, and took notice of their way and manner of performing Divine worship to God, I was ready to conclude and say in my mind, surely these are his people; and a brave, living people they really were; there being divers worthies among them, who I believe are now in the fruition of joy unspeakable, and full of glory; the earnest of which, they through mercy then at times partook of, to the satisfaction of their hungry and thirsty souls. The solid, weighty, and tender frame of spirit some of them were many times favoured with, in meetings, brought serious considerations over my mind, with this query: Why is it not so with me? And I said in my heart, these people are certainly better than I am, notwithstanding I have made a great deal more to do about religion than they.

As I was pondering on these things, the saying of the apostle, "that circumcision or uncircumcision avails nothing, but a new creature in Christ Jesus,"[2] was often brought to my mind. I saw this work must begin in the heart, and be carried on by a Divine power. This I was soon convinced of, and therefore could wait with patience, though in silence. But yet the whole work was not completed, it went on gradually, step by step, which demonstrates the paternal care of our heavenly Father, carrying the lambs in his arms, lest they should be weary and faint! Who can but admire his goodness, and celebrate his praise? His wisdom and power are great. Oh! that all would dwell under his peaceable government, and learn of him, who is pure and holy. Through the operation of Divine Goodness, great love was begotten in my heart to these people; and if at any time Friends were concerned to speak against any evil habit of the mind, I did not put it from me, but was willing to take my part, and have sometimes thought it all belonged to me.

As I continued in this humble frame, and was diligent in attending meeting when I could, Infinite Goodness was graciously pleased to favour me with a fresh and large visitation of his heavenly love, and often tendered my spirit and begot strong desires after true and saving knowledge, and that the way of life and salvation might be clearly demonstrated; and blessed be his eternal name, he heard my cries, and was pleased to send his servants both male and female, filled with life and power, who sounded forth the Gospel in Divine authority, declaring the way to the Father through Christ the Door, and opening the principles of these people, by turning our minds inward to the pure gift and manifestation of the Spirit.

This doctrine agreeing with what I had in some measure been convinced of, I was made willing to join heartily with it, and was ready to say, these are true ministers of Christ, for they speak with Divine power and authority, and not as the scribes. Now I was mightily reached unto, and stripped of all self-righteousness, and my state was opened to me in such a manner, that I was quite confounded, and concluded that though I could talk of religion, of being made a child of God, a member of his church, and an inheritor of his holy kingdom, there was as much need as ever to cry, Lord have mercy on me a poor sinner! not having yet witnessed the law of the spirit of life in Christ Jesus, to set me free from the law of sin and death. Outward ceremonies availed nothing, the new birth was wanting, and must be witnessed, in order to prepare me for the work whereunto the Lord had called me, and was about to engage me in. The baptism of the Spirit was to be known before I could be a member of Christ's church; this great work I saw, by Divine favour, I must submit unto if ever I come to be a partaker of that bread which nourishes the soul unto eternal life.

But oh, the weight and exercise I was under during this time of refinement! the days and nights of godly sorrow and penitential mourning I underwent, are far beyond my ability to set forth in words; and once being alone I wept exceedingly, and the desire of my soul was, that it might please the Almighty to show me his ways, to teach me his paths which lead to peace, and give me strength to walk therein according to his word; promising that I would endeavour to follow in the way which was most pleasing to him, for that was what my panting soul most desired. My desires were not for great things, but Divine favour; the Lord alone was become the centre of my happiness, and I believe I should have died at that time, had He not been pleased in a wonderful manner to manifest himself a present help in that needful time, and to reveal himself through his dear Son Christ Jesus, by administering consolation to my wounded soul, filling my heart with heavenly love, so that my cup ran over, and I was made to cry out; Oh, that all may know thee and thy goodness! His matchless loving kindness so overcame me, that I thought I could have gone through the world to proclaim the tender dealings of a merciful God to my soul. Here I again renewed my covenant with God, and promised obedience to his commands; and Oh! the calm, the peace, the comfort, and satisfaction wherewith my mind was clothed, like a child enjoying his father's favour, and with inexpressible delight, beholding the smiles of his countenance. I was afraid to do or say anything that might offend the Lord, lest the rod might be laid heavy on me, for this is the portion of disobedience. In that time I became a wonder to many, but was treated with great tenderness by most of the Friends and neighbours. I had laid aside all superfluity of apparel, for which I had been condemned; I attended meetings diligently, and walked three or four miles to them, sometimes alone, meditating upon the Lord, and thought the work of my present and future happiness was now completed in me, that I had nothing to do but sit contented under the enjoyment of Divine favour, rejoicing that I had left all and followed Christ, whom I loved more than my natural life. Thus I concluded in my own mind, not knowing as yet what the Lord was preparing me for, nor that there was a further work allotted me, which I was a stranger to, till one time being in a meeting, and sitting very contented under my own vine and fig-tree, a call arose in my mind, "I have chosen thee a vessel from thy youth to serve me, and to preach the Gospel of salvation to many people: and if thou wilt be faithful, I will be with thee unto the end of time, and make thee an heir of my kingdom."

These words were attended with life and power, and I knew his promises were yea, and amen forever. Yet I must confess, this awful word of Divine command shocked me exceedingly, my soul and all within me trembled at the hearing of it; yea, my outward tabernacle shook, insomuch that many present observed the deep exercise I was under. I cried in spirit, "Lord I am weak and altogether incapable of such a task, I hope thou wilt spare me from such a mortification; besides I have spoken much against women appearing in that manner." This and more such like reasonings I was filled with, which did not administer peace, but death and judgment. Great darkness began to spread over my understanding, and increased to such a degree, that nothing but horror possessed my soul. I went to meetings as usual, but I felt not the least enjoyment of the Divine presence, but on the contrary, inexpressible anguish of mind, so that I could not shed a tear, and concluded all was over with me, and that I was lost for ever. My very countenance was changed and became a true index of my deep distress, and a person that I had a great love for, told me she had the word of the Lord to declare to me, which was, that I had withstood the day of my visitation, and was now left to myself. This I readily believed, and so gave over all hope of salvation; and the grand enemy got in with his temptations and suggestions, and like a torrent which bears down all before it, made my sorrow and bitterness of soul inexpressible; and certainly he had prevailed against me with his wicked devices, had not the Almighty, by his eternal arm of power, interposed, and driven him back, saying unto me, in the hour of my deepest probation [i.e., trial], "Be obedient and all shall be forgiven; and thy soul shall be filled with joy and peace unspeakable." At the hearing of which, I broke out into tears, and in deep humility blessed his holy arm for delivering me from the mouth of the lion, who seeks to devour all he can. I renewed my covenant with the Lord, and prayed for resignation to his Divine will.

But alas! When it was again required of me to stand up in a meeting and speak the words he bid me, I again rebelled, and justly incurred the displeasure of my great and good Master. I went from this meeting in sorrow, and offered my natural life a sacrifice to be excused from this service, but it was not accepted; nothing would do but perfect obedience. In this situation I continued six or seven months; I could have but little rest night or day, by reason of the anguish of spirit I was in; yet still longed for meeting days, and made many promises that if I found the like concern, and it would please Infinite Goodness to be with me, I would submit to his Divine will, come what would. But though I went with these resolutions, when the time of trial came, I put off the work which was required of me, and came away as before, full of sorrow and anguish of soul, and knew not what to do; but often wished myself dead, hoping thereby to be exempt from pain. Yet not duly considering that if I was removed out of time in displeasure, my portion would still be more dreadful, and that it was the old liar who introduced such a thought, and intended not only to bring me to destruction, but also to make me the instrument of it myself.

Oh, I have often admired the long forbearance of a merciful God with me; and when I considered his loving kindness in preserving me from the devil's temptations, desires were begotten in my soul to conduct [myself] through time with reverence and fear, to his glory. And here a still more refined snare was laid for me, which was a conclusion to stay from the meeting, because I believed I might, when there, disturb the quiet of others; and really I was ashamed to be seen in the condition I often was in, when at meeting.

The Friends with whom I lived, and many neighbouring Friends, sympathized deeply with me, and intimated their concern that I had left off going to meetings, and begged, as those with whom I lived gave me full liberty to go, both on first and week days, that I would comply with their request, and go with them as before. Their arguments had weight with me, and I went, but had not sat long before the concern to stand up and speak a few words came powerfully upon me, with this close hint; *"this may be the last offer of this kind thou wilt be favoured with, embrace it, I will be thy strength and exceeding great reward."* I then said, "Lord I will submit, be thou with me, take away the fear of man, thou shalt have my whole heart." And sitting a while I felt the aboundings of heavenly love towards God and his people to arise in my soul, in which I stood up, and after pausing a little, like a child, spoke a few words which were given me, and sat down in the enjoyment of heavenly life. The Friends were sensibly affected, indeed as many said afterwards, it was a time not to be forgotten. And so it was to me indeed, for I went home rejoicing, and renewed my promise of future obedience; but though I cannot charge myself with wilful disobedience, yet for fear of a forward spirit, I have, I believe, been guilty of the sin of omission. And though it is dangerous and criminal to withhold the word of the Lord; yet, Oh! saith my soul, may all who are called to this honourable work of the ministry, carefully guard against being actuated by a forward spirit which leads into a ministry that will neither edify the church, nor bring honour to our holy High Priest, Christ Jesus. As the tree is known by its fruit, so is such ministry known by its effects, producing death instead of life; and such as offer this, will sooner or later sit down in sorrow and condemnation, for running before the true Guide.

In the year 1714, our worthy Friends Thomas Wilson and James Dickinson,[3] came into this province, on a religious visit to the churches. I was present at a meeting they had at Plymouth, which on account of the great gathering of people, was held under the trees. Thomas, in the exercise of his gift, was led to treat on several subjects, which making a great impression on my mind, at that time, and tending to confirm me in the faith I made open profession of, I still remember. He was led to speak of David's bringing the ark of the Lord from the house of Obededom;[4] also the festival, a sacrifice he offered to the Lord, and his dispensing the bread, flesh, and wine to the multitude, to the women as well as the men; which Thomas repeated two or three times; from thence inferring the Lord's influencing females, as well as males, with Divine authority, to preach the Gospel to the nations.

He spoke largely on the passage of the captive maid, and her service to her Lord and Master;[5] and in a powerful manner set forth the privileges which the true members of the church of Christ enjoy under his peaceable government. He also spoke prophetically concerning the work of sanctification which some were under; saying, the Lord would bring the faithful through all to his glory, and the solid comfort of the afflicted, though some might be like David, in the horrible pit, &c. These and divers other subjects which he mentioned, greatly affected me, and reached me in such a manner, that I was much broken, and said in my heart, surely all here will be not only convinced, but converted by the eternal Word of God, unto the true faith of Christ our Lord, who came to seek and to save all who should believe in his pure name. I thought none could withstand the doctrine preached, it being with great power and Divine authority, not as that of the scribes or hireling priests. What made it further remarkable to me was, that the Friend where they dined, insisted on my going with them, and it being in my way home, with fear and trembling I complied, and being sat down in the house, Thomas Wilson fixed his eyes upon me, which made me conclude he saw something in me that was wrong. I arose and went out, being much affected, but heard him say, "What young woman is that? She is like the little captive maid I have been speaking of this day.—May the God of my life strengthen her; she will meet with sore trials, but if she is faithful, the Lord will fit her for his service." He further remarked, that he saw the Lord was at work in me for good, and would in his time bring me through all.

These hints have since been of service to me, when almost overwhelmed in trouble, and I think should never be forgotten. I do not mention them in ostentation, but bow in awful reverence, as with my mouth in the dust, rendering to the great Author of all mercies, adoration and praise; may it now be given unto Him, and forever. Amen.

About this time the Lord was graciously pleased to renew his merciful visitation unto the Friends and inhabitants of North Wales, and Plymouth; many of the youth were reached, and by the effectual operation of Divine and heavenly life, brought into true submission to the cross of Christ, several were called to the ministry, and engaged to speak in the authority of the Gospel, which is now, the same as formerly, the power of God unto salvation, unto all who receive it with meekness, and truly believe in, and patiently wait for, the inward and spiritual appearance of Christ our Holy Redeemer. Among the many thus favoured, was our dear and well beloved Friend and brother John Evans, who was blessed with an excellent gift in the ministry, and being faithful to his heavenly calling, became an able publisher of the Gospel; preaching it in the demonstration and power of God. He was careful to discharge his trust according to Divine ability, yet not forward, but patient in waiting for the motions of life, by which he attained experience, and knew when to speak, and when to be silent. In this, as in his love of silence, he was exemplary—he was likewise blessed with the Christian virtues of brotherly love, and universal charity; and being endowed with a good understanding, was a man of sound judgment; wherefore I always esteemed him as an elder brother, and gave him the right hand of fellowship. He was an instrument of help and good to me in my infant state in religion, which in point of gratitude I ought never to forget. Oh, may I conduct [myself] in such a manner through this state of probation, as that my latter end may be like his.

Now, though I had in part been faithful to the call of my great Lord and holy Redeemer, yet he was pleased at times to withdraw the light of his countenance from me, and to suffer the grand enemy to buffet me severely, by tempting me to believe that the peace I had enjoyed was only a false one, that it was all delusion, that the mortifications I underwent would be of no real advantage to my soul. Besides he suggested, how did I know that the Lord required these mortifications at my hands? that the humility I pretended to, was only feigned, and therefore the Lord would never accept of it.

Here I was again brought very low in my mind, and my spirit depressed almost to despair; so that I began to think all this might be true, yet knew not whither to go for help. But after some time, these words sprang up in my mind, I will trust in the Lord, for in the Lord Jehovah is everlasting strength. And then secret breathings arose to God, that it might please him once more to favour me with his holy presence, which giveth light and life whereby to distinguish his pure voice from that of a stranger. But, Oh! the bitter whisperings of satan, and the thoughts that passed through my mind, such as my soul hated! Yet such were the suggestions of the enemy, who was a liar from the beginning. And indeed, had not the secret hand of Infinite Goodness supported me though these great temptations, I should have fainted and lain down in deep despair.

I had not long enjoyed Divine peace, before the old Accuser began again, telling me I had blasphemed against the Holy Ghost, in that I deceived the people, in pretending to preach by Divine influence, which he insinuated was a positive untruth; and for me to make a show of worshipping Him whom I had thus belied, was a sin never to be forgiven. This was a distressing state to pass through, and lasted several weeks. I went about mourning like a person bereaved of reason; and though Friends still continued their care and regard to me, I never had freedom to communicate my exercise to any mortal. I have since found that the work which the Lord required, if people would but patiently wait his time, they would be enabled to perform, and would find deliverance in a proper season. I concluded I was the worst creature ever born, and had only received life for Divine vengeance, but the Lord gave me to see otherwise; for sitting one time alone in the woods, a cry rose up in my heart, if I die it shall be at thy foot-stool, O Lord! for thy loving kindness has been great to me from my youth to this day; and falling on my knees, I prayed that he would be graciously pleased to enlighten my understanding in such a manner, that I might see clearly wherein I had offended so merciful a Father; for I thought I had offended him, because I was suffered to be so tempted. His word then became as a fire in my breast, and the answer I received was to this effect; be encouraged, thou are suffered to pass through these trying dispensations, not only on thy own account, but for the sake of others to whom, when qualified, I will, in my own time, send thee: be faithful, and I will be with thee to the end of time. At this intimation I was tendered and filled with gratitude to his Divine Majesty, who alone can deliver his children out of their afflictions. My soul at this time, under a sweet sense of his goodness, bows in awful reverence with praises to his holy name, and says, Who is like unto our God! I wish all who make profession of the Truth may conduct agreeably to the holy principle of sincerity, and then such will be good examples to their children and families, if they have any, as also to the youth in general. There were many incidents occurred during the time of my being among those Friends, to whom I was indebted for payment of my passage, which for brevity's sake I omit. When the time for which I engaged to them was expired, I served them a quarter of a year longer, in consideration of the tender regard they had shown to me, when it was in their power to have conducted otherwise, and for granting me the liberty of going to weekday meetings; which they accepted from me with reluctance.

We loved one another much, and being unwilling to part, I staid with them till the spring, and then in much love and tenderness we parted.— I am persuaded that if servants were careful to discharge their trust faithfully to their masters and mistresses, the Lord would provide suitably for their support through the world, with credit and reputation. I never was more easy and contented in mind, with regard to outward things, in any station of life, than when I was a servant; because under this circumstance, I met with that for which I had laboured many years—the true and saving knowledge of Christ Jesus, who is the only way to the Father, and whom to know is life eternal. I cannot but desire that people in every condition in this world may be thus blessed. When the soul is tendered with the love of God, it strongly desires that all may be partakers of life and salvation, as freely offered though Christ Jesus our Lord.

Notes

1. Legal action or suit.

2. A point often made by the apostle Paul in his epistles, notably Rom. 2:28–29 and Gal. 5:6.

3. Two of the great Quaker preachers of this period.

4. The story is told in 2 Sam. 6; when David returned the Ark of the Covenant to the temple from the house of Obededom, there was great rejoicing.

5. The reference is to 2 Kings 5:2.

Agnes Beaumont

1652–1720

The singular Experience and great Sufferings of Mrs. Agnes Beaumont, who was born at Edworth, in the county of Bedford, as written by herself. In An Abstract of the Gracious Dealings of God, With several Eminent Christians, in their Conversion and Sufferings. Taken from Authentic Manuscripts, and Published for the Comfort and Establishment of Serious Minds. [Comp.] by Samuel James. London: J. Ward, 1760.

Agnes Beaumont was born in 1652 in the village of Edworth in Hertfordshire. Little is known of her family beyond what can be gleaned from her narrative; she had a sister and a brother, John, and her father, John Beaumont, appears to have been a prosperous farmer. This area of Hertfordshire seems to have been a center of nonconformist creeds; there were regular Sunday meetings at the nearby towns of Gamlingay and Hitchin, and the millenarian Dissenter John Bunyan had a congregation in Bedford. In 1670 Beaumont, her father, and her brother were attending the Bedford meetings, and she was "received into fellowship" there in 1672. Her brother continued to attend meetings, despite warnings that as constable of Edworth he was expected to attend Church of England services. At the time of the "singular experience" Beaumont records, she was twenty-four years old, living in Edworth and keeping house for her elderly and widowed father; her brother lived nearby. Although her father's religious ardor has cooled, he gives her permission to attend a Gamlingay meeting escorted by a neighbor. When she instead rides to the meeting seated behind Bunyan, her enraged father locks her out of the house. The subsequent travails make up the balance of Beaumont's narrative, which concludes with her eventual justification.

Details of Beaumont's later life are sparse. She mentions a "vile scandal" (94) linking her name with Bunyan's, and a self-justifying passage in the fifth edition of his *Grace Abounding to the Chief of Sinners* (1680) is often taken as a refutation of that scandal. Beaumont married Thomas Warren of Chestnut; we know nothing more of him except that they lived in a farmhouse at Blunham and he died in 1707. Beaumont's second husband, Samuel Story, was a prosperous Highgate merchant who survived her. She died in 1720 and is buried in the Tilehouse Street meeting yard in Hitchin.

TEXT: The manuscript of Agnes Beaumont's complete narrative is in the British Library, MSS Egerton 2414 and 2128. A somewhat abbreviated version was published in 1760 in *An Abstract of the Gracious Dealings of God*; compiled by Samuel James, the *Abstract's* five spiritual autobiographies were intended to awaken "careless sinners" and alarm the "lukewarm and drowsy." Beaumont's narrative was also published separately, six times in the next forty years. Revised by Samuel Burder, it appeared in 1801 under the title *Real Religion: Exemplified in the Singular Experience and Great Sufferings of Mrs. Agnes Beaumont*. This cheap tract edition, available for "gratuitous circulation by the affluent" (Burder 2), seems analogous to the Cheap Repository Tracts distributed in large numbers after the French Revolution to counter irreligion among the lower orders. Another edition was published in 1929, and excerpts from it were performed on British radio. *Behind Mr. Bunyan*, a modernized version of the entire narrative, was published in 1962 for use as a Sunday school prize. In the excerpt (pp. 104–128 of James's *Abstract*), Beaumont is at this point in her tale staying with her brother, since her father will allow her to return to his house only if she promises never again to go to meeting.

CR BD

THIS WAS SATURDAY NIGHT. The next morning I said to my brother, let us call on my father as we go to the meeting, but, upon his telling me this would but further provoke him, we forbore. As we went along he said, Sister you are now brought upon the stage to act for Christ, I pray God help you to bear your testimony for him, I would by no means have you consent to my fathers terms. No brother, I replied, I will sooner beg my bread from door to door. While I sat at meeting, my mind was hurried, as no wonder, considering my case; but service being ended I again made the proposal to call on my father in our way home. We did so, and found him in the yard. Before we came quite to him my brother repeated his admonition to me, though I thought I stood in no need of his counsel on this particular. He talked very mildly to my father, pleading with him to be reconciled, but perceiving he still retained his anger, I whispered and desired my brother to go home. No, said he, not without you. I said, I will come presently; on which he went, though (as he told me afterwards) with many fears lest I should comply, but I then thought I could as soon part with my life.

My brother being gone I stood pleading with my father, and said, Father I will serve you in any thing that lies in my power, I only desire liberty to hear God's word on his own day, grant me this and I ask no more. Father, (continued I) you cannot answer for my sins or stand in my stead before God, I must look to the salvation of my own soul, &c. He replied, if I would promise never to go to a meeting as long as he lived, I should then go into the house, and he would provide for me as his own child; if not, I should never have one farthing from him. Father, said I, my soul is of more worth than so, I dare not make you such a promise; upon this his anger was greatly inkindled, and he bid me be gone, for he was resolved what to do; therefore promise me that you will never go to the meeting again, and I will give you the key, repeating these words several times, holding it out to me, and urging me to promise, and I as often refusing, till at last his wrath increased. What do you say? if you now refuse to comply you shall never be offered it more, and I am determined you shall never come within my doors again as long as I live. While I thus stood crying by him he repeated the same expressions; What do you say hussey? will you promise or not? Being thus urged, at last I answered, Well father I will promise you never to go to a meeting again as long as you live, without your consent. Hereupon he gave me the key and I went into the house.

But O! soon after I had entered the door, that awful scripture was brought to my mind, Matth. x. 33. *Whosoever shall deny me before men, him will I also deny before my Father which is in heaven.* Also verse 37. *He that loveth father or mother more than me is not worthy of me.* O thought I what will become of me! what have I done this night! I was so filled with terror that I was going to run out of the house again, but I thought this would not alter what I had done. Now, alas! all my comforts were gone, and, in their room, nothing but grief and guilt and rendings of conscience! In this instance I saw what all my resolutions were come to; even nothing. This was Lord's day night, and a black night it was to me.

In a little time my father came in and behaved with affection; he bid me get him some supper which I did. He also told me to come and eat with him, but it was a bitter supper to me. My brother's heart ached when he saw I did not follow him, fearing I should promise, and not coming to his house, was ready to conclude I had done so. But no tongue can express what a doleful condition I was in. I hardly durst look up to God for mercy. Now I thought I must hear the word no more. What good would it do me if my father could give me his house full of silver and gold! Thus I went about reflecting on my condition, and sorrowing till almost spent with my grief.

On Monday I withdrew into the barn to pray and give vent to my sorrow; when, as I stood sighing, with my hand [head?] inclined to the wall, and crying out, Lord what shall I do? those words surprized me, I Cor. x. 13. *There shall be a way to escape that you may be able to bear it.* Lord! thought I, what way wilt thou make for my escape? wilt thou make my father willing to let me go to thine ordinancies? if thou dost, still what a wretch was I thus to deny Christ! In the evening as we were sitting by the fire, my father asked me what was the matter? I burst into tears, saying, O father! I am distressed at the thoughts of my promise not to go to a meeting again without your consent. He was so moved that he wept like a child, bidding me not let that trouble me for we should not disagree, at which I was a little comforted, and said, Pray father forgive me where I have been undutiful to you. He then told me with tears how much he was troubled for me that night he shut me out of doors, insomuch that he could not sleep, adding, it was my riding behind John Bunyan that made him so angry.[1]

The greatest part of the next day, being Tuesday, I spent in prayer and weeping, with bitter lamentations, humbling myself before the Lord for what I had done, and begging I might be kept by his grace and spirit from denying him and his ways for the future. Before night he brought me out of this horrible pit and set my feet upon a rock, enabling me to believe the forgiveness of all my sins, by sealing many precious promises home on my soul. I could now look back with comfort on the night I spent in the barn; the sweet relish of that blessed and *beloved* return, and I believed that Jesus Christ was the same yesterday, to day, and for ever; and that scripture was much in my mind, Job, v. 19. *He shall deliver thee in six troubles, yea in seven there shall no evil touch thee.* Also Deut. xxxiii. 27. *The eternal God is thy refuge, and underneath are the everlasting arms.*

My father was as well as usual this day, and eat his dinner as heartily as ever I knew him; after supper he smoked a pipe and went to bed seemingly in perfect health. But while I was by his bed side laying his clothes on him, those words ran though my mind, Amos viii. 2. *The end is come.* I could not think what to make of these words, they seemed so very mysterious to me.

As soon therefore as I quitted the room I went to the throne of grace, where my heart was wonderfully drawn forth, especially that the Lord would shew mercy to my father, and save his soul, for which I was so importunate that I could not tell how to leave pleading; and still that word continued on my mind, *The end is come.* Another thing I entreated of the Lord was that he would stand by me and be with me in whatever trouble I had to meet with, little thinking what was coming upon me that night and the week following.

After this I went to bed, thinking on the freedom which God had given me in prayer, but had not slept long before I heard a mournful noise, which at first I apprehended had been in the yard, but soon perceived it to be my father. I immediately arose, put on a few clothes, ran and lighted a candle, and coming to him, found him sitting upright in his bed, crying to the Lord for mercy, saying, Lord have mercy on me, for I am a miserable sinner! Lord Jesus wash me in thy precious blood, &c.! I stood trembling to hear him in such distress, and to see him look so pale, enquired how long he had been ill. He said, I was struck with a pain at my heart in my sleep and shall die presently. I then kneeled down by the bed side, and which I had never done before, prayed with him, in which he seemed to join very earnestly.

This done I said, Father I will go and call some body, for I dare not stay with you alone. He replied, You shall not go out at this time of night, don't be afraid, still crying aloud for mercy. Soon after he said he would rise and put on his clothes himself, I ran and made a good fire, and got him something hot, hoping that it might relieve him. O, said he, I want mercy for my soul! Lord shew mercy to me, for I am a great sinner! If thou dost not shew me mercy I am miserable for ever! Father, said I, there is mercy in Jesus Christ for sinners, the Lord help you to lay hold on it. O, replied he, I have been against you for seeking after Jesus Christ, the Lord forgive me and lay not this sin to my charge!

I desired him to drink something warm which I had for him, but his trying to drink brought in a violent retching, and he changed black in the face. I stood by holding his head and [he was] leaning upon me with all his weight. Dreadful time indeed! If I left him I was afraid he would fall into the fire! and if I stand by him he would die in my arms, and no one person near us! What shall I do! Lord help me! Then came that scripture, Isaiah xli. 10. *Fear thou not for I am with thee, be not dismayed I am thy God; I will help thee, yea, I will uphold thee,* &c.

By this time my father revived again out of his fit of fainting, for I think he did swoon away, he repeated his cries as before, Lord have mercy upon me for I am a sinful man! Lord spare me one week more! one day more! Piercing words to me! After he had sat a while he felt an uneasiness in his bowels, and called for a candle to go into the other room. I saw him stagger as he went over the threshold, soon followed him and found him on the floor, which occasioned me to scream out, Father! father! putting my hands under his arms, lifting with all my might, first by one arm then by another, crying and striving till my strength was quite spent.[2]

I found all my attempts to raise him in vain, and therefore, though not without fears of rogues, who I thought waited at the door, ran like some distracted creature through deep snows to my brothers, where I stood crying in a deplorable manner. The family being alarmed, my brother came immediately with two of his men, and found our father risen from the ground and laid upon the bed. My brother spake to him, but he could not answer, except one word or two. On my return, they desired me not to go into the room, saying he was just departing. O dismal night, had not the Lord wonderfully supported me I must have died too, of the fears and frights which I met with.

My brother's man soon came out, and said he was departed: melancholy tidings! but in midst of my trouble I had a secret hope that he was gone to heaven, nevertheless I sat crying bitterly to think what a sudden and surprizing change death had made on my father who went to bed well and was in eternity by midnight! I said in my heart, Lord give me one seal [i.e., sign] more that I shall go to heaven when death shall make this change on me. Then that word came directly, Isaiah xxxv. 10. *The ransomed of the Lord shall return and come to Zion with songs and everlasting joy upon their heads,* &c. O I longed to be gone to heaven! thought I they are singing whilst I am sorrowing! O that I had the wings of a dove, then would I fly away and be at rest!

Quickly after my brother called in some neighbours, among whom came Mr. F. my bitter enemy,[3] who enquired if my father was dead. Some body replied, Yes, he is. He then said it is no more than what I looked for, though no notice was taken of these words till afterwards. This was Tuesday after the Friday night that I lay in the barn, when that scripture was so frequently in my mind, *Beloved think it not strange concerning the fiery trial which is to try you.* I thought now I had met with fiery trials indeed, not knowing that I had as bad or worse to come, which I shall now proceed to relate.

The day that my father died, the clergyman who met Mr. Bunyan and me at Gam'gay [i.e., Gamlingay] town's end, reported at Baldock fair, that we had been criminally conversant together; which vile report I heard the next day, but that scripture came with much sweetness and bore me up, Matth. v. 11, *Blessed are ye when men shall revile you, and say all manner of evil against you falsly for my sake.*

On Thursday we had agreed to bury my father, and accordingly invited our relations and friends to the funeral. But, on the Wednesday night, Mr. F. sends for my brother, and asked him whether he thought my father died a natural death; a question which amazed my brother, who readily answered in the affirmative, Yes, I know he died a natural death; Mr. F. replied, but I believe he did not, and I have had my horse out of the stable twice to day to fetch a surgeon, but considered that you are an officer of the parish, therefore leave it to you; pray see and do your office. Upon my brother's asking him, how he thought my father came to his end if he did not die a natural death, he answered, I believe your sister has poisoned him.

My brother returned with a heavy heart, not knowing but I might lose my life; on acquainting my sister she was likewise distressed, when they sent for a godly neighbour to pray with and counsel them, who advised them to keep it from me that night; but early in the morning my brother came and told me, to whom I immediately said, O brother! blessed be God for a clear conscience. We deferred the funeral, and sending for a surgeon, told him the case, who examined me how my father was before he went to bed, and what supper he eat, &c. I told him all the particulars, and, when he had surveyed the corps, he went to Mr. F. and told him that he wondered how he could entertain such thoughts concerning me, assuring him there were no just grounds for his suspicion. Mr. F. replied, he verily believed it was so. The surgeon perceiving that no arguments would convince him, told us we must have a coroner and jury. I readily agreed to this proposal, saying, moreover, sir, as my innocency is known to God I would have it known to men, therefore pray be pleased to open my father. This he declined, saying, there was no need for it, but promised to meet the coroner and jury the next day.

Now I had new work cut out, therefore went to the Lord and prayed that he would appear in this fiery trial. I saw my life lay at stake as well as the name of God struck at, but that word was sent for my support and comfort, and it was a blessed one to my soul, Isaiah liv. 17. *No weapon that is formed against thee shall prosper, and every tongue that shall rise against thee in judgment thou shalt condemn.* Also ch xlv 24. *All that are incensed against thee shall be ashamed.* Encouraged by these precious promises, we sent for the coroner the next morning. Mr. F. hearing it, told my brother he would have him meet the coroner and jury and agree [to] it, for, continued he, it will be found petit treason,[4] and your sister must be burnt. No, sir, replied my brother, we are not ashamed to let them come through. Upon hearing this I said I will have them come through if it costs me all that my father has left me. I did not know how far God might suffer this man and the devil to go. It also troubled me to think that in case I suffered, another as innocent as myself must suffer too, for Mr. F. reported that I poisoned my father, and Mr. Bunyan gave me the stuff to do it with; but the Lord knew our innocency in this affair both in thought, word, and deed.

Whilst thus surrounded with straits and troubles, I must own that at times I had many carnal reasonings though I knew myself clear. I thought should God suffer my enemy to prevail to the taking away of my life; how shall I endure burning? O the thoughts of burning were very terrible, and made my very heart to ach[e] within me! But that scripture which I had often thought of before my father's death, came now into my mind, Isaiah xliii. 2. *When thou passest through the fire I will be with thee*, &c. I said in my heart, Lord thou knowest my innocence, therefore if thou art pleased to suffer my enemies to take away my life, yet, surely, thou wilt be with me; thou hast been with me in all my trials hitherto, and I trust wilt not now leave me, in the greatest of all. At last I was made to believe that if I did burn at a stake the Lord would give me his presence, and, in a solemn manner, resigned myself to his disposal, either for life or death.

That forenoon in which the coroner was expected some christian friends from Gam'gay paid me a visit, and spent time in prayer; and pleaded earnestly with the Lord on my behalf, that he would graciously appear for me and glorify his name in my deliverance. This done, I retired, and was much enlarged in begging the divine presence this day, and that I might not have so much as a dejected countenance, or be in the least daunted before them. I thought to stand before a company of men for the murder of my own father, though I knew my innocence, would make me sink, unless I had much of the Lord's presence to support me. I thought should I appear dejected or daunted, people will conclude that I am guilty, therefore I begged of God that he would carry me above the fears of men, devils and death, and give me faith and courage to lift up my head before my accusers. Immediately that scripture darted into my mind, Job xvii 9. *The righteous also shall hold on his way, and he that hath clean hands shall be stronger and stronger.* Then I broke out, Lord thou knowest my heart, and my hands are clear in this matter. This was such a suitable word that I could hardly have had such another, and the Lord made every tittle of it good before the sun went down, so that I was helped to look mine enemies in the face with boldness.

Presently word was brought that the coroner and jury were come. I sat with some neighbours by the fire as they passed through the house into the room where my father lay, some of the jurymen came, and, taking me by the hand, with tears running down their cheeks, said, pray God be thy comfort, thou art as innocent as I am I believe; thus one and another spake to me, which I looked upon as a wonderful mercy to find they believed me not guilty.

When the coroner had viewed the corps, he came to warm himself by the fire where I sat, and looking stedfastly at me, he said, are you the daughter of the deceased? I answered yes. He replied, are you the person who was in the house alone with him when he was struck with death? Yes, sir, I am she. He then shook his head, at which I feared his thoughts were evil towards me.

The jury also having taken their view, they went to dine at my brother's; after which they proceeded to business, and sent for me. As I was going my heart went out much to the Lord, that he would stand by me. Then came those words, Isaiah liv. 4. *Fear not for thou shalt not be ashamed.* And before I came to my brother's house my soul was made like the chariots of Amminadib,[5] being wonderfully supported, even above what I could ask or think.

When I got there my brother sent for Mr. F. who not coming soon, he sent again; at last he came. Then the coroner called the witnesses, being my brother's men, who were sworn, he asked them whether they were present when my father died? what words they heard him speak? &c. and when they had answered, he called Mr. F. and gave him his oath, Come, said he, as you are the occasion of our meeting together, we would know about this young woman's murdering her father, and on what grounds you accuse her? Mr. F. but in a confused manner, told the coroner of the late difference between my father and me, how I was shut out of doors, and that my father died but two nights after I was admitted; nobody knew what to make of this strange preamble; but I stood in the parlour amongst them with my heart as full of comfort as it could hold, being got above the fear of men or devils.

The coroner said, this is nothing to the matter in hand; what have you to accuse this young woman with? To which Mr. F. replied little or nothing to the purpose, and, at the same time, returning cross answers, was bid to stand by. Then I was called. Come sweet-heart, saith the coroner, tell us where was you that night your father shut you out? I answered, sir, I was in the barn all night. And was you there alone? yes sir, I had nobody with me. He shook his head, and proceeded, Where did you go the next morning? sir, I staid in the yard till nine or ten o'clock, entreating my father to let me come in, but he would not.

At this he seemed concerned, and asked, Where I was the remaining part of the day? I said at my brother's, and lay there the following night. When did your father let you come in? On Lord's-day evening. Was he well when you came in? Yes, sir. How long did he live afterwards? Till Tuesday night, sir. Was he well that day? Yes, sir, as well as ever I saw him in my life, and he eat as hearty a dinner. In what manner was he taken, and at what time? Near midnight, complaining of a pain at his heart; I heard him groan and made all haste to light a candle, and when I came, I found him sitting up in his bed and crying out of a pain in his heart, and he said he should presently die, which frightened me much, so that I could scarce get on my clothes, when I made a fire, and my father rose and sat by it. I got him something warm, of which he drank a little, but straining to vomit, he swooned away while I held his head, and could not leave him to call in assistance, fearing lest in my absence he should fall into the fire.

The coroner further proceeded. Was there nobody in the house with you? No, sir, I said, I had none with me but God. At length my father came a little again to himself, and went into the other room, whither I soon followed him and found him lying upon the floor, at which sight I screamed out in a most dismal manner, yet I tried to raise him up, but in vain, till at last, being almost spent, I ran to my brother's in a frightful condition.

Having given him this relation, the coroner said, sweet-heart, I have no more to say to you; and then addressed himself to the jury, whose verdict being given, he turned himself to Mr. F. and said, you, sir, who have defamed this young woman in this publick manner, endeavouring to take away her good name, yea, her life also, if you could, ought to make it your business now to establish her reputation. She has met with enough in being alone with her father, when seized with death, you had no need to add to her affliction and sorrow, and if you were to give her five hundred pounds it would not make her amends.

He then came to me, and taking me by the hand, said, sweet-heart, do not be daunted, God will take care of thy preferment, and provide thee a husband notwithstanding the malice of this man. I confess these are hard things for one so young as thou art to meet with, but thank God for this deliverance, and never fear but he will take care of thee. Then, addressing myself to the coroner and jury, I said, sirs, if you are not all satisfied I am free my father should be opened, as my innocence is known to God, I would have it known to you also, for I am not afraid of life. No, replied the coroner, we are all satisfied, there is no need of having him opened, but bless God that the malice of this man broke out before thy father was buried.

The room was full of people, and great observation made of my looks and behaviour. Some gentlemen who were on the jury, as I was afterwards told, said, that they should never forget with what cheerful countenance I stood before them. I know not how I looked, but this I know, my heart was as full of peace and comfort, as it could hold. The jurymen were all much concerned for me, and were observed to weep when the coroner examined me. Indeed I have abundant cause to bless God that they were deeply convinced of my innocence, and I have heard that some of them were so affected with my case, that they would long after speak of me with tears.

When the coroner and company were gone, we sent again to our friends to invite them to the funeral, which was on Saturday night. I now thought my trials on this account were over, and that Mr. F. had vented all his malice, but was mistaken, for, seeing he could not take away my life, his next attempt was to deprive me of that substance my father had left me. Accordingly he sends for my brother-in-law from my father's grave, and informed him how things were left in the will, telling him that his wife was cut off with a shilling, but that he could put him in a way to come in for a share.

This was a new trouble. My brother-in-law threatened if I would not resign part of what my father had left he would begin a suit at law. Mr. F. prompted him on, saying, hang her, do not let her go away with so much more than your wife, &c. And to law we were going, to prevent which and for the sake of peace I satisfied my brother with a handsome present.

About a month after my father was buried, another report was spread at Biggleswade, that now Agnes Beaumont had confessed she poisoned her father, and was quite distracted. Is it true, said some? Yes, it is true said others. *I have heard the defaming of many report, say they, and we will report it,* Jer. xx. 10.

But I was determined, if it pleased God to spare me till next market day, I would go and let them see I was not distracted, and accordingly went, and when the market was at the height, shewed myself among the people, which put a stop to their business for a time; for their eyes were upon me while I walked through and through with this thought, if there were a thousand more of you I would lift up my head before you all. That day I was well in my soul, and therefore exceeding chearful. Many people came and spake to me, saying, we now see that you are not distracted.

Some I saw cry, but some others laughed: O, thought I, mock on, there's a day coming that will clear up all. That was a wonderful scripture, Psalm xxxvii. 6. *And he shall bring forth thy righteousness as the light, and thy judgment as the noon-day.*

After this another report was raised in a different part of the country, that Mr. Bunyan was a widower and gave me counsel to poison my father, that he might marry me, which plot was agreed on they said as we went to Gam'gay. But this report rather occasioned mirth than mourning, because Mr. Bunyan, at the same time, had a good wife living.

Now, thought I, surely Mr. F. has done with me: but the next summer a fire broke out in the town; how it came to pass no one could tell, but Mr. F. soon found a person on whom to charge it, for he affirmed that it was I who set the house on fire; but, as the Lord knoweth, I knew nothing of this fire till the doleful cry reached my ears: this malicious slander was not much regarded.

Thus have I related both the good and evil things I have met with, in past dispensations of providence, and have reason to wish it was well with my soul now as then. And one mercy the Lord added to all the rest, which I cannot but mention, namely, that he kept me from prejudice against Mr. F. for notwithstanding he had so greatly injured me, I was helped to cry to the Lord, and that with many tears, for mercy on his soul. I can truly say that I earnestly longed after his salvation, and begged of God to forgive him whatever he had said or done to my hurt.[6]

Notes

1. Some evil-minded men of the town . . . had set her father against Mr. Bunyan, for in time past he had heard him preach, and had been much melted under the word; he would pray and frequently go to the meetings. Yea, and when his daughter was first under spiritual concern he had very great awakenings himself, and would say to some of the neighbours, My daughter can scarce eat, drink, or sleep, and I have lived these threescore years, and have scarce ever thought of *my* soul, &c. [James].

2. See the remarkable dream of the apple tree, p. 20 [James]. In that dream, Beaumont tried but failed to lift an apple tree felled in a storm, just as she is here trying and failing to lift her father.

3. Mr. Ffeery, the attorney who had drawn up Beaumont's father's will; he persuaded her father to leave her more money than her sister because he wanted to marry her, but after she got religion he became her "bitter enemy" (James 125).

4. A child who killed her or his father might be charged with petit treason; this charge could also be lodged against a wife for killing her husband, an apprentice for killing her or his master, and a person for killing her or his spiritual superior.

5. I.e., her soul was exalted; see Song of Sol. 6:12.

6. [A] most excellent spirit, which every Christian should aim at [James].

Mary Churchman

1654–1734

Memoirs of Mrs. Mary Churchman, relating to her Conversion, and the difficulties she underwent from her own family, until the Lord appeared in her favour, in turning every one of them to himself. In *An Abstract of the Gracious Dealings of God, With several Eminent Christians, in their Conversion and Sufferings. Taken from Authentic Manuscripts, and Published for the Comfort and Establishment of Serious Minds.* [Comp.] by Samuel James. London: J. Ward, 1760.

The only known facts about Mary Churchman's life are either contained in her *Memoirs* or provided by its editor, Samuel James. Born in 1654, she was raised, as her first paragraph indicates, to be a zealous Anglican. After a serious illness at the age of eighteen, she was much affected by hearing Richard Holcroft, a pastor of a congregational church and well known among nonconformists as a powerful preacher. Her parents, however, were extremely opposed to "fanatick" Dissenters, and her father, as a local official, was particularly adamant in his opposition to a group considered subversive of established order. After a year of secretly attending Sunday meetings, Mary gave public witness of her new faith; her father then turned her out of his house, and she took a position as governess. Her father remained obdurate, and in 1675 she obtained another position farther from his home. During the following years she appears to have been employed by several noble families.

The arrest and harassment of Dissenters persisted during these years, and Mary's employer was one of several who hoped to escape persecution by emigrating to Protestant Holland. Churchman's decision to accompany him led to a reconciliation with her family, an event which is the high point of her text considered as a spiritual autobiography or, more specifically, as a conversion narrative: both she and her family have now followed the course of spiritual development that culminates in salvation. The final paragraph of Churchman's *Memoirs* briefly notes the existence of a husband and children, and James adds several paragraphs about her "witnessing" to her neighbors and family. She died in the arms of her daughter on 12 January 1734 at the age of eighty.

TEXT: Mary Churchman's *Memoirs* was first and last published in 1760, as one of the five spiritual autobiographies compiled in Samuel James's *Abstract of the Gracious Dealings of God*. Her text may have been edited: noting that collections such as his were "far from being suited to the present taste" (i), James abbreviated some of the manuscripts and made "some few alterations" (vi) in the authors' "style" in order to clarify the "sentiment" and "sense." Churchman's narrative is reprinted in full.

❦ ❧

AGREEABLE TO WHAT MY PARENTS educated me in I was zealous for the established church, and thought all fanatics, who dissented from it.[1] I had as much prejudice against dissenters, and as great an inclination to persecute as Paul had. There lay a way through my father's yard for Mrs. M. a godly woman, to go to the meeting,[2] which she did every Lord's day. I really thought it my duty to set his great dog to molest her, and used sometimes to encourage him for half a mile together, with the most bitter invectives, such as saying my dog would smell the blood of a fanatick, &c. The cur, though cursed to others, yet, such was the preventing providence of God, that he never once fastened upon this gracious[3] person, notwithstanding, for some time, I constantly made it my business to set him upon her.

While I was about eighteen years of age it pleased the Lord to lay on me a languishing fit of sickness, which raised in me some promises of a new life, and when recovered, at the perswasion of a neighbour, who had been very useful to me in my illness, I went with her to hear that great man of God Mr. Holcroft. He preached powerfully of hell and judgment, which made me tremble and secretly wish I had never came there. Every time he named the name of Christ it was terrible as the thunder and lightning upon mount Sinai. I wished myself covered with the mountains, and looked upon Christ as my terrible judge and enemy. This trouble I vented in floods of tears, and many wishes that I had never been born, and that I had never came there, for now thought I, they will think me one of themselves, which I at that time was fully resolved against. I seemed now to like their persons worse than ever. Satan also suggested, what would my relations say? they must never know that I had been at a meeting, and the like.

Thus in great hurry and confusion, I sat till service was ended. After sermon, staying for my neighbour, the minister came to me, and asked where I lived? who I was? and whether I knew anything of the Lord Jesus Christ? &c. But such was my ignorance, and such the hurry and confusion of my mind, that dark was my answer. I told him I believed the world was at an end. Home I came, and not one word did I speak to my neighbour, but was very angry in my mind that she should ever ask me to come amongst the dissenters. I grew worse and worse, insomuch that my mother sent for a doctor, fearing that I should be melancholy, which indeed greatly increased upon me. This was in the reign of king Charles II. at which time they were bringing in popery [at] a great pace.[4]

The next opportunity which presented I had an inclination to go to the meeting again, which I did, but very privately [i.e., secretly]. My mother began to mistrust me and repeated her charge, warning me not to go among such sort of creatures as fanaticks, for I believe, said she, they bewitch people into their perswasions. However I went on a week day, and the same minister preached from those words, Cant. ii. 16. *My beloved is mine and I am his, he feedeth among the lillies.*

He was a good Samaritan to me that day. The spirit of the Lord shone round about me. O then I saw the Lord Jesus become my husband! he was to me as a hiding place from the storm and tempest to which I saw my guilty and polluted nature had exposed me. O happy day indeed! I found him who a little before appeared as a terrible judge was now become my beloved, and I knew that I was his. O inexpressible joy! he was as a bundle of myrrh to my soul. I had not only here a little and there a little, but I had every where much. I had every thing I wanted to my decayed spirits. I well knew I should meet with hard things from my relations, but could now pray, *Father forgive them, for they know not what they do.* Luke xxiii. 34.

As soon as my father and mother knew that I went to the meeting, Satan was in a great rage. My father was then high constable,[5] and had an order from the justices to return all the names of them who frequented the meetings. This made it an hard thing for his *own* daughter to be a fanatick, which was what he could not bear. And this also increased my difficulty, in getting out on a Lord's day, with notwithstanding I sometimes did, and have walked eight, ten, yea, twelve miles to a meeting. If my father at any time understood where I was gone, he spent the day in nothing but oaths and curses, and resolves to murder me. My mother, though an enemy to fanaticks, would frequently send a servant to meet me before I could reach home, to tell me not to appear till my father was gone to bed; and I often hid [my]self in a wood stack, where I have seen him pass by, with a naked knife in his hand, declaring he would kill me before he slept.

In this bondage I lived for one year, but the Lord carried on his work with much power, and enabled me to declare in Zion what he had done for my soul, which I did on a Lord's day as the manner then was. I had some fear indeed lest my parents should hear of it, which they did within a fortnight after, by means of a basket woman, who asked my mother if she had not a daughter? she answered, yes; O, said the woman, I heard her preach such a sermon[6] at Mildred, as raised the admiration of all who heard her. This my mother obliged her to attest before my father and me, who no sooner heard of it, but he immediately turned me out of doors, not suffering me to carry any thing with me, except the clothes on my back.

I went to a godly gentleman's about four miles distant from my father's, who had often told me I should be welcome to his house, where my employ should be to be the governess to his seven children. But there the Lord was pleased to try me greatly at my first setting out; my mistress, though a good woman, soon became uneasy, thinking her husband shewed me too much favour. She was suffered to carry it [i.e., behave] very cruelly towards me, ordering my lodging with the meanest[7] of the servants, and my diet likewise as coarse as theirs. It being a time of scarcity of provisions, we under-servants lived chiefly upon barley bread. I was obliged to borrow for necessary change of linen, nor did I know for months together, what it was to have one penny in my pocket.

This great change of living, together with my grief at being banished from my father's house, brought me so low, that a sore fit of sickness ensued. My life not being long expected, the gentlewoman sent a messenger to acquaint my mother that I had a great desire to see her, but as soon as the messenger informed my father, he replied, if he did not immediately get out of his yard he would shoot him dead. However, about a fortnight after my mother sent me a box of wearing apparel, which I received with these words on my thoughts, Matth. vi. 32. *For your heavenly Father knoweth that ye have need of all these things.*

I lived in this place with difficulty three years, but in all that time never knew what it was to have one barren sabbath. I thought my mercies equal to the children of Israel's. I gathered my manna on the sabbath, and it always lasted [tasted?] sweet and good, it never cloyed, and I was always hungry, insomuch that I thought if seeing and hearing the saints sometimes here was so pleasant, what must it be to dwell for ever with them above!

I was placed indeed among those where I had frequent opportunities of being convinced that good men are subject to like passions with others. This grieved me, but God did me good by such disappointments, for hereby he brought me more off from the creature to the creator.

The year following providence placed me twenty miles another way, where I obtained a Joseph's character, and a Joseph's promotion,[8] being greatly valued by many noble families, and especially the lady M.[9] who told me she loved me years before she was personally acquainted with me; she gave me of her liberality and maintained christian communion with me. One remark this lady made I well remember, speaking of the suitableness of the spirits, applying the word to all ranks and conditions, it is well said, saith she, in holy writ, not *many* noble are called; had it been expressed not *any* noble, what a condition must I have been in!

Persecution now came on apace, the dissenters could have no meetings but in woods and corners. I myself have seen our companies often alarmed with drums and soldiers; every one was fined five pounds a month for being in their company. Here God left me to stagger; Satan suggested if you give your body to be burned, and have not charity, it is nothing, (I Corinth. xiii. 3.) But the greater the temptation the greater was the deliverance, from those words, Revelat. vii. 14. *These are they which came out of great tribulation, and have washed their robes, and made them white in the blood of the lamb.* Also chap. vi. 11. *And white robes were given to every one of them* &c. Blessed be God, Satan by this assault only bruised my heel, my head remained whole.

While I was in this family the commissioners came and searched for ministers. Mr. B. (the gentleman of the house) and Mr. Holcroft were asleep in a private arbour. I ran with some difficulty and awoke them, and they made their escape through the hedges, but as I returned the officers surprized me. They went and found some slips of their clothes on the hedges, which made them roar like blood-hounds, after which they came and seized a whole house of goods. These men were major T. and colonel C.[10]

But O! the great trial now came on, they found and seized my beloved pastor Mr. Holcroft, and carried him to Cambridge castle [prison], but even there God appeared wonderfully for him; he preached, and many souls were converted in that place. Now God was with us much; he was indeed as a pillar of fire by night, and a cloud by day. And O how do I remember his loving kindness to *me* the least of all saints; he not only delivered me from fears, but even death itself, nay the very flames with which we were threatened were made familiar to me. I was enabled to say, O death where is thy sting? The Lord was a covert from that storm and tempest, and a strong rock in that day of trouble.

Mr. B. with whom I lived, had a call[11] to Holland, and as the persecution was very threatening in England, he thought it his duty to accept the call. He gave me an invitation to go with him, assuring me that all things should be in common. As I well knew my circumstances were very precarious, not having any where to hide my head, when this worthy family was gone, this drew me into great straits. I sought the Lord time after time on this account, and it seemed as if he was providing for me in another land. Grace taught me my duty to my parents, though they were enemies to the cross of Christ. Accordingly I acquainted them with this invitation, and that I should comply with it unless their commands were to the contrary. I added in my letter I should be all obedience to them, saving in matters relating to my God, and though I had not been permitted to see them seven years past, yet could assure them my affections for them were the same as ever. I begged they would consider of it, and let me know in eight days time, for all things were ready to embark in a fortnight.

Not hearing from them in the time I set, I took their silence for a consent, and so prepared all things ready for my journey, and set out with my kind friends. Just before we reached Harwich, where we were to take shipping, a messenger from my father overtook me with a letter, the contents of which were as follows, That if I would come home I should have my liberty to worship God in my own way, but as to my leaving the land, this was what they could not bear, therefore without fail I must come back with the messenger; which I did. Great was the sorrow of parting with my friends, but my duty to my parents surmounted all.

I no sooner entered my father's house but my mother in receiving me fainted away. My father also, though a man of great spirits, offered to fall on his knees to ask my pardon for his former cruelty. O amazing work of sovereign grace! when our ways please the Lord he makes even our enemies to be at peace with us. My father immediately told me I should have my liberty in matters relating to my God. I then humbly offered my obedience to them both on my knees. At supper there was not a mouthful eaten but with tears. I well knew my God had appeared to my father on my behalf, as he did to Laban of old, and applied Jacob's promise to myself, Gen. xxxii. 12. *Thou saidst I will surely do thee good.* The next sabbath my father came into my chamber by break of day, and told me I should have a horse and a man to wait on me to the meeting, which was at a place called Taft. Mr. Oddy[12] preached from those words, Psalm cx. 3. *Thy people shall be willing in the day of thy power.* Then I could see electing love, the prime cause of all God[']s dealings with me.

There now appeared a great reformation in the whole family. My father feared to sin, for fear of grieving his daughter, and in a little time left off drinking, which was the forerunner of all his other evils. Now I thought I could give my very body to be burned for the souls of my dear relations. The Lord granted my request on their behalf. In a few years I had not only the pleasure of seeing the conversion of my three brothers, but of seeing them also eminently useful. I found my God reserved his greatest mercies for my greatest trials, for at the death of my dear sister I had not only the comfort of seeing her conversion, but the great satisfaction of seeing my dear father and mother also converted to the faith of Jesus, though at the eleventh hour. Yea such was the power and goodness of God, that he left not so much as a *hoof* behind in the whole family.

Surely now I may say that nothing but goodness and mercy hath followed me all the days of my life. When we had free liberty under our great deliverer from popery and slavery, King William,[13] many were the favours which I enjoyed. God gave me the best and tenderest of husbands; a prophet of the Lord indeed, whose good instructions abide with my children to this day. In short, the Lord has sanctified every trial to me, and followed me with pleasure and comfort in my old age.

Notes

1. The Church of England, the Anglican Church; Dissenters separated themselves from communion with this Church to establish their own sects.

2. "Meeting" here means an assembly of people for worship.

3. Filled with grace.

4. Charles II reigned from 1660 to 1685; his brother, James, heir to the throne, was a professed Roman Catholic, and it was rumored that Charles, too, had converted— hence Churchman's feeling that "popery" (Roman Catholicism) was rapidly encroaching on English Protestantism.

5. Officer of a large administrative district whose duty is to keep the peace.

6. According to James, Churchman did not so much preach a formal sermon as witness or testify.

7. Used in the class sense to mean lowest.

8. Refers to the Old Testament story (Gen. 39:1–4) in which Joseph's master, Potiphar, promotes him in the belief that he is a favorite with God.

9. Not identified.

10. Not identified.

11. Prompting to a special spiritual service or office.

12. Holcroft's assistant or fellow pastor.

13. William III, a Protestant, replaced the Catholic James II as king of England in the so-called Glorious Revolution of 1689.

Christian Davies

1667–1739

*The Life and Adventures of Mrs. Christian Davies, commonly call'd Mother Ross;
Who, in several Campaigns under King William and the Late Duke of Marlborough, In the Quality of a Foot-Soldier and Dragoon, gave many signal Proofs
of an unparallell'd Courage and personal Bravery. Taken from her own Mouth
when a Pensioner of Chelsea-Hospital, and known to be true by Many who were
engaged in those great Scenes of Action.* 2 vols. London: R. Montagu, 1740.

Christian Cavenaugh was born in 1667 into a prosperous Dublin family;
her father was a maltster and brewer with twenty employees, and her
mother managed the farm he rented. Her parents "spared no Cost" (1:2)
to educate her, but her "Love of romping" and "manly Employments"
led her to prefer helping her mother with farm work. Although she relates
some of "the wild, girlish Tricks" she played as a child, she also gives
incidents "to shew my Inclinations, while a Girl, were always masculine"
(1:4); this alternation between "feminine" and "masculine" is characteristic
of her text. Raped by a cousin when she was perhaps sixteen, Christian
persuaded her mother to send her to an aunt who kept a pub in Dublin.
She lived there for four years, behaving with "such dutiful Respect" that
she inherited the pub on her aunt's death.

Around 1687 Christian married Richard Welsh. Four years later he dis-
appeared, and another year passed before she received a letter from him
saying that he had been impressed into the British army. Determined to
find him, she enlisted as Christopher Welsh, and much of her *Life* is given
over to the battles in which she fought as well as the amours and "Wine
and Company" (1:47) she enjoyed as a soldier. She was once wounded
but, propped against a tree, she "endeavoured to animate my Brother
Soldiers" (1:53), and although hospitalized, she "narrowly escaped" discovery of her sex. Eventually she located her husband but remained in
the army as a dragoon. Only when she was again wounded was her sex
detected, and the examining officer was so "well entertained" (1:76) by
her history that he kept her on as paid cook and then sutler to the regi-

*Christian Davies ("Mother Ross"), by an unknown engraver. Courtesy of
the National Portrait Gallery, London.*

ment. In the winter of 1706 she bore a premature baby; after the infant's
death six months later, Christian resumed work as an undercook. A favorite in the regiment, she often tells of the laughter, applause, and money
she gained from exploits such as wooing the lover of a young man who
had irritated her.

When her husband died in battle in 1707(?), her grief earned her the
respectful regimental nickname "Mother Ross." Although her mourning
seems to have been sincere, she remarried within three months. This husband soon thereafter was wounded and died, but Christian appears to have
stayed with her regiment until the end of the War of the Spanish Succession in 1712. She then approached various generals and patrons, and eventually the Court, with a petition for a pension "in consideration of my

own Service and the Loss of two Husbands in her Majesty's" (2:78); she was pregnant at the time, and although Queen Anne offered to give the child a military commission, Christian was disappointed in this expectation when, "to my Sorrow" (2:82), the child proved a girl. Returning to Dublin, she made her living managing a pub; there "my Evil Genius entangled me in a third Marriage" (2:86), with Davies. This husband was careless with her money, and she concludes her *Life* by stating that, despite her pension, she is barely subsisting on donations from "the Benevolence of the Quality and Gentry of the Court" (2:104). Rather ironically considering her military service, Christian Davies died in 1739 of a cold she caught while nursing her husband. She was interred in the burial grounds of Chelsea Hospital with military honors.

TEXT: First published in 1740, Christian Davies's *Life and Adventures* rapidly went into a second edition (1741) and an abridged edition (1742), and it has occasionally been republished (in 1840, 1928, and 1973). The book was early attributed to novelist Daniel Defoe, and in 1981 it was microfilmed as part of an Early British Fiction collection, but there seems no reason to doubt Davies's existence. The two excerpts are from the 1740 edition: the first (pp. 19–22 and 25–32 of volume 1) records Davies's decision to enlist in the army, some early adventures, and an amour; in the second (pp. 35–37 and 41–43 of volume 2), Davies relates some later exploits with her regiment.

છ ૪૦

[Davies has received a letter from her husband, whom she had thought dead.] This Letter renewed my Grief, and gave new Fountains to my Eyes. I had bewailed him dead, and now I lamented him living, looking upon his unfortunate Situation [as] worse than Death, as he was deprived of all means of returning to me; for I despaired of his Officers parting with him. When I had read the Letter, I was at first stupified; I stood without Motion, and my Trouble being too great to allow of Tears, I gave a sudden Shriek and fell down, without the least Signs of Life remaining in me. When, by the Care and Charity of my Friends and Neighbours who came to my Assistance, I was brought to my Senses and Speech, I burst into a Flood of Tears; but when I was asked the Occasion of this sudden Grief, I, for some Time, answered nothing but, *my dear* Richard, *O must I never see thee more! O my dear, dear Husband! once the Comfort of my Life, now the Source of my Misfortunes, I can never support the Loss.* In a Word, I was in such Agonies, and fainted so often, that they who were about me almost despaired of my Life, or if I survived this new Affliction, of which I was not capable to give them an Account, that it would be the Loss of my Senses. Some of my Friends would watch with me that Night, and had it not been for their Care, I had certainly put an end to that Life which I thought insupportable. In the getting me to Bed, my Letter dropp'd, and their Curiosity having taught them the Cause of my distracting Trouble, they endeavoured to comfort me with the Hopes of recovering my Husband; but to no purpose, I was inconsoleable, and closed not my Eyes all that Night; in the Morning I thought of going in search of my dear *Richard,* and this gave some Ease to my tortured Mind. I began to flatter my self that I should meet no great Difficulty in finding him out, and resolved, in one of his Sutes, for we were both of a Size, to conceal my Sex, and go directly for *Flanders,* in search of him whom I prefered to every thing else the World could afford me, which, indeed, had nothing alluring, in comparison with my dear *Richard,* and whom the Hopes of seeing had lessened every Danger to which I was going to expose my self. The Pleasure I found in the Thoughts of once more regaining him, recalled my Strength, and I was grown much gayer than I had been at any Time in my supposed Widowhood. I was not long deliberating, after this Thought had possessed me; but immediately set about preparing what was necessary for my Ramble; and disposing of my Children, my eldest with my Mother, and that which was born after my Husband's Departure, with a Nurse, my second Son was dead; I told my Friends, *That I would go to* England *in search of my Husband, and return with all possible Expedition after I had found him.* My Goods I left in the Hands of such Friends as had spare House-room, and my House I let to a Cooper. Having thus ordered my Affairs, I cut off my Hair, and dressed me in a Sute of my Husband's, having had the Precaution to quilt the Waistcoat, to preserve my Breasts from hurt, which were not large enough to betray my Sex, and putting on the Wig and Hat I had prepared, I went out and bought me a Silver hilted Sword, and some Holland[1] Shirts: But was at a Loss how I should carry my Money with me, as it was contrary to Law to export above Five Pounds out of the Kingdom; I thought at last of quilting it in the Waistband of my Breeches, and by this Method I carried with me Fifty Guineas without Suspicion.

I had now nothing upon my Hands to prevent my setting out, wherefore, that I might get as soon as possible to *Holland,* I went to the Sign of the *Golden Last,* where Ensign *Herbert Laurence,* who was beating up [i.e., searching] for Recruits, kept his Rendezvous. He was in the House at the Time I got there, and I offered him my Service to go against the *French,* being desirous to shew my Zeal for his Majesty King *William,* and my Country.[2] The Hopes of soon meeting with my Husband, added a Sprightliness to my Looks, which made the Officer say, *I was a clever brisk young Fellow,* and having recommended my Zeal, he gave me a Guinea inlisting Money, and a Crown to drink the King's Health, and ordered me to be enrolled, having told him my Name was *Christopher Welsh,* in Captain *Tichbourn's* Company of Foot, in the Regiment commanded by the Marquis *de Pisare.* The Lieutenant of our Company was Mr. *Gardiner,* our Ensign Mr. *Welsh.*

We staid but a short Time in *Dublin* after this, but, with the rest of the Recruits, were shipped for *Holland,* weighed Anchor, and soon arrived at *Williamstadt,* where we landed and marched to *Gorkum.* Here our Regimentals and first Mountings[3] were given us. The next Day we set out for *Gertruydenberg,* and proceeded forward to *Landen,* where we were incorporated in our respective Regiments, and then joined the grand Army, which was in Expectation of a general Battle, the Enemy being very near within Canon Shot. Having been accustomed to Soldiers, when a Girl, and delighted with seeing them exercise, I very soon was perfect, and applauded by my Officers for my Dexterity in going through it.

In a Day or two after we arrived at *Landen,* I was ordered on the Night Guard, and, by Direction of my Officer, was posted at the Bed Chamber Door of the Elector of *Hanover.*[4] *Mustapha,* a *Turk,* and Valet de Chambre to his most Serene Highness, while I was here upon Duty, introduced to the Elector a fine, handsome, jolly Lady, who was what we call a black Beauty; she was dressed in a rich Silk, and her Gown was tied with Ribbons from her Breast to her Feet. I thought the Lady went with a great deal of Alacrity, as I believe many more of our Sex would visit a Sovereign Prince with a particular Satisfaction; especially, if agreable in his Person, as the Elector, who then wore his own Hair,[5] and the finest I ever saw, really was. When I saw his late Majesty, I told him, *I remembered him in fine Hair of his own, which became him better than that of possibly some lewd Women, which he then wore.*

Before I was relieved, the *French* drew nearer to our Army, and were engaged by some of the Troops of the Allies; I heard the Canon play, and the small Shot rattle about me, which, at first, threw me into a sort of Panick, having not been used to such rough Musick: however, I recovered from my Fear, and being ordered by Lord *Cholmondley* to repair Instantly to my Regiment, as I was going, I received a Wound from a Musket Ball, which grazed on my Leg, a little above the Ankle, but did not hurt the

Bone. Lord *Cholmondley* was present, and expressed his Concern for my Wound in very humane Terms, ordering me at the same Time to be carried off the Field. . . .[6]

I was two Months incapable of Service; after which I joined my Regiment, which was under Cover the remaining Part of the Summer, and at the Approach of Winter was ordered into Quarters at *Gertruydenberg.*

While I staid here, the Dykes near the Town were ruined by Worms, and a Village near our Quarters was drowned. As the repairing the damaged Dykes required the utmost Expedition, the *English* Soldiers were commanded to assist the *Dutch,* and we were obliged to work Day and Night up to our Waists in Water, 'till they were repaired. Ensign *Gardener* and I staying, the last Time we were at the Work, somewhat too long, being resolved to see every thing secure, narrowly escaped drowning by the Tide coming upon us; however, we supported each other, and waded out Hand in Hand, long after the others had gone off.

The following Summer was spent in Marches and Counter-marches to watch the Motion of the *French.* During this peaceful Campaign, as we were foraging, the *French* came unexpectedly upon, and took three-score of us Prisoners, stripped us, and, by very tiresome Marches, conducted us to St. *Germain's en lay.* The first Night the *Dutch* and *English* were promiscuously imprisoned, but the next Day King *James's* Queen caused the *English* to be separated, to have clean Straw every Night, while the *Dutch* had none, and allowed us Five Farthings a Day per Head, for Tobacco, a whole Pound of Bread, and a Pint of Wine a Day for each Man; and, moreover, ordered our Cloaths to be returned us. The other Prisoners had but half a Pound of Bread a Day, drank Water, and lay almost naked, in filthy dark Prisons, without other Support. The Duke of *Berwick* frequently came to see that we were well used, and not defrauded of our Allowance. He advised us to take on in the *French* Service, as seven of the *English* did: he spoke to me in particular; I answered, *That I had taken an Oath already to King* William, *and if there was no Crime in breaking it, as I was satisfied it was one of the blackest Die, I could not in Honour break my Engagement, nothing in my Opinion being more unbecoming an honest Man and a Soldier, than to break even his Word once given, and to wear a double Face.* He seemed to applaud my Principles, and only added, That *if I had accepted Conditions, I should have been well used; but the Choice depended entirely on me.*

Captain *Cavenaugh,* who was my first Couzen, and an Officer in the *French* Troops, often came to the Prison, and I was at first apprehensive of his knowing me; but afterwards, had an Inclination to discover myself to him, as I certainly had done, had my Husband been dead, or had I found him; but my Fear of such a Discovery being an Impediment to the Search of my Husband, got the better of my Inclination.

In about nine Days after our Imprisonment, Mr. *Van-Dedan*, a Trumpet,[7] and now living in *Chelsea*, came to exchange us against some *French* Prisoners, and we were set at Liberty; after which, as it was a Duty Incumbent on us, we went to the Palace to return her Majesty grateful Thanks for the good Offices she had done us, and, indeed, we were greatly endebted to her Charity. She had the Condescension to see us; she told me, *I was a pretty young Fellow, and it grieved her much that I had not my Liberty sooner.*

At our Return to the Army, we heard the melancholly News of the Death of Queen *Mary*[8] on which our Drums and Colours, &c. were put into Mourning, and we soon after drew off into Winter Quarters. I was in *Gorkham,* where my Grief for my Husband being drowned in the Hopes of finding him, I indulged to the natural Gaiety of my Temper, and lived very merrily. In my Frolicks, to kill Time, I made my Addresses to a Burgher's Daughter, who was young and pretty. As I had formerly had a great many fine Things said to myself, I was at no loss in the amorous Dialect; I ran over all the tender Nonsense (which I look upon [as] the Lovers heavy Canon, as it does the greatest Execution with raw Girls) employed on such Attacks; I squeezed her Hand, whenever I could get an Opportunity; sighed often, when in her Company; looked foolishly, and practised upon her all the ridiculous Airs which I had often laughed at, when they were used as Snares against myself. When I afterwards reflected on this unjust Way of Amusement, I heartily repented it; for it had an Effect I did not wish; the poor Girl grew really fond of me, and uneasy when I was absent: for which she never failed chiding me if it was but for half a Day. When I was with her, she always regaled me in the best Manner she could, and nothing was too good or too dear to treat me with, if she could compass it; but notwithstanding a declared Passion for me, I found her nicely virtuous; for when I pretended to take an indecent Freedom with her, she told me, *That she supposed her Tenderness for me was become irksome, since I took a Method to change it into Hatred. It was true, that she did not scruple to own she loved me as her Life, because she thought her Inclination justifiable, as well as lawful; but then she loved her Virtue better than she did her Life. If I had dishonourable Designs upon her, I was not the Man she loved, she was mistaken, and had found the Ruffian, instead of the tender Husband she hoped in me.*

I own this Rebuff gained my Heart, and taking her in my Arms, I told her, That *she had heightened the Power of her Charms by her Virtue; for which I should hold her in greater Esteem, but could not love her better, as she had already engrossed all my Tenderness;* and, indeed, I was now fond of the Girl, though mine, you know, could not go beyond a platonick Love. In the Course of this Amour, a Serjeant of our Regiment, but not of the Company I belonged to, sat down before the Cittadel of her Heart, and made regular Approaches, which cost him a Number of Sighs, and a great deal of Time; but finding I commanded there, and it was impossible to take it by a regular Siege, he resolved to give a desperate Assault, Sword in Hand. One Day, therefore, while I was under Arms, he came to her, and, without any previous Indication of his Design, a fair Opportunity offering, he very bravely, and like a Man of Honour, employed Force to obtain what he could not get by Assiduity. The Girl defended her self stoutly, and in the Scuffle she lost her Cap, and her Cloaths were most of them torn off her Back; but notwithstanding her resolute Defence, he had carried the Fortress by Storm, had not some of the Neighbours opportunely come in to her Assistance, alarmed by her Shrieks, and made him retreat in a very shameful Manner.

No sooner had she recovered, and dressed her self, than she went in search of, and found me, in my Rank standing to my Arms. She told me what had passed, and begged me to *revenge the Insult offered her.* I was so irritated at this Account, that I could hardly contain my self: I was siezed with a Tremor all over my Body; often changed Colour, and, had I not been prevented by my Duty, I should that Instant have sought and killed him. However, I stifled my Resentment till I was dismissed by the Officer, and then went in Quest of my Rival, whom having found I surlily asked, *How he durst attempt the Honour of a Woman, who was, for aught he knew, my Wife; to whom he was sensible I had long made honourable Love.* I told him, *The Action in it self was so base, that it made him unworthy of the King's Cloth, which he wore, and ought to be the Quarrel of every Man in the Regiment, as it cast a Reflection on the whole Corps; but, as I was principally concerned in this Insult, so I was sufficient to chastize his Impudence, and required immediate Satisfaction for the Affront.* He answered me, *That I was a proud, prodigal Coxcomb.* I leave, said I, *Bilingsgate Language*[9] *to Women and Cowards; I am not come to a Tongue Battle, Mr. Serjeant, but to exact a Reparation of Honour. If you have as much Courage in the Face of a Man, as you have in assaulting defenceless Women, go with me instantly to that Windmill* (which I pointed to) *and I will soon convince you that General T——n had too good an Opinion of you, when he took his Livery off your Back to put on the King's, and gave you a Halbard* [i.e., halberd]. The Fellow had been Footman to General

T——n, and this Reproach stinging him to the Quick, he only told me, *He would soon cool my Courage*, and we went together to the Windmill, where we both drew. I was so irritated at the ill Usage of my Sweetheart, and the Affront put upon me in her Person, that I thought of nothing but putting the Villain out of the World. We both drew, and the first Thrust I made, gave him a slaunt Wound in his right Pap, which had well nigh done his Business. He returned this with a long Gash on my right Arm (for his Sword was both for cutting and thrusting, as all Soldiers Swords are; I fought with that I had purchased in *Dublin*) but before he could recover his Guard, I gave him a Thrust in the right Thigh, about half a Span from the Pope's Eye;[10] the next Pass, he aimed at my Breast, but hit my right Arm; tho' it was little more than a small Prick of a Pin, he being feeble with the Loss of Blood which flowed plentifully from his Wounds. By this Time some Soldiers on Duty having seen our first Attack, a File of Musqueteers, under the Command of a Serjeant, came up, took us Prisoners, disarmed both, and sent him directly to the Hospital, and, as my Wounds were slight, as I was the Agressor, and beside, a common Soldier, conducted me to Prison, for the Serjeant was thought mortally wounded, and did not recover of a considerable Time. I sent my Sweetheart an Account of what had happened, and where I then was. She acquainted her Father with the villainous Attempt which the Serjeant had made upon her, and let him know, it was her Quarrel which I had taken up, was the Cause of my Confinement. The good Burgher made a proper representation of the Affront offered his Family, and found means, in four Days Time, to procure me a Pardon from King *William*, an Order *to release me immediately; to return me my Sword, pay my Arrears, and give me my Discharge from the Regiment;* all which were punctually performed. The Minute I was enlarged, I went to thank my Deliverer for my Liberty; she, on her Side, as gratefully acknowledged my risking my Life in revenging the Insult done her. She expressed her self with great Tenderness, and told me, *That when she heard of my Imprisonment, she heartily repented her having acquainted me with the Serjeant's villainous Attempt; blamed her self for having exposed me to so great a Danger, and wished she had buried the Action in Silence.* She proceeded, *It had been prudent in me, for the Sake of both; for you would not have ventured your Life, and I should not have given the ill-natured Part of the World any Ground to censure my Conduct; for what Interpretation may it not make of your being warm in my Cause? This Consideration makes me throw off the Restraint our Sex lies under, and propose to you what I have expected from you, the skreening my Honour by our Marriage. My dear,* said I, *you offer me the greatest Happiness this World can afford me; will you give me leave to ask you of your Father? My Father!* cried she, *you cannot imagine a rich Burgher will give his Daughter to a Foot Soldier; for tho' I think you merit every Thing, yet my Father will not view you with my Eyes.* This answer I expected, and, indeed, my being very sure that her Father would not consent, was the Reason why I proposed speaking to him. I asked her, *Since she imagined her Father would be averse to my Happiness, what could be done? I will,* said she, *run the Hazard of your Fortune, in case my Father proves irreconcileable after our Marriage. My dear Life,* said I, *There are two Obstacles to such a Proposal, which are, with me, insuperable. How could I bear to see you deserted by your Father, deprived of a Fortune, and stripped of all the Comforts of Life, exposed to Hardships and Insults, to which Women who follow a Camp are liable? And how can I, with Honour, consent to bring your Father's grey Hairs to the Grave in Sorrow, by robbing him of a Daughter, whom he tenderly loves, by way of return for having procured my Liberty? No, my Charmer, tho' I am no more than a common Centinel, this Breast is capable of as much Tenderness, and contains as much Honour, as that of a General. No, I can neither be so inhumane to you, nor so unjust to your Parent. But, as I shall know no Satisfaction in Life, if deprived of you, it will animate me to such Actions, as shall either raise me to a Rank that your Father need not be ashamed of my Alliance, or shall put an end to a Life, which must be miserable without you. The Sword, my Dear, ennobles, and I don't despair of a Commission, as I have some Reputation in the Army, many Friends, and am not destitute of Money. I think it more becoming the Character of a Soldier to gain a Commission by his Bravery, than to purchase one with money: But my Desire to call you mine, will make me, at any rate, endeavour to deserve you, and I will, if possible, purchase a Pair of Colours.*

I have heard, said she, *that Love and Reason are incompatible; this Maxim is either false, or you are not the ardent Lover you profess your self: However, I relish your Proposal of buying a Commission, and, if your Money falls short, let me know it.*

You call, said I, *the Ardour of my Passion in Question, because I love you for your self: I wish to make you, if possible, as happy in our Union as I shall be; while most other Men have their own Satisfaction alone in View, when they address the fair Sex. I accept your Offer with a grateful Sense of the Obligation; but hope I need not put you to the Proof of your Friendship, without some Misfortune should deprive me of what I have by me.*

Thus I got off from this Amour without Loss of Credit. As I was discharged from my Regiment, and loath to break into my capital Stock, which would not long maintain me, I entered with Lieutenant *Keith,* in Lord *John Hayes's* Regiment of Dragoons: For my Discharge from my Regiment was a Favour done me, lest the Serjeant, by being an Officer, and in Favour with his quondam Master, might do me some private Injury: It was not a Discharge from the Service.

My Husband's Regiment was one of those that attack'd the Citadel.[11] One Day Lord *Cobham* coming into the Trench, order'd the Engineer to point a Gun at a Wind-Mill between us and the Citadel, and promised a Guinea to whoever fired and brought it down: I immediately snatched the Match out of the Man's Hand who was going to fire, clapp'd it to the Touchhole, and down came the Wind-Mill. Major *Petit*, before I fired, bid me take care the Canon did not recoil upon me, or break the Drums of my Ears, which I had forgot to stop. I was in too much haste to get the Guinea, and not minding the Caution, I was beat backwards, and had the Noise of the Cannon a long while after in my Ears. The Officers could not refrain Laughing to see me set on my Backside; but as I was not hurt, I had according to the Proverb, *Let him laugh that wins*, the most Reason to be merry about the Mouth, for Lord *Cobham*, always better than his Word, gave me two Guineas, saying, *I was a bold Wench*, instead of one he promised me; General *Fagel* gave me another, and four Officers gave me a Ducat a Piece.

Soon after Captain *Brown* mounting the Trench had his Leg so miserably shatter'd by a Musquet Shot, that the Surgeon was obliged to cut it off. His Servants and Nurses not having the Courage to hold the Candle, I perform'd that Office, and was very intent on the Operation, which no way shock'd me, as it was absolutely necessary.

During this Siege, or indeed any other, I never lost an Opportunity of Maroding [i.e., marauding]; to this End I was furnished with a Grapling Iron and a Sword, for I must acquaint my Reader, that on the approach of an Army, the Boors[12] throw their Plate, Copper, &c. into Wells; their Linnen they bury in Chests, and for their own Security they get into fortify'd Towns or under the Shelter of some strong Place. With my Graple I searched all the Wells I met with, and got good Booty, some times Kitchen Utensils, Brass Pales, Pewter Dishes, &c. sometimes a Silver Spoon. With my Sword, which I carried to discover what was buried, I bored the Ground, where I found it had been lately stirred. This I learned of the *Dutch* Soldiers in *Ireland* when King *William* was there, for they discovered by this Method, and took away a Chest of Linnen my Mother had hid under Ground, with a large Quantity of Wheat. While I was one Day busyed in search of Plunder, I heard behind me a great burst like a sudden short Clap of Thunder, and turning nimbly round, I saw the Air full of shattered Limbs of Men. This happened, as I was informed, at my

Return, by a Spark from a Pipe of Tobacco setting Fire to a Bomb, by which fifty Shells and twenty-four of our Men were blown up; but luckily, our Magazine of Powder, though near the same Place, escaped. As I have often said, where-ever my Husband was ordered upon Duty, I always followed him, and he was sometimes of the Party that went to search for and draw the Enemy's Mines, I was often engaged with their Party under Ground, where our Engagements were more terrible than in the Field, being sometimes near suffocated with the Smoak of Straw which the *French* fired to drive us out, and the fighting with Pick-Axes and Spades, in my Opinion, was more dangerous than with Swords. I have in the Journal of the Siege, taken notice of the Number of Mines sprung; one of which blew up four hundred of our Men, and another narrowly miss'd carrying up a whole Regiment, which was just drawn off as it was fired, so that the design'd Execution was by Accident prevented, and only eight Men lost. . . .[13]

When we left *Tournay,* and before the Investing of *Mons,* as the Army marched toward the *French* Lines, I chose to go with the Camp-Colour-Men, who attended by the Forlorn Hope, march at so considerable a distance before the Army, that they are often cut off before any Force can come up to their Assistance, which though it makes it the most dangerous Post, it is the most profitable, if there is any Plunder to be got, as there are but few to share it. In our March, I espied at some Distance a great House, which I, advancing before the Camp-Colour-Men, ran to, leaving my Horse to the Care of a sick Serjeant, who was glad of the Opportunity to ride. I here found six Couple of Fowls with their Legs tied, a Basket of Pigeons and four Sheep, who were also tied, and ready to be carried off; but I suppose, upon our Appearance, the People made the best of their Way to secure Things of greater Value. One of the Sheep I killed, dressed, cut off a Leg, and all the Fat. The other three I loos'd and turned into the Yard; by the Time I had done our Men came up with me, and I put the Carcass of the Sheep on my Mare before the Serjeant; the Fowls I hung about my Neck; drove my Sheep before me, and so marched to the Place designed for the Camp, called *Havré.* Being here arrived, while they were fixing Boughs for the Disposition of the Camp, and marking out Ground for every Regiment, I pitched my Tent near a deserted Publick-House, allotted for Col. *Hamilton's* Quarters; turned my Sheep to Grass, and hung up my Mutton on a Tree to cool: I then went into the Colonel's Quarters, over which, as soon as it was appointed, a Guard was set, but by a Bribe, I struck him so blind, that he could not see me, and my Husband's Comrades, who lent a friendly Hand, carry off a large

Quantity of Faggots, Hay and Straw for my Mare and my own Bed; fill all my empty Flasks with Beer, and rowl off a whole Barrel to my Tent. Having made these Prizes, I cut up my Mutton, laid by a Shoulder to roast, the Neck and Breast to make Broth; dug a Hole with a Hatchet to boil my Pot in, which, the Fire being made, I set on with the Mutton and Sweet-herbs, and was enjoying myself by a glorious Fire when the Army came up. Col. *Hamilton* and Major *Erwood* came to my Fire, and were not a little surprised to see I had gotten so many Things in Readiness. I shew'd them my Provisions of all Sorts; upon which the Colonel suspecting that I had plundered his Quarters, asked where I had got my Barrel of strong Beer. I told him that falling in with some Boors, I drove them before me, and made them bring me what I wanted; to which he civilly replied, *D——n you, you are a lying Devil. Come,* said I, *you Mutton-Monger, will you give me Handsel?*[14] They called for a Gallon of Beer, and drinking a little, gave the Rest among some of the Men, and ordered the Shoulder of Mutton to be roasted, which I did by pitching two forked Sticks into the Ground, putting it on a jointed Spit, and setting a Soldier's Wife to turn it. I made four Crowns a-piece of my Sheep, besides the Fat which I sold to a Woman, who made mold Candles for the Men, and made a good Penny of my Fouls and Pigeons. A Body of Troopers, and some *Hussars*, being ordered out to reconnoitre in the Woods at *Taisnieres*, before the Enemy entrench'd themselves, and to cover the Foragers, with strict Charge to return, at the firing of a Cannon, I being one of the Foragers, took my Mare along with me, leaving another Horse which I had bought of a *Hussar* in an Orchard, near Brigadier *Lalo*'s quarters, and digging a Hole, I buried my Money. When we were some Distance from the Camp I pushed forward, on which Quarter Master *Hankey* and Lieutenant *Mack-enny*, bid me not be too venturesome, I answered that I saw no Danger, and hasten'd on to a large House, which I enter'd, and found a Bed ready made; two or three Tubs of Flower [*sic*]; an Oven full of hot Bread; a considerable Quantity of Bacon and Beef hanging in the Chimney, a Basket full of Cocks and Hens, with two Pots of Butter. I emptied the Feathers out of the Tick to cover my Mare with, lest the hot Bread should burn her back, then threw the Feathers out of the Bolster, into one End of which I put my Bread, and into the other my Beef and Bacon; my Pots of Butter I flung on each Side of her, took my Fowls in my Hand and mounted; which I had scarcely done when I heard the signal Gun, an alarm given the Foragers, that the whole Body of the Enemy was coming upon us, and that their seeming to march to the left, was only to cover the Fileing off their Infantry into the Woods. The Terror with which the Foragers were struck at the News is hardly credible; the Fields were strewed with Corn, Hay, and Utensils, which they had not the Courage to take along with them, nay some, whose Horses were at a little distance, rather chose to lose, than venture to fetch, them: I jogged on towards the Army, but seeing a fine Truss of Hay lying, and fearing my Horses might want, the Danger could not make me withstand the Temptation; I leaped off my Mare, clapped it upon her, and mounting again got safe to the Place where the Army lay. I was surprised to see all in Motion, however I staid to kill my Fowls, fetch my Horse and Money that I had buried, strike my Tent, with which and other Things I loaded him and followed the Army. . . .

Notes

1. Linen; called Holland because the fabric generally came to Britain from there.

2. By serving in what was known as King William's War or the Nine Years' War (1688–1697).

3. "Regimentals," the uniform proper to a particular regiment; "mountings," soldier's outfit of clothes and arms.

4. Head of the house of Hanover; became George I of England in 1715.

5. Rather than a fashionable elaborate wig.

6. An account of the battle of Landen follows.

7. Trumpeter, especially one who signals the troops.

8. Queen Mary of England, wife of William III, died December 1694.

9. Scurrilous, abusive, foul language.

10. A "span" is a measurement of 9 inches, derived from the maximum distance between tips of thumb and little finger; "pope's eye" is a rude (and anti-Catholic) term for the anus.

11. The Citadel of Tourney, attacked in 1709.

12. Peasant, especially a Dutch or German peasant.

13. Davies goes on to describe the progress and the end of the campaign against the Citadel.

14. To give handsel means to give something auspicious to open a new enterprise; from the custom of inaugurating the new year or the first day of a new business by giving a gift or one's business.

Mary Blandy

1720–1752

Miss Mary Blandy's own Account of the Affair between her and Mr. Cranstoun, from the Commencement of their Acquaintance, in the Year, 1746. To the Death of her Father, in August, 1751. With all the Circumstances leading to that unhappy Event. To which is added, An Appendix. Containing copies of some original letters, now in Possession of the Editor. Together with An exact Relation of her Behaviour, whilst under Sentence; and a Copy of the Declaration signed by herself, in the Presence of two Clergymen, two Days before her Execution. Published at her dying Request. London: A. Millar, 1752.

Mary Blandy was born in 1720 in Henley, near Oxford. Francis Blandy, her father, was an attorney; he served as town clerk of Henley and was employed as steward by most of the surrounding gentry. Mary was an only child and, by some accounts, mistress of a ladylike "accomplishments" education by the early age of fourteen. The events leading to her execution for her father's murder are somewhat murky. It is generally agreed that Francis Blandy stated his intention of dowering his daughter with the very generous sum of £10,000; whether he had that amount or was instead attempting to lure a titled suitor remains unclear. Mary did have several suitors and in fact was engaged when she first met William Cranstoun, a lieutenant in a regiment of marines, at the home of his uncle Lord Mark Kerr in the summer of 1746. Her engagement was broken off for "prudential Reasons" (1), however, and the following summer she and Captain Cranstoun met again. She claims that Cranstoun admitted to an entanglement with a Miss Murray; according to other commentators, it was his uncle who warned Mr. Blandy that under Scottish law Cranstoun was already married. Over the next two years Cranstoun paid several long visits to the Blandy home in Henley. At one point he proposed a private marriage to Mary, with her mother's knowledge, and early in 1749 he loaned Mrs. Blandy £40. Both parents seem to have approved, or at least tolerated, this unconventional courtship, and when Mrs. Blandy became very

Mary Blandy, mezzotint by T. Ryley, after F. Wilson. Courtesy of the
National Portrait Gallery, London.

ill in September 1749 she was comforted by Cranstoun's sending Mary a
solemn contract of marriage.

Following Mrs. Blandy's death, the pattern of Cranstoun's extended
stays in Henley resumed, and his final visit commenced in August 1750.
At this time Cranstoun informed Mary that, before he met her, he had
fathered a daughter by a Miss Capel. Mary forgave him, and forgave him
again the following day when she found a letter from his current mistress.
Soon thereafter Cranstoun received a letter informing him of his mother's

illness; borrowing a watch from Mary to pay his traveling expenses, he left Henley. Mary never saw him again. Wittingly or not, she then administered to her father the powder that turned out to be arsenic. Tried and convicted for his murder, she was hanged on 6 April 1752. Approximately five thousand people attended her execution; many of them, including several gentlemen from the University of Oxford, shed tears. In her final declaration Mary maintained her innocence, and almost immediately she became a cause célèbre. Her *Account* was published "at the Solicitation of several Persons of Rank and Figure in the University of Oxford" (iv), and more than thirty pamphlets and broadsides appeared shortly thereafter. References to her appear in letters and memoirs throughout the nineteenth century; her case was included in the early twentieth-century Celebrated Trials series, and she has recently received attention from feminist legal scholars.

TEXT: Mary Blandy's *Account* was published as a pamphlet soon after her execution. According to its editor, Mary wanted her case submitted to the judgment of the public (iii), and it was published in compliance with her dying request. In the excerpt (pp. 33–44), she defends her conduct before and after her father's death.

❀ ❧

MR. CRANSTOUN, soon after this,[1] taking his Leave of *Henley*, set out for *Scotland*, as has been already observed. A Day or two after his Departure, Mr. *Cranstoun* wrote me a Letter on the Road, wherein he begged me to make acceptable to my Father his most grateful Acknowledgments for his late Goodness to him. "This, he said, had made such an Impression upon him that he never should forget it as long as he lived; and that he should always entertain the same tender Sentiments for him as for his Father, the late Lord *Cranstoun* himself, had he been then alive." In the same Letter, he also desired me to permit my Letters to be directed [i.e., addressed] by some body who wrote a more masculine Hand than mine; since otherwise they might be intercepted by some one or other of Miss *Murray*'s Family,[2] as they were jealous of the Affair carried on between us two. He likewise therein insisted upon my subscribing myself *M. C.* instead of *M. B.* tho' he did not discover to me the real View he had therein. Soon after he arrived at his Mother's, he wrote me another Letter, wherein he informed me, that he told his Mother we were married, and had been so for some Time; and that she would write to me, as her Daughter, by the very next Post. This she did; and her Letter came accompanied with one from her Son, wherein he desired me, if I loved him, to answer his Mother's by the Return of the Post, and sign myself *Mary Cranstoun* at length, as I knew before God I was, by a solemn Contract, intitled to that Name. This, he pretended, would make his Mother stir more in the *Scotch* Affair. On the Supposition that I was her Daughter, she wrote many tender Letters to me, always directing to me by the name of *Mary Cranstoun*, and sent me some very handsome Presents of *Scotch* linen. He also obliged his eldest Sister, Mrs. *Selby*, and her Husband, to write to me as their Sister. Lady *Cranstoun* likewise wrote to my Father in a very complaisant Style, thanking him for the Civilities he had shewn her Son; and hinting, that she hoped it would be in her Power to return them to me, when she should have the Pleasure of seeing me in *Scotland*, which she begged might be soon. Lord *Cranstoun*, his Brother, also wrote to my Father, and returned him Thanks in the same polite Manner. During this whole Period, my Father's Behavior to me was very uncertain; but always good after he had received any of these Letters. In a few Months, however, after Mr. *Cranstoun's* Departure, my Father's Temper was much altered for the worse. He upbraided me with having rejected much better Offers than any that had come from *Scotland;* and at last ordered me to write to Mr. *Cranstoun* not to return to *Henley*, till his affair with Miss *Murray* was quite decided. I complied with this Order, writing to him in the Terms prescribed me. To this I received an Answer full of Tenderness, Grief, and Despair. He said, "He found my Father loved him no longer, and was afraid he would inspire me with the same Sentiments. He saw, he said, a Coolness throughout my whole Letter; but conjured me to remember the sacred Promises and Engagements that had passed between us." After this, I received several other Letters from him, filled with the same sort of Expostulations, and penned in the same desponding and disconsolate Strain. I likewise received several Letters from his Mother, the old Lady *Cranstoun*, and Mrs. *Selby*, his Sister, wrote in a most affectionate Style.

In *April*, or the Beginning of *May*, 1751, as I apprehend, I had another Letter from Mr. *Cranstoun*, wherein he acquainted me, that he had seen his old Friend, Mrs. *Morgan*; and that if he could procure any more of her Powder, he would send it with the *Scotch* Pebbles he intended to make me a Present of.[3] In answer to this, I told him, "I was surprized that a Man of his Sense could believe such Efficacy to be lodged in any Powder whatsoever; and that I would not give it to my Father, lest it should impair his Health." To this, in his next Letter, he replied, "That he was extremely surprized I should believe he would send any Thing that might prove prejudicial to my Father, when his own Interest was so apparently concerned in his Preservation." I took this as referring to a Conversation we had had a little before he set out for *Scotland*; wherein I told him, "I was sure my Father was not a Man of a very considerable Fortune; but that if he lived, I was persuaded he would provide very handsomely for us and ours, as he lived so retired, and his Business was every Day increasing." So far was I from imagining, that I should be a Gainer by my Father's Death, as has been so maliciously and uncharitably suggested! Mr. *Cranstoun* also seemed most cordially and sincerely to join with me in the same Notion. Soon after this, in another Letter, he informed me, "That some of the aforesaid Powder should be sent with the *Scotch* Pebbles he intended me; and that he should write upon the Paper in which the Powder was contained, *Powder to clean* Scotch *Pebbles*, lest, if he gave it its true Name, the Box should be opened, and he be laughed at by the Person opening it, and taken for a superstitious Fool, as he had been by me before." In *June* 1751, the Box with the Powder and Pebbles arrived at *Henley*, and a Letter came to me the next Day, wherein he ordered me to mix the Powder in Tea. This some Mornings after I did; but finding that it would not mix well with Tea, I flung the Liquor into which it had been thrown out of the Window. I farther declare, that looking into the Cup, I saw Nothing adhere to the Sides of it; nor was such an Adhesion probable, as the Powder swam on the top of the Liquor. My Father drank two Cups of Tea out of that Cup, before I threw the Powder into it: Nor did he drink any more out of it that Morning, it being *Sunday*, and he fearing to drink a third Cup, lest he should be too late for Church. It has been said by *Susan Gunnel*, at my Trial, that she drank out of the aforesaid Cup, and was very ill after it. In answer to which, I must beg Leave to observe, that she never before would drink out of any other Cup, than one which she called her own, different from this, and which I drank out of on that and most other Mornings. It has been farther said, that Dame *Emmet*, a Chairwoman,[4] was likewise hurt by drinking Tea at my Father's House: Be pleased to remember, Reader, that I mixed it but in one Cup, and then threw it away. *Susan* said, she drank out of the Cup and was ill, what then could hurt this Woman, who to my Knowledge was not at our House that Day? Mr. *Nicholas*, an Apothecary, attended this old Woman in the first Sickness they talk of, which, by *Susan*, I understood was a Weakness common to her, *viz.* fainting Fits and Purging;[5] and I know, that she had had fainting Fits many Times before. When I heard she was ill, I ordered *Susan* to send her Whey, Broth, or any Thing that she thought would be proper for her. She had long served the Family, would joke and divert me, and I loved her extremely. Nor can my Enemies themselves (let them paint me how they please) deny, that from my Heart I pitied the Poor. I never felt more Pleasure, than when I fed the Hungry, cloathed the Naked, and supplied the Wants of those in Distress. Had God blessed me with a more plentiful Fortune, I should have exerted myself in this more; and I flatter myself, that the Poor and Indigent of our Town will do me Justice in this Particular, and own that I was not wanting in my Duty towards them. But to proceed in my Account: I would not fix on any other Chairwoman; and *Susan* said, that Dame *Emmet* would, she thought, by my Goodness, soon get Strength to work again. I told her, was it ever so long I would stay for her. I mixed the Powder, as was said before, on the *Sunday*, and on the *Tuesday* wrote to Mr. *Cranstoun*, that it would not mix in Tea, and that I would not try it any more, lest my Father should find it out. This has been brought against me by many: But let any one consider, if the Discovery of such a Procedure as this, would not have excited Anger, and consequently have been followed by Resentment in my Father. This might have occasioned a total Separation of me from Mr. *Cranstoun*, a thing I at that Time dreaded more than even Death itself. In answer to this Letter, I had one from him to assure me the Powder was innocent, and to beg I would give it in Gruel, or something thicker than Tea. Many more Letters to the same Effect I received, before I would give it again; but most fatally, on the 5th of *August*, I gave it to my poor Father, innocent of the Effects it afterwards produced, God knows; not so stupid as to believe it would have that desired, to make him kind to us; but in Obedience to Mr. *Cranstoun*, who ever seemed superstitious to the last Degree, and had, as I thought, and have declared before, all the just Notions of the Necessity of my Father's Life for him, me, and ours. On the *Monday* the 5th, as has been said, I mixed the Powder in his Gruel, and at Night it was in a half-pint Mug, set ready for him to carry to Bed with him. It had no Taste.—The next Morning, as he had done at Dinner the Day before, he complained of a Pain in his Stomach, and the Heart-burn; which he ever did before he had the Gravel.[6] I sent for Mr. *Norton* at Eleven o'Clock in the Forenoon, who said, that a little Physick would be right for my Father to take on *Wednesday*. At Night he ordered some Water-gruel for his Supper, which his Footman went for. When it came, my Father said, Taste it *Molly*, has it not an odd Taste? I tasted it, but found no Taste different from what is to be found in all good Water-gruel. After this he went up to Bed, and my Father found himself sick, and reached [retched?]; after which he said he was better, and I went up to Bed. *Susan* gave him his Physick in the Morning, and I went into his Bed-chamber about Eight o'Clock; then I found him charming well.

Miss Mary Blandy's own Account / 121

Susan says, that on my Father's wanting Gruel on the *Wednesday*, I said, as they were busy at ironing, they might give him some of the same he had before. I do not remember this; but if I did, it was impossible I should know, that the Gruel he had on *Tuesday* was the same he had on *Monday;* as that he drank on *Monday* was made on *Saturday* or *Sunday*, I believe on *Saturday* Night; much less imagine, that she whoever made it, and managed it as she pleased, would pretend to keep such stale Gruel for her Master. *Thursday* and *Friday* he came down Stairs. I often asked Mr. *Norton*, "If he thought him in Danger: If he did, I would send for Dr. *Addington*." On *Saturday* Mr. *Norton* told me, "he thought my Father in Danger." I said, "I would send for the Doctor;" but he replied, "I had better ask my Father's Leave." I bid him speak to my Father about it, which he did; but my Father replied, "Stay till To-morrow, and if I am not better then, send for him." As soon as I was told this, I said, "That would not satisfy me; I would send immediately, which I did; and Mr. *Norton* the Apothecary attested this in Court." On the same Night, being *Saturday*, the Doctor came. I believe it was near Twelve o'Clock. He saw my Father, and wrote for him: he did not then apprehend his Case to be desperate. I have been by this Gentleman blamed, for not telling then what I had given my Father. I was in Hopes that he would have lived, and that my Folly would never have been known: In order the more effectually to conceal which, the Remainder of the Powder I had, the *Wednesday* before, thrown away, and burnt Mr. *Cranstoun's* letter: So I had Nothing to evince the Innocence of my Intention, and was moreover frightened out of my Wits. Let the good-natured Part of the World put themselves in my Place, and then condemn me if they can for this. On *Sunday* my Father said, "He was better;" but found himself obliged to keep his Bed that Day. Mr. *Blandy*, of Kingston, a Relation of ours, came to visit us, stayed with me to breakfast, and then went to Church with Mr. *Littleton*, my Father's Clerk. I went, after they were gone, to my Father, and found him seemingly inclined to sleep; so left him, retired into the Parlour, and wrote to Mr. *Cranstoun*, as I did almost every Post. I had, on the *Friday* before, a Letter from him; wherein some Secrets of his Family were disclosed. As I wrote in a hurry, I only advised him to take care what he wrote; which, as my unhappy Affairs turned out, my Enemies dressed up greatly to my Disadvantage at my Tryal. I gave this Letter, as I did all of them, to Mr. *Littleton* to direct, who opened it, carried it to a Friend of his for Advice on the Occasion, and conveyed it to a French Usher;[7] who, by the Help of it, published a Pamphlet intitled, *The Life of Miss* Mary Blandy. On *Sunday* in the Afternoon, Mrs. *Mounteny*[8] and her Sister came to see my

Father; who told them, "He hoped he should soon be able to meet them in his Parlour; since he thought himself better then." *Susan* was to sit up with her Master that Night. The Rev. Mr. *Stockwood*, Rector of the Parish, came in the Evening to visit him; the Apothecary was there likewise; and he desired the Room might be quite still; so that only *Susan*, the old Maid, was to be with him. After this I went up to my Father's Bed-side; upon which he took me in his Arms and kissed me: I went out of the Room with Mr. *Stockwood* and Mr. *Norton*, the Apothecary, almost dead, and begg'd of the latter to tell me if he thought my Father still in Danger. He said, "he was better, and hoped he would still mend. To-morrow, said he, we shall judge better, and you will hear what Dr. *Addington* will say." While Mr. *Stockwood* stayed, Mr. *Littleton* and *Betty*, my Father's Cook-maid, behaved tolerably well; but as soon as he was gone, they altered their Conduct: However, upon Mr. *Norton's* speaking to him, Mr. *Littleton* became much more civil: and *Betty* followed his Example. I took a Candle, and went up into my own Room; but in the Way I listened at my Father's Door, and found every thing still there: this induced me to hope that he was asleep. On *Monday* Morning, I went to his Door, in order to go in: His Tenderness would not let me stay up a-Nights; but I was seldom from him in the Day-time. I was deprived Access to him; which so surprised and frightened me, that I cried out, "What, not see my Father!" Upon which, I heard him reply, "My dear *Polly*, you shall presently;" and some time after I did. This Scene was inexpressibly moving. The mutual Love, Sorrow, and Grief, that then appeared, are truly described by *Susannah Gunnel*; tho', poor Soul, she is much mistaken in many other Respects. I was, as soon as Dr. *Addington* came, by his Orders, confined to my own Room; and not suffered to go near my Father, or even so much as to listen at his Door: All the Comfort I could then have had, would have been to know whether he slept or no; but this was likewise refused me. A Man was put into my Room Night and Day; no Woman suffer'd to attend me. My Garters, Keys, and Letters were taken away from me, by Dr. *Addington* himself. Dr. *Lewis*, who it seems was called in, was at this Time with him; but he behaved perfectly like a Gentleman to me. During this Confinement I had hardly any Thing to eat or drink: and once I staid from five in the Afternoon till the same hour the next Day without any Sustenance at all, as the Man with me can Witness, except a single Dish of Tea; which, I believe, I owed to the Humanity of Dr. *Lewis*. I had frequently very bad Fits, and my Head was never quite clear; yet I was sensible the Person who gave these Orders had no Right to confine me, in such a manner. But I bore it patiently, as my Room was very near my

Father's, and I was fearful of disturbing him. Dr. *Addington* and Dr. *Lewis* then came into my Room, and told me "Nothing could save my dear Father." For some Time, I sat like an Image; and then told them, that I had given him some Powders, which I received from *Cranstoun*, and feared they might have hurt him, tho' that Villain assured me they were of a very innocent Nature. At my Trial, it appeared, that Dr. *Addington* had wrote down the Questions he put to me, but none of my Answers to them. The Judge asked him the Reason of this. He said, "They were not satisfactory to him." To which his Lordship replied, "They might have been so to the Court." The Questions were these. Why I did not send for him sooner? In answer to which, I told him, that I did send for him as soon as they would let me know that my father was in the least Danger. And that even at last I sent for him against my Father's Consent. This, I added, he could not but know, by what my Father said, when he first came on *Saturday* Night into his Room. The next Question was, why I did not take some of the Powders myself, if I thought them so innocent? To this I answered, I never was desired by Mr. *Cranstoun* to take them; and that if they could produce such an Effect as was ascribed to them, I was sure I had no need of them; but that had he desired this, I should most certainly have done it. It is impossible to repeat half the Miseries I went thro', unknown, I am sure, to my poor Father. The Man that was set over me as my Guard had been an old Servant in the Family: which I at first thought was done out of Kindness; but am now convinced it was not. When Dr. *Addington* was asked, "If I express'd a Desire to preserve my Father's Life, and on this Account desired him to come again the next Day, and do all he could to save him;" he said, "I did." He then was asked his Sentiments of that Matter; to which he replied, "She seemed to me more concerned for the Consequences to herself than to her Father." However, the Doctor owned that my Behaviour shewed me to be anxious for my poor Father's Life. Could I paint the restless Days and Nights I went through, the Prayers I made to God to take me and spare my Father, whose Death alone, unattended with other Misfortunes, would have greatly shocked me, the Heart of any Person who has any Bowels[9] at all would undoubtedly bleed for me. What is here advanced, the Man that attended me knows to be true also, who cannot be suspected of Partiality. *Susan Gunnel* can attest the same. She observed at this Juncture several Instances between us both of filial Duty and paternal Affection.

On *Wednesday*, about Two o'Clock in the Afternoon, by my Father's Death, I was left one of the most wretched Orphans that ever lived. Not only indifferent and dispassionate Persons, but even some of the most cruel of mine Enemies themselves, seem to have had at least some small Compassion for me. Soon after my Father's Death I had all his Keys, except that of his Study, which I had before committed to the Care of the Rev. Mr. *Stevens* of *Fawley*, my dear unhappy Uncle, delivered to me. This Gentleman and another of my Uncles visited me that fatal Afternoon. This occasioned such a moving Scene, as is impossible for any human Pen to describe. After their Departure, I walked like a frantic distracted Person. Mr. *Skinner*, a Schoolmaster in *Henley*, who came to see me, as I have been since informed, declared that he did not take me to be in my Senses. So that no Stress ought to be laid on any Part of my Conduct at this Time. Nor will this at all surprize the candid Reader, if he will but dispassionately consider the whole Case, and put himself in my Place. I had lost mine only Parent, whose untimely Death was then imputed to me. Tho' I had no Intention to hurt him, and consequently in that Respect was innocent; yet there was great Reason to fear, that I had been made the fatal Instrument of his Death,—and that by listening to the Man I loved above all others, and even better than Life itself. I had depended upon his, as I imagined, superior Honour; but found myself deceived and deluded by him. The People about me were apprized, that I entertained, and not without Reason, a very bad Opinion of them; which could not but inspire them with vindictive Sentiments, and a firm Resolution to hurt me, if ever they had it in their Power. My Cook-maid was more inflamed against me than any of the rest; and yet, for very good Reasons, I was absolutely obliged to keep her. My Mother's Maid was disagreeable to me; but yet, on Account of Money due to her, which I could not pay, it was not then in my Power to dismiss her. But this most melancholy Subject I shall not now chuse any farther to expatiate on. I have brought down the preceding Narrative to my Father's Death, where I at first intended it should end. Besides, I have not now many Days to live, and Matters of infinitely greater Moment to think upon. May God forgive me my Follies, and my Enemies theirs! May he likewise take my poor Soul into his Protection, and receive me to Mercy, through the Merits of my Mediator and Redeemer, *Jesus Christ*, who died to save Sinners! Amen.

The foregoing Narrative, which I most earnestly desire may be published, was partly dictated and partly wrote by me, whilst under Sentence of Death; and is strictly agreeable to Truth in every Particular. Witness my Hand,

Mary Blandy

Miss Mary Blandy's own Account / 125

1. An incident in which Cranstoun, while a guest at the Blandy home, insisted he had seen Mr. Blandy sleepwalking.

2. Cranstoun had privately married Ann Murray in May 1744. She had borne him a daughter in February 1745, and the child had been baptized before members of both families. Although Cranstoun's marriage was private, under Scottish law it was binding.

3. Mrs. Morgan had earlier provided Cranstoun with a supposed "love-powder"; at Mary's trial the prosecution claimed that this powder was actually a poison. Scotch pebbles were highly polished stones, very fashionable at the time.

4. Cleaning woman (modern charwoman).

5. Emptying the bowels.

6. A disease of the urinary tract, such as kidney stones.

7. A servant of variously defined duties, e.g., admitting visitors to a hall or chamber or walking before a person of high rank; sometimes a male attendant on a lady.

8. A friend of Mary's late mother.

9. Compassion, pity, feeling; from "bowels" considered as the site of the tender and sympathetic emotions.

Charlotte Charke

1713–1760

A Narrative of the Life of Mrs. Charlotte Charke, (Youngest Daughter of Colley Cibber, Esq.) Written by Herself. London: W. Reeve, 1755.

"I always thought it proper to imitate," Charlotte Charke tells readers in *A Narrative of the Life of Mrs. Charlotte Charke*—not surprising for the daughter of the actor, playwright, and producer Colley Cibber, one of the triumvirate of managers at the Theatre Royal in Drury Lane. Born in 1713, the last of ten children, when her mother was forty-five and thought "she produc'd her last," Charlotte was a beloved child who was provided an education, both genteel and liberal such as might have been "sufficient for a Son instead of a Daughter" (14, 17). In addition to being a bright and motivated student, she was proficient in hunting, shooting, and riding—less than ladylike activities to which her father quickly put an end when he returned from one of his many journeys. Taken to the city where he could keep an eye on her, Charlotte met and fell in love with a composer and dancing master who was also one of the violinists at Drury Lane, Richard Charke. In less than a year after their marriage, Richard showed his true nature: arrogant, lazy, and unfaithful. When their daughter, Catherine (Kitty), was born in 1729, he ran off to Jamaica where he reportedly died two years later, and Charlotte was left to support herself and her child by appearing on the stage.

Charlotte Charke debuted as Mademoiselle in *The Provok'd Wife* in April 1730. To save her father and herself embarrassment if she failed in the part, the playbill for *The Provok'd Wife* credited Charke's role as performed "by a young Gentlewoman, who had never appear'd on any Stage before" (56). Until around 1739 she successfully performed numerous serious and comedic roles from Arabella to Thalia and Cleopatra in London's theater district. Charke made "breeches" appearances[1] as Plume, Archer, Pistol, George Barnwell, Macheath, Lothario, and Sir Fopling Flutter—which satirized her father (Rogers 252). She joined her brother, Theophilus, in an actor's revolt against the Drury Lane manager, John

Highmore, which ruined him. When she was fired by Charles Fleetwood, she wrote *The Art of Management: or Tragedy Expell'd*, representing Fleetwood in the character of Brainless.

By 1739 Charke had so antagonized the managers of the London theater district and alienated her father to the total loss of his support that she was forced to give up the stage. Thus began her fantastic career as a strolling player and vagabond, a career that "rival[ed] Defoe's *Moll Flanders*, Fielding's *Jonathan Wild*, and Smollett's *Ferdinand Count Fathom*" (L. Ashley xvi).

After nine years in the provinces, Charke returned destitute to London in 1755 and petitioned her father for help in a letter that included the first installment of her *Narrative*. She begged his forgiveness and asked that he pay her to withhold publication of further installments. He refused, and Charke went to press. The "scandalous" *Narrative* was published first in serial form in March and April 1755. It appeared as a book later that year, cataloging, as the title page announces, "her Birth, Education, and mad Pranks"; her "coming on the Stage . . . and sundry Theatrical Anecdotes"; "Her Adventures in Mens Cloaths, going by the Name of Mr. *Brown*"; her "being belov'd by a Lady of great Fortune"; and her "commencing Strolling-Player" (Charke i). Her leading character was always, of course, herself, acting out various roles in "the whole scene of my unaccountable Farce" (224) where dogs serve as prompters (45–46) and strolling actors— impudent, ignorant, despicable—leave good trades, become useless to themselves and a nuisance to others while true actors (bred up in the profession) are invaded by "Barbers 'Prentices, Taylors, and Journeymen Weavers" (188). When Charke found herself out of theater work, she took on menial jobs to support herself and her child—male servant to a lord, sausage seller, fish and rabbit hawker, tea and oil merchant, companion to an orphaned heiress, restaurant and inn proprietess, pastry cook and farmer, hog merchant, newswriter—testifying to the difficult life of the strolling player under the Licensing Act of 1737.[2] Charke was often arrested as a vagrant and fined or imprisoned for failure to pay her debts. After nearly a decade of poverty and misfortune, she returned to London, where she embarked on a writing career that earned her a paltry living until she died in 1760.

In the first of the two excerpts, Charke introduces her readers to her purposes for writing and to her earliest character part, playing her father, Colley Cibber. While this performance in wig, waistcoat, and silver-hilted sword entertained her readers, the episode was also intended to remind her father of his once-tender feelings toward her. The next performance finds her riding through Hampton-Town on the tiny foal of an ass, with

*Charlotte Charke, engraving by L. P. Boitard, after a painting by
B. Dandridge. By permission of the British Library.*

a cast of young "Gentlemen and Ladies" of "low birth" making up her
retinue. Charke has enlarged her role; she is now both actress and director,
reconstructing and directing herself to entertain her readers and to win
back her father's affection through the means of a long-past family joke.
The second excerpt presents Charke in her role as Mr. Charles Brown,
the "husband" of Mrs. Brown, a young woman who was her companion
in her wanderings through the provinces. The name "Brown" was chosen
as a slap at her older sister, Catherine Brown, who was responsible for

much of Cibber's rejection of Charlotte (Mackie 863). The Mr. Brown role, the larger role she played throughout her strolling player years, is also the one given most attention by current Charke scholars.[3] Charke invites this interest from the first and continues to titillate her readers' curiosity by refusing to fully reveal her reasons for taking on the Mr. Brown role. In the excerpt, Mr. and Mrs. Brown are the typical heterosexual couple as portrayed in Restoration and early eighteenth-century comedies. Mr. Brown collects, takes possession of, and squanders Mrs. Brown's legacy on being a "worthy Gentleman" (Baruth 48).

TEXT: Charlotte Charke's *A Narrative of the Life of Mrs. Charlotte Charke* first appeared as eight numbers in serial form in the *Bristol Weekly Intelligencer*, edited by Edward Ward, from 8 March to 19 April 1755. The selection (pp. 14–22 and 230–236) is from the second full-text edition published in London by W. Reeve, 1755.

CR ED

I SHALL NOW BEGIN my Detail of the several Stages I have pass'd thro' since my Birth, which made me the last-born of Mr. *Colley Cibber,* at a Time my Mother began to think, without this additional Blessing (meaning my sweet Self) she had fully answer'd the End of her Creation, being just Forty-five Years of Age when she produc'd her last, "THO' NOT LEAST IN LOVE". Nor was I exempted from an equal Share in my Father's Heart; yet, partly thro' my own Indiscretion (and, I am too well convinc'd, from the cruel Censure of false and evil Tongues) since my Maturity, I lost that Blessing: Which, if strongest Compunction and uninterrupted Hours of Anguish, blended with Self-conviction and filial Love, can move his Heart to Pity and Forgiveness, I shall, with Pride and unutterable Transport, throw myself at his Feet, to implore the only Benefit I desire or expect, his BLESSING, and his PARDON.

But of that, more hereafter—And I hope, ere this small Treatise is finish'd, to have it in my Power to inform my Readers, my painful Separation from my once tender Father will be more than amply repaid, by a happy Interview; as I am certain neither my present or future Conduct, shall ever give him Cause to blush at what I should esteem a justifiable and necessary Reconciliation, as 'tis the absolute Ordination of the Supreme that we should forgive, when the Offender becomes a sincere and hearty Penitent. And I positively declare, were I to expire this Instant, I have no self-interested Views, in regard to worldly Matters; but confess myself a Miser in my Wishes so far, as having the transcendant Joy of knowing that I am restor'd to a Happiness, which not only will clear my Reputation to the World, in Regard to a former Want of Duty, but, at the same Time, give a convincing Proof that there are yet some Sparks of Tenderness remaining in my Father's Bosom, for his REPENTANT CHILD.

I confess, I believe I came not only an unexpected, but an unwelcome Guest into the Family, (exclusive of my Parents,) as my Mother had borne no Children for some few Years before; so that I was rather regarded as an impertinent Intruder, than one who had a natural Right to make up the circular Number of my Father's Fire-Side: Yet, be it as it may, the Jealousy of me, from her other Children, laid no Restraint on her Fondness for me, which my Father and she both testified in their tender Care of my Education. His paternal Love omitted nothing that could improve any natural Talents Heaven had been pleased to endow me with; the Mention of which, I hope, won't be imputed to me as a vain Self-conceit, of knowing more, or thinking better, than any other of my Sister Females. No! far be it from me; for as all Advantages from Nature are the favourable Gifts of the Power Divine, consequently no Praise can be arrogated to ourselves, for that which is not in ourselves POSSIBLE TO BESTOW.

I should not have made this Remark, but, as 'tis likely my Works may fall into the Hands of People of disproportion'd Understandings, I was willing to prevent an Error a weak Judgment might have run into, by inconsiderately throwing an Odium upon me, I could not possibly deserve—FOR, ALAS! ALL CANNOT JUDGE ALIKE.

As I have instanc'd, that my Education was not only a genteel, but in Fact a liberal one, and such indeed as might have been sufficient for a Son instead of a Daughter; I must beg Leave to add, that I was never made much acquainted with that necessary Utensil which forms the housewifely Part of a young Lady's Education, call'd a Needle; which I handle with the same clumsey Awkwardness a Monkey does a Kitten, and am equally capable of using the one, as Pug[4] is of nursing the other.

This is not much to be wondered at, as my Education consisted chiefly in Studies of various Kinds, and gave me a different Turn of Mind than what I might have had, if my Time had been employ'd in ornamenting a Piece of Canvas with Beasts, Birds and the Alphabet; the latter of which I understood in *French*, rather before I was able to speak *English*.

As I have promised to conceal nothing that might raise a Laugh, I shall begin with a small Specimen of my former Madness, when I was but four Years of Age. Having, even then, a passionate Fondness for a Periwig,[5] I crawl'd out of Bed one Summer's Morning at *Twickenham*, where my Father had Part of a House and Gardens for the Season, and, taking it into my small Pate, that by Dint of a Wig and a Waistcoat, I should be the perfect Representative of my Sire, I crept softly into the Servants-Hall, where I had the Night before espied all Things in Order, to perpetrate the happy Design I had framed for the next Morning's Expedition. Accordingly I paddled down Stairs, taking with me my Shoes, Stockings, and little Dimity Coat;[6] which I artfully contrived to pin up, as well as I could, to supply the Want of a Pair of Breeches. By the Help of a long Broom, I took down a Waistcoat of my Brother's, and an enormous bushy Tie-wig of my Father's, which entirely enclos'd my Head and Body, with the Knots of the Ties thumping my little Heels as I marched along, with slow and solemn Pace. The Covert of Hair in which I was concealed, with the Weight of a monstrous Belt and large Silver-hilted Sword, that I could scarce drag along, was a vast Impediment in my Procession: And, what still added to the other Inconveniences I laboured under, was whelming myself under one of my Father's large Beaver-hats, laden with Lace, as thick and broad as a Brickbat.

Being thus accoutred, I began to consider that 'twould be impossible for me to pass for Mr. *Cibber* in Girl's Shoes, therefore took an Opportunity to slip out of Doors after the Gardener, who went to his Work, and roll'd myself into a dry Ditch, which was as deep as I was high; and in this Grotesque Pigmy-State, walked up and down the Ditch bowing to all who came by me. But, behold, the Oddity of my Appearance soon assembled a Croud about me; which yielded me no small Joy, as I conceived their Risibility on this Occasion to be Marks of Approbation, and walked myself into a Fever, in the happy Thought of being taken for the 'Squire.

When the Family arose, 'till which Time I had employ'd myself in this regular March in my Ditch, I was the first Thing enquir'd after, and miss'd; 'till Mrs. *Heron*, the Mother of the late celebrated Actress of that Name,[7] happily espied me, and directly call'd forth the whole Family to be Witness of my State and Dignity.

The Drollery of my Figure rendered it impossible, assisted by the Fondness of both Father and Mother, to be angry with me; but, alas! I was borne off on the Footman's Shoulders, to my Shame and Disgrace, and forc'd into my proper Habiliments.

The Summer following our Family resided at *Hampton-Town*, near the Court. My Mother being indisposed, at her first coming there, drank every Morning and Night Asses Milk.[8] I observed one of those little health-restoring Animals was attended by its Fole, which was about the Height of a sizeable Greyhound.

I immediately formed a Resolution of following the Fashion of taking the Air early next Morning, and fix'd upon this young Ass for a Padnag;[9] and, in order to bring this Matter to bear, I communicated my Design to a small Troop of young Gentlemen and Ladies, whose low Births and adverse States rendered it entirely convenient for them to come into any Scheme, Miss *Charlotte Cibber* could possibly propose. Accordingly my Mother's Bridle and Saddle were secretly procured, but the riper Judgments of some of my Followers soon convinced me of the unnecessary Trouble of carrying the Saddle, as the little destin'd Beast was too small, and indeed too weak, to bear the Burden; upon which 'twas concluded to take the Bridle only, and away went Miss and her Attendants, who soon arrived at the happy Field where the poor harmless Creature was sucking. We soon seiz'd, and endeavour'd to bridle it; but, I remember, 'twas impossible to bring that Point to bear, the Head of the Fole being so very small, the Trappings fell off as fast as they strove to put them on. One of the small Crew, who was wiser than the rest, propos'd their Garters being converted to that Use; which was soon effected, and I rode triumphantly into Town astride, with a numerous Retinue, whose Huzzas were drown'd by the dreadful Braying of the tender Dam, who pursued us with agonizing Sounds of Sorrow, for her oppress'd young one.

Upon making this Grand-Entry into the Town, I remember my Father, from the violent Acclamations of Joy on so glorious an Occasion, was excited to enquire into the Meaning, of what he perhaps imagin'd to be an Insurrection; when, to his Amazement, he beheld his Daughter mounted as before described, preceded by a Lad, who scrap'd upon a Twelve-penny Fiddle of my own, to add to the Dignity and Grandeur of this extraordinary Enterprize.

I perfectly remember, young as I was then, the strong Mixture of Surprize, Pleasure, Pain and Shame in his Countenance, on his viewing me seated on my infantical *Rosinante*;[10] which, tho' I had not then Sense enough to distinguish, my Memory has since afforded me the Power to describe, and also to repeat his very Words, at his looking out of Window, *Gad demme! An Ass upon an Ass!*

For near six Months my Friend and I resided in this terrible Abode of Infamy and Guilt;[11] but being ignorant, at our first coming, of what Kind of Mortals they were, we settled amongst them, and did not find it an easy Matter to remove, though we went trembling to Bed every Night, with dreadful Apprehensions of some ill Treatment before the Break of Day.

I took a little Shop, and because I was resolved to set off my Matters as grand as possible, I had a Board put over my Door, with this Inscription,

BROWN, PASTRY-COOK, FROM LONDON:

At which Place I can't charge myself with ever having, in the Course of my Life, attempted to spoil the Ingredients necessary in the Composition of a Tart. But that did not signify, as long as I was a *Londoner*, to be sure my Pastry must be good.

While the Ships were coming in from *Ireland* (which is in the Months of *June, July,* and *August*) I had a good running Trade; but, alas! the Winter was most terrible, and if an Uncle of my Friend's (who died while we were there) had not left her a Legacy, we must inevitably have perished.

About the Time the News came of her Money, we were involved to the Amount of about Four or Five and Thirty Shillings; and, if a Shilling would have saved us from total Destruction, we did not know where to raise it.

On the Receipt of the Letter I showed it to the Landlord, hoping he would lend me a Guinea to bear my Charges to Mrs. *Brown's* Aunt, who lives in *Oxfordshire*, where I was to go to receive her Legacy, which was a genteel one, and I should have left her as a Hostage 'till my Return.

But the incredulous Blockhead conceived the Letter to be forged; and, as he himself was capable of such a Fraud, imagined we had artfully contrived to get a Guinea out of him, and reward him by running away in his Debt. But he was quite mistaken, as he was afterwards convinced, and made a Thousand aukward Excuses for his Unkindness when we received the Money, and had discharged his trifling Demands.

I consulted on my Pillow what was best to be done, and communicated my Thoughts to my Friend; upon which we concluded, without speaking a Word to any Body, both to set out and fetch the Money, according to Order, from her Relation's, though there was two very great Bars to such Progress, in the Eye of Reason, but I stepped over both.

One was, having no more than a single Groat in the World between us: And the other, my having been obliged to pledge my Hat at *Bristol* a Fortnight before for Half a Crown, to carry on the anatomical Business,[12] we haplessly pursued.

Yet notwithstanding these terrible Disasters I was resolved, at all Events, to go the Journey. I took my Fellow-Sufferer with me, who was lost in Wonder at so daring an Enterprize, to set out, without either Hat or Money, fourscore Miles on Foot. But I soon eased the Anxiety of Mind she laboured under, by assuring her, that when we got to *Bristol* I would apply to a Friend, who would furnish me with a small Matter to carry us on to *Bath*.

This pacified the poor Soul, who could scarce see her Way for Tears, before I told her my Design; which never entered my Imagination, 'till we had got two Miles beyond the detested Place we lived in. Our Circumstances were then so desperate, I thought

> "*What ever World we next were thrown upon,*
> "*Cou'd not be worse than* Pill."

As we were on our March, we were met by some of our unneighbourly Neighbours, who took Notice of my being in full Career,[13] without a Hat; and of Mrs. *Brown*, with a Bundle in her Hand, which contained only a Change of Linnen for us, on our Travel.

They soon alarmed our Landlord with the Interview, with many Conjectures of our being gone off; and concluded, my being bare-headed was intended as a blind for our Excursion: But let their Thoughts be what they would, we were safe in *Bristol* by the Time they got Home to make their political Report; and I obtained, at the first Word, the timely Assistance our Necessities required to procure a Supper and Bed that Night, besides what served to bear our Charges to *Bath* next Morning.

The only Distress I had to overcome, was to procure a Covering for my unthinking Head; but Providence kindly directed us to a House where there was a young Journeyman, a Sort of a *Jemmy-Smart*,[14] who dress'd entirely in Taste, that lodg'd where we lay that Night. As I appeared, barring the want of a Hat, as smart as himself in Dress, he entered into Conversation with me; and, finding him a good-natur'd Man, ventured (as I was urged by downright Necessity) to beg the Favour of him to lend me a Hat, which, by being very dusty, I was well assured had not been worn some Time, from which I conceived he would not be in a violent Hurry to have it restored; and, framing an Excuse of having sent my own to be dress'd, easily obtained the Boon.

Next Morning, at the Hour of Five, we set out, and staid at *Bath* 'till the Morning following: Though I remember I was obliged to give the Landlady my Waistcoat for the Payment of my Lodging before we went to Bed, which I had the Comfort of redeeming, by the Help of Mr. *Kennedy* and Company,[15] and set forwards on my Journey with the Favour they were pleased to bestow on me.

I never received an Obligation in my Life that I was ashamed to acknowledge, though I have very lately incurred the Displeasure of a fine

Lady, for mentioning a Person in my third Number, to whom I shall ever think myself most TRANSCENDANTLY OBLIGED; and shall never be perswaded to forget their Humanity, *or to reconcile Contradictions, and believe in Impossibilities.*

As soon as I was empowered, by the Help of a little Cash, we set out from *Bath* to *Oxfordshire*; and, in three Days, arrived at the happy Spot, where we were furnished with that Opiate for Grief,[16] the want of which had many tedious Night kept us waking.

Our Journey Home was expedited, by taking a Double-Horse from *Whitney* to *Cirencester*; and now and then, for the rest of the Way, mounting up into a Hay-Cart, or a timely Waggon.

When we returned to *Bristol*, we met with several of the *Pill* Gentry, who were surprized to see us, and informed us how terribly we had been exploded,[17] as being Cheats and Run-aways; and though they themselves, in our Absence, were as inveterate as the rest of the vulgar Crew, were the first to condemn others for a Fault they were equally guilty of.

I returned the borrowed Hat, and went Home triumphant in my own—Paid my Landlord, and, as long as the Money lasted, was the worthiest Gentleman in the county.

Notes

1. The adoption of male roles and attire by female actresses was at its height in the 1730s. By the end of the eighteenth century, "discourse about the cross-dressed actress is . . . more condemnatory of the practice," considering it a "mere travesty . . . which left gender boundaries unquestioned" (Straub 127).

2. See the Introduction for a discussion of the Licensing Act of 1737.

3. See Smith, "A Narrative"; Wanko; Straub; P. Rogers; Nussbaum, *Autobiographical Subject; and* Minter Strange, for various takes on gender and sexuality in the *Narrative*.

4. Generic name for a pet dog; cf. modern Rover or Spot.

5. Periwig is a corrupt form of the French *perruque*, a very large wig, the wearing of which had begun to wane in the reign of George III.

6. A coat made from a strong, thin, corded cotton.

7. The celebrated actress is Mary Heron (?–1736); in 1734 she joined Charke and her brother, Theophilus Cibber, in their protest against the management of Drury Lane Theatre.

8. This rich milk would be available from the ass only during the time it was nursing a new foal.

9. A horse with a slow, easy pace.

10. Don Quixote's trusty steed.

11. Pill, England, a tiny harbor town five miles from Bristol. Charke thought the town pleasant enough, but of the inhabitants she remarks, "the Villainies of these Wretches are of so heinous and unlimited a Nature, they render the Place so unlike any

other Part of the habitable World, that I can compare it only to the Anti-Chamber of that Abode we are admonish'd to avoid in the next life" (228).

12. Not specifically identified; may be the "hog business" in which Charke bought what she thought was a sow with pig but which turned out to be a barrow, or castrated male.

13. Full travel dress.

14. Term for a dandy.

15. Probably the Mr. Kennedy (first name unknown) who acted in various London and touring companies from 1737 to the early 1750s.

16. The money from Mrs. Brown's legacy.

17. Discredited; also, hissed or hooted off the stage.

Catherine Jemmat

?–1766

The Memoirs of Mrs. Catherine Jemmat, daughter of the late Admiral Yeo, of Plymouth, written by herself. 2 vols. London: Mr. Walker's, 1762.

Catherine Yeo's birthdate is unknown; we do know that she was born in Exeter, that her father was Admiral John Yeo, and that her mother died when she was five. Nine weeks later the admiral married a girl of nineteen, and Catherine was sent off to boarding school with her sister. When she returned home, she was subjected to what she considered the persecution of her stepmother and the ill-temper of her father: "whatever might be deficient in his character as a commander on the liquid element, he was a finish'd tar in his own house" (1:5), she complains. Catherine's *Memoirs* reveals a high-spirited young woman, and much of the first volume is taken up with her japes and flirtations. Of her many suitors, she most favored a Mr. B., but the courtship did not prosper: Admiral Yeo forbade it, and eventually Mr. B.—nobly, in Catherine's view—gave up his suit because he had no money. Her next admirer was the son of a rich trades-man, but their differences in religion gave her "a plausible pretext" (1:20) for rejecting him. To discourage another swain's fondling she kicked him in the nose and was then rescued from his further attentions by a passing farmer. Soon thereafter she ran away from home, first to the farmer and then to a Mr. S. Her letters to her father remained unanswered, and Cath-erine decided to marry "the first person who should propose himself to me" (1:167).

Unfortunately, the successful aspirant was Jemmat. Although he kept a fabric shop and convinced the admiral that he could support a wife, he soon revealed himself to be a drunkard and a wastrel who had married Catherine for money to pay his debts. Furthermore, he insulted and beat his pregnant wife, once so severely as to bring on child-bed fever (2:56). For a time Catherine was reconciled with her stepmother and hitherto hostile stepbrother, and she nursed her father through an attack of gout. When her husband later went bankrupt, however, her father refused to take her in. What happened next is decorously concealed in the *Memoirs*. A somewhat racy concluding anecdote, along with allusions to misrepresentations (1:ii) and aspersions (1:2) by her relatives, suggests that Catherine's subsequent career was less than respectable. Yet the list of subscribers—those who contributed money to have the *Memoirs* published—runs to twelve pages, and the book was dedicated by permission to the duke of York, which perhaps indicates these patrons agreed with Catherine that her family's conduct was "some excuse for any foibles I may since have been led into" (2:58). In 1766 she published a book, *Miscellanies in Prose and Verse*, again by subscription; she died the same year.

TEXT: Catherine Jemmat's *Memoirs* was first published in 1762; other editions appeared in 1765 and 1771. Although she intended the book to "arraign my words, thoughts, and actions, with the minutest truth, at the tribunal of publick justice" (1:3), she may also have needed money. The excerpt (pp. 16–46 of volume one) is written with a self-deprecating wit characteristic of the *Memoirs*.

C&Ə

AS TO MYSELF, without being the least partial, I was endow'd with a quick genius, and a propensity to learn whatever was within the reach of my capacity; I was indeed as the poet has happily express'd it,

> "Wild as colt untamed."[1]

but quite inoffensively so.

I was removed from the boarding school to learn plain work,[2] under the care of three gentlewomen, the daughters of a deceas'd clergyman.

With regard to my person, I never could boast of it; for I was never a beauty. I was what you might call a comely black girl, with a blooming country complexion; I was remarkable indeed for an easy, obliging disposition, which perhaps was the only attraction of the many addresses I was afterwards honoured with.

When I left this school, and returned to my father's, a master was employed to teach my sister and myself the harpsichord; but she, neither having a taste, or an ear for divine harmony, left off learning at the end of three months, without being in the least improved. Indeed, she

> "Had not musick in her soul,
> "Nor was she touch'd with the concord of sweet sounds."

The reader may apply the remaining part of this speech, which I think is in the Merchant of Venice, in what manner he pleases.[3]

My further progress was, however, shortly after retarded, as my father was ordered to Spithead; and both my musick-master, and captain S. a veteran acquaintance of my father's, who took infinite pains to improve me in time and the thorough bass,[4] were, by the prudent advice of my mother-in-law,[5] forbid the house, during my father's absence, lest her character should again be censured.[6]

About this time an elegant and brilliant assembly[7] was opened at Plymouth, and Miss C. the then agent-victualer's[8] daughter, with myself, were admitted as subscribers,[9] though yet dressed in robe-coats. As this gave some umbrage to the graver sort,[10] it was specified, in the articles set up in each room, that no more young ladies, under such an age, should be subscribers for the future; but as we were introduced by a majority of votes, we were permitted to continue.

The antiquated virgins considered this as advantageous to them, who knew no country dances that had been in use since the deluge; whereas we, who attended twice a week on the best dancing master in that part of the world, who had all the new dances, as they came out in London, constantly sent down to him, were allowed to trip it extremely well; and had generally the best partners; a circumstance not very pleasing to our competitors.

I can't help taking notice here of a melancholly accident that happened the first night of our assembly.

Lady P. mother to the present dutchess dowager of L. was seized with a fit of apoplexy while she sat at cards, and died early the next morning: There were present her ladyship's two daughters, and their husbands; namely, the marchioness and marquess of C; Mrs. T. the other daughter, and Mr. T. her husband, then master of the king's houshold;[11] who, though she lived at Plymton, but four miles from Plymouth, could never afterwards be persuaded to come into it; so deeply was she affected by this event.

Various constructions were put upon this accident, which might, and undoubtedly would have happened in any other place; and I very well remember to have heard a religious old lady declare, that all meetings of that kind were an abomination to good and virtuous people; and that she verily believed the death of the above lady was a judgment from heaven: but, continued she, very satyrically, what commenced in the death of her ladyship, will probably terminate in the birth of others; which must be the consequence of mixing youth of both sexes promiscuously together.

In this pious conjecture she was, however, mistaken; for the utmost decency and good order were inviolably preserved, which continued without the smallest infringment as long as I frequented it.

As this assembly was the resort of the gay and sprightly, particularly the navy officers, it was no wonder that the daughter of a commander should attract their notice and compliments; many of whom are now general officers, and daily reaping laurels by their courage and conduct.

Amongst the many who paid their addresses to me, by bows at church, nods and emphatical motions at the assembly, serenades under my window, and the many powerful yet natural enchantments with which Love instructs his votaries; I noticed none so much as those of a young surgeon,[12] just set up for himself; not that I had the least tincture of passion for the man, but that I thought him a genteel person, and fit to lead the vanguard of my train of idolaters. I had frequently noticed him passing and repassing under my window; where

"Revolving in his love-sick soul,
     "The various state of things below,
"Now and then a sigh he stole,
     "And tears began to flow."[13]

Compassion and curiosity; come, I'll e'en add vanity, inclined me to know what he had to say for himself; and a favourable opportunity for it soon after offered: I stood, in the cool of a summer's evening, at the street-door of my father's house; and left my mother-in-law at cards in the parlour; but perhaps I should not have found this indulgence, had not my father been at the assembly.

Soon after my spark[14] made his appearance, and began to chat on the beauties of the evening, and other common-place conversation, stupid enough of all conscience, tho' I thought it very pleasing: he certainly was a young man of good sense; but lovers are not always happy in the talent of expression, particularly on the first interview.

My sister (ever a most zealous marplot)[15] standing in the passage, and hearing me converse with a man, ran into the kitchen, and declared to the servants (her favourite companions)[16] that she had seen an apparition, and that the ghost of Jack S. was absolutely conversing with her sister at the door.

As I have mentioned this young gentleman, it may not be improper to observe, that he was the son of an alderman at Plymouth, who was deemed a man of great property: he had no children but this youth, and a younger son: his father having intended him for the study of physic, sent him to the university at Oxford; where, having a warm contest with some of his fellow-students, about an atheistical book then on the table; Mr. S. took up the book (as he thought) and threw it into the fire, where it was consumed to ashes; but, when his passion subsided, he found it was his own Greek testament, exactly of the same size and bind, that he had unwillingly destroyed; this fact being represented to his tutor, by the other lads, as done in contempt of that sacred legislature; his tutor severely reprimanded him for his want of circumspection in an affair of that moment: here it would probably have ended, but that the story was related to doctor C. then head of the college, with a thousand aggravating circumstances; and, notwithstanding the most pathetic asseverations on his part, of his innocence, and the kindest remonstrances of his tutor in his favour, to which were added, the articles of his faith, drawn up by himself, and inclosed in a letter to the doctor, he was cruelly expelled, and was obliged to return to his father's house, till he went over to Leyden[17] to finish his studies.

During this interval, I had an opportunity of commencing an acquaintance with him. He was a pretty youth, but rather foppish, and too effeminate: these foibles, however, were far from depreciating him in my eyes; and I had the pleasure to be a peculiar favourite of his, insomuch that, by the assistance of a maid-servant, we had many private meetings; and frequently walked together in a garden of my father's some distance from the house: but these excursions were always very early in the morning, and might have continued to our mutual delight, for some time longer, had we not been discovered by an antiquated aunt of mine, who, rising one morning unusually early, discovered us in earnest confabulation together: she immediately retired without seeming to have noticed what she had seen. The gentleman made off as well as he could, and left me to stand the shock of a very severe lecture; for my father, having cognizance of this matter, swore he would turn me out of his house, if ever he heard any thing of this kind for the future. Before Mr. S. left England, he sent me the following lines.

> To Miss Catherine Yeo.
>   What passion dictates, and what love recites,
> See my hand tremble while my heart indites;
> Health to my dearest maid, these strains I send,

Health, which my dearest maid, alone can lend;
Believe the honest verse, or let my blood
Write the sad accents in a purple flood;
Believe the falling tear, the rising sigh
That heaves my breast, and swells upon my eye:
On the fair page see briny drops appear,
Anxious to drown the tidings which they bear.
Did fate propitious to my vows incline,
And kindly fix my golden lot with thine,
With how much rapture would the moments roll,
Blest with the darling object of my soul;
But now accurs'd, by ill-starr'd fate's decree,
I fly my country, my content, and thee.
Farewell my charmer, oh! these lines review,
Then judge what pangs I feel to bid adieu!

After this expressive epistle he went abroad; but not till he had received in answer the little piece annexed, which, as the first poetical attempt of a flighty girl, I hope the critics will be favourable to.

To Mr. S.
   Go, virtuous S. and with you ever go,
All you can taste of happiness below:
By time at length grown wiser, I resign
A bliss, for me too perfect and divine;
As bounteous clouds, that teem with liquid show'rs,
Now here, now there, diffuse their useful stores,
So you, from place to place should ever range,
Rejoicing every climate with the change;
For, wheresoe'er your devious [i.e., wandering] footsteps stray,
The spot must glow with intellectual day;
Blest with the beams of knowledge which you shed,
And rich with treasures of your virtue bred.
But must I then, whose soul like lightning flew,
To meet the kindred soul it found in you,
(Forgive my pride) so soon alas! resign
The new-born joy, nor call it longer mine?
It must be so, stern fate will have its way;
My tyrant stars command, and I obey.

But to return to the young surgeon, who so terribly alarm'd my sister, and the servants; he march'd off on the first outcry of an apparition; and gave me a fair scene to display the excellencies of my tragick abilities in; I had overheard what my sister bellow'd out in the kitchen; and being assured he was beyond the reach of a pursuit; I suddenly dropp'd down in the passage, just when the servants had assum'd courage enough to take a peep at the supernatural visitant; seeing me in that position, confirmed their suggestions, for it has been the opinion of all the learned old women in the country, since the days of Popish superstition, that any person who sees a spirit, faints at the sight of a candle; my mother-in-law, who did not want for credulity, applied restoratives to my mouth and nostrils, but to very little seeming effect; I continued quite motionless, and in that posture, suffered the maids to undress me, and put me in bed.

My mother-in-law, in the mean time, dispatch'd two expresses, one to the physician, and the other to my father, then at the assembly, and who instantly obeyed the summons; but did not arrive as soon as the doctor, who was in my bed-chamber when he entered, and was followed by my mother, my sister, and all the servants; who in reality were afraid to stay below; and as I roll'd my eyes about, I could plainly perceive they look'd as if the spirit had been behind them.

My father enquir'd the cause of all this, and they all attempted to explain it at once, which made a Babylonian confusion that was highly entertaining to me.

G——d d——mn you all, said my father, speak one at a time, or I'll run my cane down some of your throats. My mother then gave a circumstantial detail of all she knew of the matter, and declared she believed the poor child had seen some evil thing: Upon this I burst out a laughing, and continued it a full half hour, till my spirits were quite exhausted, which made a fit of weeping the less difficult to affect. My father, who had intervals of good-nature, or at least could pretend to them before company, very seriously consulted the physician what was to be done.

The doctor having very deliberately felt my pulse, advised some blood to be immediately taken from me; upon this a surgeon was sent for, who blooded me, and left me to take some rest.

The next morning I was much better, but the doctor would prescribe some medicines which I was oblig'd to swallow, in order to save appearances; tho' I was impatient to finish the farce, in order to get news of my spark; but would give no account of what had occasioned my disorder.

Fortune, who is frequently the foe of enterprizing geniuses, had like to have overturn'd all the machinery of my brain: The young surgeon, not knowing the methods I had used to prevent a suspicion of him, and being impatient at not seeing me, or hearing from me in two or three days, during which it was absolutely necessary I should confine myself to my room, wrote a letter which was unluckily deliver'd to a creature of my mother's; but she, like a prudent lady, sent it back unopened; or else she might thereby have unravell'd the whole mystery; this circumstance, she thought proper to acquaint my father of; who, when he thought I was able to come down stairs, sent for me, and adddress'd me in these terms: What fellow is this you correspond with? I assur'd him I could not comprehend his meaning; Pray, said he to his wife, Did not you tell me she receiv'd letters? No my dear, but I told you a letter came, from whom I know not; and I thought it incumbent on me both to inform you of the matter, and to send the letter back unopen'd. However, I was well pleas'd to find things were no worse. And after attending a lecture not replete with the most elegant terms, from my vociferous pappa, blended with threats of the severest punishment if I ever encouraged any manner of courtship; I was dismiss'd with a heart as light as a feather, to lay new schemes for the advancement of our future correspondence.

I had been some time tampering with our chambermaid, whom I for that purpose permitted to sleep with me, to give me her aid and assistance; she enumerated the hazards she shou'd run in embarking in such a cause; as being turn'd out of doors, or sent to the house of correction,[18] if she was discover'd; but withal told me, that if she once undertook it, she would go thro' with it.

I plainly understood this significant If; which imply'd no more than the mock-doctor's asking for the symptoms, i.e. the money; but I was not at that time mistress of any, therefore was oblig'd for the present, to suspend further importunities.

A day or two after, she came into my chamber, with joy dancing in her eyes, and after carefully locking the door behind her, cry'd, here Miss, here's something will make you happy; she then pull'd from her breast a letter, which I rapturously received, and after enjoining her to perpetual secresy, began to examine; Lord, madam, said she, the dear gentleman gave me half a guinea, and I am sure that's more than any one in the house will do except yourself.

I thought the letter written with the elegance of an Addison,[19] joined to the passionate softness of an Ovid or a Sappho;[20] which left me no room to doubt, that it was dictated by a heart truly sincere.

I sat up all night to answer it, and whatever defects might have been in my stile, I took care that no parts of it shou'd exceed the limits of modesty and moderation: Many letters from this æra continued to pass between us, and by the means of the maid, a place was appointed where we frequently met; till at length he put the grand question to me, namely,—Will you marry me? your father probably may not consent to it, but it may be done in another manner; and I am willing to trust to his generosity for a fortune, when he knows how long and how tenderly I have lov'd you, and that the thing once done is irrevocable.—This was going an octave beyond my compass; for tho' I lov'd adulation immensely, I had by no means settled my affections on him, nor had I any serious intentions of becoming his wife, tho' his merit might justly entitle him to one infinitely superior: I therefore thought proper to break off the correspondence, at least, till he could find some method to persuade my father into his opinion.

After this, tho' we frequently met at publick places, we never noticed each other for a full year.

In the mean time, many advantageous matches for me were propos'd both to my father and myself: but his parsimony on one side, and my prudence on the other, prevented any of them from succeeding.

Notes

1. Source unidentified.

2. Plain sewing.

3. In *The Merchant of Venice* 5.1.83–88, such a person is said to be "fit for treasons, strategems, and spoils."

4. In music, the bass part written with figures which indicate the harmony.

5. In eighteenth-century usage, stepmother.

6. Earlier, a neighbor had hinted to Yeo that his new wife was entertaining men while he was at sea.

7. Gathering for purposes of entertainment, such as dancing, conversation, cards.

8. One who furnishes a navy or ship with provisions.

9. Members, on payment of a subscription or fee.

10. Robe-coats were worn by children; "the graver sort" would be objecting to the admission of such young members to the assembly.

11. Minor functionary in the management of the king's household.

12. Not at this time a particularly prestigious occupation.

13. Freely rendered lines from John Dryden's poem "Alexander's Feast."

14. A witty or lively young man; the term is often, as here, used dismissively.

15. Marplot is a character in Susanna Centlivre's play *The Busy Body* (1709), described as "very inquisitive to know everybody's business" and thus "generally spoil[ing] all he undertakes, but without design."

16. Note the class-based nature of this insult.

17. At this time medical students often took their degrees from Dutch universities.

18. Something like a combination of prison and workhouse.

19. Joseph Addison (1672–1719), English dramatist and essayist much admired for his prose style.

20. Classical poets known for their love lyrics.

Lady Mary Wortley Montagu

1689–1762

Letters of the Right Honourable Lady M——y W——y M——e, Written, during her Travels in Europe, Asia and Africa, to Persons of Distinction, Men of Letters, &c. in different Parts of Europe. 4 vols. London: T. Becket and P. A. de Hondt, 1763.

Lady Mary Wortley Montagu was born in 1689, the same year her father, Evelyn Pierrepont, earl of Kingston and marquis of Dorchester, was elected to Parliament. Her mother, Lady Mary Fielding, daughter of the earl of Denbigh, died when Lady Mary was only four years old. Lord Kingston was heavily involved in politics and sent Lady Mary, her two sisters, and brother to live with their grandmother, Elizabeth Pierrepont, until her death in 1698. Lady Mary then moved back and forth between London and the family country house in Thoresby, engaging in the flurry of activities proper to a young woman of her class.

Angered that Lord Kingston and her suitor, Edward Wortley Montagu, grandson of the first earl of Sandwich, could not agree on the financial arrangements for their marriage and at Wortley's too great interest in the size of her dowry, Lady Mary broke off their engagement for a time.[1] In 1712, when her father attempted to force her to marry the Honorable Clotworthy Skeffington or lose her inheritance, Lady Mary and Wortley eloped in the romantic fashion of the French novels she read as an adolescent and with all the confusion of a Restoration comedy (Desai xiii).

Wortley, a man of considerable wealth and political ambition, was elected to Parliament when George I was crowned king and the Whigs returned to power. He was then appointed ambassador extraordinary to the Court of Turkey. Lady Mary was twenty-six years of age and recovering from a virulent case of smallpox when Wortley was assigned to effect a truce between Turkey and the Venetian Republic. Wortley met with Ahmed III, the Turkish sultan who agreed to a truce. When negotiations failed, Wortley was recalled to England, having served less than two years.

The *Letters* details Lady Mary's travels to and from Turkey and her

Lady Mary Wortley Montagu, painting by Jonathan Richardson. Courtesy of the National Portrait Gallery, London.

experiences during her stay there. They share literary traditions with seventeenth- and eighteenth-century men's travel narratives by beginning with "familiar moral didacticism," drawing oriental geography, defining oriental culture, and remarking on differences and novelty (Aravamudan 72–73). Believing her "anthropological skills of cultural decipherment far superior to her [male] predecessors," however, she hurls scathing comments at the travel narratives of Richard Knolles, Sir Paul Rycaut, Aaron Hill, and Jean Dumont (74).[2] Lady Mary challenges these male versions of the Orient from what she believes is a superior position as woman and skeptical intellectual. "As a woman traveller, Lady Mary Wortley Montagu was uniquely privileged. When she went to Turkey in 1716 . . . she was assured access to the upper echelons of Ottoman society. Her gender, in addition, gained her entry to distinctive institutions of that society which were off limits even to privileged men" (Bohls, "Aesthetics" 179). Lady Mary also *wrote* from a position of privilege. Traveling in all available luxury, she wrote almost exclusively of her encounters with Turkish royalty, court life, and her associations with the international aristocracy. Her primary audience, the first recipients of the letters, was also drawn from the privileged class: ladies-in-waiting, countesses, and men of letters.

The five letters in this selection were composed in the Turkish city of Adrianople,[3] now known as Edirne, which stands at the convergence of several important trade routes, a little more than a hundred miles north of old Constantinople. Written during a single day, 1 April 1717, the letters are a microcosm of Lady Mary's world, revealing her values and beliefs and the range of her interests. Even as they give insight into her character, they reshape the travel literature of her day.

The first letter, addressed "To Lady ———," describes her visit to the Turkish bagnio, or bath house. While she believes that the account of this experience will entertain and amaze her readers, she also attempts to rewrite the exotic. She replaces the rude, degrading, and inaccurate characterizations of the Turkish bagnio—misrepresented in men's travel narratives—with respectful language in the artistic style of a painter who sees beauty all around.[4] In the voice of the social critic, she compares the baths to the English coffeehouse: "In short, 'tis the women's coffee-house, where all the news of the town is told."[5] She seems to imply that, while English women are shut out of the coffeehouses, Turkish women have places where they are the sole authorities. Examining the positive aspects of Turkish manners and religion, her letter to Abbé Conti overturns contemporary Western misconceptions of the Moslem religion and condemns the "quackery of all churches." The letter to the countess of Bristol, discussing Turkish government and court life, critiques the tiresome "forms and ceremonies" expected of foreign ambassadors and of court life in general. In a letter to her sister, Lady Mary shows her flair for vivid detail as she describes the Turkish dress she adopts and the customs and conduct that Turkish women observe with regard to marriage vows, infidelity, divorce, wealth, and property. While she declares that the Turkish women are "the only free people in the Empire," she thoughtlessly ignores women of other classes or lower stations. The letter to Alexander Pope is a continuation of a game of poetic seduction in which the two have been engaged—exchanging, translating, revising, and rewriting love poems—since Lady Mary left for the Orient. Filled with poetry—her own and that of a Turkish prince—she refutes the notion that Turkish poetry is inferior, finding the poems of Ibrahim Bassa very much like the verses of the Song of Solomon.[6] The final selection, addressed to Sarah Chiswell, her childhood friend, shows Lady Mary's humanitarianism. In this letter she tells how smallpox, so fatal in England and the disease that horribly scarred her face for life, "is here entirely harmless, by the invention of *engrafting*" (an early form of vaccination whereby the smallpox virus is implanted in four or five veins). She vows to try it on her own son and to bring it to England on her return; Chiswell died of smallpox in 1726.

After they returned from Turkey in 1718, Lady Mary lived apart from Wortley, settling in a house near Alexander Pope in Twickenham, on the Thames. But the close relationship between the two soon deteriorated, and they began to attack each other in poems and squibs, sharp, witty verbal attacks. Pope lampooned Lady Mary as the "pox'd Sappho" and "lewd lesbia" in his "Capon's Tale." She retaliated, in "Verses Addressed to the Imitator of Horace, by a Lady," with scathing lines on his crooked mind and crooked back.

In 1739 Lady Mary traveled to Italy, hoping to establish a residence with Francesco Algarotti, an Italian scientist with whom she had fallen in love. Both the affair and her health failing, she embarked on a series of extensive travels that took her from Italy to Switzerland, France, Germany, and Holland. She returned to England after an absence of twenty-three years when her husband died in 1761. Stopping at Rotterdam, she left her *Letters* with the Reverend Benjamin Sowden, "to be disposed of as he thinks proper. This is the will and design of M. Wortley Montagu."[7]

After Lady Mary's death in 1762 her daughter, Lady Bute, burned all her mother's diaries and journals. Only the *Letters*, written between August 1716 and November 1718, were saved. To avoid their publication, Lady Bute and her husband bought the manuscript from Sowden for £500. They were shocked when the *Letters* appeared in the *London Chronicle* in 1763. Two Englishmen had borrowed the letters and had copied and published them.

There is clear evidence of the accomplished writer in the *Letters*. Lady Mary had been creating poems since the age of fourteen and is credited with numerous political and social essays, town eclogues, translations, criticism, satirical works, and poetry volumes. This superior writing talent, coupled with her privileged status and gender, allows Lady Mary to introduce a new type of "exotic" subgenre with bold new elements into the travel literature of the eighteenth-century British canon. The *Letters,* however, are not "the original letters sent to various correspondents during Wortley's embassy. Lady Mary polished copies of these original letters after her return, perhaps revising (in the senses both of re-writing and re-seeing) them extensively in the course of her long life" (Lew 433). These selections show Lady Mary as elitist and humanitarian, as poet and critic, as deeply interested in philosophy as she is preoccupied with court dress and intrigue. She is to be acknowledged for her attempts to mediate differences "after encountering an Ottoman empire that tolerated the social mixture of multinational, multiethnic, and multireligious populations in a manner that would have bewildered the still provincial English" (Aravamudan 92).

TEXT: Lady Mary Wortley Montagu's *Letters* first appeared in the *London Chronicle* in 1763 and was afterward published the same year by T. Becket and P. A. de Hondt, from which the excerpts are taken. Subsequent editions followed: R. Phillips (1801), Dallaway (1803), Donaldson (1818), Thomas (1861), Halsband (1965–1967), Pick (1988), Everyman (1992), and Jack (1994). We are indebted to the Beinecke Rare Book and Manuscript Library for the copyflow prints of the Montagu microfilm. The letters excerpted are from volume one, pages 157–165, and volume two, pages 1–63.

ଔ ౙ

LETTER XXVI.
To Lady ———.[8]
Adrianople, April 1, O.S. 1717.

I am now got into a new world, where every thing I see, appears to me a change of scene; and I write to your ladyship with some content of mind, hoping, at least, that you will find the charm of novelty in my letters, and no longer reproach me, that I tell you nothing extraordinary. I won't trouble you with a relation of our tedious journey; but I must not omit what I saw remarkable at *Sophia,*[9] one of the most beautiful towns in the Turkish Empire, and famous for its hot baths, that are resorted to both for diversion and health. I stop'd here one day, on purpose to see them; and designing to go *incognito,* I hired a Turkish coach. The voitures [i.e., carriages] are not at all like ours, but much more convenient for the country, the heat being so great that glasses [i.e., windows] would be very troublesome. They are made a good deal in the manner of the Dutch stage coaches, having wooden lattices painted and gilded; the inside being also painted with baskets and nosegays of flowers, intermixed commonly with little poetical motto's. They are covered all over with scarlet cloth, lined with silk, and very often richly embroidered and fringed. This covering entirely hides the persons in them, but may be thrown back at pleasure, and thus permit the ladies to peep through the lattices. They hold four people very conveniently, seated on cushions, but not raised.

In one of these covered waggons, I went to the *Bagnio* about ten a clock. It was already full of women. It is built of a stone, in the shape of a dome, with no windows but in the roof, which gives light enough. There were five of these domes joined together, the outmost being less than the rest, and serving only as a hall, where the *Portress* stood at the door. Ladies of quality generally give this woman a crown or ten shillings, and I did not forget that ceremony. The next room is a very large one, paved with marble, and all round it are two raised Sofas of marble, one above another. There were four fountains of cold water in this room, falling first into marble basons, and then running on the floor in little channels made for that purpose, which carried the streams into the next room, something less than this, with the same sort of marble Sofas, but so hot with steams of sulphur proceeding from the baths joining to it, 'twas impossible to stay there with one's cloaths on. The two other domes were the hot baths, one of which had cocks[10] of cold water turning into it, to temper it to what degree of warmth the bathers pleased to have.

I was in my travelling habit, which is a riding dress, and certainly appeared very extraordinary to them. Yet there was not one of them that shewed the least surprize or impertinent curiosity, but received me with all the obliging civility possible. I know no European court, where the ladies would have behaved themselves in so polite a manner to such a stranger. I believe, upon the whole, there were two hundred women, and yet none of those disdainful smiles, and satyrical whispers, that never fail in our assemblies, when any body appears that is not dressed exactly in the fashion. They repeated over and over to me: "UZELLE, PEK, UZELLE," which is nothing but, *"Charming, very charming."*—The first Sofas were covered with cushions and rich carpets, on which sat the ladies; and on the second, their slaves behind them, but without any distinction of rank by their dress, all being in the state of nature, that is, in plain English, stark naked, without any beauty or defect concealed. Yet there was not the least wanton smile or immodest gesture amongst them. They walked and moved with the same majestic grace, which Milton describes our General Mother with. There were many amongst them, as exactly proportioned as ever any goddess was drawn by the pencil of a Guido[11] or Titian,[12]—And most of their skins shiningly white, only adorned by their beautiful hair, divided into many tresses, hanging on their shoulders, braided either with pearl or ribbon, perfectly representing the figures of the graces.

I was here convinced of the truth of a reflection I have often made, *that if it were the fashion to go naked, the face would be hardly observed.* I perceived that the ladies of the most delicate skins and finest shapes, had the greatest share of my admiration, though their faces were sometimes less beautiful than those of their companions. To tell you the truth, I had wickedness enough, to wish secretly, that Mr. *Gervais*[13] could have been there invisible. I fancy it would have very much improved his art, to see so many fine women naked, in different postures, some in conversation, some working, other drinking coffee or sherbet, and many negligently lying on their cushions, while their slaves (generally pretty girls of seventeen, or eighteen) were employ'd in braiding their hair in several pretty fancies. In short, 'tis the women's coffee-house, where all the news of the town is told, scandal invented, &c.—They generally take this diversion once a week, and stay there at least four or five hours, without getting cold, by immediate coming out of the hot-bath into the cool room, which was very surprizing to me. The lady, that seemed the most considerable amongst them, entreated me to sit by her, and would fain have undressed me for the bath. I excused myself with some difficulty. They being however all so earnest in persuading me, I was at last forced to open my shirt, and show them my stays, which satisfied them very well; for, I saw, they believed I was locked up in that machine, and that it was not in my own power to open it, which contrivance they attributed to my husband.—I was charmed with their civility and beauty, and should have been very glad to pass more time with them; but Mr. W—— resolving to pursue his journey the next morning early, I was in haste to see the ruins of Justinian's church,[14] which did not afford me so agreeable a prospect as I had left, being little more than a heap of stones.

Adieu, madam, I am sure I have now entertained you, with an account of such a sight as you never saw in your life, and what no book of travels could inform you of, as 'tis no less than death for a man to be found in one of these places.

LETTER XXVII
To the Abbot ———.[15]

Adrianople, April 1, O.S. 1717.

You see that I am very exact in keeping the promise you engaged me to make. I know not, however, whether your curiosity will be satisfied with the accounts I shall give you, tho' I can assure you, the desire I have to oblige you to the utmost of my power, has made me very diligent in my inquiries, and observations. 'Tis certain we have but very imperfect accounts of the manners and religion of these people. This part of the world being seldom visited, but by merchants, who mind little but their own affairs; or travellers, who make too short a stay to be able to report any thing exactly of their own knowledge. The Turks are too proud to converse familiarly with merchants, who can only pick up some confused informations, which are generally false, and can give no better account of the ways here, than a French Refugée, lodging in a garret in Greek-street,[16] could write of the court of England. The journey we have made from Belgrade[17] hither, cannot possibly be passed by any out of a public character. The desert woods of Servia, are the common refuge of thieves, who rob, fifty in a company, so that we had need of all our guards to secure us; and the villages are so poor, that only force could extort from them necessary provisions. Indeed the Janizaries[18] had no mercy on their poverty, killing all the poultry and sheep they could find, without asking to whom they belonged; while the wretched owners durst not put in their claim for fear of being beaten. Lambs just fallen, geese and turkies big with egg, all massacred without distinction! I fancied I heard the complaints of *Melibeus,*[19] for the hope of his flock. When the Bassas[20] travel, 'tis yet worse. Those oppressors are not content, with eating all that is to be eaten belonging to the peasants; after they have crammed themselves and their numerous retinue, they have the impudence to exact what they call *Teeth-money,* a contribution for their use of their teeth, worn with doing them the honour of devouring their meat. This is literally and exactly true, however extravagant it may seem; and such is the natural corruption of a military government, their religion not allowing of this barbarity, any more than our does.

I had the advantage of lodging three weeks at Belgrade, with a principal Effendi, that is to say, a scholar. This set of men are equally capable of preferments in the law or the church; those two sciences being cast into one, and a lawyer and a priest being the same word in the Turkish language. They are the only men really considerable in the Empire, all the profitable employments and church revenues are in their hands. The Grand Signior,[21] though general heir to his people, never presumes to touch their lands or money, which go, in an uninterrupted succession, to their children. 'Tis true, they lose this privilege, by accepting a place at court, or the title of Bassa; but there are few examples of such fools among them. You may easily judge of the power of these men, who have engrossed all the learning, and almost all the wealth of the Empire. 'Tis they that are the real authors, tho' the soldiers are the actors, of revolutions. They deposed the late Sultan *Mustapha*,[22] and their power is so well known, that 'tis the Emperor's interest to flatter them.

This is a long digression. I was going to tell you, that an intimate, daily conversation with the Effendi *Achmet-beg*, gave me an opportunity of knowing their religion and morals in a more particular manner than perhaps any Christian ever did. I explained to him the difference between the religion of England and Rome; and he was pleased to hear there were Christians, that did not worship images, or adore the Virgin *Mary*. The ridicule of *Transubstantiation*[23] appeared very strong to him.— Upon comparing our creeds together, I am convinced that if our friend Dr. ———[24] had free liberty of preaching here, it would be very easy to persuade the generality to Christianity, whose notions are very little different from his. Mr. *Whiston*[25] would make a very good Apostle here. I don't doubt but his zeal will be much fired, if you communicate this account to him; but tell him, he must first have the gift of tongues, before he can possibly be of any use.— Mahometism is divided into as many sects as Christianity, and the first institution as much neglected, and obscured by interpretations. I cannot here forbear reflecting on the natural inclination of mankind, to make mysteries and novelties.— The *Zeidi, Kudi, Jabari*, &c.[26] put me in mind of the *Catholics, Lutherans*, and *Calvinists*, and are equally zealous against one another. But the most prevailing opinion, if you search into the secret of the Effendi's, is plain Deism.[27] This is indeed kept from the people, who are amused with a thousand different notions, according to the different interest of their preachers.— There are very few amongst them (*Achmet-beg* denied there were any) so absurd, as to set up for wit, by declaring they believe no God at all. And Sir *Paul Rycaut*[28] is mistaken (as he commonly is) in calling the sect *Muterin* (i.e. *the secret with us*) Atheists, they being Deists, whose impiety consists in making a jest of their prophet. *Achmet-beg* did not own to me, that he was of this opinion, but made no scruple of deviating from some part of Mahomet's law, by drinking wine with the same freedom we did. When I asked him how he came to allow himself that liberty; he made answer, That all the creatures of God are good, and designed for the use of man; however, that the prohibition of wine was a very wise maxim, and meant for the common people, being the source of all disorders amongst them; but that the prophet never designed to confine those that knew how to use it with moderation; nevertheless, he said, that scandal ought to be avoided, and that he never drank it in public. This is the general way of thinking amongst them, and very few forbear drinking wine, that are able to afford it. He assured me, that if I understood Arabic, I should be very well pleased with reading the Alcoran,[29] which is so far from the nonsense we charge it with, that 'tis the purest morality, delivered in the very best language. I have since heard impartial Christians speak of it in the same manner; and I don't doubt but that all our translations are from copies got from the Greek priests, who would not fail to falsify it with the extremity of malice. No body of men ever were more ignorant, or more corrupt; yet they differ so little from the Romish[30] Church, that, I confess, nothing gives me a greater abhorrence of the cruelty of your clergy, than the barbarous persecution of them, whenever they have been their masters, for no other reason, than their not acknowledging the Pope. The dissenting in that one article, has got them the titles of Heretics, and Schismatics; and what is worse, the same treatment. I found at Phillippopolis,[31] a sect of Christians that call themselves *Paulines*. They shew an old church where, they say, St. *Paul* preached, and he is their favourite Saint, after the same manner as St. *Peter* is at Rome; neither do they forget to give him the same preference over the rest of the Apostles.

But of all the religions I have seen, that of the *Arnounts*[32] seems to me the most particular; they are natives of *Arnountlich*, the antient *Macedonia*, and still retain the courage and hardiness, tho' they have lost the name of Macedonians, being the best militia in the Turkish Empire, and the only check upon the Janizaries. They are foot soldiers; we had a guard of them, relieved in every considerable town we passed; they are all cloathed and armed at their own expence, dressed in clean white coarse cloth, carrying guns of a prodigious length, which they run with upon their shoulders, as if they did not feel the weight of them, the leader singing a sort of rude tune, not unpleasant, and the rest making up the chorus. These people living between Christians and Mahometans, and not being skilled in controversy, declare, that they are utterly unable to judge which religion is best; but to be certain of not entirely rejecting the truth, they very prudently follow both. They go to the mosques on Fridays, and to the church on Sunday, saying for their excuse, that at the day of judgment they are sure of protection from the true prophet; but which that is, they are not able to determine in this world. I believe there is no other race of mankind, who have so modest an opinion of their own capacity.

These are the remarks I have made, on the diversity of religions I have seen. I don't ask your pardon for the liberty I have taken in speaking of the Roman. I know you equally condemn the quackery of all churches, as much as you revere the sacred truths, in which we both agree.

You will expect I should say something to you of the antiquities of this country, but there are few remains of antient Greece. We passed near the piece of an arch which is commonly call *Trajan's gate*, from a supposition that he made it to shut up the passage over the mountains, between Sophia and Phillippopolis. But I rather believe it the remains of some triumphal arch (though I could not see any inscription;) for if that passage had been shut up, there are many others, that would serve for the march of an army; and notwithstanding the story of *Baldwin* Earl of Flanders,[33] being overthrown in these straits, after he won Constantinople, I don't fancy the Germans would find themselves stopped by them at this day. 'Tis true, the road is now made (with great industry) as commodious as possible, for the march of the Turkish army; there is not one ditch or puddle between this place and Belgrade, that has not a large strong bridge of planks built over it; but the precipices are not so terrible as I had heard them represented. At these mountains, we lay at the little village Kiskoi,[34] wholly inhabited by Christians, as all the peasants of Bulgaria are. Their houses are nothing but little huts, raised of dirt baked in the sun, and they leave them and fly into the mountains, some months before the march of the Turkish army, who would else entirely ruin them, by driving away their whole flocks. This precaution secures them in a sort of plenty; for such vast tracts of land lying in common, they have the liberty of sowing what they please, and are generally very industrious husbandmen. I drank here several sorts of delicious wine. The women dress themselves in a great variety of coloured glass-beads, and are not ugly, but of tawney complexions. I have now told you all, that is worth telling you, and perhaps more, relating to my journey. When I am at Constantinople, I'll try to pick up some curiosities, and then you shall hear again from,

Yours, &c.[35]

LETTER XXVIII.
To the Countess of B——.[36]

Adrianople, April 1, O. S. 171[7].

As I never can forget the smallest of your ladyship's commands, my first business here, has been to enquire after the stuffs [i.e., fabrics], you ordered me to look for, without being able to find what you would like. The difference of the dress here and at London is so great, the same sort of things are not proper for *Caftans* and *Manteaus*.³⁷ However, I will not give over my search, but renew it again at Constantinople, though I have reason to believe there is nothing finer than what is to be found here, as this place is at present the residence of the court. The Grand Signior's eldest daughter was married some few days before I came hither, and upon that occasion the Turkish Ladies display all their magnificence. The bride was conducted to her husband's house in very great splendor. She is widow of the later Vizier, who was killed at Peterwaradin,³⁸ though that ought rather to be called a *contract*, than a *marriage*, since she never has lived with him; however, the greatest part of his wealth is hers. He had the permission of visiting her in the Seraglio; and being one of the handsomest men in the Empire, had very much engaged her affections— When she saw this second husband, who is at least fifty, she could not forbear bursting into tears. He is indeed a man of merit, and the declared favorite of the Sultan, (which they call *Mosayp*) but that is not enough to make him pleasing in the eyes of a girl of thirteen.

The government here is entirely in the hands of the army. The Grand Signior, with all his absolute power, is as much a slave as any of his subjects, and trembles at a Janizary's frown. Here is, indeed, a much greater appearance of subjection than amongst us; a minister of state is not spoke to, but upon the knee; should a reflection on his conduct be dropped in a coffee-house (for they have spies every where) the house would be raz'd to the ground, and perhaps the whole company put to the torture. No *huzzaing mobs, senseless pamphlets, and tavern disputes about politics;*

A consequential ill that freedom draws;
A bad effect,—but from a noble cause.³⁹

None of our harmless calling names! but when a minister here displeases the people, in three hours time he is dragged even from his master's arms. They cut off his hands, head and feet, and throw them before the palace gate, with all the respect in the world; while the Sultan (to whom they all profess an unlimited adoration) sits trembling in his apartment, and dare neither defend nor revenge his favorite. This is the blessed condition of the most absolute monarch upon earth, who owns no *Law* but his *Will*.

I cannot help wishing, in the loyalty of my heart, that the Parliament would send hither a ship load of your passive-obedient men, that they might see arbitrary government in its clearest strongest light, where 'tis hard to judge, whether the Prince, People, or Ministers, are most miserable. I could make many reflections on this subject; but I know, Madam, your own good sense, has already furnished you with better than I am capable of.

I went yesterday with the French Ambassadress[40] to see the Grand Signior in his passage to the Mosque. He was preceded by a numerous guard of Janizaries, with vast white feathers on their heads, as also by the *Spahis* and *Bostangees,* (these are foot and horse guards) and Royal Gardeners, which are a very considerable body of men, dressed in different habits of fine lively colours, so that, at a distance, they appeared like a parterre[41] of tulips. After them the Aga of the Janizaries, in a robe of purple velvet, lined with silver tissue, his horse led by two slaves richly dressed. Next him the *Kyzlier-Aga,* (your ladyship knows, this is the chief guardian of the Seraglio Ladies) in a deep yellow cloth (which suited very well to his black face) lined with sables. Last came his *Sublimity* himself, arrayed in green, lined with the fur of a black Muscovite fox, which is supposed worth a thousand pounds sterling, and mounted on a fine horse, with furniture embroidered with jewels. Six more horses richly caparisoned [i.e., furnished] were led after him; and two of his principal courtiers bore, one his gold, and the other his silver coffee-pot, on a staff; another carried a silver stool on his head, for him to sit on.— It would be too tedious to tell your ladyship, the various dresses and turbants by which their rank is distinguished; but they were all extremely rich and gay, to the number of some thousands; so that perhaps there cannot be seen a more beautiful procession. The Sultan appeared to us a handsome man of about forty, with something, however, severe in his countenance, and his eyes very full and black. He happened to stop under the window where we stood, and (I suppose being told who we were) looked upon us very attentively, so that we had full leisure to consider him. The French Ambassadress agreed with me as to his good mien: I see that lady very often; she is young, and her conversation would be a great relief to me, if I could persuade her to live without those forms and ceremonies that make life formal and tiresome. But she is so delighted with her guards, her four and twenty footmen, gentlemen-ushers, &c. that she would rather die than make me a visit without them; not to reckon a coachful of attending damsels yclep'd [i.e., called] maids of honour. What vexes me is, that as long as she will visit me with a troublesome equipage, I am obliged to do the same; however, our mutual interest makes us much together. I went with her the other day all round the town, in an open gilt chariot, with our joint train of attendants, preceded by our guards, who might have summoned the people to see what they had never seen, nor ever perhaps would see again, two young Christian Ambassadresses at the same time. Your ladyship may easily imagine, we drew a vast crowd of spectators, but all silent as death. If any of them had taken the liberties of our mobs upon any strange sight, our Janizaries had made no scruple of falling on them with their scymitars, without danger for so doing, being above law. These people however (I mean the Janizaries) have some good qualities; they are very zealous and faithful where they serve, and look upon it as their business to fight for you on all occasions. Of this I had a very pleasant instance in a village on this side Phillippopolis, where we were met by our domestic guards. I happened to bespeak pigeons for supper, upon which one of my Janizaries went immediately to the *Cadi* (the chief civil officer of the town) and ordered him to send in some dozens. The poor man answered, that he had already sent about, but could get none. My Janizary, in the height of his zeal for my service, immediately locked him up prisoner in his room, telling him he deserved death for his impudence, in offering to excuse his not obeying my command; but, out of respect to me, he would not punish him but by my order. Accordingly he came very gravely to me, to ask what should be done to him; adding, by way of compliment, that if I pleased he would bring me his head.— This may give you some idea of the unlimited power of these fellows, who are all sworn brothers, and bound to revenge the injuries done to one another, whether at Cairo, Aleppo,[42] or any part of the world. This inviolable league makes them so powerful, that the greatest man at court never speaks to them, but in a flattering tone; and in Asia, any man that is rich, is forced to enroll himself a Janizary to secure his estate.— But I have already said enough, and I dare swear, dear Madam, that, by this time, 'tis a very comfortable reflection to you, that there is no possibility of your receiving such a tedious letter but once in six months; 'tis that consideration has given me the assurance of entertaining you so long, and will, I hope, plead the excuse of, dear Madam,

Yours, &c.

LETTER XXIX
To the Countess of ————.[43]

Adrianople, April 1, O.S. 1717.

I wish to God, dear sister, that you were as regular in letting me know what passes on your side of the globe, as I am careful in endeavouring to amuse you by the account of all I see here, that I think worth your notice. You content yourself with telling me over and over, that the town is very dull; it may, possibly, be dull to you, when every day does not present you with something new; but for me, that am in arrears, at least two months news, all that seems very stale with you, would be very fresh and sweet here. Pray let me into more particulars, and I will try to awaken your gratitude, by giving you a full and true relation of the novelties of this place, none of which would surprize you more than a sight of my person, as I am now in my Turkish habit, though I believe you would be of my opinion, that 'tis admirably becoming.— I intend to send you my picture; in the mean time accept of it here.

The first part of my dress is a pair of drawers, very full, that reach to my shoes, and conceal the legs more modestly than your petticoats. They are of a thin rose coloured damask, brocaded with silver flowers. My shoes are of white kid leather, embroidered with gold. Over this hangs my smock, of a fine white silk gauze, edged with embroidery. This smock has wide sleeves, hanging half-way down the arm, and is closed at the neck with a diamond button; but the shape and colour of the bosom is very well to be distinguished through it.— The *Antery* is a waistcoat, made close to the shape, of white and gold damask, with very long sleeves falling back, and fringed with deep gold fringe, and should have diamond or pearl buttons. My *Caftan,* of the same stuff with my drawers, is a robe exactly fitted to my shape and reaching to my feet, with very long straight falling sleeves. Over this is the girdle, of about four fingers broad, which, all that can afford it, have entirely of diamonds or other precious stones; those, who will not be at that expence, have it of exquisite embroidery on sattin; but it must be fastened before with a clasp of diamonds.— The *Curdée* is a loose robe they throw off, or put on, according to the weather, being of a rich brocade (mine is green and gold) either lined with ermine or sables; the sleeves reach very little below the shoulders. The headdress is composed of a cap, called *Talpock,* which is, in winter, of fine velvet embroidered with pearls or diamonds, and, in summer, of a light shining silver stuff. This is fixed on one side of the head, hanging a little way down with a gold tassel, and bound on, either with a circle of diamonds (as I have seen several) or a rich embroidered handkerchief. On the other side of the head, the hair is laid flat; and here the ladies are at liberty to show their fancies; some putting flowers, others a plume of heron's feathers, and, in short, what they please; but the most general fashion is, a large *Bouquet* of jewels, made like natural flowers, that is, the *buds* of pearl; the *roses* of different coloured rubies; the *jessamines* of diamonds; the *jonquils* of topazes, &c. so well set and enamelled, 'tis hard to imagine any thing of that kind so beautiful. The hair hangs at its full length behind, divided into tresses braided with pearl or ribbon, which is always in great quantity. I never saw in my life, so many fine heads of hair. In one lady's I have counted a hundred and ten of the tresses, all natural; but it must be owned, that every kind of beauty is more common here than with us. 'Tis surprising to see a young woman that is not very handsome. They have naturally the most beautiful complexions in the world, and generally large black eyes. I can assure you with great truth, that the court of England (though I believe it the fairest in Christendom) does not contain so many beauties as are under our protection here. They generally shape their eyebrows, and both Greeks and Turks have the custom of putting round their eyes a black tincture, that, at distance, or by candle light, adds very much to the blackness of them. I fancy many of our ladies would be overjoyed to know this secret; but 'tis too visible by day. They dye their nails a rose-colour; but I own, I cannot enough accustom myself to this fashion, to find any beauty in it.

As to their morality or good conduct, I can say, like Harlequin, that 'tis just as 'tis with you;[44] and the Turkish ladies don't commit one sin the less for not being Christians. Now that I am a little acquainted with their ways, I cannot forbear admiring, either the exemplary discretion, or extreme stupidity of all the writers that have given accounts of them. 'Tis very easy to see, they have in reality more liberty than we have. No woman, of what rank soever, is permitted to go into the streets without two *Murlins,* one that covers her face, all but her eyes; and another, that hides the whole dress of her head, and hangs half way down her back. Their shapes are also wholly concealed, by a thing they call a *Ferigee,* which no woman of any sort appears without; this has straight sleeves, that reach to their fingers ends, and it laps all round them, not unlike a riding-hood. In winter, 'tis of cloth; and in summer, of plain stuff or silk. You may guess then, how effectually this disguises them, so that there is no distinguishing the great lady from her slave. 'Tis impossible for the most jealous husband to know his wife, when he meets her, and no man dare touch or follow a woman in the street.

This perpetual masquerade gives them entire liberty of following their inclinations without danger of discovery. The most usual method of intrigue is, to send an appointment to the lover to meet the lady at a Jews shop, which are as notoriously convenient as our Indian-houses;[45] and yet, even those who don't make use of them, do not scruple to go to buy penny-worths, and tumble over rich goods, which are chiefly to be found amongst that sort of people. The great ladies seldom let their gallants know who they are; and 'tis so difficult to find it out, that they can very seldom guess at her name, whom they have corresponded with for above half a year together. You may easily imagine the number of faithful wives very small in a country where they have nothing to fear from a lover's indiscretion, since we see so many have the courage to expose themselves to that in this world, and all the threatned punishment of the next, which is never preached to the Turkish damsels. Neither have they much to apprehend from the resentment of their husbands; those ladies that are rich, having all their money in their own hands. Upon the whole, I look upon the Turkish women, as the only free people in the Empire; the very Divan[46] pays a respect to them, and the Grand Signior himself, when a *Bassa* is executed, never violates the privileges of the *Haram*, (or womens apartment) which remains unsearched and entire to the widow. They are Queens of their slaves, whom the husband has no permission so much as to look upon, except it be an old woman or two that his lady chuses. 'Tis true, their law permits them four wives, but there is no instance of a man of quality that makes use of this liberty, or of a woman of rank that would suffer it. When a husband happens to be inconstant (as those things will happen) he keeps his mistress in a house apart, and visits her as privately as he can, just as 'tis with you. Amongst all the great men here, I only know the *Testerdar (i. e.* Treasurer) that keeps a number of she-slaves, for his own use, (that is, on his own side of the house, for a slave once given to serve a lady, is entirely at her disposal) and he is spoke of as a libertine, or what we should call a rake; and his wife won't see him, though she continues to live in his house. Thus you see, dear sister, the manners of mankind do not differ so widely, as our voyage writers would make us believe. Perhaps, it would be more entertaining to add a few surprizing customs of my own invention; but nothing seems to me so agreeable as truth, and I believe nothing so acceptable to you. I conclude therefore, with repeating the great truth of my being,

Dear Sister, &c.

LETTER XXX
To Mr. Pope.[47]

Adrianople, April 1, o.s. [1717]

I dare say you expect, at least, something very new in this letter, after I have gone a journey, not undertaken, by any Christian, for some hundred years. The most remarkable accident that happened to me, was my being very near over-turned into the Hebrus;[48] and, if I had much regard for the glories that one's name enjoys after death, I should certainly be sorry for having missed the romantic conclusion of swimming down the same river in which the musical head of *Orpheus*[49] repeated verses, so many ages since:

> "*Caput a cervice revulsum,*
> "*Gurgite cum medio, portans O agrius Hebrus*
> "*Volveret, Euridicen vox ipsa, et frigida lingua.*
> "*Ah! miseram Euridicen! anima fugiente vocabat,*
> "*Euridicen toto referebant flumine ripae.*"[50]

Who knows but some of your bright wits, might have found it a subject affording many poetical turns, and have told the world, in an heroic Elegy, that,

> As equal were our souls, so equal were our fates.

I despair of ever hearing so many fine things said of me, as so extraordinary a death would have given occasion for.

I am at this present moment writing in a house situated on the banks of the Hebrus, which runs under my chamber window. My garden is full of tall cypress trees upon the branches of which, several couple of true turtles[51] are saying soft things to one another from morning till night. How naturally do *boughs* and *vows* come into my mind, at this minute? And must not you confess, to my praise, that 'tis more than an ordinary discretion, that can resist the wicked suggestions of poetry, in a place where truth, for once, furnishes all the ideas of pastoral. The summer is already far advanced, in this part of the world; and for some miles around Adrianople, the whole ground is laid out in gardens, and the banks of the rivers are set with rows of fruit trees, under which all the most considerable Turks divert themselves every evening, not with walking, that is not one of their pleasures; but a set party of them choose out a green spot, where the shade is very thick, and there they spread a carpet, on which they sit drinking their coffee, and are generally attended by some slave with a fine voice, or that plays on some instrument. Every twenty paces you may see one of these little companies, listening to the dashing of the river; and this taste is so universal, that the very gardeners are not without it. I have often seen them and their children sitting on the banks of the river, and playing on a rural instrument, perfectly answering the description of the ancient *Fistula*, being composed of unequal reeds, with a simple but agreeable softness in the sound.

Mr. *Addison*[52] might here make the experiment he speaks of in his travels; there not being one instrument of music among the Greek or Roman Statues, that is not to be found in the hands of the people of this country. The young lads generally divert themselves with making garlands for their favourite lambs, which I have often seen painted and adorned with flowers, lying at their feet, while they sung or played. It is not that they ever read Romances. But these are the ancient amusements here, and as natural to them as cudgel-playing and foot-ball to our British swains; the softness and warmth of the climate forbidding all rough exercises, which were never so much as heard of amongst them, and naturally inspiring a laziness and aversion to labour, which the great plenty indulges. These gardeners are the only happy race of country people in Turkey. They furnish all the city with fruit and herbs, and seem to live very easily. They are most of them Greeks, and have little houses in the midst of their gardens, where their wives and daughters take a liberty, not permitted in the town, I mean to go unveiled. These wenches are very neat and handsome, and pass their time at their looms under the shade of their trees.

I no longer look upon *Theocritus*[53] as a romantic writer;[54] he has only given a plain image of the way of life amongst the peasants of his country; who, before oppression had reduced them to want, were, I suppose, all employed as the better sort of them are now. I don't doubt, had he been born a Briton, but his *Idylliums* had been filled with descriptions of thrashing and churning, both which are unknown here, the corn being all trod out by oxen; and butter (I speak it with sorrow) unheard of.

I read over your *Homer*[55] here, with an infinite pleasure, and find several little passages explained, that I did not before entirely comprehend the beauty of: Many of the customs, and much of the dress then in fashion, being yet retained, I don't wonder to find more remains here, of an age so distant, than is to be found in any other country, the Turks not taking that pains to introduce their own manners, as has been generally practised by other nations, that imagine themselves more polite. It would be too tedious to you to point out all the passages that relate to present customs. But I can assure you, that the Princesses and great ladies pass their time at their looms, embroidering veils and robes, surrounded by their maids, which are always very numerous, in the same manner as we find *Andromache* and *Helen* described. The description of the belt of *Menelaus*,[56] exactly resembles those that are now worn by the great men, fastened before with broad golden clasps, and embroidered round with rich work. The snowy veil, that *Helen* throws over her face, is still fashionable; and I never see half a dozen of old Bashaws (as I do very often) with their reverend beards,

sitting basking in the sun, but I recollect good King *Priam*[57] and his coun-
sellors. Their manner of dancing is certainly the same that *Diana*[58] is *sung*
to have danced on the banks of *Eurotas.*[59] The great lady still leads the
dance, and is followed by a troop of young girls, who imitate her steps,
and, if she sings, make up the chorus. The tunes are extreme gay and
lively, yet with something in them wonderfully soft. The steps are varied
according to the pleasure of her that leads the dance, but always in exact
time, and infinitely more agreeable than any of our dances, at least in my
opinion. I sometimes make one in the train, but am not skilful enough to
lead; these are the Grecian dances, the Turkish being very different.

I should have told you, in the first place, that the Eastern manners[60]
give a great light into many Scripture-passages, that appear odd to us, their
phrases being commonly what we should call Scripture language. The
vulgar Turk is very different from what is spoke at court, or amongst the
people of figure; who always mix so much Arabic and Persian in their
discourse, that it may very well be called another language. And 'tis as
ridiculous to make use of the expressions commonly used, in speaking to
a great man or lady, as it would be to speak broad Yorkshire, or Somersetshire, in the drawing-room. Besides this distinction, they have what
they call, the *sublime,* that is, a stile proper for poetry, and which is the
exact Scripture stile. I believe you would be pleased to see a genuine
example of this; and I am very glad I have it in my power to satisfy your
curiosity, by sending you a faithful copy of the verses that *Ibrahim Bassa,*
the reigning favourite, has made for the young Princess, his contracted
Wife, whom he is not yet permitted to visit without witnesses, though
she is gone home to his house. He is a man of wit and learning; and
whether or no he is capable of writing good verse, you may be sure that,
on such an occasion, he would not want the assistance of the best poets
in the Empire. Thus the verses may be looked upon as a sample of their
finest poetry, and I don't doubt you'll be of my mind, that it is most
wonderfully resembling the *Song of Solomon,* which was also addressed to
a Royal Bride.

TURKISH VERSES addressed to the *Sultana,*
eldest daughter of SULTAN ACHMET III.

STANZA I.

Ver.   The nightingale now wanders in the vines;
1.   Her passion is to seek roses.

2. I went down to admire the beauty of the vines;
   The sweetness of your charms has ravished my soul.

3. Your eyes are black and lovely,
   But wild and disdainful as those of a stag;

STANZA II.

1. The wished possession is delayed from day to day,
   The cruel Sultan ACHMET will not permit me
   To see those cheeks, more vermillion than roses.

2. I dare not snatch one of your kisses,
   The sweetness of your charms has ravish'd my soul.

3. Your eyes are black and lovely,
   But wild and disdainful as those of a stag.

STANZA III.

1. The wretched IBRAHIM sighs in these verses,
   One dart from your eyes has pierc'd thro' my heart.

2. Ah! when will the hour of possession arrive?
   Must I yet wait a long time?
   The sweetness of your charms has ravished my soul.

3. Ah! SULTANA! stag-ey'd—an angel amongst angels!
   I desire,—and, my desire remains unsatisfied.
   Can you take delight to prey upon my heart?

STANZA IV.

1. My cries pierce the heavens!
   My eyes are without sleep!
   Turn to me, SULTANA—let me gaze on thy beauty.

2. Adieu—I go down to the grave.
   If you call me—I return.
   My heart is—hot as sulphur;—sigh and it will flame.

3. Crown of my life, fair light of my eyes!
      My SULTANA! my princess!
   I rub my face against the earth;—I am drown'd in scalding tears—
      I rave!
   Have you no compassion? will you not turn to look upon me.

168 / *Lady Mary Wortley Montagu*

I have taken abundance of pains to get these verses in a literal translation; and if you were acquainted with my interpreters, I might spare myself the trouble of assuring you, that they have received no poetical touches from their hands. In my opinion, (allowing for the inevitable faults of a prose translation into a language so very different) there is a good deal of beauty in them. The epithet of *stag-ey'd* (though the sound is not very agreeable in English) pleases me extremely; and I think it a very lively image of the fire and indifference in his mistress's eyes.— Monsieur *Boileau*[61] has very justly observed, that we are never to judge of the elevation of an expression in an antient author, by the sound it carries with us; since it may be extremely fine with them, when, at the same time, it appears low or uncouth to us. You are so well acquainted with *Homer*, you cannot but have observed the same thing, and you must have the same indulgence for all oriental poetry. The repetitions at the end of the two first Stanza's are meant for a sort of *Chorus*, and are agreeable to the antient manner of writing. The music of the verses apparently changes in the third Stanza, where the burden is altered; and I think he very artfully seems more passionate at the conclusion, as 'tis natural for people to warm themselves by their own discourse, especially on a subject in which one is deeply concerned; 'tis certainly far more touching, than our modern custom of concluding a song of passion, with a turn which is inconsistent with it. The first verse is a description of the season of the year; all the country being now full of Nightingales, whose amours with roses, is an Arabian fable, as well known here, as any part of *Ovid*[62] amongst us, and is much the same as if an English poem should begin, by saying,— *"Now Philomela sings."* Or what if I turned the whole into the stile of English poetry, to see how it would look.

STANZA I.

"Now Philomel renews her tender strain,
"Indulging all the night her pleasing pain;

"I sought the groves to hear the wanton sing,
"There saw a face, more beauteous than the spring.

"Your large stags-eyes where thousand glories play,
"As bright, as lively, but as wild as they.

STANZA II.

"In vain I'm promis'd such a heavenly prize.
"Ah! cruel SULTAN! who delay'st my joys!

"While piercing charms transfix my amorous heart,
"I dare not snatch one kiss, to ease the smart.

"Those eyes like, &c.

STANZA III.
"Your wretched lover in these lines complains;
"From those dear beauties rise his killing pains.

"When will the hour of wished-for bliss arrive?
"Must I wait longer?—Can I wait and live?

"Ah! bright Sultana! Maid divinely fair!
"Can you, unpitying, see the pains I bear?

STANZA IV.
"The Heavens relenting hear my piercing cries,
"I loath the light, and sleep forsakes my eyes,
"Turn thee, Sultana, 'ere thy lover dies;

"Sinking to earth, I sigh the last adieu,
"Call me, my Goddess, and my life renew.

"My Queen! My Angel! My fond heart's desire.
"I rave—my bosom burns with heavenly fire!
"Pity that passion, which thy charms inspire.

I have taken the liberty in the second verse, of following what I suppose the true sense of the author, though not literally expressed. *By his saying he went down to admire the beauty of the Vines, and her charms ravished his soul:* I understand a poetical fiction, of having first seen her in a garden, where he was admiring the beauty of the spring. But I could not forbear retaining the comparison of her eyes with those of a stag, though perhaps the novelty of it may give it a burlesque sound in our language. I cannot determine, upon the whole, how well I have succeeded in the translation, neither do I think our English proper to express such violence of passion, which is very seldom felt amongst us. We want, also, those compound words which are very frequent and strong in the Turkish language.

You see I am pretty far gone in Oriental learning, and to say truth, I study very hard. I wish my studies may give me an occasion of entertaining your curiosity, which will be the utmost advantage hoped for from them, by,

Yours, &c.

LETTER XXXI.
To Mrs. S. C.[63]

Adrianople, April 1, o.s. [1717]

In my opinion, dear S. I ought rather to quarrel with you, for not answering my Nimeguen[64] letter of August, till December, than to excuse my not writing again till now. I am sure there is on my side a very good excuse for silence, having gone such tiresome land-journies, though I don't find the conclusion of them so bad as you seem to imagine. I am very easy here, and not in the solitude you fancy me. The great number of Greeks, French, English and Italians, that are under our protection, make their court to me from morning till night; and I'll assure you, are, many of them, very fine ladies; for there is no possibility for a Christian to live easily under this government, but by the protection of an Ambassador— and the richer they are, the greater is their danger.

Those dreadful stories you have heard of the *Plague*, have very little foundation in truth. I own, I have much ado to reconcile myself to the sound of a word, which has always given me such terrible ideas; though I am convinced there is little more in it, than in a fever. As a proof of this, let me tell you, that we passed through two or three towns most violently infected. In the very next house where we lay, (in one of those places) two persons died of it. Luckily for me, I was so well received, that I knew nothing of the matter; and I was made believe, that our second cook had only a great cold. However, we left our doctor to take care of him, and yesterday they both arrived here in good health; and I am now let into the secret, that he has had the *Plague*. There are many that escape it, neither is the air ever infected. I am persuaded that it would be as easy a matter to root it out here, as out of Italy and France; but it does so little mischief, they are not very solicitous about it, and are contented to suffer this distemper, instead of our variety, which they are utterly unacquainted with.

A propós of distempers, I am going to tell you a thing, that will make you wish yourself here. The *small-pox,* so fatal, and so general amongst us, is here entirely harmless, by the invention of *engrafting*, which is the term they give it. There is a set of old women, who make it their business to perform the operation, every autumn, in the month of September, when the great heat is abated. People send to one another to know if any of their family has a mind to have the small-pox; they make parties for this purpose, and when they are met (commonly fifteen or sixteen together) the old woman comes with a nut-shell full of the matter of the best sort of small-pox, and asks what veins you please to have open'd. She immediately rips open that you offer to her, with a large needle (which gives you no more pain than a common scratch) and puts into the vein, as much matter as can lie upon the head of her needle, and after that, binds up the little wound with a hollow bit of shell, and in this manner opens four or five veins. The Grecians have commonly the superstition of opening one in the middle of the forehead, one in each arm, and one on the breast, to mark the sign of the cross; but this has a very ill effect, all these wounds leaving little scars, and is not done by those that are not superstitious, who chuse to have them in the legs, or that part of the arm that is concealed. The children or young patients play together all the rest of the day, and are in perfect health to the eighth. Then the fever begins to seize them, and they keep their beds two days, very seldom three. They have very rarely above twenty or thirty [smallpox blisters] in their faces, which never mark, and in eight days time they are as well as before their illness. Where they are wounded, there remains running sores during the distemper, which I don't doubt is a great relief to it. Every year thousands undergo this operation, and the French Ambassador says pleasantly, that they take the small-pox here by way of diversion, as they take the waters in other countries. There is no example of any one that has died in it, and you may believe I am well satisfied of the safety of this experiment, since I intend to try it on my dear little son. I am patriot enough to take pains to bring this useful invention into fashion in England, and I should not fail to write to some of our Doctors very particularly about it, if I knew any one of them that I thought had virtue enough to destroy such a considerable branch of their revenue, for the good of mankind. But that distemper is too beneficial to them, not to expose to all their resentment, the hardy wight[65] that should undertake to put an end to it. Perhaps, if I live to return, I may, however, have courage to war with them. Upon this occasion, admire the heroism in the heart of,

Your friend, &c. &c.

Notes

1. Much later Lady Mary wrote an anonymous essay, "On the Mischief of Giving Fortunes with Women in Marriage" (1726), challenging these practices.

2. Richard Knolles wrote *The Turkish History, from the Original of that Nation, to the Growth of the Ottoman Empire* (1687); Sir Paul Rycaut wrote *The Present State of the Ottoman Empire Containing the Maxims of the Turkish Polity* (1686); Aaron Hill wrote *A Full and Just Account of the Present State of the Ottoman Empire in all its Branches* (1709); Jean Dumont wrote *A New Voyage to the Levant* (1705) (Aravamudan nn. 10–12).

3. City in northwestern Turkey near the Greek border.

4. Jean-Auguste-Dominique Ingres's famous painting *Le Bain turc*, completed nearly

a century after *Letters* was published, owes its origins to Lady Mary's "accounts of Turkish women at their bath" (Yeazell 111).

5. For an excellent discussion of the way in which Lady Mary uses the aesthetic, then moves to the political, to create subject positions for the women of the Turkish bagnio, see Bohls, "Aesthetics."

6. A book of the Bible's Old Testament. Like Ibrahim's poem, Solomon's songs are addressed to a royal bride.

7. Annotated in the Malcolm Jack edition of the *Letters:* "From a facsimile of the note written on the cover of the volumes left with Sowden dated 11 December 1761; in *The Works of Lady Mary Wortley Montagu*, ed. I. Dallaway, 5 vols. (London, 1803), 1:30."

8. Most scholars identify the addressee as Lady Rich, Elisabeth Griffin (1692–1773), wife of Sir Robert Rich and lady-in-waiting to Queen Caroline; however, Robert Halsband does not identify the recipient in his edition of the *Letters*.

9. Sofia, the present capital of Bulgaria, captured by the Turks in 1382, after which many buildings were replaced, giving the city an oriental appearance.

10. A spout or short pipe serving as a channel for liquids and having an appliance for regulating or stopping the flow; a tap.

11. Guido Reni (1575–1642), Bolognese painter with 200 to 300 works to his credit, painted Fortuna, goddess of fortune, and Aurora, goddess of dawn.

12. Tiziano Vecelli (1490?–1576). Of the Venetian school, Titian is considered one of the world's greatest painters. Among the many goddesses he painted were Ariadne, Venus, Europa, and Diana.

13. Charles Jervas (1675?–1739), Irish painter and friend of Alexander Pope's.

14. Justinian I (483–565), emperor of the Eastern Roman Empire, A.D. 527–565: known for his legal reforms, empirical administration, and ecclesiastical and foreign policies; he had the giant Hagia Sophia church built with the intent of leaving a lasting legacy.

15. Abbé Antonio Conti (1677–1749), Italian dramatist and scholar.

16. Many French Protestants fled to London in 1685 to avoid persecution when the Edict of Nantes was revoked. They settled in the Soho district of London, in the Greek Street area.

17. Modern day capital of Serbia. Its attractive position had led to numerous conflicts over the city; it was held by the Turks in 1717.

18. An infantry force of Turkish soldiers first organized by Sultan Orhan around 1330. At one time the regular troops numbered 60,000 and the irregular troops 400,000. They became so dangerous that the corps was finally abolished in 1826.

19. From Chaucer's *Canterbury Tales*, the "Tale of Melibeus" relates how Melibeus's enemies break into his house, beat his wife, and kill his daughter. "Whan Melibeus retourned was into his hous, and saugh al this meschief, he, lyk a mad man rentynge his clothes, gan to wepe and crie" (Chaucer 217).

20. A form of "*bashaw*," Turkish for military commander.

21. Sultan Ahmed III, Ottoman emperor 1703–1730.

22. Mustafa II, Ottoman emperor 1695–1703.

23. According to Catholic doctrine, the conversation in the Eucharist of the whole substance of the bread into the body and of the wine into the blood of Christ, only the appearances of bread and wine remaining.

24. Dr. Samuel Clarke (1675–1729), English theological and philosophical writer; author of *A Discourse on Natural Religion*; later appointed chaplain to Queen Anne.

25. William Whiston (1667–1752), English theologian and mathematician; deputy professor of mathematics to Sir Isaac Newton at Cambridge; founded a society for the promotion of primitive Christianity.

26. Various sects of Islam.

27. Belief in God on rational grounds rather than through revelation. During the seventeenth and eighteenth centuries, Deists believed that God created the world and its natural laws and then took no part in its further functioning.

28. Served as a British representative in Constantinople in the mid-seventeenth century. Also see note 2.

29. The Koran, or sacred book of the Moslems, written in Arabic.

30. Roman Catholic.

31. Present-day Plovdiv, Bulgaria, held by the Turks in 1717.

32. Natives of present-day Albania.

33. Baldwin I (1171–1205) led the Fourth Crusade (1202–1204); crowned first Latin emperor of Constantinople; served from 1204 to 1205 before he was defeated by the Greeks and Bulgarians.

34. A small village in the Balkan Mountains near Sofia.

35. It was customary to conclude letters with an elaborate complimentary formula and to indicate the omission of this formula by "&c."

36. Elizabeth Felton, countess of Bristol (1676–1741); close friend of Lady Mary's; second wife of John Hervey, first earl of Bristol.

37. Caftans are long, loose tunics; manteaus are cloaks or women's capes.

38. A city in Serbia; site of the battle where the Austrians routed the Turks in 1716.

39. From *A Portrait of Sir Robert Walpole*, written by Lady Mary and published in 1729.

40. Madeline-Françoise de Gontaut-Biron (1698–1739), wife of the French ambassador Jean Louis d'Usson, marquis of Bonac.

41. Section of a formal garden in which the flowers are arranged in ornamental patterns.

42. Second-largest city in Syria, the mercantile center of the country at the time.

43. Frances Pierrepont, Lady Mar (1690–1761); younger sister of Lady Mary; wife of John Erskine, earl of Mar.

44. In Aphra Behn's *The Emperor of the Moon*, Harlequin announces that morality on the earth and the moon are the same.

45. Shops displaying wares from India.

46. The Turkish Council of State.

47. Alexander Pope (1688–1744), English poet and satirist; at one time a passionate friend and correspondent of Lady Mary's. Pope biographer Maynard Mack, in discussing the breakup of this relationship and the particularly vicious personal attacks that followed, offers a number of possible causes—lack of interest on her part, jealousy on his. For a new reading of this conflict, see Wall. Noting that Pope's letters to Lady Mary "transform the limits" of the tradition of epistolary gallantry "in which elegant sexual innuendo and fantasy create an atmosphere of mock-seduction," Wall argues that Pope's attempts to engage Lady Mary in a literary seduction failed because she refused to be fully engaged; yet he succeeded "precisely because, in the end, Pope [wrote] the real Lady Mary out of the texts in exchange for a more satisfactory poetic reality" (222).

48. The Maritza River.

49. Mythological figure representing excellence in singing and poetry.

50. Lady Mary quotes Virgil's famous passage in which Orpheus's severed head floats down the Hebrus crying for Eurydice.

51. Turtledoves, birds associated with thoughts of love and affection, conjugal fidelity, and purity.

52. Joseph Addison (1672–1719), English essayist who, with Richard Steele, is noted for his political writings in the *Tatler* and the *Spectator*. From 1699 to 1703, Addison traveled through France, Switzerland, Germany, Holland, and Italy. His *Letter from Italy* in verse and his *Remarks on Italy* in prose mark the interest in classical art and literature to which Lady Mary refers.

53. Greek poet; flourished around 280 B.C.; credited with more than thirty idylls, or pastoral poems, some of which are probably by other writers.

54. A writer of romances—tales of wondrous and extraordinary events.

55. Pope's first translation of the *Iliad* appeared in 1715.

56. Mythological figures from Homer's *Iliad*: Andromache was princess of Thebes, wife of the Trojan leader, Hector. After the fall of Troy she was awarded to Achilles' son as a slave and concubine. Helen was daughter of Zeus, queen of Sparta, and wife of Menelaus, who was king of Sparta and brother of Agamemnon.

57. King of Troy when it fell to the Greeks.

58. An ancient Roman goddess of the moon and hunting, associated with Artemis, Apollo's sister. Diana's dances were the subject of poets' songs.

59. Erymanthus, the mythological mountain and river in Arcadia.

60. Oriental laws, manners, and customs as mischaracterized by Westerners.

61. Nicolas Boileau-Despréaux (1636–1711), French writer and critic; his treatise on poetry, *L'Art poétique*, holds a significant place in aesthetics and literary criticism.

62. Roman poet (43 B.C.–17 A.D.) admired for his *Metamorphoses*, as well as his love lyrics.

63. Sarah Chiswell.

64. City in the East Netherlands on the Waal River.

65. Archaic term for creature or person.

Jemima Kindersley

1741–1809

Letters from the Island of Teneriffe, Brazil, the Cape of Good Hope, and the East Indies. London: J. Nourse, 1777.

Very little is known of Jemima Kindersley. Born Jemima Wicksted in 1741, she married Colonel Nathaniel Kindersley of the Bengal Artillery in 1762 at Great Yarmouth. He preceded her to India, and in June 1764 she began the journey to join him of which the *Letters* is a record. The first letter notes her promise to give "a particular account" (1) of everything "worthy of notice" on her journey and in India, and the book is a very detailed record of the manners and customs she encountered during her five-year absence from England. Judging from the *Letters*, she was well educated; she seems familiar with travel literature and with such stalwarts of Enlightenment thought as Montesquieu. Her *Letters* begins with a history of the Canary Islands. As her journey continues she makes observations on the political and social state of Tenerife under Spanish rule and of Brazil under Portuguese rule, and during a five-month stay at the Cape of Good Hope she observed and described the Hottentots. Kindersley arrived at Pondicherry in June 1765, and the remainder of the *Letters* is an exhaustive record of India's history and its current situation, including commentary on the East India Company's government. Her topics range from an English factory for preparing raw silk, to the revolutions whereby Mohammedans became masters of India, to "the pomp of eastern kings!" (213), to the English in India and their way of life (289); she pays particular attention to the lives of Indian women. Kindersley left India in 1769, perhaps with her son, Nathaniel Edward, later an employee of the Madras civil service. In 1781 she published a translation of Antoine Thomas's *Essay on the Character, Manners, and Understanding of Women*, to which she appended two essays of her own defending the capacities of women. She died in 1809.

TEXT: Jemima Kindersley's *Letters* was first published in 1777. The work immediately attracted the disapproving attention of one Reverend Hodgson, who wrote a series of letters to the *London Chronicle* decrying what he considered its dangerous pro-popery propaganda. Excerpted here are six letters (pp. 113–139), written in July 1767 from Allahabad, which give her view of the Hindu religion and caste system.

CR BD

LETTER XXIX.

Allahabad, July 1767

However pure the system of religion might originally be, it is certain the *Hindoos* have no reason, at present, to boast; for the whole of it, at this time, consists in absurd unaccountable ceremonies, which the people do not understand the meaning of; nor, I may venture to say, do many of the *Brahmins* themselves.

The number of holidays their religion commands, engross at least one third part of their time: these days are either feasts or fasts, devoted to some or other of their gods, of whom they tell the most ridiculous stories: there is not a god amongst them but some-how or other has signalized himself on some day, which is kept in remembrance of him: many of them, according to their accounts, have descended on earth on particular occasions.

It is observable, that in all translations from Eastern manuscripts, both antient and modern, the expressions are figurative: the *Shastah*[1] is quite in this stile; the power, wisdom, goodness, and other attributes of the Almighty are emblematically described; the Almighty is represented with many heads, many hands, many eyes; wisdom is depicted in the figure of a snake; and, in short, almost the whole class of animals is taken in to represent some or other of his attributes.

These emblematical figures have furnished them with a set of inferior gods; and, through a long course of time, the extreme ignorance and credulity of the people, and the *Brahmins* keeping the knowledge of the *Shastah* entirely to themselves, are become the essential parts of their worship; and taken, not in a figurative, but a real sense.

They believe, that the god whom they worship, is the god of the *Hindoos*, of the Musselmen,[2] and of the Christians; but that it pleases him to be worshiped different ways; that no one must change his religion, therefore it is a fundamental part of theirs, that no person can become a *Hindoo* but those who are born such.

Whether Pythagoras[3] learned any of his opinions from the *Brahmins*, is, at this distance of time, difficult to determine; but it is certain that the *Hindoos* have similar opinions concerning the transmigration of souls; for which reason, they never eat of any thing which has had life, or ever put any insects, not even those of venomous natures, to death. The effect of this is seen all over the country, particularly in Benaras, a province where only *Hindoos* reside; the animals are so unused to fear the hand of man, that birds of all sorts will walk into the rooms, alight on the tables where people are at meals, and feed out of their hands.

The approach of death is by no means terrible to the *Hindoos*, as the soul is immediately to pass into some other animal. Nevertheless, they have an idea of what we call heaven, where the souls of the virtuous are to be received by the Almighty, after they have gone through an infinite number of transmigrations.

The beast they have the greatest veneration for, and are said to worship, is the cow; these they cherish and guard with particular care. If they can redeem a cow, a bull, or a calf, which is doomed to be slain by Mahomedans or Christians, it is a meritorious act; and this is not unfrequently done.

It would be a vain attempt to enumerate all their superstitious opinions and ceremonies. In some of the fasts they undergo great punishments of their own inflicting, beating themselves with rods of iron, and hanging extended in the air by the flesh of their backs upon iron hooks: but the superior *casts* [i.e., castes] of people neither put themselves to these tortures, or join in the processions, which have all the appearance of a mad rabble running in crouds along the streets, their faces disfigured with marks of *channam*, or red power, which they throw over each other as a sort of compliment or blessing.

The *Brahmins* practise incredible austerities in matters of no importance; at *Benaras* is one who is revered almost as a god, for keeping a vow he had made many years since, never to sit or lay down, but to stand, with his arms extended above his head; it is not known that he has broke through it. This is one instance, amongst many others of similar kinds, and of equal use to society. It would fill a volume, was I to recount a hundredth part of the variety of punishments and tortures the *Brahmins* condemn themselves to.

LETTER XXX.

Allahabad, July 1767

The great virtue of the *Hindoos* is their extensive charity: the *Brahmins* inculcate, with the utmost zeal, the necessity of building and endowing *pagodas* [i.e., temples] (where themselves are maintained in ease and plenty) feeding the hungry, relieving the poor, and providing against the distresses of their fellow-creatures, whether of their own religion or strangers.

They are simple, and temperate in their diet; the common people live cheifly upon rice; their superiors have the addition of *gee*,[4] milk, sweet-meats, &c.; it is surprising to think how little their usual expence is, but still they are not without extravagance, for although they live in this ab-stemious manner, they spend vast sums of money in *tamashes*:[5] this they do on the marriage of their children, or in honour of their gods; all ranks of people have *tamashes*, according to their different abilities; the money spent in them is in lights (for they illuminate the houses in the inside), ornament, music, dancers, and perfumes.

They are mild and inoffensive in their manners, even to timidity, and a dastardly submission to superiors: this is the characteristic of the gener-ality of the *Hindoos*: but the fighting *casts*, the principal of which are the *Rajapoots* and the *Mahrattars*, are an exception to this rule; the last of these are a bold, hardy nation; and the most formidable of any now in *Hin-doston*.[6]

The *Mahrattors* fight chiefly on horse-back, and every man finds [i.e., provides] his own horse: besides the frequent incursions they have made into different parts of the country, under various pretences, on their own account; armies of them sometimes enter into the service of the Maho-medan powers. Notwithstanding the pay they are promised by these pow-ers, and perhaps sometimes receive, their chief aim is plunder; therefore when two armies are engaged, they pour upon the rear of the enemy, amongst the women and baggage, where they cause great confusion, and leave nothing behind them which they can possibly carry off.

They are formidable enemies, but unsteady friends; as they follow the constant maxim of all black powers, changing sides as the face of affairs alters, and never keep to any engagement they enter into if they find it more convenient to break it.

They are excellent horsemen; and curious[7] in their breed of horses, which are much valued all over India, as being uncommonly hardy and very swift.

The *Mahrattors*, though *Hindoos*, differ from the other nations in Hin-dostán, in many material points, and appear to be quite another people; their country is near our settlement of Bombay, on the coast of *Malabár*, but they are scattered across the peninsula almost to the coast of Coro-mandél.

The *Hindoos* never bury their dead; those whose friends can afford the expense are burned; others are thrown into the nearest river; and it is not uncommon for them, when very near their end, to be, by their own desire, carried and laid at the water's edge, especially if the river has any sacred character in the history of their religion, that, when they expire, their bodies may be washed away by the tide. It sometimes happens that the poor creatures lay in this state a day or two; but the apprehension they are under of not being thrown into the river, or their dead bodies being touched by any but those of their own *cast*, makes them readily undergo this punishment.

There is a particular *cast* who always carry their dying parents and relations to the water's edge, and fill their mouths, ears, and noses, with mud, and then leave them to their fate.

LETTER XXXI.

Allahabad, July 1767

The *Hindoo* women we can know little of, as none but the very lowest are visible: they are almost in their infancy married by the care of their parents to some of their own *cast*. Every *Hindoo* is obliged to marry once: and polygamy is allowed, but there is generally one wife who is held as superior to the rest. The women have no education given them, they live retired in the *zanannahs*,[8] and amuse themselves with each other, smoaking the *hooker* [i.e., hookah], bathing, and seeing their servants dance.

There is one well-known circumstance relative to the women, which is the most extraordinary and astonishing custom in the world: I mean their burning themselves with the dead bodies of their husbands: this custom is not at present so frequent as formerly, they cannot burn without permission from the Nabób of the province, and it is much to be hoped, that the English will in future prevent those Nabóbs we are in alliance with, from giving any such permission, but there has been within a very short time at least one instance.

I have endeavoured to find out what could give rise (if you'll permit me the expression)[9] to such a barbarous exertion of virtue; but it is difficult to find out the cause of institutions of so antient a date, therefore I do not depend on either of the following reasons, although they have each their advocates, who insist strongly that their opinion is the right one.

The first is, that it was so common for women to poison their husbands, that this institution was necessary to prevent it.

The other is, that the *Brahmins*, to promote their own interest, first persuaded the women that it was for the ever-lasting good of their families; that their souls would not enter into any groveling insects, but animate a cow, or some such noble animal, and that their term of purgation would be shortened, and they would have the fewer transmigrations to go through, before they become pure enough to be received by the Almighty in Heaven.

Whatever may be the cause, it is however certain, that the *Brahmins* greatly encourage this practice, and that they receive great benefits from it; for the woman, when she is brought out to sacrifice herself, is dressed with all her jewels, which are often of considerable value; when the [funeral] pile is prepared, and the woman has taken leave of her friends, she throws all her ornaments from her, which the priests take for themselves.

It is said, that the strict rule of *casts* is on this occasion sometimes dispensed with; and the daughter of a mother who has burned, may be married to a man of a higher rank.

I cannot myself subscribe to the first opinion of the cause of this custom, because they have many of them more than one wife, and only one is permitted to have the honour of burning.

No people in the world have stricter notions of the honour of their women, particularly those of the higher *casts*. If any one has an improper connexion, such a woman has not only lost her *cast*, but it is an indelible stain upon the honour of her family: and in case of an elopement, it has been known that the girl has been pursued and recovered by her parents, who have put her immediately to death, to expiate, by her blood, part of the disgrace she has brought upon them.

Nevertheless, the retirement of the women does not appear to be a part of the religion, or caused by the jealousy of the men, so much as an idea of delicacy and dignity, in concealing themselves from vulgar eyes.

LETTER XXXII.

Allahabad, July 1767

The tribe of *Hindoos* the English have most connexion with, and are obliged to put most confidence in, are in the third great division, called *Banians*, who are a kind of merchants, or rather brokers in every kind of merchandize. Every European both civil and military, who has either trade, or troops under him to pay, is obliged to have one of them in his service, who is a sort of steward: one of them is likewise necessary at the head of every family, to hire and pay the servants, and purchase whatever is wanting, for nothing can be bought or sold without them.

They are exceedingly indolent; crafty and artful to an astonishing degree; and shew in all their dealings the most despicable low cunning, which makes them not to be depended upon for any thing: they have not only a secret premium out of whatever they pay to servants, tradespeople, &c. but keep them out of their money long after the master supposes they have been paid.

They are the most tedious in the world, for besides the holidays, which they will on no account break through, they have a method of putting every thing off till to-morrow: when it is found out, as it often is, that they have told an untruth, they have no shame for it, but immediately tell another and another; nothing can hurry them, nothing can discompose or put them out of countenance, nothing can make them angry; provided their gains are sure, the master may fret to find his business go on slowly, may abuse them for want of honesty, may argue with them for their ingratitude, may convict them of falshood and double dealing, it signifies nothing; the same mild and placid countenance remains, without the least symptom of fear, anger, or shame.

Those who are concerned with us usually speak pretty tolerable English; they are many of them worth large sums of money, and frequently lend a great deal to their masters, mostly at the interest of nine or ten per cent.

By being in the service of an English gentleman, particularly if he has any considerable rank or employment in the company's[10] service, they have great advantages, not only from all his concerns, out of which they have a profit, but it enables them to carry on their own with the greater security; besides their wages, which, according to their master's situation and their own importance, is from a hundred to ten *rupees* a month, they are many of them of consequence amongst their own people, keep a palanqueen [i.e., palanquin], horses, and a number of servants.

Those who act in that capacity to a Governor or Commander in Chief, pretend to a superior rank, and take the title of *Duan* instead of *Banian*.

LETTER XXXIII.

Allahabád, July 1767

The temples of the *Hindoos* are called *pagodas*, they are generally square high buildings of brick or stone, but with very little taste. In the Decan and Carnatic [regions] are many of these *pagodas;* but in Bengal and up the Ganges very few, except in the province of Benaras. I must observe in favour of the *Hindoos*, that, in spite of the absurdity and unmeaningness of most of their ceremonies and customs, their strict observation of them does them honour.

To sum up their general character in few words, they are gentle, patient, temperate, regular in their lives, charitable, and strict observers of their religious ceremonies. They are superstitious, effeminate, avaritious, and crafty; deceitful and dishonest in their dealings, void of every principle of honour, generosity, or gratitude. Gain is the predominant principle; and as a part of their gains bestowed in gifts to their priests, or charities to the poor, will procure their pardon, they can cheat without fearing the anger of their gods.

But for the *Brahmins*, to whom alone all their learning is confined, it is a circumstance not much to their credit; that while all other nations, those in Europe particularly, have been making constant improvements and new discoveries in science, they have contented themselves with that which has been handed down to them from their forefathers; and still less, that they have made so ill a use of their learning; and, instead of informing those whose *casts* forbid them to enquire into the laws and religion, in such plain and simple truths as might tend to virtue and happiness, they have encumbered them with forms, and filled their heads with stories, which can tend to no other purpose but to raise their own importance.

LETTER XXXIV.

Allahabád, July 1767

Whenever a *Hindoo* has occasion to cross the *Carramnassa*, or the *Accursed River*, which in the dry season is fordable, he gives a Mahomedan money to carry him over upon his back, that his feet may not be wet with the accursed water, which is a thing forbidden by their religion. In this, and many other instances, the letter of the commandment is observed, while the spirit of it is lost; for I think one cannot doubt, but that the intention of this law, was to keep them within their own provinces.

Their being forbid to eat or drink of what has been touched but by those of their own *casts*, is likewise a great bar to migration, as they cannot always meet with those of their own *cast* to provide what they want; and is particularly calculated to prevent their taking voyages by sea. It is astonishing with what strictness the *Hindoos* observe these rules, even to starving themselves to death rather than break through them.

The children of the *Hindoos* are not to be tempted to eat any thing forbidden, either by persuasion, or by offering them the greatest delicacies; which I have often been witness of.

It is the first impression their minds receive; they are used to seeing it strictly observed by their own and other *casts;* it grows up with them as the first, and most absolute law; and is perhaps observed with more strictness than any other law, religious or civil, by any nation under the sun.

It must be acknowledged, that the religion of the *Hindoos* is now so overgrown with absurd and ridiculous ceremonies, that it is difficult to believe there has ever been any degree of common sense in it.

And yet, upon a closer examination, one must admit, that the division into *casts* and tribes promotes subordination. It is not peculiar to this country, but has been observed by other nations in the early ages: amongst the Romans, the sacerdotal office was likewise confined to the Patricians; as amongst the *Hindoos*, it is to the *Brahmins*; and in the Levitical law we are told, that the ark was carried by the tribe of Levi, and to them was the priesthood for ever. Something like it likewise exists at present in the ideas of noble blood amongst the French and Germans.

The impossibility of rising to any higher *cast* checks ambition in the bud. Their abstinence from animal food promotes temperance. Their being forbid to eat of certain food, and with none but those of their own *casts*, prevents migration. Their belief in the transmigration of souls makes them tender of the lives of all animals, and produces an aversion and horror at the idea of shedding blood.

It is no wonder, that, being taught to revere and preserve a cow on account of its utility, or to admire an elephant for its sagacity and strength; and the river Ganges, as causing the fertility, and facilitating the commerce of their country; and these opinions delivered to them in the lofty and figurative stile of the East; it is no wonder, I say, that they should rank the two first in the number of their demy gods, and believe that the other is able to cure diseases, and wash away sin.

When the priests of the Christian religion were first compelled to celibacy, it seems to have been intended, that the acknowledged purity of their characters should gain the most perfect veneration. But long after it was known that this end was not answered by it, it was still held to be a sin for any priest to marry.

If this and other institutions in the Christian church, were held sacred after the first intention of them was forgot; it is not at all surprising, that the antient customs of the *Hindoos* should be yet observed, although the use of them is either lost, or not understood.

No Martin Luther has arisen to open their eyes; and was it possible that any *Brahmin* by translating the *Shastah* from the *Sanscrit* to the vulgar tongue, or by explaining it according to common sense, was to endeavour to free them from their absurdities, they are too ignorant, and too indolent, to be benefited by it.

Monsieur Montesquieu,[11] who has unravelled the causes of different manners, says:

"Si avec cette foiblesse d'organes qui fait recevoir aux peuples d'orient les impressions du monde les plus fortes, vous joignez une certain paresse dans l'esprit, naturellement liée avec celle du corps, qui fasse que cet esprit ne foit capable d'aucune action, d'aucune contention; vous comprendrez que l'ame que a un fois reçû des impressions, ne peut plus en changer, c'est ce que fait que les loix, les mœurs, & les manieres, même celles que paroissent indifferentes, comme la façon de se vetir, sont aujourd'hui en orient, comme elles étoient il y a mille ans."[12]

Notes

1. Shastrah: any of the sacred writings of the Hindus.

2. In the eighteenth century a common term for Muslims.

3. Sixth century B.C. Greek philosopher, center of a religious brotherhood, one of whose doctrines was the immortality and transmigration of the soul.

4. *Gee* [ghee], made of milk, generally that of buffaloes, almost to the consistence of butter, but will keep much longer [Kindersley].

5. *Tamashes*, all kinds of shews, entertainments, or processions [Kindersley].

6. Usually spelled Hindustan; in the eighteenth century, a common name for India.

7. Particular, difficult to satisfy.

8. A walled city of women.

9. "Give rise" is apparently a slang, or at least informal, expression.

10. The East India Company; "a government owned by businessmen" (Gardner 11), it in effect ruled India.

11. Charles-Louis de Secondat, baron de La Brède et de Montesquieu (1689–1755), an extremely influential political philosopher best known at this time for his *Persian Letters* (1721) and *The Spirit of Laws* (1748).

12. The passage comprises section 4 of Book 14 of *The Spirit of Laws* (1748). As translated by Thomas Nugent (1949), it reads: "If to that delicacy of organs which renders the eastern nations so susceptible of every impression, you add likewise a sort of indolence of mind, naturally connected with that of the body, by means of which they grow incapable of any exertion or effort, it is easy to comprehend that when once the soul has received an impression it cannot change it. This is the reason that the laws, manners, and customs, even those which seem quite indifferent, such as their mode of dress, are the same to this very day in eastern countries as they were a thousand years ago."

Eliza Fay

1756–1816

Original Letters from India; containing a narrative of a Journey through Egypt, and the author's imprisonment at Calicut by Hyder Ally. To which is added an Abstract of three subsequent voyages to India. Calcutta: n.p., 1821.

All we know of Eliza Fay's maiden name is that it began with a C. She was born in 1756, possibly at Blackheath; her father may have been a sailor. Eliza probably received a "vaguely commercial" education (Forster 9), but she had a reading knowledge of French and Italian and taught herself Portuguese and shorthand. She married Anthony Fay, an attorney. By 18 April 1779, the date of the first letter of her text, the Fays were traveling through Europe en route to India. England had declared war on France in 1778, and Eliza's letters from Europe record the effects there, but the war did not touch her directly until her arrival in India, when the Fays and their fellow passengers on the *Nathalia* were captured by Haidar Ali, an ally of France. Released after a fifteen-week captivity, the Fays reached Calcutta in May 1780. Soon thereafter Anthony began to intrigue against the East India Company government and to neglect his work for "low and unworthy pursuits" (282). Eventually he fathered an illegitimate child, and by the end of July 1781 he had left his wife. From the beginning the *Letters* hints Eliza's dissatisfaction with her husband, and she seems to have reacted to his conduct with spirit. She demanded a legal separation and by 11 August 1781 had obtained a deed rendering her "wholly independent of Mr. F——'s authority" in "the strongest terms our language could supply" (289). Prior to this point, her letters had been gossipy accounts of sword-swallowers and company scandal; in contrast, and perhaps in response to her new independence, the later letters show an interest in customs that affected Indian women.

Ill and "destitute" (288), Eliza returned to England in February 1783. After a year of recuperation and various failed "plans in pursuit of independence" (338), she set sail for Bombay, having obtained a cheap passage

Eliza Fay, frontispiece to Original Letters from India, *engraving by T. Alais, after a drawing by A. W. Devis. By permission of the British Library.*

in exchange for serving as "protectress" to four ladies during the voyage. The *Abstract* records an array of business ventures she then engaged in. She ran a millinery business for four years, and although the enterprise failed in 1788, she eventually settled her debts and got together a little property. For the next ten years she traded in various goods, traveling between Europe and India; a business venture in America in 1797, however, was "the grave of that property, for which I had toiled so long" (404). Almost nothing is known of the following twenty years of Eliza's life. In 1815, because a woman author was no longer "an object of derision" (v), she was preparing to publish her "unembellished narrative of simple facts and real sufferings" (iii). She died intestate and insolvent at Calcutta in 1816.

TEXT: After her death, Eliza Fay's administrator published the *Original Letters from India* with the *Abstract of three subsequent voyages to India*. The latter is incomplete, either because the manuscripts were lost or because the publisher considered them uninteresting. The book was republished in 1817 and in 1821; a badly edited edition appeared in 1908. E. M. Forster edited a more faithful version in 1925, and that edition was reissued in paperback by Hogarth Press in 1986. The selection (pp. 167–201 of the first edition) is Fay's journal of her captivity.

ଓ ଫ

I WILL HERE by way of relaxation transcribe a few passages from my Journal, as nothing happened for some time worthy of a particular recital; reserving to myself, however, the option of resuming the narrative style, whenever I shall deem it necessary.

14th November, 1779.

Mr. F—— was sent for, this morning, to the Governor,[1] who asked him what he wanted? he replied, *Liberty*:—there was no observation made on this answer, nor can we conceive what Sudder Khan can mean by the detention of so many persons, who never bore arms. They gave Mr. Tulloh 30 rupees for our support.[2] All we are able to procure is tough, lean, old beef, goat's flesh, and a not unpleasant rice cake, but too sweet to be palatable with meat; we preserve either with difficulty from our perpetual visitors the crows, having no cup-board or place to put our victuals in.—Of all existing creatures crows are surely the most voracious, and the most persevering—I have seen one with his eye fixed for a full half hour on a person, and the instant that person's eye was averted, pounce on the bread or whatever has been prepared and bear away the prize. Mem.[3]—Ayres[4] is remarkably like these crows, he has exactly their *thievish* expression of countenance, and the form of his head resembles their's.

15th November, 1779.

The Gentlemen waited all day at the Governor's house, being promised their baggage, but he thought proper to disappoint them—received 10 rupees subsistence money.

A most impudent message brought from the Governor, requiring all the gentlemen to enter into the Nabob's service; which they unanimously refused, with every mark of contempt, and were in consequence ordered to be more closely confined—One of Mr. F——'s trunks brought on shore containing wearing apparel, and law books, probably much damaged, yet certainly valuable to him as he has *none* remaining. Made application for it but without success. Tulloh received 20 rupees.

20th November

Received notice to prepare immediately to set off for Seringapatnam, a large City about three hundred miles distant, where Hyder Ally usually resides—How can I support this journey over the mountains!—Mr. F—— is about drawing up a petition, representing the bad state of my health, and entreating permission for me to proceed to Cochin.[5] We hope to prevail on Isaac[6] to present it.

21st November

Discover that the journey to Seringapatnam was merely a vile plot of the Governor's to put us off our guard, and thereby gain possession of what property had hitherto been concealed; thank God this feint miscarried. A letter reached us from Mr. O'Donnell,[7] stating the arrival of the St. Helena[8] at Cochin. He laments our misfortune and promises to take such methods as shall compel the Nabob to do us speedy and effectual justice. Heaven speed his endeavours; this life is horrible.

22d November

The gentlemen waited five hours at the Governor's for their effects, but returned without them. He takes evident satisfaction in seeing them like slaves attendant on his *nod*.—Five ships supposed to be English passed in front of our prison. How peculiarly distressing did I feel this sight!

23d November, 1779.

Mrs. Tulloh being taken ill of a fever, application was made to the Governor for medicines; but this happening to be a high festival, he, like the Pharisees in Scripture, refused to profane it by doing good—Should the woman die in the interim what cares he?

24th November, 1779.

This morning got some medicines from the ship's chest—many flying reports of hostilities having actually commenced between Hyder Ally, and the English—should this really prove true, our fate will be sealed *for life*. Little did I think when pleading the cause of the Chevalier de St. Lubin at Mocha,[9] that he had been raising a storm whose effects would so materially involve us. Mem.—The lady is well again.

28th November, 1779.[10]

It is now certain that the Nayhirs have laid seige to Tellicherry; a settlement of our's about a degree to the northward; seven miles nearer lies Mahey which the French held, 'till we took it from them in March last; but not finding it worth keeping, have since evacuated it, after dismantling the fortifications.

29th November, 1779.

Sudder Khan is about to March a thousand troops into Mahey, under pretence of resuming it in the Nabob's name, but every one guesses this to be merely a feint to cover his real intentions of privately assisting the Nayhirs;—should they succeed in their attack, Hyder will then throw off the mask and declare war; but if the English conquer, he will disavow the whole affair.

30th November

I have now a lamentable tale to relate. We were this morning hurried away at a moments warning to the fort, and crouded together in a horrid dark place scarcely twenty foot square, swarming with rats, and almost suffocating for want of air. Mr. and Mrs. Tulloh secured a small room to themselves, but my husband and I, were obliged to pass the night among our companions in misery—rats continually gnawing the feet of my couch, whose perpetual squeaking would have prevented sleep, had our harrassing reflections permitted us to court its approach.

1st December, 1779.

Luckily discovered a trap-door, which led to some rooms, or rather lofts, where no human foot had trod for many *many* years. These had been the store rooms of Angria the Pirate,[11] and they certainly contain "a remnant of all things"[12]—Broken chairs—tables—looking-glasses—books, even a spinet was among the articles, but beyond all repair, and vast quantities of broken bottles, which had been filled with liquors of all kinds: but the rats in their gambols had made havoc among them. I remember when I should have shuddered at the thoughts of sleeping in such a wretched place; but now privacy gave it irresistible charms; so having with difficulty obtained leave to occupy it, we exerted every nerve to get a spot cleared out before dark, for my couch; likewise so to arrange some bolts of canvas which were among the spoils, as to form a sort of mattress for Mr. F——; here we lay down, comparatively happy in the hope of enjoying a tolerable nights rest; my husband being provided with a long pole to keep off the rats; but surely never were poor mortals so completely disappointed and for my part I may add, terrified.—No sooner was the light extinguished, than we heard a fluttering noise, attended at intervals with squeaking— by degrees it approached the *beds*, and we felt that several creatures were hovering over us, but of what description we were totally ignorant— sometimes their wings swept our faces, seeming to fly heavily—then again they would remove farther off, but still continued squeaking.—Good God! what horrors I felt. Mr. F—— protested that whole legions of evil spirits had taken possession of our apartment, and were determined to expel the intruders. The rats also acted their part in the Comedy; every now and then jumping towards the beds, as we could hear;—however Mr. F—— on these occasions laid about him stoutly with his pole, and thus kept *them* at bay; but our winged adversaries were not so easily foiled; —they persisted in their assaults 'till day-break, when what should we find had caused all this disturbance, but a parcel of poor harmless bats! whose "ancient solitary reign we had molested."[13] To any one accustomed to see or hear these creatures our terror must appear ridiculous, but to me who had never chanced to meet with any such, the idea never occurred, nor did even Mr. Fay suggest any probable or natural cause of alarm. We cannot help laughing very heartily at it ourselves now, and you are at full liberty to do the same.

2d December

Ayres called to tell us that two ships of the line, and a frigate[14] had just passed towards Tellichery.—We shall soon hear news from hence; Oh! that it may change our hard destiny!—The Governor marched at the head of his Troops towards Tellichery.

10th December

Application was made this morning to the Lieutenant Governor by Mr. Isaac, who I am now convinced is our warm friend, representing that this air disagreeing with me I required permission to remove to Cochin, and that my husband, on account of my extreme ill health, might accompany me. He promised to consult Sudder Khan upon it. The Quelladar or Governor of the Fort spent some time with us this morning;—he is a fine old man, with a long red beard, and has altogether a most interesting appearance:—and here I may as well give a short description of this place.

Calicut then, is situated on the coast of Malabar in 11 degree north latitude and 75 degree east longitude. It was formerly a very considerable town governed by a Zamorin,[15] who also held the adjoining country; but has been some years in the possession of Hyder Ally, of whom you must have heard on occasion of his war with the English in 1770.[16] They would certainly have put an end to the reign of this Usurper, had he not discovered a *method* of influencing the principal persons in power, in consequence of which he obtained a peace, much more honourable and advantageous to himself than to those who granted it. Having acquired by his genius and intrepidity every thing that he enjoys, he makes his name both feared and respected; so that nobody chooses to quarrel with him. I have indeed heard a comparison drawn between him and the King of Prussia, though I think much to the disadvantage of the latter; as supposing their *natural* abilities to be equal,—the great Frederick ought *infinitely* to surpass a man who can neither write nor read, which is the case with Hyder. The lawful Prince of the country of which he has usurped the Government is held by him in actual confinement, though with every outward shew of respect, by which means he prevents the people from rising, lest their legitimate sovereign should fall a victim to his resentment.

The fort must have formerly been a strong place, but is now in a dilapidated state—the walls are very thick, and they mount guard regularly; which was one inducement for sending us here; as Ayres told the Governor it was not worth while to keep a hundred seapoys [i.e., sepoys] watching us, when they were wanted elsewhere and that the fort was quite good enough for us to live in;—these arguments prevailed and here we were sent. When I first arrived I was so extremely ill, as to be scarcely sensible of what passed for some hours; but I remember H——[17] burst into a violent flood of tears, declaring that we were all doomed to death by our removal to this wretched spot, which being completely surrounded by stagnant water, could not fail to produce some of those disorders so fatal to Europeans. We have not however hitherto experienced any complaint. The loft we sleep in is indeed disgusting beyond belief, and the Quelladar, I suppose at the suggestion of Ayres, has ordered the easier of the two ways of entrance, that discovered by Mr. F——, to be blocked up; so that there is no way left but by means of a ladder placed almost in a perpendicular direction:—there is a rope by which to hold, or it would be impossible for any person to descend, but even with this assistance, I have great difficulty to reach the bottom.

11th December, 1779.
Peremptorily ordered to make ready for a journey to Seringapatnam. By the Governor's desire delivered an Inventory of our losses:[18] he promises full restitution, but has given no answer to my request.[19] I am full of solicitude on this subject; but would submit to any thing rather than remain in this wretched place.

12th December, 1779.
Mr. F—— waited twice on the Lieut. Governor but without effect. What can he mean by thus trifling with us? is it merely a wanton exercise of power, or intended to hide some dark design? these perpetual surmises distract me. Mem. Tulloh received 144 rupees to pay *all* our debts but took especial care not to let us have a single rupee, what wretches we are cast among! my very soul rises at them.

13th Dececember, 1779.
Mr. F—— was sent for by the Governor, who told him, that we might both have permission to go to Cochin whenever we thought proper; that he would furnish a boat and pay every incidental expense, besides making entire satisfaction for damages sustained,—Can all this good news be true? How suspicious I grow! what a change from being credulous—yet where is the wonder after being so frequently deceived?

14th December, 1779.
Preparations are going on briskly all day with our fellow passengers, who are eager for their departure, as well they may [be]. Every thing which was taken from them on shore, has been this day restored, but those left in the ship are irrecoverable; of course we benefit nothing by this restitution—Mr. F—— could not obtain our promised licence [i.e., passport] to-day.—These delays, weigh down my spirits, and increase all my complaints. I have still much pain in my breast; Oh that I fear, will prove a fatal blow—I shall have a great loss in Mr. Taylor.[20]

15th December, 1779.
The Governor still withholding our licence under pretence of business, I advised Mr. F—— to insist on being *immediately* dispatched, or in case of refusal, by all means to declare himself ready to accompany the others; for I saw clearly that should they once leave us, it must then be entirely at this fellow's option, whether we went all or not, and who would not rather run the risk of even *dying* of fatigue on the journey, than hazard remaining at

the mercy of such wretches! I dread, lest this should be part of the old plan[21] of which I have since never heard, and had almost forgotten it. It is much easier to practise against two individuals than a whole company.

16th December

The Doolies (a kind of shabby Palanquin in which a person sits upright and is carried between two men) arrived this A.M. about ten. The gentlemen went to take leave, when Tulloh urgently represented our case, to which the Governor replied, that he could not possibly attend to other matters till they were gone, but pledged his word that nothing should arise on his part to detain us a single hour afterwards; every one agreed with me how dangerous it was to trust such fallacious promises. On my knees I entreated Mr. F—— to pursue the method I had before pointed out,[22] but my advice was despised. At nine in the evening the party commenced their journey, having first stripped the place of provisions and every thing else, which having been bought out of the general purse we had an undoubted right to share. They even took my tea kettle, but luckily the man who had it in charge forgot it amidst the hurry of departure, by which means I recovered it. My heart sunk within me at seeing them quit the fort, not from motives of personal esteem or regret you may suppose, for it was impossible to grieve for the loss of some of the company; we parted with as much indifference as absolute strangers; after a fellowship in misfortune sufficient to have united almost any other society more closely than an intercourse of *years* under common circumstances. I went to bed, but inspite of every endeavour to calm the agitation of my mind, passed a *sleepless* night.

17th December

Rose in extreme anxiety which was far from being diminished by a message from the Governor, ordering Mr. F—— not to attend him 'till the evening; accordingly at four o'clock he set out, and as I felt extremely ill, the certain consequence of fretting and want of rest, I lay down and had just sunk into a doze, when my poor husband flew into the room like a madman, uttering a thousand extravagant expressions. Starting up in new and indescribable terror, and wringing my hands, I begged only to know what had happened. "Happened!" cried he "why we are betrayed, ruined, utterly undone; you must leave this place instantly, or you may be made a prisoner here for ever." Where are we to go? I very naturally asked! I *heard* not the answer, my head swam, and I dropped on the floor completely overpowered.—Whatever happened at that *fearful* moment I forget and endeavour to banish from my mind, as the effect of insanity.—How he accomplished it I know not, but Mr. F—— actually carried me in his arms down that almost perpendicular ladder which I have described and placed me on a kind of bier: I was in this manner conveyed to my former habitation—I opened my eyes and became for a few moments sensible of the motion, but soon fainted again, and did not recover 'till I found myself once more entering the English Factory[23] as a prisoner.

I now inquired, what was the cause of this change in our abode: and learnt that Mr. F—— being refused leave to depart, had become so exasperated as wholly to lose all self-command; and rushing up to the musnud (throne) of the Lieutenant Governor had actually seized him, peremptorily insisting on the immediate fulfilment of his promise. Such conduct might have been expected to bring down *instant* destruction; but fortunately every one present was persuaded that grief and vexation had literally turned his brain; and they are not only much terrified at every species of madness, but from their religious prejudices, regard the sufferers under these complaints with a superstitious awe. Swayed by these mingled emotions the wicked Governor condescended to temporize with my husband, acknowledging that he had no *power* to release us without the Nabob's order which in consideration of my ill health he would endeavour to procure; and to pacify him further, he permitted our return to this place, where we are certainly in every respect more comfortably situated. But these concessions went little towards allaying that fever of passion, which his continual and cruel delays had excited: thence arose the alarm I experienced and which for a time so materially affected my health.

19th December, 1779.

Received five rupees subsistence money which we were informed were the last we should ever have. I cannot conceived what they mean to do with us or what will be our fate at last.

21st December, 1779.

The Governor sent for Mr. F—— to offer him a commission in the Nabob's service and on his absolute refusal, swore that he might subsist how he could; that his masters money should no longer be lavished on idlers, then in a rage ordered Palanquins "you shall go to Seringapatnam" said he "they will soon teach you better manners there." Mr. F—— joyfully acquiesed in this mandate,—we provided necessaries for our journey which was fixed for the 24th; but the other knew better than to keep his word, so this like all our former views, and expectations of liberty ends in smoke, shall I say?

26th December, 1779.

A very melancholy Christmas-day passed yesterday. My dear friends little imagined they were drinking the health of a poor prisoner, (for I know you did not forget us) neither were we forgotten here, if empty compliments can be styled remembrance. All the Europeans and several of the natives attended our Lévee.[24] But alas! what relief can mere ceremonious visits afford to misfortune! say rather that *aided by recollection,* such shadowy comforts add *keenness* to afflictions sting. I feel my mind insensibly raised whenever I attempt to expatiate on any subject which tends to revive the ideas of our separation. Even now I tread forbidden ground; for your sakes as well as my own, let me hasten to escape by passing over this dangerous season of Christmas. I therefore pass on.

10th January, 1780.

The little money saved was nearly expended, and we must soon have been reduced to our last mite had not providence sent us relief from a quarter little dreamed of. Mr. F—— wrote about a week ago to Mr. Church, Governor of Tellicherry inclosing a memorial of our case, which he requested might be translated into the language of the country and proper methods used for its safe delivery to Hyder Ally himself. This morning brought in reply, a most generous humane letter from Mr. Church; which, after acknowledging himself honoured by our application, and promising his utmost concurrence in every measure we may think necessary, concludes thus "my heart bleeds for your distresses, and those of Mrs. F—— she in particular must have suffered greatly. I have taken the liberty to accompany this letter by an order for two hundred rupees to serve *present* occasions: Any sum you may in future require a line to me shall always command it, as I know the difficulty of procuring remittances where you are. Englishmen ought to feel for each other; we are not without our share of troubles *here*; and I verily believe Hyder is at the bottom of all." Now pray does not this letter deserve more than I have said of it! just thus would my dear father have treated a distressed countryman.—Methinks I see his benevolent heart venting itself in tears of sympathy at the recital. Precious tears! why am I not permitted to mingle mine with them! for they will flow in spite of my endeavours to restrain their course.

Having now money to bribe with, we began to think of attempting an escape; for besides the silence observed on the fate of our companions, though near a month has elapsed since their departure, we live in continual dread of being forced up the country and perhaps massacred there: Every one who leaves this place must first obtain permission from the Governor, but as these passes only mention generally *so many people* and are granted indiscriminately to whoever applies for them, provided they be not suspected persons, one may easily be procured under feigned pretences (it is a matter frequently done). A Friar belonging to the Portuguese convent, usually manages these affairs when properly instructed. This information we have from a Native Portuguese named Pereira, an officer in Hyder's service, with whom Mr. F—— commenced an intimacy while we were in the Fort, and who is now quartered here at his special request. Tho' I must confess I cannot like this man, yet am I obliged to trust him. The visits we receive from Ayres are terrible trials to one who loathes dissimulation as I do. This wretch has once or twice mentioned a cow that annoyed him by entering the little garden, or paddock, in which it appears his house is placed; this morning he entered the factory with his scymitar in his hand unsheathed, and bloody, and with an expression of diabolical joy informed me that he had just caught the animal entering and being armed had completely chined her.[25] You cannot imagine said he, how *sweetly* the sword did the business; my very heart shuddered with horror and indignation, yet dared I not give vent to those feelings. I doubt not he would murder me with as much pleasure as he killed the cow with; and have no reason to suppose he would be punished for the act.

12th January, 1780.

Some quarrel unknown to me has certainly taken place between Pereira and Mr. F—— the looks of the former alarm me: his dark scowling eye is frequently directed towards him, with an expression of dreadful import; yet he appears desirous of forwarding our escape.—He has introduced us to father Ricardo, who engages to provide us all things for our departure to Cochin.

13th January, 1780.

The priest breakfasted with us, and promised to set about the business without loss of time; he is to receive twenty rupees, on our setting off from hence, and twenty more on our arrival at Cochin or Tellichery, through the medium of Isaac, on whom the order from Mr. Church was drawn, by which means we received it without suspicion.

A Licence or Passport is procured for us as two Frenchmen going to Mahey. We have paid twenty rupees boat-hire to a smuggler; these are commonly very courageous men; which is some comfort to me: under Mr. F——'s protection and his, I will endeavour to think myself secure. His house is admirably situated for our purpose, close by the sea side; this is to be our place of rendezvous. The precise time is not yet fixed upon: the intervening hours how anxiously will they pass!

15th January, 1780.

The boatman called to desire we would be at his house at six this evening;—gave him our little baggage (we had been required to purchase many necessaries) and four rupees to buy provisions. When it grew dark, Mr. F—— put on a sailor's dress and I equipped myself in a nankeen[26] jacket—a pair of long striped trowsers—a man's night cap, and over that a *mighty* smart hat,—with a pair of Mr. F——'s shoes tied on my feet, and a stick in my hand. In this dress Mr. F—— declared that I was the very image of my dear father, which highly gratified me. I had tied the clothes we took off, in a handkerchief; with that in one hand and brandishing my stick in the other, I boldly sallied forth,—taking care, however, to secure a retreat in case of accidents, a most fortunate precaution as the event proved.—Father Ricardo met us at the smuggler's according to appointment and we paid him twenty rupees, and gave him security for the other twenty; when this was settled, nothing remained as we supposed, but to step into the boat,—when behold! news was brought that the sailors had made their escape no one knew whither! after waiting two hours in that dangerous situation, to see if they would return, and raving in all the folly of angry disappointment against those who had misled us, we made a virtue of necessity and trudged back to our prison, where we lucking effected an entrance without exciting suspicion.

17th January, 1780.

Had all arranged for our escape last night but so many people were about us, that we dared not make the attempt.

19th January, 1780.

Father Ricardo has once more arranged all things for to-night,—we must give more money, but that is no object. Once free and we shall doubtless find means of proceeding on our journey.

Every day has this wicked priest contrived some scheme, to amuse us with false hopes of escaping; every *night* have we lain down in the full persuasion that it was the last we should pass in confinement; and as constantly have we awoke to meet bitter disappointments.—This continued alternation of hope and fear preys on my spirits and prevents me from gaining strength, but yesterday I received a *serious* shock from the behaviour of Pereira, and which excited more alarm than almost any circumstance that has occurred to me.—I had long marked his hatred to Mr. F—— and dreaded his revenge—I was setting at work when he entered the room— naked from the middle just as Mr. F—— was going into the next room. His strange appearance and the quick step with which he followed my husband caught my attention; and I perceived that he held a short dagger close under his arm, nearly all concealed by his handkerchief and the exigency of the moment gave me courage.—I sprung between him and the door through which Mr. F—— had just passed, drawing it close and securing it to prevent his return, and then gently expostulated with P—— on the oddness of his conduct and appearance; he slunk away, and I hope, will never trouble us again, especially as he has adopted another mode of revenge which may perhaps be equally effectual, though more slow in its operation. He went to Ayres and informed him that we had endeavoured to escape, mentioning every particular of our scheme, and, as far as I can learn, telling the whole truth; but fortunately naming a different evening from the one on which our unsuccessful attempt really was made, on which Ayres exclaimed "well Pereira you have made up a very fine story, but without a word of truth, for on the very night you mention, F—— was setting with me over a bottle of wine, I'll take my oath of that, for it was my birth night" this was true likewise, so we were saved for that time; but as Ayres knows that escape is in our heads, he will, I fear, guard us with redoubled vigilance, and so far Pereira's design has taken effect.

Mr. F—— has completely detected the pious father Ricardo, and his worthy colleague the smuggler, and sorely against their will compelled them to refund his money all to about twenty three rupees, which they pretend has been disbursed. We now discovered, that although our offers might tempt their avarice and lead them to deceive us, yet they dared not persevere in assisting our escape; as the consequence of detection would to them be inevitable death.

10th February, 1780.

At length I begin to cherish hopes of our speedy release, as Sudder Khan returned last night from Seringapatnam; but is encamped without the Town, waiting for a lucky day, till when he dares not enter his own house—So how long we may still be detained, Heaven knows.—Mr. F—— and our friend Isaac propose paying him a visit to-morrow.

13th February, 1780.

They went out on Friday and again to-day but have not yet been able to obtain an audience; and thus we may perhaps be led on a fortnight longer, by his ridiculous superstitions. Mr. Isaac, however, assures my husband, that from all he can learn it is really intended to release us, which makes me comparatively easy; yet it is impossible not to feel severely this delay, at such a critical period; for should Hyder commence hostilities against the English, whilst we remain in his power, not all Isaac's influence will be sufficient to extricate us from it: our doom must be sealed for life.

14th February

Our indefatigable advocate walked out with Mr. F—— (I should have mentioned that the distance is about three miles) but they were again disappointed, Sudder Khan being still closely shut up at his devotions, which are to continue two days longer at least.—How very distressing to be kept in this horrible suspense! But our friend still comforts us with the assurance, that *all* will be well.—He really behaves to me like a father, and as I have now acquired some knowledge of Portuguese, we are enabled to converse tolerably well. I do not recollect having described his person, and will therefore endeavour to give you some, though a very inadequate idea of it.

Isaac then is a fine venerable old man, about eighty-five with a long white beard; his complexion by no means dark, and his countenance benign yet majestic; I could look at him 'till I almost fancied that he resembled exactly the Patriarch whose name he bears, were it not for his eye, which is still brilliant. His family I find according to ancient custom in the East, consists of two wives, to whom I am to have an introduction.

15th February

Saw a letter today from Mr. Tulloh, to Mr. Passavant the Danish Factor, dated 19th January, which mentions, that they were fifteen days on their journey to Seringapatnam and twelve more confined in a shed, half starved to death, as no one was permitted to assist them except with the coarsest food in small quantities; at length the Nabob granted them an audience, when having listened to their complaint, he sent for Sudder Khan, to answer the charge. "Three successive days" says Tulloh "we were all sent for, and confronted with him, when Hyder commanded him to make instant restitution, however, we have as yet received nothing except that yesterday on taking leave his highness presented us with five hundred rupees for our journey to Madras, besides ordering Palanquins, carriages for our baggage, and every other convenience, likewise a guard of a hundred seapoys to conduct us into the English bounds. I spoke to him for Mr. and Mrs. F—— and obtained an order for their release also. Whether the ship will be returned or not, *God Knows*, we are just going to set off." Thus far Tulloh. Now the man who brought this letter, saw them all go and remained at Seringapatnam ten days afterwards, without hearing further; so I hope we may conclude they are out of *their* troubles. Mrs. Tulloh has now seen enough poor woman to satisfy her taste for adventures. From all I can learn, it would have been utterly impossible for me to have supported the various hardships of their journey, in my precarious state of health; poor Mr. Taylor how sincerely do I pity him.[27]

17th February, 1780.

Mr. Isaac called by appointment about two o'clock and took my husband with him, to wait *once more* on the Governor. He seems to entertain no doubt of bringing back the order for our release. I endeavour to be calm and to rest with confidence on his assurance; but when I contemplate the dreadful alternative, should he meet a peremptory refusal, and recollect the deep machinations that have been practised to keep us here, my heart recoils at the idea. It is now eight in the evening; every thing is packed up and ready for our departure yet they return not. Some obstacle I fear must have been thrown in the way by that vile Sudder Khan to prevent our liberation, and we are destined to remain his wretched prisoners. How shall I support the intelligence [i.e., news]? Heaven inspire me with fortitude! I can neither write, nor attend to any thing![28]

Notes

1. Sirdar (Sudder) Khan, governor of Calicut and Haidar Ali's brother-in-law.
2. Other passengers on the *Nathalia* had been taken from the ship with the Fays but not imprisoned; among them was Mr. Tulloh, who is acting as liaison for the Fays.
3. Abbreviation for "memorandum," or note to oneself.
4. Captain Ayres, an Englishman in Haidar Ali's service; he had removed the passengers from the *Nathalia*.

5. Dutch settlement on the Malabar coast, south of Calicut.

6. Mr. Isaac, a wealthy merchant and a favorite of Sirdar Khan; he had taken pity on Eliza, hence the Fays' hope that he will present their petition.

7. John O'Donnell, an English merchant and deputy paymaster to the nabob of Oudh.

8. A merchant ship.

9. Resident in Mocha while the *Nathalia* was docked there, the chevalier was rumored to be on a diplomatic mission to disrupt relations between Haidar Ali and the British; Eliza had "pleaded his cause" by opposing another passenger's plan to prevent him from returning to France.

10. The events in this entry and the next relate to the Anglo-French War (1778–1783) being fought over both nations' Indian as well as American colonies. In March 1779 the British forces won Mahé ("Mahey") from the French; the Nairs ("Nayhirs"), a Hindu community that was ruled by matriarchs and (to some extent) practiced polyandry, took this opportunity to rebel against Haidar Ali's rule. The uprising was supported, if not instigated, by the English but suppressed, and the French retook Mahé in 1780 with Haidar Ali's aid.

11. The Angria dynasty of pirate kings (ca. 1704–1756), a Muslim family of black Africans, was very successful marauding along the west coast of India against European ships.

12. Source unidentified.

13. A reference to stanza three of Thomas Gray's poem "Elegy Written in a Country Churchyard."

14. A ship of the line is a warship large enough to have a place in the line of battle. A frigate is a somewhat smaller warship.

15. Title for a Hindu sovereign.

16. During the first Anglo-Mysore War (1767–1769), Haidar Ali's successes had embarrassed the East India Company troops; after the war he continued to harass the company for failing to honor the terms of the peace treaty.

17. Hare, a passenger on the *Nathalia*.

18. The goods confiscated from the *Nathalia*.

19. To be allowed to go to Cochin accompanied by her husband.

20. Earlier a guard had closed a door on Eliza so violently that a large key, still in the door, struck her right breast with great force; Taylor, a fellow passenger and a surgeon, was treating the injury.

21. The governor's initial plan was to release the "people of consequence," in other words, everyone but the Fays.

22. See the entry for 15 December.

23. Establishment for traders doing business in a foreign country, or a merchant company's trading station.

24. Morning or afternoon reception of visitors.

25. Cut her through the backbone with his scimitar.

26. Yellowish cotton, so called for the fabric's association with Nanking, where it was originally hand-loomed.

27. Taylor had been very ill during an earlier journey with the Fays.

28. The Fays were in fact released on this day and proceeded to Calcutta via Cochin and Madras.

Mary Tonkin

FL. 1781–1783

Facts. The Female Spy; or Mrs. Tonkin's Account of her Journey through France, In the War, at the Hazard of her Life, at the express order of the Rt. Hon. Charles James Fox, Secretary of State; For which she has been refused any Indemnity or Compensation. N.p.: Vaughan and Davis, 1783.

Information about Mary Tonkin must be gleaned from her pamphlet *Facts*—and with care: since she was a spy, the account she gives of herself may well be a cover story. According to her narrative, Tonkin was shipwrecked on the French coast in 1781. Allied with the American colonies, France was at war with Britain, and in the following months she gathered information about French fortifications. When Tonkin returned to England in 1782, she gave this information to government officials and offered to return to France as a spy. After much delay, the offer was accepted, and Tonkin set sail for France on 17 May 1782. Once in Saint-Malo, she claimed to be an American wanting passage to Boston, but on 5 June she was arrested as a spy. Taken before the governor, Tonkin showed him a letter purportedly written by her husband, Zachariah Adams, directing her to leave their children with her aunt and return to Boston. The governor promised her a passport, and within a few days Tonkin arrived at her real destination, Brest, where she met with a trusted friend and gathered information about fortifications. For the next two weeks she continued her travels, compiling data, meeting with American ship captains and agents, and attempting to obtain a passport for Amsterdam. By 27 June she was back in Paris; there she obtained a passport from the American ambassador, Ben Franklin, and followed his recommendation to visit Versailles.

Returning to London on 6 July 1782, Tonkin delivered her information to the authorities and began a year of fruitless effort to be paid for her labors. To some extent the delay was understandable, for the British government was in a state of disarray amounting to constitutional crisis (L. G. Mitchell 46). Partly as a result of disputes over the management of the war in America, from 1782 to 1784 the government changed hands four times, and many of the ministers going in and out of office were Tonkin's contacts. When she first approached the government in January 1782, Lord North's government was in power; within two months, Lord North had been replaced by a coalition ministry under the earl of Shelburne and the marquis of Rockingham. Rockingham died on 1 July, and three days later Charles James Fox resigned as secretary of state in protest against King George III's conduct during this crisis. After a period of infighting among the Whigs, a coalition ministry of Fox and North took control in February 1783, negotiated peace terms, and governed until George III dissolved Parliament in March 1784. These changes in government personnel, particularly in Fox's position, directly affected Tonkin's efforts to obtain compensation, and she tried to force Fox's hand by publishing *Facts* in July 1783 and a longer version in 1785. It is not known whether she succeeded, and in fact nothing more is known of her.

TEXT: According to the title page, *Facts* was "printed for and sold by the author," which suggests that Mary Tonkin hoped to recoup some of her losses with sales of the pamphlet. The excerpts from the 1783 text are the dedication (pp. iii–v), the opening of her narrative (pp. 7–12), and the conclusion (pp. 22–27 and 30–32); all are characteristic of Tonkin's style of invective.

CR BO

To the Queen's most excellent Majesty.[1]

MAY IT PLEASE YOUR MAJESTY,

I wish my education had enabled me to present the following case in a better and more elegant dress; for being under the necessity of telling my own tale, it must be in my own way, or it may not have that exact truth, on which I rest my pretensions to public attention and favor.

While *England* is the contempt of *Europe*, as the theatre of dishonorable factions,[2] contending for the fragments of its broken fortunes, for the purposes of dissipation and profligacy: the industrious and meritorious, those who have hazarded their lives in important services to their king and country, are pining in wretchedness; and soliciting from the hand of charity, what they should receive from the justice and gratitude of the public.

You will pardon an injured and distressed woman, for laying at your Majesty's feet, the particulars of her extraordinary case. You will perceive that the fate of His Majesty's dominions, and the fortunes of your numerous and illustrious family, are often affected by the resolution of an obscure individual, as the lion may have owed his life to a gnat.

That no prince in *Europe* has been, or is worse served than the King of *England*, is a truth too notorious to all the world, to require any proofs from me to corroborate. It will not be the least affecting misfortune of the royal house, that while the public revenues are the prey of adventurers, its compassion will be long and repeatedly called upon, to save from misery the only persons who have rendered it actual and essential services.

That your Majesty and your family may be preserved from all the disagreeable consequences of the ignorance and wickedness which have almost ruined your country; is the sincere and humble prayer of,

Madam,

Your Majesty's

Most devoted Subject,

M. Tonkin

A SHORT ACCOUNT.

—Boreas' Blast, and Neptune's Wave,

Have toss'd me to and fro![3]

In the year 1781 I had the misfortune to be shipwrecked on the coast of *France* which detained me there several months: In *January* 1782 I came to *England*, and wrote to that mean spirited man Stephens, at the Admiralty,[4] that the combined fleets would be in the chanel in the course of the summer: and likewise an account of what was doing in all the seaport towns between *Grandeville* and *Boulogne*. If he doubted the truth of what I said, I desired him to apply to an able officer, who was in the service, for my character, who was at *Portsmouth;* and who knew me from a child. Receiving no answer, I returned to *Portsmouth;* where I communicated the secret to my friend, who reported it to the admiral. I was sent for, had an audience of the squeaking admiral Pye;[5] and told him that the supplies going to *Gibraltar* for the garrison, and then at *Spithead*, would be intercepted by the Spaniards: for they knew in *France* there was but one frigate to go as convoy. I informed Sir Thomas Pye there were a great many spies about *Portsmouth* and *Gosport* who transmitted every thing that was going on at *Portsmouth*, every week, to *France:* that I had seen the *Winchester* and *Southampton* papers on the continent within 30 hours after they were printed. And told Sir Thomas, if he would be so condescending to advance me a few guineas I could soon find out the villainy, and put a stop to it. Instead of granting my request, he grinned like a monkey, and said he would see farther into it. On my moving to leave the room, I was desired to stay: Sir Thomas was so kind to tell me, that in the year 1740 he went to *France* upon discoveries himself; he was some weeks at *Morlaix,* took a ride one day 14 or 15 miles up the country, and returned safe, without any accident; being a stranger to the *Bretagne* language, but having an honest welchman on board, he stood interpreter for the whole ship's company. I answered Sir Thomas, that it was a surprizing undertaking, and that I hoped he was promoted on his return: He replied he was; not long after his return. I said, Sir, I'll tell you a secret; I have been 48 times in *France,* and once had the courage to go to the top of the spire of the cathedral of St. Paul's de *Lyons,* which is a mark for vessels to come in for the *Isle of Baas:* He replied, that he had been in the *church,* but never went to the *look-out:* I said he was in the right of it; so, wishing the admiral a good morning, I retreated. On my return down stairs I met my friend, and told him that poor old *England* now feels the loss of Boscawen and Hawke.[6] Not being any ways satisfied with the admiral's behavior, and greatly distressed to see my country so imposed upon, I wrote a letter to the *slippery* lord Stormont, then secretary of state,[7] and informed likewise his lordship where he might apply for my character: his answer was he knew nothing of Mrs. T——, and could say nothing to the letter. I then wrote a letter to lord North, then at the head of the treasury,[8] requesting his lordship not to suffer such villainy to go on; but his lordship being governor of the cinque ports,[9] took no notice of the letter.

1782, *May* 1st. On hearing that the late Marquis of Rockingham was at the head of the treasury,[10] and was supported by Fox, who was then a general favourite, I sett off for *London:* on my arrival I had an audience of the secretary of state, Mr. Fox;[11] to whom I communicated the whole of the affair: He was surprized, and told me a stop should be put to it immediately. A few days after I had another audience of the said gentleman, and was ordered to be at the secretary's office the following day. I attended, and there were several gentlemen present: I was asked if I could undertake to go to some particular places in *Holland;* I excused myself by saying I was a stranger to the country and the language, but was thoroughly acquainted about *Brest* and *Morlaix;*[12] being asked if I could either get to Brest or Morlaix; I answered I would undertake to get to *Morlaix,* and if possible into *Brest;* if not, I had two or three friends in *Morlaix,* whose integrity I could rely on, who should go there for me, and get the best intelligence they could; for I knew them to be trusty slaves to captain Walker, when he was employed during the peace for six years at *Morlaix,* by Lord Sandwich;[13] and that I was several times entrusted with Captain Walker's secrets from *Morlaix* to *London.* On the 15th of *May* I was ordered to get myself ready to depart that night. From two in the afternoon till twelve at night I was at the secretary's office, settled my plan for my said voyage and journey, received a private order from Lord Keppel,[14] to go directly down to *Plymouth*, to Lord Shuldham, who was to furnish me with a sloop of war, to take me on the French coast, and land me where I thought proper. On my complaining that I was very much fatigued, and wishing to go to my lodging, to get a little rest; I was answered by an insignificant puppy behind me, and one of my own country, whose name is Kempthorn; but being in a new uniform I did not know him at first, having seen him in a jacket and trowsers; but found he had, like Harlequin, jumped out of a Dutchman's pipe,[15] and was metamorphosed into a captain of the 50th regiment of foot: he said I must sleep in the carriage; but being assured by that *lying, deceitful puppy*[16] *Sheridan*, together with that *pitiful mean spirited Scotch pebble Fraser*,[17] that I should be honorably rewarded for my trouble on my return: and that they would not serve me as Lord North had done. On the 16th, at three o'clock in the morning, I set off from the secretary's office on my journey; thinking, or reflecting within myself, that if the nation's affairs were to be conducted by such clever fellows as the old gormandizing Todd at the post office, who never sailed ten leagues in the pacquet[18] in his life; and the thick headed Rogers, admiral Keppel's secretary, together with my old friends, the under secretaries Sheridan and Fraser, with Kempthorn and the poor old and blind Mr. Sneyd, that brings up the rear, we should defy all the world.

. . . The 30th [June], left *Paris*, and arrived at *Ostend* the 2d of *July;* the wind proving contrary, no pacquet passed: there was an express boat went off, but that pittiful monkey Peters, the English commissary,[19] would not give me leave to go in it. I arrived in *London* the 6th, and on hearing that the noble marquis of Rockingham was dead, and Mr. Fox, who employed me, out of office, and not in town, I was distressed to my soul. The 27th, gave lord Keppel the contents of my voyage, &c. was seized with a fever myself, and confined for six weeks. As soon as I was able to go abroad, I waited on lord Keppel, and was told by his secretary, that I must go to general Conway.[20] I gave general Conway a copy of my whole proceedings: after waiting upon him two or three times, he told me, (like a *hero* as he is) that he had no business with it: and *keeping* my journal, without so much as thanking me for it, said I must go to lord Grantham.[21]

The next day I wrote to his lordship, as follows:

My Lord,
Being some time since employed by the honourable Mr. Fox, to go to *France*, in order to obtain intelligence privately; I obeyed his orders ac-

cordingly, gained the particulars wanted, and much more than I have expressed in my journal.

I have taken the liberty of enclosing a copy of the minutes of my voyage, journey, &c. for your lordship's perusal and inspection.

I most humbly entreat your lordship will be pleased to permit me to explain, if necessary, to your lordship, the contents thereof; and that your lordship will favor me with an audience for that purpose.

Humbly soliciting your lordship's interest and favor, I beg leave to subscribe myself,

My Lord,

Your lordship's obedient,

And faithful servant,

September 12, 1782.   M. T.

(COPY.)

The next day I had an audience of his lordship, who told me he never heard of such an enterprize undertaken by a woman, in his life: said he must see me again, and desired I would leave my address. Hearing nothing from his lordship, I waited on his lordship a second time, and told him, that I was in the utmost distress, for that I had expended £142 on my last expedition, and was now without a shilling to support me. The secretary replied, like a brave fellow, that my information was of no use to him; and as Mr. Fox had employed me, I must go to him to be paid. Struck with the barbarity, and inhuman expression of his lordship, I desired him to be kind enough to give me back my journal; which he nobly refused: I then saw clearly, that his lordship was very short sighted. The next day I wrote a letter to the hide-bound lord Shelburne,[22] but received no answer: I then wrote to the sly Mr. Fraser as follows:

SIR,

I beg leave to inform you of my friend's arrival, who was at *Morlaix*, in *France*. By this event I am encouraged to remind you of your engagement with me, in conjunction with Mr. Sheridan.

When I set out on my journey, you was pleased to promise me, that on my return, I should receive an honourable recompence for my trouble; and from the high opinion I entertain, Sir, of your integrity, the purity of your intentions, and the consideration of the many dangers and difficulties that I experienced, in travelling abroad for the benefit of my country, I flatter myself with the hopes of a speedy performance of your promise;

and that I shall receive such a reward as I am entitled to for my faithful services.

I am now, Sir, 360 miles distant from home, without five shillings in my pocket, for the supply of my daily wants; much less to defray the expence of returning thither. This unhappy situation will, I hope, influence you to be speedy in your relief, to extricate me out of it: but if my reasonable request is not complied with, I must beg leave to observe, that I shall be under the disagreeable necessity (though much against my inclination) of publishing my case; and thereby exposing to the world the hardships I have suffered, and the cruel treatment I have received; which I could wish might be timely prevented.

I attend personally with this letter, and request that you, Sir, will be pleased to favor me with an answer.

I have the honor to be, with the greatest respect,

SIR,

Your most obedient,

And very humble servant,

Nov. 6, 1782   M. T.

[———— Fraser, Esq.]

The answer I received from Mr. Fraser was as follows.

"Mrs. T. I cannot, nor will not have any thing to say in the affair." A clever fellow to be employed to write the gazette![23]

The next day I wrote lord Keppel the following letter.

My Lord,

I flattered myself before this, I should have received sufficient recompence for the business I did, by order of the right honourable Charles James Fox; but yet have received no satisfaction. Without I receive some immediate relief, am under the necessity to acquaint your lordship, I must publish the whole of my case.

I am, my Lord,

With the utmost respect,

Your faithful humble servant,

Nov. 8, 1782   M.T.

The answer I received from his lordship, was, "You must go to Mr. Fraser."

A few days after, I met with the *sly* Sheridan, who told me in a great hurry, he would speak to Mr. Stephens concerning the affair, as it was a shame and a scandal they did not pay me. I have seen the *puppy* several times since he has been made secretary of the treasury, who very genteelly told me, he did not belong to Mr. Fox's office now: I told him he was a clever fellow, and deserved to be preferred. . . .

The day after, I waited upon Mr. Stephens with the said letter,[24] and had an audience: he told me he had seen a letter the same morning, which admiral Keppel had received from my said friend, almost to the same purport. He likewise added, that it was very cruel I was not paid, notwithstanding Mr. Fox was out [of office]; that it was in Mr. Fraser's power to pay me, as he knew the whole contents; and promised me that he would enquire about it: but I never could have an audience afterwards. The 7th of *December,* going to try whether I could see the said gentleman, I had the misfortune to meet with an accident, and broke my leg in two places. In *January* 1783, I wrote a letter to Mr. Fox, acquainting him with my misfortune. A gentleman of credit, who is an acquaintance of mine, and a staunch friend to Mr. Fox, undertook to carry the above. Mr. Fox said he was very sorry for my misfortune; that he had employed me to go abroad, but it was not in his power to pay me; he hoped things would be better soon: sent me two guineas, and said he would speak to lord Grantham concerning the affair, acknowledging it to be cruel usage.

When the *coalition* took place between him and lord North; and Mr. Fox was re-established in his former post, as secretary of state; my friend waited on him several times, but was put off by saying he must call again, I will see about it. When the right honourable secretary saw that my friend was determined to have a final answer, and would not be put off any longer, he gave him five guineas; and genteelly enough told him he had enquired in the office, and he could do nothing for me. On my friend saying that I was a cripple, and ruined by the affair; between three and four hundred miles from home; and nothing to carry me there: he said he was very sorry for it, but he could not pay me; and left my friend in a violent hurry, like a *turncoat,* and a *deceitful fellow* as he is. Every one that reads this journal will probably be of the same opinion. I hope the freemen of the city of *Westminster* will take warning, not to put confidence in such a man as this, for the future. Was he a *wise* or an *honest* man, he would see me honourably paid; not only for the sake of policy, but from a principle of humanity.

FINIS

I delivered to the hon. Mr. Fox, one of these pamphlets, with the following letter, dated the 7th of *July,* 1783.

Honoured Sir,

Before I proceed to extremities, I think it proper to apprize you of the steps, which in justice to myself, you have driven me to the necessity of taking. It depends on yourself, to prevent my carrying my intentions into execution. The case being printed, the publication or suppression of it to-morrow morning will depend on your answer, as I am now waiting for it. I remain,

Honoured Sir,
Your most obedient,
Humble Servant,
Mary Tonkin.

Right Hon. Charles James Fox, Esq.

The Answer I received, after waiting three or four hours, was to this purpose:

It was peace now,[25] and Mr. Fox's turn was served.

Notes

1. Queen Charlotte, wife of George III.
2. While "faction" is a common charge in eighteenth-century politics, Tonkin is referring to the particularly virulent infighting of 1782–1784 among factions of the Whig party.
3. Source unidentified.
4. Sir Philip Stephens (1725–1809), secretary of the Admiralty.
5. Sir Thomas Pye (1713?–1785).
6. Edward Boscawen (1711–1761) and Edward Hawke (1705–1781), regarded as heroes for naval victories during the Seven Years' War (1757–1763) against the French in Canada.
7. David Murray, earl of Stormont (1727–1796).
8. Frederick, earl of Guilford, Lord North (1732–1793); head of one Whig faction and, by the time Tonkin writes, of the ministry.
9. Group of five seaports on southeast coast of England, incorporated under one governor.
10. Charles Watson Wentworth, marquis of Rockingham (1730–1782), head of the ministry from March 1782 until his sudden death on 1 July 1782.
11. Charles James Fox (1749–1806); influential Whig politician also known for his high-stakes gambling and relentless wenching; in 1783 he joined Lord North in a coalition ministry.
12. Towns in France.
13. John Montagu, earl of Sandwich (1718–1792), First Lord of the Admiralty 1771–1782.

14. Augustus, Viscount Keppel (1725–1786), succeeded Lord Sandwich as First Lord of the Admiralty.

15. Such antics were characteristic of Harlequin, a stock character in the popular form of improvisational comedy known as *commedia dell'arte*.

16. I am no writer by profession: I describe people as I found them, in plain language; and write, as most people *speak*, of the characters in this pamphlet [Tonkin].

17. Richard Brinsley Sheridan (1751–1816), playwright, politician, and at this time undersecretary of state for foreign affairs; Archibald Campbell Fraser (1736–1815) was another undersecretary. A Scotch pebble is a highly polished stone; Tonkin appears to be insulting Fraser's Scots heritage.

18. Packet, a mail or passenger ship.

19. Officer in charge of providing food, stores, and transport for a body of soldiers.

20. Henry Seymour Conway (1721–1795), commander in chief during Rockingham's ministry.

21. Thomas Robinson, Baron Grantham (1738–1786), secretary of state for foreign affairs in Shelburne's short-lived cabinet.

22. William Petty, second earl of Shelburne (1737–1805); head of Whig faction opposed to both Fox and Rockingham.

23. An official publication, including announcements of various sorts; the nature of Tonkin's insult is unclear.

24. From her friend T. P. in Morlaix.

25. The American War of Independence, in which France supported the colonies, concluded in 1783 with a peace negotiated by Fox.

George Anne Bellamy

1733?–1788

An Apology for the Life of George Anne Bellamy. Late of Covent-Garden Theatre. Written by herself. To which is annexed, her original Letter to John Calcraft, Esq; advertised to be published in October, 1767, but which was then violently suppressed. 2 vols. Dublin: Moncrieffe et al., 1785.

In her *Apology* George Anne Bellamy claims a birthdate of 1733, but she may have been born in 1731, and, according to some commentators, her narrative as a whole is "by no means reliable" (Highfill et al. 2:3). Certainly the *Apology* is cavalier about dates, so the course of Bellamy's career is difficult to follow. Her mother's maiden name was Seal and the family were Quakers, but her mother was less than devout: at fourteen she ran away from school to become the mistress of James O'Hara, baron of Tyrawley. When Lord Tyrawley was made ambassador to the Court of Lisbon in 1728, she went on the stage in Dublin, but she later joined him in Lisbon. At his instigation she then married Captain Bellamy, master of a trading vessel; a few months later, to the captain's "inexpressible astonishment and dissatisfaction" (1:14), George Anne was born. Bellamy departed and Lord Tyrawley acknowledged paternity of George Anne. When she was five, he sent her to be educated in a convent at Boulogne, in northern France, where she remained for six years. On her return to London he lodged her with one of his ex-servants, but he refused to support her when she began to live with her mother.

George Anne Bellamy claims she began her theatrical career at the age of fourteen, which would make the date 1745 or 1747; according to one biographer, however, she first performed in 1741. It is certain that she acted with the Covent Garden Theatre company in London in 1744, then with Dublin's Smock Lane Theatre from 1745 to 1747. She returned to Covent Garden for the 1748–1749 season, and she claims to have been kidnapped by an admirer (William, fifth Lord Byron), but this may have been a publicity stunt (Highfill et al. 2.11). After a short stay with her Quaker cousins, Bellamy was engaged by the Theatre Royal in Dublin. During this period she was befriended by Lady Cardigan and the duchess of Queensbury, courted by Sir George Metham, and reconciled with her father. When he insisted that she marry a Mr. Crump, however, she ran off with Metham and lived with him in the hope that he would eventually marry her. Bellamy also developed "a taste for expence" (1:177), and much of the *Apology* from this point on records periodic indebtedness.

After numerous tiffs with Metham, Bellamy took up with John Calcraft of Grantham, "an eminent politician" (Highfill et al. 2:13). At his insistence they signed a contract stipulating that he would marry her within seven years, a delay he claimed was necessitated by his "dependence" on Charles James Fox, who forbade him to "enter into a serious engagement with a woman in public life." Bellamy bore Calcraft two children, but when she learned that he had not only a mistress but a wife, she demanded that he pay her debts and left him. Engaged by a Dublin theater company, she lived with the actor West Digges for two years, possibly marrying him in Scotland in 1763. Returning to London and learning that she was £10,000 in debt, Bellamy signed a release of the marriage contract with Calcraft and departed for Scotland to escape her creditors. She acted in Edinburgh and Glasgow, then accepted a contract to return to Covent Garden, but a scandal over her relations with Calcraft broke in 1767 (the year her public letter of defense was "violently suppressed"), and it seems to have affected her theatrical career. Her contract with Covent Garden lapsed at the end of the 1767–1768 season, and the balance of the *Apology* records recurring debts. Other troubles included the scrapes of her two sons, the death of the elder son, and the loss of several expected legacies. By the end of the *Apology* Bellamy was reduced to applying for a position as housekeeper, and the profits from the book went to her creditors. She died in 1788.

TEXT: George Anne Bellamy's *Apology* takes the form of letters to "The Hon. Miss ———," written "in compliance with the solicitations of yourself and many other friends" (1:1). Some commentators believe that the book was ghostwritten by Alexander Bicknell from events and sentiments she provided. If Bicknell is responsible for the first-person narrator's flatulent style and oceanic self-absorption, one can only wonder at his taste. In any event, if Bellamy was involved in the production of the *Apology*, then the book can be seen as an authentic representation—if not record—of an eighteenth-century public woman. Although the *Apology* is often classified as a *mémoire scandaleuse*, the narrative is hardly titillating, and the author claims it was

George Anne Bellamy, portrait by F. Lindo, from the collection of the Garrick Club. Courtesy of e.t.archive/Garrick Club.

written to "rescue my character"; perhaps sincerely, she also hopes that "the recapitulation of my errors and misfortunes" (1:2) may serve as a warning to "the young and thoughtless of my own sex." In the excerpt (pp. 79–94 of volume one), Bellamy recounts two early career feuds (which Highfill et al. claim did not occur) and reflects on her profession.

An Apology for the Life of George Anne Bellamy /

LETTER XX

To show my readiness to obey your commands, Madam (for the request of a friend is as obligatory as a command) I employ almost every hour on the continuation of my narrative; and shall esteem myself sufficiently re-paid, if I can prevent it from proving tiresome. You must remember that it is the history of a weak woman, recited by the same weak woman. Be, therefore, to her faults, whether relative to her conduct, or her literary ones, *a little blind*. But a truce with apologies. Such as it is, I give it unto you.

The next winter, when our theatrical campaign commenced, we were very apprehensive that we should feel the desertion of so able a general as Garrick.[1] But through the exertions of the manager, who was deservedly a great favourite with the gentlemen of the college, at which he was bred, as the provost and professors had been his fellow-students, our success was not less than when we were aided by his powerful assistance—He who, *in himself alone*, was a tower of invincible strength.

A droll circumstance happened about this time, which I must not omit. Going one evening to Fishamble-Street concert, I happened to be seated next to Lord Chief Baron Bowes.[2] A gentleman, who was lately come to Dublin, entering into conversation with his Lordship, remarked to him (at the same time fixing his eyes upon me) that his daughter was vastly like him. We were at this period reviving at the theatre, "The Merchant of Venice;" upon which it instantly occurred to me, to make particular observations on the manner of the person I was thus supposed to resemble, in order to adopt it in the part of Portia, which I was to play.

I accordingly did so; and succeeded so happily, that when I made my appearance as the counsellor, the audience, struck with the similitude, universally exclaimed "Here comes the young Lord Chief Baron." And I retained that title during my residence in the kingdom.

The Lord Chief Baron himself was so much pleased with the imitation, that he paid me many compliments upon the occasion. He humorously remarked that I had even got his cough in the middle of a long word. This indeed was true, but it proceeded entirely from accident; as I never had the pleasure of hearing his Lordship speak in any of the courts. I however, luckily hit off this peculiarity in repeating the word *predicament*. Was it not that I am apprehensive of incurring the imputation of vanity, I would give you the conclusion of his Lordship's complimentary address to me. I will therefore omit it; but guess something very flattering, and even then, I assure you, that you will fall far short of the purport of it.

Early in the season, the tragedy of "All for love, or the World well Lost,"[3] was revived; in which Barry and Sheridan[4] stood unrivalled in the characters of Antony and Ventidius. The getting it up produced the following extraordinary incidents. The manager in an excursion he had made during the summer to London, had purchased a superb suit of clothes that had belonged to the Princess of Wales, and had only been worn by her on the birth-day. This was made into a dress for me to play the character of Cleopatra; and as the ground of it was silver tissue, my mother thought that by turning the body of it in, it would be a no[t] unbecoming addition to my waist, which was remarkably small. My maid-servant was accordingly sent to the theatre to assist the dresser and mantua-maker in preparing it; and also in sewing on a number of diamonds, my patroness not only having furnished me with her own, but borrowed several others of her acquaintance for me. When the women had finished the work, they all went out of the room, and left the door of it indiscreetly open.

Mrs. Furnival (who owed me a grudge, on account of my eclipsing her, as the more favourable reception I met with from the public, gave her room to conclude I did; and likewise for the stir which had been made last season about the character of Constance)[5] accidentally passed by the door of my dressing-room in the way to her own, as it stood open. Seeing my rich dress thus lying exposed, and observing no person by to prevent her, she stepped in, and carried off the Queen of Egypt's paraphernalia, to adorn herself in the character of Octavia, the Roman matron, which she was to perform. By remarking from time to time my dress, which was very different from the generality of heroines, Mrs. Furnival had just acquired taste enough to despise the black velvet in which those ladies were usually habited. And without considering the impropriety of enrobing a Roman matron in the habiliments of the Egyptian Queen; or perhaps not knowing that there was any impropriety in it, she determined, for once in her life-time, to be as fine as myself, and that at my expence. She accordingly set to work to let out the clothes, which, through my mother's œconomical advice, had been taken in.

When my servant returned to the room, and found the valuable dress, that had been committed to her charge, missing, her fright and agitation were beyond expression. She ran like a mad creature about the theatre, inquiring of every one whether they had seen any thing of it. At length she was informed that Mrs. Furnival had got possession of it. When running to that lady's dressing-room, she was nearly petrified at beholding the work, which had cost her so much pains, undone. My damsel's veins, unfortunately for Mrs. Furnival, were rich with the blood of the O'Bryens. And though she had not been blest with so polished an education as such a name was entitled to, she inherited at least the *spirit* of the Kings of Ulster. Thus qualified for carrying on an attack even of a more important nature, she at first demanded the dress with tolerable civility; but meeting with a peremptory refusal, the blood of her great fore-fathers boiled within her veins, and without any more ado, she fell tooth and nail upon poor Mrs. Furnival. So violent was the assault, that had not assistance arrived in time to rescue her from the fangs of the enraged Hibernian nymph, my theatrical rival would probably have never had an opportunity of appearing once in her life adorned with *real* jewels.

When I came to the theatre, I found my servant dissolved in tears at the sad disaster; for notwithstanding her heroic exertions, she had not been able to bring off the cause of the contest. But so far was I from partaking of her grief, that I could not help being highly diverted at the absurdity of the incident. Nothing concerning a theatre could at that time affect my temper. And I acknowledge I enjoyed a secret pleasure in the expectation of what the result would be. I sent indeed for the jewels; but the lady, rendered courageous by Nantz [brandy], and the presence of her paramour, Morgan,[6] who was not yet dead, she condescended to send me word, that I should have them after the play.

In this situation I had no other resource than to reverse the dresses, and appear as plain in the character of the luxurious Queen of Egypt, as Antony's good wife, although the sister of Caesar, ought to have been. In the room of precious stones, with which my head should have been decorated, I substituted pearls; and of all my finery I retained only my diadem, that indispensable mark of royalty.

Every transaction that takes place in the theatre, and every circumstance relative to it, are as well known in Dublin as they would be in a country town. The report of the richness and elegance of my dress had been universally the subject of conversation, for some time before the night of performance; when, to the surprise of the audience, I appeared in white satin. My kind patroness, who sat in the stage-box, seemed not to be able to account for such an unexpected circumstance. And not seeing me adorned with the jewels she had lent me, she naturally supposed I had reserved my regalia till the scene in which I was to meet my Antony.

When I had first entered the green-room, the manager, who expected to see me splendidly dressed, as it was natural to suppose the enchanting Cleopatra would have been upon such an occasion, expressed with some warmth his surprise at a disappointment, which he could only impute to caprice. Without being in the least discomposed by his warmth, I coolly told him, "that I had taken the advice Ventidius had sent me by Alexis, and had parted with both my clothes and jewels to Antony's wife." Mr. Sheridan could not conceive my meaning; but as it was now too late to make any alteration, he said no more upon the subject. He was not however long at a loss for an explanation; for going to introduce Octavia to the Emperor, he discovered the jay in all her borrowed plumes. An apparition could not have more astonished him. He was so confounded, that it was some time before he could go on with his part. At the same instant Mrs. Butler exclaimed aloud, "Good Heaven, the woman has got on my diamonds!" The gentlemen in the pit concluding that Mrs. Butler had been robbed of them by Mrs. Furnival; and the general consternation, occasioned by so extraordinary a scene, is not to be described. But the house observing Mr. Sheridan to smile, they supposed there was some mystery in the affair, which induced them to wait with patience till the conclusion of the act. As soon as it was finished, they bestowed their applause upon Antony and his faithful veteran, but as if they had all been animated by the same mind, they cried out, "No more Furnival! No more Furnival!" The fine dressed lady, disappointed of the acclamations she expected to receive on account of the grandeur of her habiliments, and thus hooted for the impropriety of her conduct, very prudently called fits to her aid, which incapacitated her from appearing again. And the audience had the good nature to wait patiently till Mrs. Elmy, whom curiosity had led to the theatre, had dressed to finish the part. Had the character of Octavia been originally cast according to merit, Mrs. Elmy would certainly have had the preference; as the softness of her manner, and the propriety with which she spoke, justly entitled her to it.

The impropriety of Mrs. Furnival's conduct in the affair, just related, warrants my troubling you with an observation I have frequently made, which is, that every attempt to obtain a desirable end, if the means are not consistent with honour and rectitude, mar instead of promoting it. If I recollect aright, I have made a remark somewhat similar to this in a former letter, but it cannot be too often repeated, "Honesty will be always found to be the best policy."—"More proverbs, and preaching again?" methinks I hear you say; "Pray go on with your narrative!"—I will, my dear Madam, when I have reminded you that it was by your permission I now and then preach, as you are pleased to term it.

With these interruptions the piece could not appear to so much advantage, on its first representation, as there was reason to hope it would. But the next night, either inspired with the brilliancy of my ornaments, or animated by the sight of his Excellency Lord Chesterfield, who together with his Lady, graced the theatre, it was the general opinion that I never played with so much spirit, or did greater justice to a part. The applause I received was universal.

A gentleman, who stood near the stage-door, took a very unallowable method of shewing his approbation. Being a little flushed with liquor, or otherwise I am persuaded he would not have been capable of the rudeness, he put his lips to the back of my neck as I passed him. Justly enraged at so great an insult, and not considering that the Lord Lieutenant was present, or that it was committed before such a number of spectators, I instantly turned about, and gave the gentleman a slap in the face. Violent and unbecoming as this sudden token of resentment appeared, it received the approbation of Lord Chesterfield, who rose from his seat and applauded me for some time with his hands; the whole audience, as you may suppose, following his example. At the conclusion of the act, Major Macartney came, by order [of] his Excellency, to Mr. St. Leger (that was the gentleman's name) requesting that he would make a public apology for this forgetfulness of decorum; which he accordingly did. I have reason to believe that this incident contributed, in a great measure, to a reform that Mr. Sheridan, with great propriety, soon after made. Agreeable to this regulation, no gentlemen, in future, were to be admitted behind the scenes.

G. A. B.

LETTER XXI.

March 25, 17—.

"Proceed, and indulge yourself in any manner you please, whenever fancy prompts you to wander from the road of your history; for I read with inexpressible pleasure every part of your letters."—Do you really write thus, my dear Madam? And does my humble attempt to afford you entertainment answer the intended purpose? It does, it does. You tell me so; and I know you are too sincere to flatter me. Thus encouraged, I *will* proceed. Nor shall one reluctant sigh at the length of the way which still lies before me, or a further fear of proving tiresome to you, escape me.

Notwithstanding the applause bestowed upon my theatrical talents by the people of Dublin, was an indubitable proof of my possessing no mean degree of merit, yet I was apprehensive (though naturally vain) that this was rather exaggerated by their partiality, and the support I received on account of my family from the higher ranks. I endeavoured therefore, by *intense application*, as I have already told you, to render them more justly deserving of the public approbation.

Mr. Garrick having about this time purchased a half-share of the patent of Drury Lane theatre, and my success in Dublin having reached his ears, he wished to engage me for the ensuing season. And Mr. Delany,[7] an actor then of the first rate, being obliged to visit Ireland to take possession of an estate left him by his mother, Mr. Garrick deputed him to make me an offer of ten pounds a week. This offer however I refused; and I acknowledge my indiscretion in so doing. I must here just observe, that the applause I met with in comedy was equal, if not superior, to that which was bestowed upon me when I played in tragedy. And by playing the character of Biddy in "Miss in her Teens,"[8] I convinced the town, that I was no less qualified to perform in *low* than in *genteel* comedy.

I was about this time informed that Mr. Quin had been so displeased with me for my apparent ingratitude,[9] that he had consented to be reconciled to Mrs. Cibber;[10] and now bestowed that generous attention on her that I should otherwise have shared in. He had been greatly offended with that lady also, on account of her desertion from Covent-Garden theatre to Drury-Lane. She lay under as many obligations to him for *real* favours as I did for intentional ones; for she had not only been necessitated to accept of those of a pecuniary nature, but had been obliged to him for her re-establishment on the English stage, from which she had been precluded, for some time, by the machinations of her husband. Her ingratitude was, notwithstanding, now obliterated from Mr. Quin's mind, and he took her once more under his protection.

My refusal of Mr. Garrick's offer offended him so highly, that, it was said, he formed a resolution never to engage me upon any terms whatever. But the resolutions of managers are seldom considered as binding, when opposed by their interest. Self-interest, with them, as with the greatest part of mankind, is the grand moving principle. Pique, resentment, prejudice, in an instant dissolve before it. Even pride and arrogance bend submissive to it. It may therefore be truly said, however degrading the thought, to be the *ruling passion* of the human mind.

Just at this period an event happened, which, if it had been attended with the expected consequences, would have broken Mrs. O'Hara's heart, have greatly affected the mind of my patroness, and have ruined my reputation for ever. One night, as I was performing the part of Lady Townley in "The Provoked Husband,"[11] I received a card from Mrs. Butler, wrote in a servant's hand, requesting me to come to her house as soon as I should be at liberty. As the note was delivered to me during the performance of the play, I had only leisure just to send verbally, with my compliments, that the fatigue of the evening would prevent me from being able to do myself that honour.

Had I attended to the circumstance of the card's being written by a servant, I must have been convinced that something was wrong; as my dear friend Miss Butler was always happy in seizing every occasion to write to me. It, however, passed unnoticed. Not long after, I received another note, informing me, that I must absolutely come the moment I had finished, and even without waiting to change my dress. So very pressing an invitation, I own excited my curiosity, and made me impatient for the conclusion of my business. I was to have played Miss Biddy in the entertainment; but the gentleman who was to have performed Fribble being suddenly taken ill, the after-piece was obliged to be changed; which enabled me to make my curtsey much sooner than I had reason to expect.

My task being done, I got into my chair in the same dress in which I had played the character of Lady Townley, and hastened away to Stephen's-Green. As the dress I wore was a modern one, there was no great impropriety in my appearing in it off the stage. Just as I entered one door of the parlour in which Mrs. Butler and her female visitors were, the Colonel, and several gentlemen, who had just risen from their bottle, were ushered in at the opposite one. The company was numerous; and the elegance of my dress attracted the attention of all the gentlemen; but not one of the ladies condescended to speak to me. Even the lady whose guest I was, only deigned to welcome me, on my entrance, with a formal declination of her head.

A reception so indifferent from what I had been accustomed to in that hospitable mansion, not only surprised, but greatly shocked me. In this agitation of mind, I made up to Mrs. O'Hara, who was present, and requested she would inform me what was the occasion of it. The answer I received from her was, that a few minutes would determine whether she should ever notice me again. The coolness of her manner, whilst she uttered this, as I was conscious of my innocence, and my aunt must have been well assured of the sincerity of my heart, piqued my pride for a moment; but this emotion soon went off, and I assumed, at least in appearance, my usual tranquillity.

A gentleman now made his *entrée*, whose figure, shape, dress, and address, exceeded every thing I had ever beheld before. The ladies, notwithstanding, continued to look as serious and demure as a convocation of old maids met on purpose to dissect the reputation of a giddy thoughtless young one. Nor did this beautiful stranger, with all his attractions, seem to be less neglected than myself. From being in such company, and in such a splendid dress, for my head was adorned with the jewels of my patroness, the gentleman might naturally conclude, that I was a person of quality. And as a young lady of distinction had lately taken an airing, on a moonlight night, with a noble lord, he imagined, in all probability, from the reserve with which he saw me received by the ladies, that I was the very identical girl who had made that *faux pas*, and who had now *obtruded* herself into the first circle in the kingdom. What other opinion could he form of me from the present appearance of things.

From this motive, or some other, his attention appeared to be fixed upon me, in preference to any of the other ladies; and he introduced himself to me with an air so easy and confident, that I knew immediately that he had travelled. He acquainted me, that he was just returned from making the *grand tour*, and was come to take possession of his estate, and settle for the remainder of his days in Ireland. We then entered into conversation on different subjects, in which I acquitted myself with more ease than I expected I could have done in a state of such suspense. My affected cheerfulness was so well counterfeited, that it appeared to be real; and I kept up the ball with so much spirit, that my companion seemed to entertain a better opinion of me than he had done at first.

The test intended for the discovery of some dubious points, which will presently be known, having now been carried on as long as necessary, Miss Butler was sent to put a stop to our *tête à tête*. When my *Ganymede*,[12] whose curiosity had been on tiptoe to find out who I was, went to the upper end of the room, to make the needful inquiries of the lady of the house. Having in a whisper asked the question, Mrs. Butler answered *aloud*, "Surely, you must know her. I am certain you know her; nay, that you are well acquainted with her." The gentleman, not a little disconcerted at this want, in a lady of fashion, of what is usually termed *du monde*,[13] that is, among other things, replying to a whisper in an audible voice; assured her, still in a low tone, that he had never seen me before, and now felt himself greatly interested in the inquiry. "Fye, fye, Mr. Medlicote," returned my patroness, "what can you say for yourself, when I inform you, that this is the dear girl whose character you so cruelly aspersed at dinner?"

I now plainly perceived, that this accomplished gentleman, vain of his attractive graces, had boasted, like too many others, of favours he had never received; not knowing that he did so in the presence of my best friends, and that there was a certainty of his false assertions being detected. The pencil of Hogarth[14] alone could justly depicture the confusion of the gentleman at this discovery of his treachery; or of my petrefaction at finding myself the subject of his slander. It for some time totally deprived me of the use of every faculty till at length my patroness kindly relieved me from the situation in which I was absorbed. Coming up to me, she took me by the hand, and with a smile on her countenance thus addressed me: "My dear child, you have gone through a fiery trial; but it was a very necessary one. This gentleman has vilely traduced your character. We were all perfectly convinced that you did not merit what he said of you; but had he seen you first at the theatre, instead of here, he would, doubtlessly, have maintained his assertions with oaths, and there would then have been no possibility of contradicting them, however favourably we may have thought of you, notwithstanding. By the method we have pursued, though it has been somewhat irksome to you, his falsehoods have been so palpably disproved, as not to admit of the least palliation." Having said this, she embraced me in the most cordial manner. And as soon as I got from her embrace, I ran and threw myself into the arms of my dear aunt, who seemed to feel the utmost satisfaction at my triumph.

As for my traducer, it may be supposed he did not long disgust us with his company. Charming and accomplished as he was, there did not appear to be a wish among us all to detain him.—How much more charming and accomplished would he have been, had truth spread her refulgent beams over those perfections with which nature in so bounteous a manner had favoured him!—Of all human failings that of *detraction* is certainly one of the worst. The venom of the tongue is more fatal in its consequences than the deadly poison of the asp. It not only proves destructive to individuals, but to the peace and happiness of whole families.—But its fatal effects are so pointedly and beautifully described by that great master of nature, Shakspere,[15] in the following well-known passage, that were I to fill up a whole letter with the severest censures reason and experience could dictate, I should not be able to say the twentieth part the tithe of what he has said in these *few* immortal lines.

> "*Good name* in man and woman
> "Is the immediate jewel of their souls;
> "Who steals my purse steals trash, 'tis something, nothing;
> " 'Twas mine, 'tis his, and has been slave to thousands;
> "But he that filches from me my good name,
> "Robs me of that which not enriches him,
> "And makes me poor indeed."

G. A. B

March 31, 17—.

When Mr. Medlicote was gone, one of the gentlemen present acquainted us, that during his travels, he became enamoured with a beautiful Italian lady; who listening to his professions of love, left her family, and became the partner of his flight. Her brother, being informed of the seduction, pursued the fair fugitive and her paramour, and overtaking them, gave the gentleman his choice either to marry his sister, or settle the affair in the field of honour. Mr. Medlicote, finding there was no alternative, prudently chose the former, and they were accordingly united in indissoluble bonds.

All the company at Colonel Butler's seemed to agree in opinion, that had my family and fortune equalled his expectations, he would have considered his union with the Italian lady invalid, from its being an act of compulsion on his part, and without the least scruple have made an offer of his hand, in defiance of honour, humanity, and every tender feeling. Mrs. Butler observed, that nothing could equal her pleasure at this public testimony of the falsity of Medlicote's accusation; for notwithstanding she was convinced of my innocence, and had found it fully confirmed by the propriety of my conduct since I had resided in that kingdom, she could not have permitted her daughter to live in terms of strict intimacy with one whose reputation was not perfectly *unsullied*.

The last word *unsullied* struck me, at the time Mrs. Butler made use of it, with inexpressible force; and as there is no crime, as I have frequently said, that I hold in equal detestation with deceit, I determined, let what would be the consequence, to inform that lady the first opportunity that offered, that I was, unhappily, an unfit person for an intimate with her daughter, my character having been *sullied*, though very undeservedly, by the rude breath of scandal, through the wicked machinations of the noblemen formerly mentioned.[16] For the present I contented myself with entering into a vindication of those of the profession in which I was engaged.

I told the company, that though many young men, through levity, were so inhuman as to blast the character of most of those females who were in the theatrical line, merely because they supposed their reputation was of so little consequence, that they were fit subjects for their sportive fancy; yet there were many, I was persuaded, who trod the stage, and were truly virtuous. I brought as examples a Pritchard and a Clive;[17] to whom I said, I doubted not but many others might be added. I observed, that were actresses as chaste as vestals, such a tongue as a Medlicote's may by infamous insinuations blast their fame for ever, notwithstanding there were as

An Apology for the Life of George Anne Bellamy / 225

little foundation for them, as those with regard to myself had just been discovered to have. I concluded with declaring that I thought a woman who preserved an unblemished reputation on the stage, to be infinitely more praiseworthy, than those who retained a good name, merely because they were secured by rank or fortune from the temptations actresses are exposed to; or than such as, through their mediocrity in life, do not fall in the way of the gay and dissolute. Here Colonel Butler interrupted my declamation by singing, "And she may be chaste that never was tried."[18] This sally of his, which came in so *a-propos*, and tended to confirm the propositions I had just been striving to establish, restored cheerfulness; who, though she returned so late, was a very welcome visitor.

When I returned home, though it was very late, I could not sleep for the reflections which arose in my mind, on a review of the incidents of the day. "How much," cried I, "are the world mistaken in their ideas of *virtue*, as well as of *happiness!* the generality of mankind seem to comprise every virtue in that of *chastity*. Without doubt, chastity is one of the first and most justly admired virtues that adorns the female mind; yet when we consider, that punishment certainly attends a breach of that virtue; that the great monitor conscience is perpetually preying on the heart of every frail one capable of reflection; and that disgrace is their consequent portion; surely the *truly* virtuous ought rather to pity, and pour balm into the bosom of those who are thus unfortunately condemned to an earthly purgatory, and may have many extenuations to plead, than add to their afflictions by reproaches or contempt."—Such were my sentiments at that period, young as I was, and such are they at this hour. But though I thus plead the cause of the unfortunate, it is not because I have unhappily a claim to the same lenity myself, or that I wish to extenuate a deviation from the path of rectitude in this point; I have as high a veneration for chastity and her *true* votaries, and I as much regret the loss of innocence (my mind still retaining its native purity) as the most unerring of my sex can do.—But as Hamlet says, "Somewhat too much of this."

In the morning, after a restless night, I found myself in a fever. The different passions with which my mind had been agitated during the preceding evening, had been more than my body could bear, and a fever ensued. I was not in the least concerned at my indisposition, as it gave me an opportunity of staying at home without offending any one. My friends, however, were greatly alarmed. Mrs. Butler and her beloved daughter did me the honour to pay me a visit, and my absence from the theatre was considered as a general calamity. During my confinement I could not help indulging my reflections on the subject which had lately taken possession of my mind; and I never before viewed the profession I had embraced in so humiliating a light as I now did through Medlicote's aspersions. That every fool who happened to be possessed of a fortune, should think himself licensed to take liberties with me; or even that my own footman, upon any dislike, should be able to go for a shilling into the theatre, and insult me; was what I could not bear to think of. The very idea affected me so much, that I never could regain, from this time, the self-sufficiency I possessed before. My indisposition increased from these corroding thoughts; and it was several days before I was able to attend at the theatre. When I did so, a disagreeable event happened, which retarded my perfect recovery, and, with some other concurrent circumstances, was the cause of my leaving Ireland.

Mr. Sheridan, in consequence of the insult I had received from Mr. St. Leger, as before related, and on account of the inconveniences arising from the custom, had given a general order at the doors of the theatre, and notice in all the public papers, that no gentleman was, on any account, to be admitted behind the scenes. It happened one night, just as I was so far recovered as to venture to the house, but not to perform; that an officer, who had more wine in his head, than humanity in his heart, insisted on passing the centry placed at the stage-door. The poor fellow persisting in his refusal of admittance, the officer drew his sword and stabbed him in the thigh, with so much violence, that the weapon broke, and left a piece in the most dangerous part. Hearing a riot on the stage, I ran from the box in which I sat, and flew in my fright to the next centinel for protection. This happening to be the man who had been wounded, I found myself in a moment encompassed by numbers, and was obliged to be a witness to the broken steel being taken out. The unexpectedness of this scene, and the terrors I was thrown into by it, as I was not perfectly restored to health, were productive of a relapse. The man, however, happily recovered through the placidness of his disposition; but having lost the use of his leg, the offender, who was a man of quality, provided for him for life.

Notes

1. David Garrick (1717–1779), playwright and manager of Drury Lane Theatre 1747–1776, considered the finest actor of his generation.
2. John Bowes (1690–1767), at the time baron of the Exchequer in Ireland.
3. John Dryden's 1678 adaption of Shakespeare's *Antony and Cleopatra*.

4. Spranger Barry (1719–1797), actor; Thomas Sheridan (1719–1788), actor, father of playwright and politician Richard Brinsley Sheridan, and manager of Dublin's Theatre Royal ca. 1744–1754.

5. Furnival, another actress in the company, the previous season played Constance in Shakespeare's *King John*, a role Bellamy wanted and eventually obtained after Furnival—with the help of the "stir" created by Bellamy's claque—bombed in the part.

6. An actor; nothing more is known of him.

7. Dennis Delane (?–1750), an actor best known for his performances in tragedy.

8. Very popular two-act farce written by Garrick in 1747.

9. James Quin (1693–1766), an actor who had taken Bellamy under his wing, was "displeased" because he believed she had accepted an offer from another theater company.

10. Susannah Cibber (1714–1766), an actress and singer; wife of Theophilus Cibber. After the theatrical season of 1749–1750, she and Spranger Barry defected to the Covent Garden Theatre company, where they starred in a production of *Romeo and Juliet* intended to rival the Drury Lane production starring Garrick and Bellamy.

11. Begun by John Vanbrugh as a sequel to his *The Provok'd Wife* (1697) and completed by Colley Cibber in 1728.

12. In Greek mythology, a human boy whom Zeus, enamored of his beauty, kidnapped and made his cup-bearer; in eighteenth-century usage, often a facetious term for a server, but it also suggests a boy kept by an older man for sexual purposes. It is not clear how Bellamy is using the term.

13. Knowledge of the ways of the fashionable world.

14. William Hogarth (1697–1764), painter, engraver, and printmaker best known for his series of satiric prints, such as *The Rake's Progress* and *Marriage à la Mode*.

15. Othello, Act III. Scene V [Bellamy].

16. Presumably her abductor, William, Lord Byron, and his cronies.

17. Hannah Pritchard (1711–1768) and Kitty Clive (1711–1785), actresses much admired for their sexual respectability.

18. Source unidentified.

Jane Elizabeth Moore

1738–AFTER 1796

Genuine Memoirs of Jane Elizabeth Moore, Lately of Bermondsey, in the County of Surry. Written by Herself: Containing / The singular adventures of Herself and Family. / Her Sentimental Journey through Great Britain; specifying the various Manufactures carried on at each Town. / A comprehensive Treatise on the Trade, Manufactures, Navigation, Laws and Police of this Kingdom, and the necessity of a Country Hospital. To which is prefixed a Poetic Index. 3 vols. London: Logographic Press/J. Bew, [1785].

Jane Elizabeth Gobeil was born on 30 September 1738 into a family of merchants and traders. Her maternal grandfather had been indentured to a silversmith and engraver, and her father was engaged in leather trade and manufacture. Jane's mother died three years after her birth, and for the next three years she was raised by her maternal great-grandmother. When her father married a woman he had known for fifteen days, Jane returned to his house but was soon sent to her stepmother's sister. The couple separated when Jane was ten, and for the next three years she alternated between home and schools. Jane had early demonstrated a "talent at trade" (1:129–30), transacting "business of consequence" when she was only twelve, so when she returned home in May 1753 she was "put to the desk" and began to handle her father's accounts; eventually she was, in effect, running his business (1:185). Although initially she preferred business to marriage, when Moore proposed she accepted him; determined "not to be obligated to any man breathing" (1:297), she also bullied her father into dowering her with "a daughter's share" of the business. She was married on 10 October 1761. In the next three years she bore two children, both of whom died, and continued in both her father's and her husband's businesses. When her father died, she learned that he had not provided for the promised dower; "I may be pardoned if I say my grief much sooner subsided, th[a]n it would otherwise have done" (2:54–55), and she engaged in a six-year lawsuit contesting the will.

Much of the second volume of Jane's *Memoirs* alternates among descriptions of her subsequent business concerns, her illnesses brought on by overwork, and her travels throughout the United Kingdom. In 1773, amid the difficulties of wartime trade, she learned that her husband was having an affair with her maid, and the following five years are punctuated with further discoveries of his mistresses and her stepson's various peccadilloes. Moore suffered several strokes and then a relapse after being abused by his drunken son; by the spring of 1781 "widowhood seemed inevitable" (316), and Jane too was ill. This volume of the *Memoirs* concludes somewhat rapidly with her husband's death and the subsequent financial difficulties. Volume three is an analysis of Britain's economic state. Jane justifies such a treatise "from a female pen" (1:1) by reminding the reader that she is "wholly conversant" with trade and manufacture, and the volume ranges from fisheries and "mechanism and ingenuity in general" (3:24) to coinage, customs and excise, and several chapters on English law. She published a volume of *Miscellaneous Poems* in 1796. The date of her death is unknown.

TEXT: Jane Elizabeth Moore published three volumes of *Memoirs* in 1785, perhaps in the hope of attracting "patrons" (2:347). The excerpt (pp. 321–348 of volume two) covers her business and domestic trials at the time she was completing the book.

♋ ♋

THE TWENTY-SIXTH OF AUGUST, (this last event[1] happening in July) closed the scene of this mortal life with Mr. Moore, but this did not happen till I was enabled again to travel and attend business; nor till he had extorted from me a promise to give his son one more trial, by adopting him my clerk and assistant; this I promised to do on his conduct being such as should enable me to give him countenance. This scene of mortality affected me very sensibly, as notwithstanding every effort to the contrary, and every reflection I could bring to my ideas, I felt the separation from a husband more keenly, than I had ever done that of my children,[2] who had never offended, and seeing myself unguarded in the true sense of the word, and exposed to every evil in life, and that under the most precarious and perplexed fate, that I believe ever followed any single individual, I stood aghast and unable almost to turn my eyes to heaven; yet knowing there was no confidence in man, I had no remedy but to redouble my supplication to the All-wise-disposer of events here, who can in his good time, or in eternity, baffle the evil designs of both temporal and spiritual enemies, whenever he sees it consistent with his divine wisdom.

The kindness of my private friends, and the assistance held out by my connexions in trade on this melancholy occasion, did equal honour to both parties, as every nerve was strained to oblige me in this trying moment; but the will having laid me under the disagreeable necessity of procuring joint securities for the payment of the legacy to my son-in-law,[3] in one month, or have my premises entered, I was obliged to look accordingly among my friends, for such as I thought would acquiese in my request, and unfortunately (as it has since proved) I succeeded too well, for my dependance in that case being on gentlemen who were then in the country, one of those I made choice of, proposing to me (instead of taking the whole term of five years specified in the will) to pay by instalments, in five distinct payments, I procured my *ruin*, by yielding to his request, and a negative being put upon almost every thing I undertook after signing the bond; nothing but the most adverse fate, far exceeding all I had before seen, succeeded as fast as one event could follow another, near twenty per cent loss upon stock in hand, fifty advance upon an article which must in my consumption at least lose me five hundred pounds annually (from the usual standard price) the depricated value of the most staple article for emolument, being from the year 1778 to 1782, ninety per cent loss upon that year's returns in one single article, and some others nearly in the same proportion. I hope my candid friends will admit of my being under such circumstances a great sufferer; yet by the rigid œconomy I adhered to, I through all those difficulties made an advantage not despicable in the two years and an half I followed my business, in one of which from a disagreement among the men, in the next branch from me, two months past under a total stagnation of trade, and on my exposing a large quantity of goods (for which there was then no current demand) to public sale, a malicious information was laid against me in the excise,[4] by some malignant neighbour, who stopped the proceedings, the goods being immediately seized; in this as in other cases, I could boast of support, from the opinion mankind had of the rectitude of my general conduct. The officers who surveyed me, were ready to declare my innocence in the matter, and accordingly informed the commissioners what thoughts they entertained on the subject, when I was informed I might have the goods restored, but how the message was misconstrued that I sent, I am not able to say, but the goods which they retained were ordered to the Exchequer, and they lay some time in suspence, but on personal application they were restored; in this business, I received from those who examined the petition (which was my own drawing and writing) many encomiums, and as I succeeded with out expence in law, I thought myself rather fortunate on the whole, notwithstanding I must have sustained a loss to a large amount in extra expences, and the disappointment I met with in the sale.

On my return, from the great fatigue I underwent at the Excise Office, (as only personal attendance could be admitted of) I soon after received back my papers from Jamaica[5] by the gentleman who took them out untouched, the attorney whom I had there appointed to do the business, being deprived of his reason, no steps could be taken till another was fixed on, which must be attended with additional expence and much time. The same week my out-door collector of cash, was impressed and detained all night with a large sum about him, and no release could be had but on personal application, and which was at last with difficulty obtained; this was about the month of September 1782, that little more than one year had elapsed for all those adventures, and this bringing on the time of payment, for one of the instalments, the executors of Mr. Moore's will made their demand accordingly, but by my paying many of my unfortunate, or rather imprudent husband's debts, and many other pressing occasions, I was not able at that time to do. This second winter passed very gloomy indeed, (the first I adopted a young friend as a companion) but in January 1783, I fulfilled my contract respecting the payment, and peace taking place my hope once more revived, trusting there might yet a ray of hope transcend in my favour, but that was not to be the case, for except in two articles, no difference was perceptible, and those were not adequate to the drop which continued in the markets; if it could render me any consolation, I certainly saw others in the same situation (except that they had more care taken by their friends) respecting trade, but their family connexions being (where needed) at hand, and their not having the obligation against them I unfortunately had, these have (I am happy to say) been able to stand against the storm that has burst over my head, and I sincerely hope they ever will.

I omitted in my last observations, to mention that nothing could be done respecting the wish I had, to have countenanced my son-in-law, who instead of attending the compting house[6] properly, sometimes could not be seen more than twice in the week, and what connexions he kept, it was not in my power to discover, more then that the expensive education he had, could not keep him from company of the lowest sort. I mean those on whom vice, and its concomitants were constant attendants in his stead, I was so fortunate as to be able to put a person fully deserving my confidence, (who had been of tried fidelity in the oil trade) but from too great a desire of saving expence, I denied myself the indulgence of having him constantly at the desk. My assistant in the active part of the trade, beginning the world on his own account, I had likewise the good luck to procure another, who had been formerly with us seven years, that I then thought myself enabled to do a considerable stroke in business, still looking forward for the advantages expected from a composure of the state, but the revolutions in the average of the funds, being much against trade, no prospect seemed to flatter my expectations, equal to my payments on the bond, and the second coming due, I could only lodge securities (such as I then thought valid) in the hands of the executors, on which, (whether by their permission or not, I am not able to say,) my son-in-law took the liberty of propagating to my dealers and neighbours, (as many as were in his reach) that as I had failed in the payment then due, my premises would be immediately entered by those who had the bond in possession. This for some considerable time was kept from me, but each person to whom I was indebted, delivering in their accounts and demanding payment without ceremony; I shewed so much anxiety, that at last the secret was disclosed, and I was necessitated to sell an estate in Holborn, to pay some debts of a delicate nature, and much more fell a sacrifice by being obligated to provide for those of my creditors, where my future dependance must lay, if I continued my trade. But as from such repeated persecutions, I could by no means have any prospect of satisfaction, I one evening in coming from the country, fixed a determined resolution to decline business, part with my premises, and if possible discharge everything I owed, and take my chance in life, trusting for that succour from the hand of the Almighty, that did not seem to portend me, from those whom I trusted would have rendered me every assistance, especially as their own interest was essentially concerned, (one being dead) and two of them being creditors to Mr. Moore's estate for money borrowed by him, part of which I had paid to both of them.

This winter certainly was productive of far more evils than any of the preceding, (even bad as I have announced them) for in the month of November coming from Richmond Park with a friend, with whom I had been on business, we on this side Wandsworth, were attacked by a single highwayman who with the most horrid imprecations imaginable, notwithstanding he had many pounds of us, threatened with death many times both the coachman and myself, nor could the interference of the gentleman with me, (whose agitation of mind is still impressed on my memory) scarcely prevent his snap[p]ing the pistol, which he held some minutes to my mouth, and this because he was not content with having my money, but insisted on having the purse which the money was taken out of, and which in my haste I could not find, but I must confess, that even at that moment my courage did not forsake me sufficiently, to admit of any behaviour bordering on reproach, and indeed my companion displayed no fear bordering on cowardice, but protected me in the most becoming manner. I was equally unsuccessful this season, in all my undertakings, for on my doing business for some of my principals in trade, who wished me to engage in that branch, thinking it might promote my interest more essentially, an accident which no one could account for, blasted again my hopes, and prevented me taking such steps, as might have continued me in my situation, and had I really been possessed of Job's patience, the scenes I went through must have almost totally annihilated it.

I determined if possible, to quit my trade and premises by lady-day[7] following, (to say in 1784) but the long frost prevented the latter being exposed to public sale, till the twenty-second of April, when the Middlesex election being fixed for that day, I met another disappointment, and the fifth of May was next appointed, in which intervening time, the discovery of the steam engines being made public I lost another chance, water property then yielding no amount, and there was a flaw in the deeds, which could it have been rectified in time, might as I was assured, have in some measure prevented the disagreeable proceedings of my adopted guardians. But this being literally prevented, by every method contrary to the dictates of humanity, I think it proper after noticing a few more particulars, to give the heads [i.e., main points] of the most melancholly part of my singular narrative, which has yet occurred. I omitted to mention one particular, which in the month of February 1783, in some measure relieved my anxiety, which was, the satisfaction I received in seeing my first cousin on the mothers side, whom I noticed in the preceeding part of this account, and on whom time had operated to much more advantage, than to myself; he had a great part of the seventeen years I had not seen him been, in Spain, where he now is, in an exalted station in the mercantile line, and whose correspondence I still enjoy; and as I informed him when in England, of some part of my ill success, it did not cause so great an alarm to him, as it otherwise would, especially as in my letters, I occasionally informed him of my situation, and fully intended, after yielding up all I possest, to have been a few months fostered under his roof, by way of consulting him, on what mode I could with propriety fix for my future subsistence, which being interpreted to my disadvantage, or at least to cover other proceedings, was charged to me as a collusive idea, notwithstanding I had by public advertisements offered my effects for sale, which proceedings alone, had I been sufficiently fortunate to have fallen into the hands of social beings, would have justified my conduct, and had not my various misfortunes and disappointments been known, to the very identical persons who have so severely persecuted me, much might have been said, but as my extraordinary case can be vouched, by the most respectable people in the trade and neighbourhood, where I was born and lived, I trust the candid and pathetic readers of this plain narrative, will, if not shed a tear, at least so far apply my case, as to urge them to take such part in my troubles as to wish me a more calm autumn than I have experienced either in the spring or summer of my life, especially when I declare, that from Michaelmas 1784, to Christmas 1785, being only the space of fifteen months, I endured the very extraordinary experience of being robbed once on the high road, had once my own waggon robbed, once lost a large quantity of linen and other things out of a neighbour's waggon, which was likewise robbed, sustained damage in trade to a large amount, suffered a great loss by horses, had nine different accidents at the risk of my life, by attending my occupation, had a confirmation from Jamaica of the loss of near a thousand pounds, lost the sale of my premises, was six weeks under a surgeon, with a contusion in my left shoulder, (which will never I believe be again as before) was arrested by Mr. Moore's executors, and lay six weeks in a spunging house,[8] and from thence was obligated to remove to the King's Bench Prison, during which time I was made a bankrupt, for a debt contracted by my husband, to which statute I duly surrendered, and received many encomiums, for the labour I had bestowed, from the commissioners, yet notwithstanding all this diligence I have ever since been kept in prison on the first action, and had judgment signed against me sixteen days after I had legally yielded up the last guinea; I am not delicate in this declaration, as when in the presence of my most respectable friends, who had well known my distresses, and how they had been agitated, I offered every assistance in my power, provided I could be liberated, when fraught with all the venom that the evil genius of man could suggest, I received for answer, that I might as well assist in prison as elsewhere; (when to gratify the desire of keeping a widow, divested of every family connexions, and the whole of her property, by a singularity of fate uncommon, I hope to the generality of the world) in so horrid a situation, the proceedings against me were as above, and that without the least aggravation on my part, having not so much us [sic] put in a plea to the declaration. If any party is in this offended, for answer let it suffice to say, that on every application my friends have made in my behalf, to Mr. Moore's executors, their answer has been, that I was not kept in prison at their suit, and as among the rest of my misfortunes, I lost my own solicitor who died two days after the return of my writ, or something might e'er now, have been construed to my relief; or had there been a man employed by my persecutors, who had been enough a Christian, to have paid the least regard either to age, sex or education, I am led to believe, that I should not have been now in the eighth month of imprisonment, where I blush not to say, that had not that benevolence of heart (for which this country is so remarked) extended itself to my situation, from the most cordial friends, I must in the true sense of the word have wanted the necessaries of life, notwithstanding I have declared my readiness and willingness, to do every thing in my power to extricate every party concerned in this unfortunate business.

I am bound by every adherence to true politeness, to apologize in the most scrupulous manner, to those of my readers, who cannot (from a want of personal knowledge of me) be any way interested in the particulars of this declaration, than as directed by their own tender feelings; but if truth, solid truth can hold out any merit in the performance, I hope it may be admitted as a palliative, and I trust may obliterate in idea, the many faults which must be unavoidably perceptible to a criticizing pen; but when it is duly considered, how poignantly I must be affected at the partial descriptions I pledged myself to hold out to the public, and those of such persons as should have attended most particularly to my interest, I flatter myself, that that candor and generosity which has so frequently distinguished itself on this fertile spot, will sufficiently do away my present inaccuracies, to encourage me to proceed on literary ground, when, I hope, on more general subjects presenting themselves, my abilities may be more amply liberated. I should have here exhibited some specimens of my performances in poetry, but my friends at whose request I publish this, expressing a desire to have the account of my excursions journalized, so far, as to be useful to travellers, I have been unavoidably obliged to put them by towards a second publication, having extended this so far, and the desire that is shewn for my opinion on matters of trade, to which no part of my misfortunes can be attributed, I am of necessity obliged to reserve that needful part, with a dissertation on the laws of this country, for the third volume, which under Providence, I hope to accomplish on a plan of amusement and instruction.

On maturely considering the works of Providence, I have on that score only, been reconciled to the severity of my fate, which has greatly enabled me to submit under the heavy load of affliction, I have hitherto sustained, during a life of more than forty years, thirty of which has been sacrificed to that desire of accumulation, which sufficiently succeeded, to have in that time earned, on a moderate computation, between twenty and thirty thousand pounds; with which, had prudence in my family, been united with my endeavours, I might have attended to those kind offices to those of my fellow creatures, which are now through my inability, deprived almost of needful subsistence, owing to the want of employ in that staple[9] manufactory I was placed in; and trust, that as I am ready on being called on, to attest to the authenticity of this account, that no fallacious endeavours of my enemies, will be attended to, to controvert the opinion the world have hitherto entertained of me, nor will prejudice me in the esteem of that impartial community, of which I am a member, but hope that as a mortal being, I may be considered liable to the errors of life, in general with others, so far as not to be able to bar that inevitable fate, which resisted every effort human art could suggest, as far as consistent with honesty to avert, but to no purpose, in which case I can only add to this, my sincere and most ardent request, for the protection of that giver of all good, who alone can fortify the works of his own hands, from those temptations and troubles, to which we are equally liable in this state of trial and probation, and can after this our solvent situation ended, take us to the realms above, to those mansions for just men made perfect, and where the "wicked cease from troubling, and the weary be at rest."[10]

JANE ELIZABETH MOORE

28th of October, 1785.

It will no doubt be satisfactory to my readers in general, to announce that a few days succeeding the above conclusion, justice took place in my behalf, and on the third of May, I obtained my liberty and am once more launched on the tempestuous ocean of life, relying on my patrons for a more calm situation to console my languid soul in future, and enable me to act in a sphere of use to the community, if such my weak abilities will permit me to do; and should this my earnest wish be accomplished, I trust that gratitude which is ever an incentive to upright principles, will sufficiently urge me to that rectitude of conduct that may testify in practice, what I have so often recommended in theory, in the sincere desire of both being accomplished; I remain ever, and on all occasions with due respect,

the publick's
most faithful
and diligent
humble Servant,
JANE ELIZ. MOORE.

Notes

1. Jane's serious illness; the year is 1781.
2. Both of whom died very young.
3. In eighteenth-century usage, a stepson.
4. The government excise office, in charge of collecting taxes on domestic and imported goods.
5. Relating to one of her business ventures.
6. Building in which a business's accounts are kept.
7. Any of the four days celebrating events in the life of the mother of Christ ("our lady"); here 25 March, feast of the Annunciation.
8. Places of preliminary confinement for debtors.
9. Unprocessed wool.
10. Job 3:17.

Lady Elisabeth Craven

LATER MARGRAVINE OF ANSPACH

1750–1828

Letters from the Right Honorable Lady Craven, to His Serene Highness the Mar-
grave of Anspach, during her travels through France, Germany, and Russia in 1785
and 1786. 2d ed, including a variety of Letters not before published. London:
A. J. Valpy, 1814.

Lady Elisabeth was born in 1750, daughter of the fourth earl of Berkeley
and Elizabeth Drax. She married William Craven, later the sixth earl of
Craven, in 1767. They are variously reported to have had six or seven
children; possibly only six survived. Lady Craven's social position gave her
an opportunity to purse various interests, such as studying landscape gar-
dening with the well-known landscaper Capability Brown (in 1806 she
published a *Treatise on the art of pruning fruit trees*). During her marriage
Lady Craven frequented literary as well as social circles. Her poetry was
published throughout the 1770s. Her first plays, *La Folle de Jour* and *Abdoul*
et Nourjad, were written for the French court theater, and her next four
plays were produced on the commercial stage in England. Lady Craven
and her husband separated in 1783. Although both appear to have had
affairs, the fact that she was deprived of her jointure and her children
suggests that, at least in the eyes of the law, she was the injuring rather
than injured party. Leaving England with her youngest son, Keppel, she
began traveling through Europe, eventually arriving at the court of Anspach in Prussia, which was ruled by the Margrave Christian Frederick
Charles Alexander. There she lingered. Although she felt that her "first
duty, that of a mother, . . . lay in England" (v), she explains, the margrave
"tempt[ed]" her with his request that she establish and direct a school for
daughters of the nobility. In 1785 and 1786 Lady Craven resumed her
travels, from Paris through Europe into Russia and Turkey. Her complaints
while in France, that the "vulgar English . . . are busily inventing, as usual,
about me" (12) and that she is being "pursued" (13) by "*Liberty of the Press*
Men," suggest that she was rather notorious.

Some of the letters she wrote during this journey may have constituted the *Journey through the Crimea to Constantinople*, published in 1789. Although these letters were perhaps written to "a fictitious male friend" (Melman 49), when she republished them in the 1814 *Letters* the addressee seems to be the margrave. Despite her own shaky class position, as a traveler Lady Craven exhibits the least attractive traits of an aristocratic observer. Revolutionary Frenchwomen are dismissed as "*she* freemasons" (26) and "*she* philosophers," Muslim religious practices as "mummery" (168) and "nonsense." Kraków consists of "dirty suburbs filled with Jews" (128) and Greek music is "nothing but discordant sounds" (238). While Turkish women enjoy great "liberty, and free from all reproach" (188), Turkish men are "the most ignorant and uninformed men upon earth" (191). In November 1786 she returned to the court of Anspach, at the invitation of the margrave and his wife the margravine. While there she founded a literary club, wrote plays, and formed an amateur theatrical company to perform them; she is also thought to have been the margrave's mistress. In 1791 both the margravine and Lord Craven died, and Lady Elisabeth married the margrave. They settled in England, where she resumed her playwriting: *Yorkshire Ghost* (1794), *Puss-in-Boots* (1799), and *Love in a Convent* (1805). The margrave died in Naples in 1806, and Lady Elisabeth turned her attention to projects of social and horticultural improvement as well as writing. She published an autobiography in 1825. She died in 1828 at the age of seventy-eight.

TEXT: According to Lady Elisabeth Craven, the letters published in the 1789 *Journey* were "mutilated" (iv) and other letters were omitted because "common prudence and gratitude commanded then that my merit as a correspondent should be sacrificed . . . in pity to my children." Because she declares that the 1814 text constitutes her authentic letters and accounts, the excerpt is from that edition (pp. 131–147). The letters show her eye for detail and her ear for court gossip.

cଌ ⁊⁊

LETTER L.

Petersburgh, February 8, 1786.

Between Warsaw and this place, the road is one insipid flat; except just in and about the town of Nerva, where I took a sledge and flew hither. When I wrote last, I was upon the point of making a visit to the Princess C——.[1] I passed two days with her, at a country house of the Princess Lubomirska's, her sister-in-law. We were sincerely glad to see each other, and parted with regret.

Lady Elisabeth Craven. Copyright by the Tate Gallery, London, 1999.

I received a very civil message from the King;[2] and M. de Stackelberg[3] sent me six bottles of bishop,[4] which was very acceptable. I did not stop at Warsaw on my return from the Princess. The messenger caught me just one post on this side of it. Nothing can be conceived so *ennuyant,*[5] as travelling in such a country as this, one flat plain, the view terminated by a forest, which you drive through, only to arrive at the same scene you have quitted. The frost was not hard enough to make the road good, till I arrived at Nerva. Like a country Miss, I am gaping at the window all day. Every creature that goes about seems as if in a violent hurry. They drive full gallop. Traineaus[6] with one horse ply at the corners of the streets, as do our hackney-coaches and chairs.

Mr. S—— informed me, it belonged to my dignity to have six horses to my coach, in order to pay my visits. You will judge of my surprise, when, with a coachman on the box, I found there was a postilion[7] to each pair of horses, and those sitting on the off side. I go thus, full gallop, running races with every other *attelage*,[8] that falls in my way. The streets are luckily wide, and custom makes the danger less than might be imagined.

I am interrupted, and must therefore wish you a good night.

LETTER LI.

Petersburgh, Friday, February 18, 1786.

I was to have been presented to the Empress[9] next Sunday, but she graciously sent me word to be at the Hermitage on Thursday, where every week she keeps her court in the evening, and has alternately a French play or an Italian opera. Marchesini and Madame Todi[10] are the first singers. Nothing can be more magnificent, it is but justice to say, than the appearance of the Empress on entering the drawing-room. She has a lively good-humoured look, and her politeness to me was very great: but somebody had told her I was not an Englishwoman, for she asked me if I were not of a Scotch family.

I cannot conceive why this building, which she has added to the palace, should be called the Hermitage. It consists of a long suite of rooms, full of fine pictures. You are not ignorant of the many collections the Empress has purchased; among the rest Lord Orford's: all these fine paintings want arrangement according to their shades and size, and the Empress will find a proper person, no doubt, for that purpose.

Petersburgh is a cheerful fine-looking city, with streets extremely wide and long. The houses are stuccoed to imitate white stone. None of them are above three stories high, which certainly adds to their lively and airy appearance. I think, Sir, if a young woman might be permitted to judge of things otherwise than *en détail*,[11] that not only the town, but the manner of living is upon too large a scale. The nobles seem to vie with each other in extravagancies of every sort, particularly in foreign luxuries. The fashion of the day is ridiculous, and most improper for this climate. French gauzes and flowers were never intended for Russian beauties. They are sold too at a price which must ruin the buyers.

Buildings for the reception of the Arts and Sciences, are erected here.

Artists or amateurs, though but the surplus of Italy, France, and England, would find a dwelling with handsome encouragement from the Empress; whose respect for talents, and generosity to those who possess them, have already induced some, and will probably many more to take up their abode in the capital of this vast empire. But, alas! Sir, eight months continuance of winter, and the severe cold, must congeal the warmest imagination. Poets and painters require verdant lawns: and where spring is not to be found, the flowers of fancy must fade and die.

The Empress and the Princess d'Ashkow are the only ladies who wear the Russian dress. It is very handsome, and I am more surprised daily, that nations do not preserve their own fashions, instead of copying one country which at present is the ape of every other. From Cherson, the new town on the Turkish frontiers, which is one thousand six hundred miles hence, are brought many provisions. From Archangel likewise this city is provided: and from Astracan on the Caspian Sea, near two thousand miles distant, all the dainties, such as grapes, pease, beans, artichokes, are brought.

From these circumstances it might be natural to suppose, that the necessaries of life would be dear, but some of them are extremely cheap; and, if French wines and fashions, and English comforts can be dispensed with, Russia is perhaps one of the cheapest countries in the world. I never felt so much attachment as at this moment to the last. At the houses *Dans La Ligne anglaise*, a quarter of this town, where the English merchants reside, I find English grates, English coal, and English hospitality, to make me welcome, and the fire-side cheerful.

I have never yet been fortunate enough to make any acquaintance in the world of commerce; but if all English merchants and their families are as well informed and civil as those that are here, I should be very glad to be admitted into the city of London as a visitor, to enjoy a little rational conversation, which at the court-end of the town is seldom to be found. How should it be otherwise? A little Latin and Greek acquired in the schools of Westminster and Eton, and a great deal of vulgar rioting, make our young men a strange compound of pedantry and vice, which can only produce impudence and folly. Thus tutored, at sixteen they are turned upon the hands of some unhappy man, who is to present them at foreign courts, with no other improvement or alteration in their heads, than that of their hair being powdered and tied behind.

The careful citizen, conscious that fair dealing and knowledge can alone promote the well-being of his family, brings up his son to business: and that only, as you know well, makes the idle moments of life happy. Peter the First thought commerce an essential pillar to his empire, and the English trader was encouraged. Our little island is a proof of the consequence which trade alone can give any country; and the new acquired possessions of the largest empires may only become additional trouble to their masters, unless the advantages of trade give them new life.

The French Ambassador, and the Comte Sergé de Romanzow (named to Berlin) are men of wit. Mr. Ellis is with Mr. Fitzherbert;[12] and conversation does not languish or grow insipid in their company. We are in the concluding part of the carnival, and have magnificent balls. Those given by the Ambassadors are very superb. Mr. de Segur,[13] and the Duc de Serra Capriola, the Neapolitan Minister, have each given one in a very magnificent style.

I was presented to the Grand Duchess the same night that I waited upon the Empress. She [i.e., the duchess] has since been brought to bed. There are some young Russian ladies very pretty and much accomplished. Many of them sigh after a different climate from their own. Mousken-Pousken[14] told me, he could form no idea of happiness like that of returning to England as a private man, and purchasing a farm. He speaks very good English.

Indeed, Sir, the elegance produced by that cleanliness and order which is so conspicuous in us, is not any where to be found out of England. Here the houses are decorated with the most sumptuous furniture, from every country; but you pass into a drawing-room, where the floor is of the finest inlaid woods, through a staircase of the coarsest, made in the rudest manner, and stinking with dirt. The postilions wear sheep-skins, and at a ball, when a nobleman has proposed his hand to a fair lady, he often kisses her before the whole company. A propos to this custom—I must tell you an anecdote of Madame Dashhow's son, as I am told, who was supposed to be growing into favor with the Empress, and by that raising the jealousy of Potemkin,[15] went to a ball at court, previously having been elevated with wine, and embraced his partner, which offended so much, that he was banished the next day to Riga, where his regiment was.

Thus you perceive, he was nearly in the same predicament as the Chevalier dans la Fée Urgele; and might have said, *pour un baiser faut-il perdre la vie?*[16]

You shall have some account in my next of what I have seen at the [Hermitage] Museum.

You may have heard much of Prince Potemkin. I see him every where, but he is reserved and converses very little with ladies. I was invited by him to dine in an immense palace he is building in the suburbs. The only room finished is too particular not to be described. It is three hundred feet in length, and on the side opposite the windows there are two rows of stone pillars, whose height and breadth are proportioned to the immense size of the room, which is an oblong square. In the centre, on the side the windows are, is formed a semi-circle, or what we call a bow; which bow forms another large space, independent of, though in, the room. This space was laid out by his English gardener into a shrubbery, with borders of flowers, hyacinths, and narcissuses, myrtles, orange-trees, &c. were in plenty too. The party consisted of seven or eight ladies, and as many men. Immense stoves, concealed by the pillars, were heated, for the purpose of making such a hall, in such a climate, supportable; but I returned home quite ill with cold.

It was there I heard that extraordinary music, performed by men and boys; each blowing a straight horn, adapted to his size. Sixty-five of these musicians produce a very harmonious melody, something like an immense organ. The music, the room, the cold, all was gigantic. I sat by Prince Potemkin at dinner; but except his asking me to eat and drink, I cannot say I heard the sound of his voice. I am, therefore, unable to tell you what species of *esprit*[17] has raised him to the fortunes and dignities he possesses; or what induces Mr. S——, and others, to call him a sensible man.

I have seen the cabinet of medals and the Museum here.[18] The last, when finished, will be a very beautiful suite of rooms. Peter the Great sitting in his chair, with a coat of his amiable Catharine's embroidery, I have likewise seen. Notwithstanding he transferred his capital to this place, and the Empress, Prince Potemkin, and others, may build palaces of the finest orders of architecture, to contain productions of learning and commerce; I frequently think that a time will yet arrive when the heads of an empire, extending from the South to the North, will prefer basking in the rays of the sun, which alike cheer the mind and the body, to eternal frost. These stately buildings will probably, in that case, be converted into store-houses.

Justice compels me to say, the Empress does all in her power to invite politeness, science, and comforts from other countries, to cheer these regions of ice; but, until she can alter the climate, I believe it will prove a fruitless trial. I am informed the spring, or rather the time of year we call the spring, is more gloomy than even winter. I shall therefore hasten my departure; but a conversation I had a few days past with the Swedish minister will make me entirely give up all thoughts of returning into Germany through Sweden and Denmark. I shall in my next have the honor of repeating it to you.

LETTER LII.

Petersburgh, February 21, 1786.

I promised you in my last an account of the conversation with the Minister. Here it is. . . .[19]

I shall now prepare every thing to visit the Crimea, or rather the Tauride. It has been described to me as a very beautiful country. I am not sorry this *enfant perdu* gives me a good excuse for turning my steps towards Constantinople.

There are ladies here whom I shall be sorry to quit; who in youth possess many talents, and with whom I could form an agreeable society. Italian music, the pedal harp, and our English poets are perfectly understood by them. I often think that I can trace Grecian features among the females of this country, and the subtle wit of the Greek in the men: that pliability of genius which causes them to speak so many different languages well, and to adopt all the arts and inventions of other countries that are good.

I am speaking without any partiality, dear Sir, but I do not see here the prejudices of the English, the conceit of the French, or the stiff pride of the Germans; which national foibles make good people of each nation extremely disagreeable. I am assured the Russians are deceitful. It may be so; but as I do not desire to have intimacies, I am much better pleased to find new acquaintances pleasant and civil, than morose or pert.

Mine at present is a geographical intercourse with the world; and I like to find the road I travel on smooth. Wit and talents will always be objects of importance to me. I have found them here, and shall be sorry to quit them. Prince Repnin and his nephew Prince Kourakin, whom I often saw in England, are both here; and I look upon them as old acquaintants, it is thirteen years since our last meeting. The latter has grown fat.

The Grand Duchess was brought to bed[20] five days after my arrival; so that I have only seen her the night of my presentation, which was on the same that I was presented to the Empress. Her affability to strangers is great, for Mr. S—— had not announced me to her; but seeing me move from one seat to another at the opera, by the desire of the Empress, and being told most likely who I was, she sent for me after the spectacle.

A most ridiculous thing happened on my return; for although there were no less than three carriages waiting for me, I was above an hour getting at one. This was owing to the great distance of the Grand Duchess's apartments from the theatre, and Mr. S——'s saying he should wait for me at the Hermitage. I went three times through the whole palace, and while I was at one door, two of the carriages were at the other. Prince Kourakin, who had conducted me back from the Grand Duchess, and who was engaged to sup with the Grand Duke, was not a little embarrassed; for the doors, opened to let in company, were shut; and I had no resource but to sit in the guard-room, till Prince Kourakin's servant should find one of the carriages belonging either to me or my party.

The Prince went in to sup, and the Grand Duchess on hearing of this circumstance sent me a very fine pelisse, which I told the Prince I really did not want; but he insisted on my putting it on, which, at his request, I did, and in a few minutes I had a carriage. The most ridiculous thing of all was, that the Saxon minister's wife, whom I had accompanied to court, thought I was gone home in my own carriage, the company in that, concluded I had gone with her; and after parading on the outside of the palace from door to door, as I had done within, they gave me up. My servants took it for granted I had been invited to sup at the palace.

The Grand Duchess is fair and tall. The Duchess of Wirtemberg, who is the Duchess of Brunswick's daughter, is pretty, and very like our royal family, and she was very civil to me. I have not seen the Grand Duchess's children: I am told they are fine and healthy.

It surprises me not a little to hear people say, I shall inherit so many hundred peasants, or such a one has lost a village. The number of men, it seems, and not of acres, makes a fortune great in this country: so that a plague, or any distemper, that would prove mortal to the peasants, would be death likewise to the pockets of the nobles.

I have taken leave of the Empress, and you may judge whether I do not leave Petersburgh with a good impression of her politeness. Before the opera, she told me, that my intention was known to her; but as we defer disagreeable things as long as possible, you shall not take leave till after the spectacle. These words she pronounced with the most gracious smile; and asked me if I was satisfied with the amusements and civilities I met with. I told her I must be both stupid and ungrateful, not to regret infinitely that I could not stay any longer, to show how sensible I was of the hospitality and magnificence with which I had been treated.

The Vice-chancellor, Comte d'Osterman, is obliged to have a table for sixty foreigners every Wednesday; and a Dowager Princess de Galitzin, a supper once a week. At Mons. d'Osterman's there is a ball, too, every Sunday night. The Empress is at the expense of these entertainments; and,

I confess, I think it an excellent and royal idea, to be certain of having houses open for the reception of foreign ministers and strangers of distinction. You know, my dear Sir, that private houses, for various reasons, are seldom now open to strangers in most countries.

I am also told there are many Princes here who keep a public day, as we do in England, for the convenience of our country neighbours; and that they expect people, with whom they leave a card, to dine with them on such a day. But if I *was* to stay here ten years, I should never be prevailed on to go to those houses without invitation: nor can I believe it possible the masters of them can expect a foreigner to grace their table, without being desired even by word of mouth. I am assured I shall affront Czernitcheff, and ———— but as I meet them every where, I cannot think they should be so totally ignorant of the manners of other countries, as to expect me to dine at their house without their asking me.

There is a custom here, which is a very abominable one. Noblemen, who are engaged to marry young ladies, make no ceremony of[21] embracing them, in the midst of a large company at a ball.

I have mentioned to a few people my intention of seeing the Crimea. I am told the air is unwholesome, the waters poisonous, and that I shall certainly die if I go there. But as in the great world, a new acquired country, like a new beauty, finds detractors, I am not in the least alarmed. On the contrary, a person, not a Russian, who has been there on speculation, has given me so charming a description of it, that I should not be sorry to purchase a Tartarian estate.

LETTER LIII.

Moscow, February 29, 1786.

I left my coach at Petersburgh, and hired for myself and my small suite the carriages of the country, called Kibitkas. They are exactly like cradles, the head having windows to the front which let down. I can sit or lie at length; and feel in one like an over-grown baby, comfortably defended from the cold by pillows and blankets. These carriages are upon sledges, and where the road is good, this conveyance is comfortable and not fatiguing: but from the incredible number of sledges that go constantly upon the track of snow, it is worn into ruts like a road; and from the shaking and violent thumps the carriage receives, the hardest head might be easily broken.

I was overturned twice. The postilions, I fancy, are used to such accidents; for they get quietly off their horse, set the carriage up again, and never ask if the traveller is hurt. Their method of driving is singular; they sit behind three horses harnessed abreast: a shrill whistling noise, or a savage kind of shriek, is the signal for the horses to set off, which they do full gallop. When their pace slackens, the driver waves his right-hand, shrieks, or whistles, and the horses obey. I am told the whip is unmercifully used in the stables. I observed a postilion never strikes a horse in driving, which caused my astonishment at their being so tractable to the raising of a hand only.

I would never advise a traveller to set out from Petersburgh as I have, just at the end of the carnival. With some reason he might suppose it was a religious duty for the Russian peasant to be intoxicated. In most villages I saw a sledge loaded with young men and women in such a manner, that four horses would have been more proper to draw it than one. This wretched beast was obliged to fly with his noisy company up and down the village, which is generally composed of houses in straight rows on each side of the public road. The girls are dressed in their holiday-clothes, some of whom are beautiful; nor do they look less so from various colored handkerchiefs being tied over their forehead, in a becoming and *pittoresque*[22] manner.

Upon travellers is practised a shameful piece of roguery, after this diversion, to which there ought to be put an immediate end. The poor animal, employed on these festive occasions, is generally upon the point of death; and, for the first post-horse that is wanted, is harnessed to a kibitka in his place; because a traveller is obliged to pay the value of any horse, that expires in his service. I had one that died thus, though I remonstrated against his being put to the collar, seeing that he was in a state of approaching dissolution: but unless I could have armed six servants with good cudgels, my arguments were as fruitless, as those I employed at the next post, to prove how unreasonable it was, that I should be called on to make restitution for a horse, that was actually dying when put to the carriage.

The Russian peasant is a fine, stout, straight, well-looking man. Some of the women are uncommonly pretty, but the general whiteness of their teeth is something which cannot be conceived. It frequently happened that all the men of the village, were in a circle round my carriages; and rows of the most beautiful oriental pearl, could not be more regular and white than their teeth.

How the infants outlive the treatment they receive, till they are able to crawl into the air, is astonishing. There is a kind of space, or *entresol*, over every stove, in which the husband, wife, and children, lie the greater part of the day. Here too they sleep at night. The heat appeared to me so excessive, that I have no conception how they endure it. They, however, were as much surprised, at my seeking a door or window in every house I entered; as I could possibly be, at their living without air. All the children look pale and sickly, till they are five or six years old.

The houses and dresses of the peasants are by no means uncomfortable. The first is generally composed of wood; the latter of sheep-skins: but trees laid horizontally one upon another make a very strong wall, and the climate requires a warm skin for clothing.

It may appear to English minds, that peasants who in a manner are the property of their lord, suffer many of the afflictions which are supposed to attend slavery. But the very circumstance of their persons being the property, insures them the indulgence of their master; who stands between them and the power of a despotic government, or a brutal soldiery, for the preservation of their lives. Besides, the invaluable advantage which these peasants possess, in paying annually a very small sum, and cultivating as many acres of land as they think fit, make their fortunes depend entirely upon their own industry. Each man only pays about the value of half-a-guinea a year. If the lord were to raise this tax too high, or to make his peasants suffer; misery and desertion would ruin his fortune, not theirs. He is obliged, it is true, to furnish a recruit yearly, but only one out of three or four hundred men; so that, notwithstanding this vast empire is said to be not populated in proportion to the extent of it, when you consider the number of troops the Empress has, and these kept up by this method, the Russian people must be more numerous, than strangers in travelling through their country might imagine. To reflect, without prejudice, on the ridiculous notions of liberty and property entertained by our common people is very amusing.

And now, my dear and most honored brother,[23] that I have given you so pretty a picture of English freedom, I shall wish you a good night.

Notes

1. Princess Czartoriska, a member of a powerful Polish noble family and an old acquaintance of Lady Elisabeth.

2. Stanisław Augustus Poniatowski (1732–1798), last king of Poland (1764–1795).

3. Baron Otto Staekelburg, Russian ambassador to Poland 1773–1790.

4. A mulled and spiced port wine.

5. Tedious (Fr.).

6. Sleigh or sled.

7. Ordinarily substitutes for coachman (riding on one of the horses rather than the coach)—hence Lady Elisabeth's surprise.

8. Similar to equipage; general term for vehicle plus horses and attendants.

9. Catherine II or Catherine the Great, empress of Russia 1762–1796.

10. Luigi Marchesi (1755–1829), known as Marchesini; Italian castrato and composer. Luisa Rosa Todi (1753–1833), Portuguese mezzo-soprano.

11. Women were often thought incapable of "judging," or drawing general conclusions from specific instances.

12. Mr. Ellis is probably author George Ellis (1753–1815); Mr. Fitzherbert is probably Alleyne Fitzherbert (1753–1839), Britain's envoy extraordinary to Catherine II 1783–1787.

13. The Russian minister.

14. Count Valentin Musin-Pushkin, a high-ranking general in the Russian army.

15. Prince Grigory Potemkin, one of Catherine II's court favorites.

16. Must I lose my life for a kiss? (Fr.). The reference is to a 1765 opera composed by Egidio Romoaldo Duni and written by C. S. Favart entitled *La Fée Urgèle*.

17. Mind or wit (Fr.).

18. A complete set of harness made of white leather, stitched with colored silks, for six dogs, with a sledge for one person, brought from Kamskatka, was the lightest, neatest, and most curious piece of workmanship I ever saw [Lady Elisabeth].

19. The conversation omitted here, which Lady Elisabeth records in French, amounts to the minister's warning her about the dangers of traveling over ice.

20. Began labor.

21. Have no hesitation in.

22. Picturesque (Fr.).

23. Lady Elisabeth repeatedly addresses the margrave as her brother, to insist on the innocence of their relationship.

Phillippina Burton Hill

1754?–AFTER 1791

Mrs. Hill's Apology for having been induced, by particular Desire, and the most specious Allurements that could tempt Female Weakness, to appear in the Character of Scrub, Beaux Stratagem, for one night only, at Brighthelmstone last Year, 1786, when the theatre was applied for by the Honourable George Hanger, and engaged for that purpose; with an address to Mrs. Fitzherbert. Also, some of Mrs. Hill's Letters to his Royal Highness the Prince of Wales, Mrs. Fitzherbert, and others. The Dénoûment, with Events and Remarks, that may not be deemed uninteresting to this Nation at large. London: G. Kearsley and E. Harlow, [1787].

Little is known of Phillippina Burton's early life. In 1768 she included *The Memoirs of a Lady Now in the Bloom of Life* with her *Miscellaneous Poems*, but it is unclear whether this text is autobiographical. In her *Apology* she claims descent in the female line from Thomas Cranmer, archbishop of Canterbury. At some point she married an Ensign Robert Hill; he died some time before 1768, despite her claim to the curative powers associated with the then fashionable practice of mesmerism. Although Hill often represents herself as "defenseless" (5) and "helpless," after she was widowed she used her "weak unaided talents" (9) to support herself. She first performed as an actress in 1770 at the age of sixteen. Thomas Sheridan— much impressed, according to Hill, by her "brilliancy of voice and powers" (21)—engaged her for his Haymarket Theatre company, and she played the principal role in her own comedy, *Fashion Displayed*. Having published some works by subscription, she traveled to Windsor to seek the patronage of the Prince of Wales. His liaison with Mary "Perdita" Robinson (see page 369) was well known, and Hill perhaps hoped to follow in Perdita's footsteps: "Hope it will not be deemed a crime," she writes, "if I declare that I was surprised and captivated with his appearance, felt that flame rekindling in my breast, every spark of which I thought extinguished" (10). Broke and lovelorn, Hill proceeded to Richmond, where she was pestered by the attentions of "idle fellows of fortune" (14), perhaps because of her habit of entertaining gentleman callers until 2 A.M.

Back in Brighton, she eventually obtained permission to add the prince to her list of subscribers, but his coterie seems to have gone out of its way to humiliate her. The *Apology* concerns one such scheme, George Hanger's encouraging her to perform a "breeches" part in George Farquhar's *The Beaux' Stratagem*. Hill assented, but the production left her out of pocket; besieged by creditors, she repeatedly wrote to the prince for aid until he threatened to prosecute her. She then left Brighton but returned in April 1787, with a manuscript discoursing on "the Head and Heart" (4). Having successfully performed this work (complete with "an exhibition of the heads dressed in character") for "a select party," she attempted a public performance at the Castle Assembly Rooms, only to be hooted from the stage by her bête noire, Hanger, and his "female troop." By 1790 Hill was living in Dublin and publishing occasional poems by subscription. Although her narrative concludes with the possibility of a second *Apology*, she seems not to have made good on the threat, and nothing more is known of her.

TEXT: Phillippina Burton Hill intended the *Apology* as a final effort to "regain [the] royal sanction" (4). It was published late in 1787 with a dedication to the Prince of Wales and a heavily ironic dedicatory letter to his consort, Mrs. Fitzherbert. The excerpt (pp. 26–36) well represents Hill's humorless self-absorption and convoluted style.

☙ ❧

THE LEADERS OF MY ANCLE[1] having, through rest, nearly acquired their usual tone of elasticity, I took a walk, and, for the first time, saw Mrs. Fitzherbert.[2]—We looked at each other, I believe with mutual curiosity. She was in a phaeton, with royal favour sanctioned round and graced, I humbly on my feet; therefore I resigned the gaze to sphere and power!—Oh, that my spirit had instantly forsook this frame of frailty! or sued where blessings sure transcend true royalty—blessings worthy of their source. But, alas! I wrote to Mrs. Fitzherbert, who had subscribed to my works, and received them in town.—I was her neighbour here, Lord Brudenel's house only separated us.—And now, gentle Reader, drop the sympathizing tear of soft compassion for an innocent, unsuspecting, friendless female, who from this time may date her peace of mind destroyed, and in the event her royal Patron lost.—I wrote to Mrs. Fitzherbert, thanking her for that sanction she had shewn to my weak talents; and informed her I was writing the anecdotes of that season at Brighthelm-

Mrs. Hill's Apology / 253

stone, and would recite my Novel Display[3] if she would patronize it.—
This letter was sent to her house in the morning; soon after I heard a
voice under my window, pronouncing words to this effect: "This will be
made an anecdote of;"—the express words of my letter to Mrs. Fitzherbert.—I hastened to my window, where I saw Mrs. Fitzherbert and a
gentleman, caught in a slight shower. The gentleman looked up, and saluted me; I returned the compliment, enquired who he was.—The next
day wrote him a note, wherein I begged leave to assure him, that any
accident occasioned by the clouds of the atmosphere, malevolence, or
envy, should form no subject for my blithsome Muse, which delighted in
the sunshine of peace—to promote happiness, not to destroy it; sent him
my works, and he very politely subscribed to them.—The same evening
I went to the play, where the Hon. George Hanger[4] joined me—paid me
many compliments—a repetition of what he had said some years ago;—
they never produced the desired effect. What reason he had for thinking
they would prevail at this time, I am yet to learn. He entreated permission
to call on me after the play;—I positively refused it;—he however said he
would call. And as it was out of my power to prevent his knocking at my
door, I resolved not to let him in. The play ended, I retired, with a child
I had taken to see the play. At the foot of the stairs met some persons I
esteem and respect; indeed their hearts are so noble, and sentiments so
good, that every body almost adores both father and son—they are an
honour to nobility. While I was speaking to the Hon. ———, a gentleman
I did not recollect addressed me by name with great good-nature and
pleasing affability. I replied, he had the advantage of me. He informed me
his name was Coleman; that I had honoured him with my poems; offered
me his arm to conduct me home. I gave the child to the care of a servant,
and put myself under his protection, as he was my neighbour. Found him
very facetious and chatty. When we got home, he told me Mrs. Fitzherbert
had desired him to call, wishing to see the Anecdotes of the Season.[5] I
told him they were in so imperfect a state, as to render them unfit for
perusal: promised to send them to Mrs. Fitzherbert when I had made out
a fair copy, which could not be done till my return to town. He observed,
that he was fearful I should want subjects, as that place did not abound
with much pleasing variety:—I answered, a trifling subject, with a fertile
imagination, would give great scope. Acquainted him with my intention
of reciting my Novel Display, and gave him a specimen of my powers.
He seemed much pleased; extolled my abilities and good taste; assured me
his friend Mrs. Fitzherbert would sanction my undertaking; desired me to
draw up the form of what I intended to recite, and send it to his lodgings

in the morning: that he would give one to Mrs. Fitzherbert, and present his Royal Highness with the other, being engaged to dine with him the next day. A double knock interrupted the conversation; it proved to be the Hon. George Hanger; I did not admit him; but the street door opening at once into the parlour, he would have rushed in, if he had not seen or heard the person that was with me.—These are the insults helpless widows are exposed to!—There is no preventing the intrusion of vain, self-conceited coxcombs entirely, say or do what you can; for when repulsed, their vanity is hurt; then, coward like, they meanly seek revenge by defaming the very character they should extol. But men of sense disdain their conduct, and avoid their company.

Mr. C. now wished me a good night.—I retired to rest; in the morning drew up the form of what I intended to recite with all the judgment I was able; sent them, as advised, in the morning of the following day. Mr. C. did me the favour of calling, and informed me that he had mentioned it to his Royal Highness, who was graciously pleased to say he would come to my recital. But Mr. Hanger had acquainted the Prince that Mr. C. was with me in the evening, and represented his friendly visit agreeable to his *own ideas*. I did not love him for it, but kept my peace.

Highly flattered by the promised sanction, I sent for the manager of the theatre, to whom I was an entire stranger; he came, and behaved with great respect to me, as much as he was capable of; indeed I have had reason since to think that it was more than he possessed, and that he borrowed all the civility he shewed me on the occasion of gentlemen that had called him Manager. I informed him I wanted to engage the theatre, and for what purpose.—I could only have it on a ball night, unless I paid the exorbitant price of twenty pounds, which I did not think prudent; and not this without the approbation of Mr. Wade. Indeed, Mr. Fox said, he did not care for Mr. Wade; but as he was Master of the Ceremonies,[6] he wished to avoid altercation with him; labouring to make me believe that he was not in awe of him, and to enhance his own consequence. I called on Mr. Wade, informed him of my intention and patronage.—He asked me why I did not have it at the Rooms;[7] said it was contrary to the established rules for him to patronize any thing from the Rooms on a ball-night; gave me a friendly caution to take care of myself if I had it at the theatre; informed me fully of Fox's character; which, indeed, I found not only applicable to his name, but surpassing it in savage talents; for I never saw him, but he brought to my remembrance the wild boars I have frequently seen at the King of France's hunt; it being the fashion there for ladies of the first distinction to partake of this diversion; even the princesses, riding in open splendid cars, making a most charming appearance in the woods, which are prepared for that purpose, with spacious avenues, pruned, to open the view, and disclose the hunt.

I engaged the theatre conditionally, if it suited my patroness.—The manager heard me recite, and announced my abilities equal to any character I chose to perform; said I might play, get money, and fame, if I pleased. This he said in the presence of Mr. Thomas.[8] I informed him, that after I had recited my Novel Display, I would think of something, and perform it for his benefit and my own; to which he agreed:—was very attentive to me indeed, rather too much so; but I would not see it. I desired to know if the evening I had fixed on suited Mrs. Fitzherbert.— She sent her compliments, informing me it suited her very well, and that all her interest should be exerted in my favour. Relying on this promise, I did not solicit the patronage of any other lady or gentleman; being convinced all here was governed by party, and as I had her's, could not expect any other, which I did not think numerous; having never seen any lady walk with, or speak to her, Mrs. Walpole[9] only excepted. This was no cause of uneasiness to me, for I knew it was in her power to make it worth my trouble; nor had I a doubt to the contrary. His Royal Highness the Prince of Wales, with his suite, Mrs. Fitzherbert, and Mrs. Walpole honoured the recital, staid the whole time, and gave great applause. Mrs. Fitzherbert took six tickets; and in the morning sent her compliments, and two guineas, sealed up. This, with all her interest, did not amount to the expences of the house, although only five guineas; as I suppose she made presents of her tickets to those, who, had they sent for them to my house, would have complimented me with a guinea each for their tickets, as my own friends did. Indeed, on such an occasion, as a gentlewoman reciting the productions of her own pen, to relieve herself from oppression, it was natural to expect that Liberality would shine. His Royal Highness would have acted like himself, a most gracious, compassionate, condescending Prince, as he is. But I received nothing more from her, or her party, notwithstanding all her promised patronage and interest; which had I properly considered, this proof of her liberality should have prevented me from trusting to her generosity in future. But what could I do?—I had applied for her sanction and support; was promised it, and had apparently obtained it, as she was seemingly very gracious and kind to me. And I am certain a person of great distinction, as well as myself, believed, from the nobleness of his own heart, that she was in reality my friend:— she could have no pretext for being otherwise. Nor could I now consistently retreat, without fear of offending one whom I am most anxious to obey. I was obliged still to look on her as my patroness; nor dared presume to solicit his Royal Highness, lest it should be imagined I had not set a proper value on her interest. Still I was much distressed, having expended my own property, instead of adding to it. I was silent on the subject to all but Mrs. Fitzherbert.—It is the sincerity of my heart (whose dictates I in general most sacredly adhere to, frankly speaking the true sentiments of my mind to the very parties that are envious of my abilities, or that praise which the world, perhaps unmerited, allows me; watching for an opportunity to degrade, prompted by their baser passions) that exposeth me to become a sacrifice. I wrote to Mrs. Fitzherbert, informing her, notwithstanding all she had promised to do for me, I was a loser, which added greatly to my oppression. I was so low spirited and lost, that if not awed through fear of offending Divine Providence, I would go down to the sea-side, and sit on the sand till the waves removed me from my grief, and from being troublesome to any, (for I almost despaired now, having exerted my faint abilities, gained applause, the feather of adornment, but nothing else.)

'Tis very strange, but during this period I dreamed I was walking on roads of glass, and many other alarming subjects; that mad cows ran after me, if I spoke, or breathed but loud, they were immediately in an uproar; that a mighty ox pursued me till I outran him, and took shelter in a fine meadow, amidst a flock of sheep, with their lambs. I do most solemnly declare this relation is true, although I have no faith in dreams, or other events that derive their origin from superstition.

In this letter to Mrs. Fitzherbert I informed her I should be happy to find a proper subject to exert my humble talents for her amusement, and that of her party, so I could do it without expence, that the emolument might be appropriated to my own use, my circumstances having been embarrassed so long, which I fully informed Mrs. Fitzherbert of. I proposed selecting some passages from favourite comedies and tragedies, or to write something new, and have it at the rooms;—in short, to do any thing that was not unbecoming the character of a gentlewoman, to better my circumstances. Soon after this, I think on Monday, September the 27th, 1786, in the evening, I heard a double knock at my door;—I was indisposed in bed, with lowness of spirits;—my servant looked from the window, and asked, Who was there? When a gentleman answered, in these very ominous terms, It is neither a thief or robber, but Mr. Hanger, come with a message to Mrs. Hill, from his Royal Highness the Prince of Wales, or from Mrs. Fitzherbert.—I desired her to say I could not see him, concluding within myself that it was only to get admittance, and not wanting to see him. She ran down stairs, said 'twas from the Prince, or Mrs. Fitz-herbert, and he was in the apartment in a minute:—behaved with such politeness, courtesy, and respect, that I forgot his former solicitation, and beheld him not as a foe. He expressed great concern for my indisposition, hoped I should soon recover, &c. &c.;—then thus began, with suppliant mien and flatteries, magic force—not the serpent, when he beguiled the fair queen of Paradise, more artfully addressed her unsuspecting heart—I come, Mrs. Hill, with Mrs. Fitzherbert's compliments; she desired me to say, in answer to your letter, which indeed I saw, that all her interest, in whatever you undertake, should be exerted to promote it, but that she could not point out what was proper for you to do—this is her message.—Next, his Royal Highness, with whom I have been shooting this morning, and we were talking about you; he sent his compliments, and said, that he should be glad to assist you, and that whatever you undertake his patronage should sanction it.—What could be more pleasing to a drooping mind than this high honour?—I was transported with sudden joy!—begged him to say that my gratitude was too great for expression—sub-dued with the sense of his great favours already conferred, and promised to be continued.

Mr. Hanger, after making an apology for what he was going to propose (by observing, that it was a character Mr. Garrick and Mrs. Abington[10] had both performed) gave it a name; the mighty part was *Scrub—Beaux Stratagem!*—Had a poisoned arrow shot through my heart, I could not have felt a pang more dreadful![11]—I asked him if Mrs. Fitzherbert would come to see it?—He replied,—*Certainly.*—I thought perhaps it was only to try how far my pride would yield, having been represented by some that have sought my acquaintance without success, that my disposition was haughty, proud, and imperious;—that I had no condescension, and would not do any thing except my own pride was gratified.—My situation being now, in point of circumstances, similar to a drowning person catch-ing at every straw which my kind and officious patroness well knew, I had no time to chuse, nor was I left a choice—without a pause consented to undertake it;—never consulting my best feelings, Reason, Genius, any friend, acquaintance, or the more charming Muse!—He caught me at my word; said he would let the Prince know that I would do it. He was going from me to Mrs. Fitzherbert. The manager of the theatre should be spoke to, and the playhouse engaged—I should have a week to study the part—apologized he was obliged to go out of town, and asked if I would see the pages as occasion should require?—I assented—he took his leave—this was Monday evening.

As a proof of my unwillingness, I never spoke or did any thing in the business until the Wednesday, when the manager of the playhouse waited on me, to inform me that the Hon. Mr. Hanger had spoke to him for the house, for me to perform a character:—that as it was for the Prince he could not refuse it. And in the evening of that day, or soon after, a page called on me (Mr. Hicks) and informed me that the Hon. George Hanger ordered him to wait on me, to know if I was getting ready, and had fixed on the day. Added, that he came by authority, to desire me to be prepared. I informed him Mr. Fox had not a dress to fit me for the character:—that I believed the printer was gone to Lewes. He replied, Then you must get cloaths made to be sure; and the printer must be sent for. I told him I would do all in my power; that I was but one, and could not answer for all. Said he would speak to Mr. Fox the same evening to be attentive to me.—I wrote the next day to Mrs. Fitzherbert—informed her that I could be ready by Tuesday, if that day suited. She approved of it, to my great surprize; (for I was in hopes she would have made some excuse or other for not coming to the play).—Sent her compliments— that it was very well—she should go, and all her interest would be in my favour. This was a new cause of grief to me; but I had given my word.— Mr. Hanger had told the Prince that I would do it—it was the talk of the whole place—and I could not recede. Studied the character, and to possess it drove every pleasing idea from my brain, one only excepted, a very powerful one to me, that I was doing it to comply with the desire of him for whom I would have resigned my life. It was an innocent frolic; and I well knew I should be amply rewarded by that royal and liberal bounty which had extended to me, when I had only wrote that, which gave me pleasure, in the best of causes, Virtue and Honour. Still my feelings were hurt; and I most anxiously wished Mrs. Fitzherbert would cease to coun- tenance it:—but, to my perpetual disappointment, she apparently redou- bled her zeal. When I wrote, expressing my fears, and a wish it might be expressed in the bills that it was by command of his Royal Highness, she ordered my servant into her dressing-room, placing her hand upon her heart, desired her to assure Mrs. Hill, that it was the same thing: but as his Royal Highness had never allowed his name to be put in the bills; if he did it now, it would be expected in future— That all would be well— behaved with such affability and seeming affection, that my servant re- turned quite charmed with her; but my spirits still were sinking.—A Bar- onet, who was on a visit to Lord Gage, at whose house they were to dine on the Tuesday, but it was put off on account of my playing, called on me;—found me employed in writing an epilogue for the occasion, and so low in spirits, that I burst into tears before him, as he had known me at Brighthelmstone in affluence, &c. &c.—He bid me be of comfort, and act the part;—that he well knew, and so did every body, for whom it was done, which would be a sufficient apology for my appearing in it.— Repined that neither him nor his lady had heard me recite, as they did not know that it was me, there being another person at Brighthelmstone, calling herself Mrs. Hill at the same time—And was pleased to add, that a gentleman, who was at the performance, acquainted them I acquitted myself with great ability and unbounded applause; desired me to keep up my spirits—That a nobleman, his friend, and indeed brother-in-law, desired his respects to me; that he remembered me well, and spoke in high terms of my conduct, which they had heard of:—the great tenderness and constant attention which I had shewn to my husband; and the loss I had sustained by his death.—Also added, that his lady remembered me; whom he spoke of with so much delight, declaring that, except the Queen, he did not think she had her equal for goodness.—It gave me pleasure to hear him; but I still wept. He encouraged me all in his power; and said, "Mrs. Hill, this condescension in performing the part will immortalize you:"—then took his leave, after subscribing to my works.

I got a complete dress made from head to foot, as my credit was good; having, as I observed before, frequented this place for years, and never left a bill unpaid. My embarrassments were only known to a few people of rank; to whom I had communicated them. I had sent a letter (Mr. Fox wrote me, wherein he acquainted me that I must get cloaths, for he had none to fit me with decency to my sex) to Mrs. Fitzherbert, that she might know of this expence.—As she knew my circumstances, and declared herself my patroness, I could not think that she would suffer this, or any other, to fall on me, which she knew must at this time ruin me, being in such hands. It would have been imprudent in the extreme if I had even asked or hinted the question of who is to pay for all, and reward me in the end for the trouble and expence I am now at.—'Twas impossible an idea of doubt could arise in my mind, as it was expressed in the bills that it was by particular desire.

Under every disadvantage I appeared in the character on the Tuesday, October the 3d, having only two rehearsals; not a person I knew amongst the company I was to play with; who seemed so far from wishing to assist me, (for to say truly, the low and indecent attempts at wit by the male players quite disgusted me; not by any means discouraged by the manager, whom I had been obliged to affront, for an officiousness I did not approve, and threatened to slap his face, ordering him to leave my house. He very highly resented it, if we may guess from the change in his behaviour, which will appear in its place;) that I thought it prudent to keep from them, abiding behind the scenes the whole time I was off the stage, lest they should disconcert me, a thing which might have been easily done, in so tottering a situation as I found myself, being hurried into a public appearance in a character, the disagreeableness of which put my natural and acquired talents, and every feeling I had, to the torture. I most solemnly declare, that at intervals I felt my reason reel, and best resolves stagger, even while I was on the stage; and every time I went off, did not think I could return. When it is considered the short time I had to study the character, get the dress, bills, &c. &c. and the difficulties I had to encounter; with my ancle weak, having taken off the bandage for the occasion; exposed to the cold, and draught of air behind the scenes, never having sat but in a drawing or comfortable room, with every attention and indulgence as a gentlewoman, it will not seem strange that I was so affected; and had it not been for the very kind attention of Mr. Thomas at the library, who stood always ready to receive me when I came off the stage, and remained with me the whole time, it would have been impossible for me to have gone through with it. However, there was a most brilliant audience, and such applause, that 'twas said no person ever received in that character, the immortal Garrick only excepted; not that I think it any feather of adornment to have shown in so ridiculous a point of view. Still I should be ungrateful in the extreme if I did not acknowledge myself sensible of the high honour conferred on me by the great and condescending applause which his Royal Highness gave, and all the nobility and gentry:—but there was a little hissing from two persons, which a gentleman took great pains to find out; one of whom proved to be an intimate of the Hon. Major; however the applause was so superior, that I had apparently triumphed. But, alas! the uncertainty of human events.— I forgot to mention that I was advised to place a man to take care of the checques, which I objected to; but Mr. Thomas, who was my adviser, said that it would be giving them a proof of my prudence, in taking care that no imposition was made, as no one could appear in it; and Fox might do what he pleased, if I did not ask for the key.—This was a new cause of offence to the Manager, who expressed himself to this purport: "Do you think I want to cheat?"—and shewed me as much disrespect in the course of the evening, and ever since, as his situation would admit of.

The play being over, I hastened to undress, and dress to speak my epilogue. Fearful of making them wait, hurried myself to such a degree, that I was sick, and almost fainting when I went on the stage, having been but a few minutes off; still there were some that had not the smallest compassion:—there was a sculking spirit of opposition through the whole, which seemed unwilling to be revealed, other than in its pernicious efforts to disturb: they much succeeded during my attempting to speak my epilogue; which so distressed me, that I thought I should have fainted on the stage. However the applause was great and incessant. I finished the epilogue, and withdrew;—was getting into my chair, when the man that had the checques desired Mr. Thomas to see them counted. We went into the wardrobe, the checques were counted; and, notwithstanding there appeared so fine a house, there were but a very few pounds above the expence, all of which Mr. Fox kept.—I got into my chair, went home; not best pleased at receiving no money, when I had exhausted my last guinea in supporting the expence of my own Recital, and this last appearance. However I went to bed, very much fatigued.—I should have mentioned, that Mr. Thomas had the goodness to see me safe home, although I was in a chair; and that my parlour door being open, the master of the house spoke to Mr. Thomas, and asked me how I found myself.— He had been at the play, he said; and was so provoked at some proceedings, that he lost his patience; could not bear it, and went out—Seemed to hint that all was not fair.—During this interval the maid came to call him several times.—I went to bed without the least refreshment;—in the morning my doors were besieged below, and even my bed-room, by a set of petty tradespeople, to whom I was not known, insisting on the immediate payment of trifles. I desired the mistress of the house not to let me be disturbed, as I was very ill; but it was to no purpose.

Notes

1. Tendons of the ankle which she had sprained.

2. Believed to be mistress of the Prince of Wales, she had, in fact, secretly married him in 1785.

3. Perhaps *Fashion Displayed*, Hill's comedy.

4. Crony of the Prince of Wales and a "notorious rake and dandy" (O'Toole 185).

5. Hill's current opus, perhaps a sequel to her *Portraits, Characters, Pursuits, and Amusements of the present fashionable world, interspersed with poetic flights of fancy* (1785?).

6. As the next sentences indicate, in fashionable spa towns like Brighton and Bath a master of the ceremonies maintained "the established rules" and customs for entertainments, introductions, and so forth.

7. The Castle Assembly Rooms.

8. A friend of Hill's late husband.

9. Perhaps the wife of Horace Walpole (1717–1797), novelist and indefatigable letter writer.

10. David Garrick (1717–1779), considered the finest actor of his generation; Fanny Abington (1737–1815), highly regarded as a comedienne.

11. "Scrub" is a male servant in George Farquhar's comedy *The Beaux' Stratagem* (1707); Abington had recently bombed playing it as a "breeches" part—hence, perhaps, Hill's "pang."

Ann Sheldon

FL. 1787

Authentic and Interesting Memoirs of Miss Ann Sheldon; (Now Mrs. Archer:) A Lady who figured, during several Years, in the highest Line of public Life, and in whose History will be found, all the Vicissitudes, which so constantly attend on women of her Description. Written by herself. 4 vols. London: n.p., 1787.

Since Ann Sheldon's *Memoirs* eschews dates, her date of birth is not known. Her parents are also unknown, although she claims to be the daughter of an eminent shipbuilder turned ship's captain. The first hundred pages of her narrative tell a familiar tale of the innocent maiden seduced, but the fact that her story conforms to conventions of fiction does not necessarily mean it is untrue. Like Mr. Walsingham, her seducer, many of her later lovers are historical personages, and some of them (for example, Sir George Brudenel) appear frequently in other *mémoires scandaleuses*. Installed in a farmhouse near Windsor under Walsingham's protection, Sheldon hired servants and a footman and was visited by "persons of rank, wealth, and generosity." Her spirits "very readily conformed" to the "extravagant gaiety" of her career as a public woman (1:185–186). The first volumes of the *Memoirs,* in fact, consist mainly of "gaiety" anecdotes as well as unapologetic accounts of Sheldon's business transactions: a letter from a Colonel Murray contains "love and admiration" (1:196) and, "what was in fact superior to either," a bank note for £20; after a night of negotiation, she comes to an arrangement for £800 per year with a "doting old peer" (1:240); and so on. Walsingham reappeared periodically, giving her money, lecturing her on her extravagance, and eventually arranging both her marriage to a Mr. Archer and a post for her husband in New York so that she would not be inconvenienced by his presence.

For a time Sheldon's lovers were titled and generous (the list includes Lord Bateman, Sir George Brudenel, and the duke of Northumberland). However, soon she was being arrested for debt, and the narrative shifts slightly from "extravagant gaiety" to more mercenary arrangements: at one point, for example, Sir Clement Trafford paid her debts on condition that she live solely with him, and later Sheldon began to make her acquaintances at "public houses of reception" (3:107) and with the aid of various women panders. Yet she retained her sense of independence—"I got too much money by seeing a variety of friends, to attach myself to the uncertain protection of anyone" (3:216)—as well as her taste for "frolic"; during one imprisonment for debt, she had a swing installed for exercise and amusement. Volume four of the *Memoirs* turns somewhat darker. Alternating between periods of "eclat and figure" (68) and "chance and change" (107), Sheldon was eventually reduced to initiating young girls into prostitution, and the grief she suffered at Walsingham's death seems genuine. Periods of respectability—managing a sewing business, letting lodgings—were succeeded by periods of status-loss as a camp follower and procurer. By the end of the *Memoirs* Sheldon has been reduced to poverty by the expenses of her father's illness and then burial. She concludes with the hope that "my follies, which, in their acting, brought me to my present state of humility, will, by their history, which I now present to the public, in some measure relieve me from it" (247).

TEXT: Ann Sheldon published her *Memoirs* in 1787 in the hope of profiting from the current "public curiosity" (1:4) about women of her sort, but she also claimed other motives: demonstrating by her "absolutely true" story (1:5) the dangers of seduction, the ill effects of "the loss of female virtue" (1:2), and the "slender, transitory objects, [on which] the short lived prosperity of public women depends" (1:3). The excerpt (pp. 49–81 of volume three) is less didactic and more characteristic of Sheldon's high spirits.

෬ ෨

CHAP. XXXVII.

My acquaintance with Mr. Sweedland renewed—Jaunt to Northampton with Mr. Brudenell and Mr. Manners, who were ordered to join their Regiment—Proceed with them to Market Harborough; but, they being ordered to Glasgow, I return to Town with a Promise to follow them—Change my Resolution, and endeavour to bring about a Reconciliation with Lord Bateman—Adventures at Barrow's Hedges, with Capt. Madden, &c.

I was now again favoured with an embassy from Mr. *Sweedland*,[1] with proposals to renew his alliance with me; and the day following he paid me a visit, in order to confirm them. In answer to the abundant professions which he made of life and fortune—and all that—I told him, in very plain terms, that, if he returned to me, a new mode of conduct must be adopted by him. I represented to his consideration, the folly of my suffering any one to live with me, who cost me as much, if not more, than I received from him; and I brought back to his recollection, the power he had been used to assume in my house, and the continual expence which arose from its being constantly filled with his acquaintance—A treaty, however, was concluded between us, on the sole condition, that he was to abandon his former mode of proceeding. As I wanted, at this time, to quit my house at *Chelsea*, and to discharge a few other little pressing demands, he indulged me with a draft for fifty pounds on Mr. *Child*, the Banker—but this act of generosity was of little consequence; for our treaty, like those of greater powers, was not regarded; and my house, and its mistress, were subject to the same inconveniences, which I had before suffered, and against which I had so strongly remonstrated: but I was forced to submit, for the moment, and waited, with impatience, for some opportunity to extricate myself from my present dilemma; and, thanks to Mr. *Brudenell* and Mr. *Manners*, such an opportunity soon occurred.

One afternoon, these gentlemen called upon me, and proposed my accompanying them immediately to *Northampton*, where they were going to join their regiment. At the time they came, I was under the hands of the *friseur*;[2] and Mr. *Brudenell*, with his usual crazy spirit, positively declared, that I should go with them as I was, with one side of my head full dressed, and the other in complete disorder—nay, they would scarce give me time to throw a few clothes into a trunk; I insisted, however, upon that indulgence, though I was as well pleased as themselves to give Mr. *Sweedland* the slip. So away we went to St. *James's-street*, where a post-chaise and four was ready to receive us. By this time the evening was far advanced; and, to preserve us from being robbed, Mr. *Brudenell* bought a blunderbuss, and gave it to his servant, who was a *Swiss*, and could speak but very little *English,* with orders to shoot the first man who should attempt to stop us.—This direction, however, had very nearly proved fatal; for being stopped by a Toll-gatherer, at a Turnpike, the faithful domestic presented the blunderbuss, and would have prevented the poor man from ever stopping another carriage, if he had not been prevented by some drovers, who were, at that moment, very fortunately on the spot, settling the account for the passage of their cattle.—This circumstance, however, brought on a dispute; and as the *Madeira* in the chaise had elevated my friends beyond the spirit of decorum and prudence, a very serious bustle took place; and the Turnpike-man being joined by some travelling Farmers, we were fairly discomfitted—and, after sustaining a very severe attack of mud and dirt, were driven, in a very filthy condition, from the field of battle.

On our arrival at *Dunstable*, Mr. *Brudenell* begun, as usual, to play every kind of trick, which his unlucky fancy could suggest. Here he put on a bears-skin; and, after crawling about in this character, to the astonishment of every one in the house, he gave notice that he should exhibit a *magic lantern;* and this raree show he displayed with so much noise, &c. &c. that the people of the inn were, I believe, heartily glad when we bid them adieu. The next day we arrived at *Northampton*, where we joined the troop, which was almost immediately ordered for *Market Harborough*, to which place I had the honour of attending my unlucky soldiers. Here I remained for some days; when one of them, Mr. *Brudenell*, conducted me to an hill, in the neighbourhood of the place, in order to shew me the country—and, after I had waded through the dirt to the top of it, under a pretence of returning to the town to fetch a chaise, he left me to enjoy the prospect for at least five hours—for, in attempting to descend from this delightful eminence, I lost one of my shoes in the mud; and was, therefore, obliged to wait, 'till he thought the joke had lasted long enough—when he and his party came, and restored me to the comfort of a good fire, and other good things.

While we were enjoying ourselves at *Market Harborough*, an order came for the regiment to proceed—no farther than *Glasgow;* and I was made to promise, that I would follow my friends into *Scotland*, after I had been to arrange my affairs in *London*. Mr. *Brudenell* gave me an hundred guineas to pay my expences, and I set out for *London*, without the least intention of directing my steps towards the North. I travelled in the stage-coach for safety, and arrived in town so very indifferent, from the morning I spent on the hill, that I was obliged to confine and nurse myself for several days after my arrival.

The moment I was sufficiently re-established to venture abroad, I set about getting the sight of Lord *Bateman*[3]—and, in order to be secure in attaining it, I called upon a lady of my acquaintance, and persuaded her to accompany me to *Barrows Hedges*, where I thought myself certain of meeting his Lordship; but the hounds did not go out the day of our arrival: so that we determined to wait 'till the next hunt, when he was expected, as some of his people were there already.

Some sporting gentlemen being at the inn, desired the favour of our company.—They were Capt. *Madden*, of the Guards, Capt. *Crew*, and a Mr. *Hart*, who treated us with the utmost politeness. Lord *Bateman* had not the same disposition; for, whether it was on my account, or for any other reason, I could not tell, but he never came near the place for six weeks, but sent orders to his yeomen[4] to conduct the hunt without him—I therefore consoled myself with Captain *Madden*, who possessed the most certain means of consolation, as he had lately received a legacy of seven thousand pounds. He was a generous character—and, finding myself very comfortable, I agreed to remain with him, during the whole hunting season—nor were we here without our gambols, which consisted chiefly in dressing ourselves like beggars, and perambulating the country, at different times, in as great a change of appearance, as such ragged characters would allow. Indeed, we acted our parts so well, that, at *Carshalton*, we were driven out of the place by the Parish Officers, as some of us threatened a very speedy lying-in, and narrowly escaped the Beadle's lash.[5]

As I was now informed that Lord *Bateman* would not come down to *Barrows Hedges*, while I was there, I was determined to play him a trick; and Captain *Madden* being obliged to go to town, to mount guard, I bribed the Chambermaid to tell Lord *Bateman's* servants, that I was gone to town with him—and, as I kept myself a close prisoner to my bedchamber, the story was soon conveyed to his Lordship, and the very next morning he arrived. As he was getting out of his chaise, I threw up the window, and, to his great surprise, asked him, If he was come at last?—"Yes," answered his Lordship,—"here I am—and extremely surprised to see you." He then gave me a very polite invitation to breakfast with him, which I accepted; and then ordered a chaise for me to go and see the deer turned out. When I had viewed this very animating scene, I returned to the house, and was soon followed by several gentlemen, who did not wish to see any more of the chace, than myself.—Among these were Mr. *Astley*, of *Pall-Mall*, Mr. *Farrer*, my good friend Mr. *Sweedland*, with Mr. *Arthur*, and Mr. *Kit Blake*. They ordered dinner, before Lord *Bateman* and his company returned, and invited me to dine with them—When it was ready, we sat down to table: and I expected every moment that the noble Lord and his company would make their appearance; but I soon found, to my very great disappointment, that they had been returned some time, and were at dinner in another room. I now enquired, if any message had been sent to me?—and, being answered in the negative, I determined to make my appearance among them, whether I was invited or not—when, to my great surprise, I found the room door fastened against me, and was told, that it was by my Lord's order. I made no observation upon this circumstance, but went directly into the garden; and, lifting up one of the sashes, I contrived to step into the parlour, where his Lordship, and his

Lordship's good company were assembled—and, without any ceremony, ordered the servant to bring me a chair, and took my place among them. The gentlemen were very officious in their attentions to me; and even the noble Lord, at last, deigned to say, that he thought I had dined, or he should otherwise have desired my company.

After a certain time, the party dropped off, one after another, 'till Lord *Bateman* and myself were left alone. He then asked me, who the fellow was that I lived with there?—when I told him, he was a gentleman, as good as himself, and that they both had one master. He then answered, rather pettishly, that he had no master, nor would have any; but I insisted, that an Officer of his Majesty's Guards, and the Master of his Majesty's buck-hounds, were both servants to the King. This little sparring grew, by degrees, into a more animated stile of altercation—'till, at length, such very high words ensued, that the offended nobleman ordered his chaise, and set off for *London*—leaving me in no common state of mortification, at his cold and ungenerous treatment, after the many sacrifices I had made to him, and the many promises he had made to me.

The next day Captain *Madden* returned, and I found that the master of the house had been waiting for him on the road, merely to inform him that I had the day before, been upwards of an hour alone with Lord *Bateman*. This little mischievous tale had its effect, and when my friend came into the house, I immediately perceived that he was no longer a friend to me.—His conduct was totally altered, and from the most agreeable ease and freedom, it was now changed to the most unpleasant formality and reserve. In short, he would hardly take any notice of me, refused to help me at table, and shewed every tranquil mark of the highest disapprobation. After repeated enquiries concerning the reason of his behaviour, he deigned to tell me at last, that he was no stranger to my manœuvre with Lord *Bateman*, and that I was perfectly welcome to follow him to town.—I replied that I had no occasion to follow him or any one, as I had an house of my own, and that I should immediately order a chaise and return to it.—He said there was no chaise to be had that night; but he would take care that one should be ordered at my own time, the following morning. I now quitted the room, and retired to my chamber, where I drank my tea, and sat the whole evening by myself, being convinced that he only sought this circumstance of my late conversation with Lord *Bateman*, as an excuse to break his connection with me. About eleven o'clock I ordered the maid to warm my bed, when I was informed that Captain *Madden* had taken possession of another chamber. This contemptuous conduct did not quite suit with my high spirit, I therefore determined to pay him a visit in his new apartment, and on finding the door locked against me, I made such an use of my hands and feet, as soon gained me a forcible admittance. He immediately rose and went into another room, but like his evil genius I followed from one chamber to another, till he rang for his servant, and ordered his horses to be immediately saddled.—I then returned into my own room, and reposed myself on the bed for a few hours. On my rising to breakfast the chambermaid delivered me a note from Mr. *Madden*, in which he informed me that a chaise was ready to attend my orders, and that he had enclosed a bank bill for ten pounds to discharge the expences of it. I therefore, packed up my cloaths and bidding adieu to *Barrow's Hedges*, set off for London.

CHAP. XXXVIII

A Fresh pursuit after me by Bailiffs.—Escape in Boy's Cloaths to Barrow's Hedges.—Am obliged to continue my Disguise there, and have a New Suit made for the Purpose—Various Incidents arise in Consequence of it.—Am again extricated from all my Difficulties, and form a Connexion with Baron de Bertie, A Swedish Nobleman, &c

During my stay with Captain *Madden* at *Barrow's Hedges*, I had frequent occasion to go to town for cloaths and other little matters, but as I never stayed there but for a very few hours at a time, I kept my servants at board wages.[6]—During my country residence, my creditors were the principal visitors at my door, and one of them had bribed a woman servant, who was rather in my confidence, to give him information whenever I paid an occasional visit to my town habitation.—Accordingly, she contrived, on one of these occasions, to conduct them to my mantua-makers; where I happened to be, of which, however, an apprentice boy in the house gave me very friendly notice. This was by no means a pleasant circumstance at any time, but particularly at the present moment, when a post-chaise was in waiting, near *Westminster Bridge*, to take me back to *Barrow's Hedges*. The harpies[7] in pursuit of me watched too narrowly for me to escape without employing some stratagem; I accordingly dressed myself in a suit of cloaths belonging to the apprentice boy, and tying my own in a bundle, which I carried in my hand; the watchful eyes of the caitiff catchpoles,[8] were deceived, and while they were making enquiries about me, with Mr. *Rider*, my creditor, at their head, I passed through them without suspicion; and, making the best of my way to a Pawnbroker's in *Bridge-street*, whose shop had two doors, I passed in at one of them, and so out of the other, in order to throw my blood-hounds off their scent, in case they should follow me. Nor had I acted with an improper precaution, for I had scarce got into the chaise and told the postilions my dilemma, when the Bailiffs came running down the street;—but crack went the whips, and off we sprung, to my no small joy and happy deliverance. At the first convenient place I stopped to change my boys apparel for my own dress; and arrived safe at my destination, where I did not fail to reward my conductors as they well deserved.

I informed Captain *Madden* of the circumstance of my escape, which, he said pleased him in one sense, but gave him pain in another; for that he had won a considerable bet on my returning so soon; at the same time, it was by no means a pleasant idea, that I should be in a continual state of apprehension; and in order to cure me of it, he desired me to endeavour to make a composition with my just creditors, and he would pay the money. In the mean time, in case I should be pursued he ordered his taylor to make me a smart suit of cloaths, and I now no longer appeared as a flaunting girl, but as an elegant and well dressed macaroni.[9] But all application to my creditors proved in vain; for as they were persuaded my friends would not suffer me to go to gaol, they would not abate a single farthing of their demands.[10] On this principle they were determined to get hold of me, and having discovered from whence the chaise came, which had borne me away from their clutches; they sent down their myrmidons to *Barrow's Hedges*, in order to entrap me, but my disguise prevented their knowing me; and so completely did it shroud me from their recollection, that I was not afraid to stand at the door of the inn, when they were prowling about before it.

These circumstances were therefore, more than sufficient, when I finally left the place to make me very cautious on my arrival in town; and, in order to keep clear of danger I went and remained at my mantua-maker's till Sunday morning, when I returned home. Among my other visitors, my father had been more than once at my door, and had left a letter, in which he desired to see me. I immediately ordered a coach, and after having given orders to the other servants, if the woman, who had already betrayed me, went out, to watch where she went; I proceeded to call on my father, whom I found very much dejected from some losses which he had recently sustained; to see him in that situation, gave me infinite pain; and I felt that to relieve him would be the first of pleasures; the money therefore, which I had by me, and was enough to have discharged all my debts, I gave into his reluctant hand, and turned my thoughts to other means of dis-encumbering myself of the demands against me.

As I had been so much out of town for some time past, I thought it right to examine a little how matters stood in my house; and on looking it over, I observed that a great many things were missing; such as linen, some of my silver trinkets, &c. to the amount of about an hundred pounds—all of which, after many threats, and no little trouble, I found in the trunk of the servant, who had been a constant spy upon my actions, and given the information to my creditors, which I have already described. I need not add, that she was immediately discharged; and I felt no small addition to my comfort, when this domestic enemy was removed from me.

But I thought the most effectual way to keep myself out of the power of enemies, was to pay my debts; and as they did not amount to more than two hundred pounds, I sent for Mr. *Squires*, a pawnbroker, to look at my jewels and laces; which he accordingly did, and immediately advanced upon a part of them the sum I wanted. The attorney was then employed to arrange the business with my creditors; which being soon completed, I was again in the enjoyment of that unapprehensive situation, which is more pleasant than all the jewels and laces in the world.

The first event which took place after this little arrangement, was a very singular and unaccountable connexion with a *Swedish* nobleman, who went by the title of *Baron Deberti*. My acquaintance with this amiable person commenced, where many others had originated, in the street; for, as I was proceeding through *Whitehall*, on a little errand to my milliner, he passed me in his chair—when, ordering his chairmen to set him down, he immediately accosted me, and begged leave to attend me home, to which I had not the least objection. He then told me, in very good English, who he was, and that he lived in *Suffolk-street*, where he saw so much company, that he should rather prefer visiting me at my own house, than receiving me at his; and therefore begged permission to dine with me the next day, and he would order an elegant dinner from an adjoining tavern. This visit was but short, and was interrupted by a Mr. *Mow*, a surgeon to one of the regiments of Guards, who brought a penitential message from Captain *Madden*, desiring permission to renew his visits to me; and that very evening he himself came;—but notwithstanding all his apologies, and he offered plenty of them, he was not received with any great degree of cordiality—his late treatment was not worn off my recollection, and I was not in that state of distress which rendered it necessary for me to practise any unpleasant submissions.

The next day *Baron Deberti* came to dinner, and a very pleasant afternoon we passed. Never had I been so flattered before—and so many proposals were made, and left to my choice, as to the manner in which I would arrange my living with him, that I was at a loss which to accept.

However, it was at length agreed, that he should take an apartment for me at Mrs. *Corrregi's*, in *Suffolk-street*, keep me a carriage, pay all my expences, and allow me forty guineas a month. The next day I received a letter from him to inform me that my apartments were ready to receive me, and that he had enclosed me the first monthly payment in two bank notes to that amount.

As there was something of a very singular appearance in this business, I desired Miss *O'Neal*, a very sensible and accomplished woman, who happened to call upon me at this moment, to accompany me in my first visit to my Swedish friend. We accordingly went, and a very brilliant company there was, but consisting entirely of foreigners. The Baron was in the highest spirits; sometimes he danced about the room, and at others played upon his guitar, and accompanied the instrument with his voice. After an evening of much glitter, and as great a confusion of languages as ever took place at the Tower of Babel, the company separated, Miss *O'Neal* returned home, and I stayed to occupy one side of the Baron's large bed, without knowing, till I awoke in the morning, that any one occupied the other; when I beheld the Baron, or rather his head, decorated with all the luxury of lace and ribbon.

Miss *O'Neal* came to me at breakfast, which was no sooner over, than there was such a succession of visitors to the Baron, that I ordered the carriage, and took my friend, on a shopping ramble, through different parts of the town. As the gentleman who took this lady from her friends was in the country, she was almost entirely with me; and if having a coach at our command, partaking of a most elegant table, and seeing the best company, could have made us happy, we had every reason to be so. But still I remained at a loss as to the sex of my protector;—and one day when he was from home, Miss *O'Neal* and myself examined his wardrobe, expecting to find some remnants of female dress, which might lead us to determine on the business; but we found no clue to the mystery, and were obliged to remain contented with our ignorance. I was then, and am still of opinion, that the Baron *Deberti* was a female spy, in the exterior of a man; or at best, that his errand to this country was for some political consideration; for not a day passed but some foreign minister was in consultation with him; and his levee[11] was constantly crouded with foreigners of every denomination.

After having been with the Baron for about a week, he proposed taking me to Bath—but with all his effeminacy and insignificance, there was something about him, generous as he was to me, which made me fearful of trusting myself in the country with him. I certainly had no reason to complain of him, as he spared no expence in gratifying my wishes, as far as related to dress, and the associated objects of female vanity.

Notes

1. A previous swain.
2. Literally, curler (Fr.); a hairdresser.
3. Sheldon's current lover, with whom she is feuding.
4. Servants, usually of a superior grade.
5. Under the Poor Laws, a person was entitled to relief from the parish in which he or she was born; parish officers such as a beadle thus discouraged (sometimes by whipping) women vagrants from giving birth in their districts.
6. Reduced wages that covered only board.
7. In Greek mythology harpies are ministers of divine vengeance; hence, as here, rapacious predators.
8. "Caitiff," despicable; "catchpoles," petty officers of justice, especially those who arrest for debt.
9. A man who dressed in the height of Italian fashion, e.g., tight-fitting clothes, red-heeled shoes, and blue hair powder; cf. Yankee Doodle, who "stuck a feather in his hat and called it macaroni."
10. Sheldon's creditors refused to accept partial payment for her debts, believing that her friends would prevent her arrest by paying the debts in full.
11. Morning or afternoon reception of visitors.

Elizabeth Gooch

1756–AFTER 1806

An Appeal to the Public, on the conduct of Mrs. Gooch, the wife of William Gooch, Esq. Written by herself. London: G. Kearsley, 1788.

Elizabeth Gooch began life in 1756 as Elizabeth Sarah Villa-Real. Three years later, at the death of her father, William Villa-Real, her mother and Lord Galway (husband of her father's sister) became her joint guardians. In 1764 her mother remarried, but four years later this potential father and guardian died; furthermore, her mother left her in total ignorance of the worldly wisdom necessary to a girl of fortune. Thus, when Elizabeth accompanied her mother to Bath in April 1775, sole heiress to her father's estates in Edwinstow, she found herself hurried into marriage with William Gooch six weeks after they met. The subsequent events are recorded in the *Appeal* and at greater length in *The Life of Mrs. Gooch* which she wrote in 1792. Soon after the marriage, Elizabeth learned of her husband's mistress, but she bore him two children and lived relatively happily with him for three years, until her husband's family accused her of having an affair with her music-master. "My property having been secured as Mr. *Gooch* wished, my person was deemed an incumbrance" (18), and she was threatened with a scandal unless she left Bath. In December 1778 her husband escorted her as far as Lille and left her there, a "folly and cruelty" (19) that "must entirely exculpate me, in the eye of Reason," from her subsequent misconduct. Seduced by a man named Semple and convinced by false friends that returning to her family or husband was impossible, Elizabeth began a series of liaisons. Wooed by a M. DuBuque, she attempted to obtain a divorce but succeeded only in signing away her estates in return for an annual allowance of £200. DuBuque's affection then waned, and she took up with Baron d'Arthaud and his mother, who ran a gambling house. After losing all her cash she was requested by the baroness to depart and eventually returned to England.

From this point on Gooch alternated between Paris and London, sometimes under the protection of various princes and chevaliers, sometimes in considerable debt, especially when her annual allowance was reduced to £150. Under the stage name of Mrs. Freeman, she acted with the Portsmouth theater company for a while, but by 1786 she was imprisoned for debt in Lille. Released and later kept by the duc de Lauzun for a time, Gooch ran further into debt. The *Appeal,* written from the Fleet Prison for debtors, concludes at this low point in her fortunes. According to the *Life,* the advertised publication of the *Appeal* spurred her family to pay her debts. Gooch then lived with a Mr. Lindsey, accompanying his regiment to Glasgow and Ayrshire; volume three of the *Life* describes several excursions in Scotland. After the regiment returned to England, Gooch persuaded Lindsey to rejoin it without her. Despite his continued financial assistance, the *Life* concludes as the *Appeal* had, with Gooch's arrest for debt and a plea to the public for funds. One assumes Gooch was released, at least temporarily, and in the following years she turned to literature. A collection, *Poems on various subjects,* published in 1793, was followed by a book of essays (*The Wanderings of the Imagination* [1796]) and several novels: *The Contrast* (1795), *Fancied Events* (1799), *Truth and Fiction* (1801), *Sherwood Forest* (1804), and *Can We Doubt It* (1806). Nothing is known of Gooch's subsequent life and death.

TEXT: Elizabeth Gooch wrote her *Appeal* in 1788 for money to clear her debts. Although the *Appeal* was not republished, the story was again told in the *Life of Mrs. Gooch,* out of "NECESSITY" (*Life* 1:15), but also to demand "justice" and to argue that "the want of a *friend*" (1:16) rather than her "depraved mind" was responsible for her misfortunes. The excerpts from the *Appeal* (the preface, pp. 1–6, and pp. 56–68) indicate similar claims.

c8 8ɔ

SOME ALLEVIATION OF OUR DISTRESSES is always derived from communication; and it is one of the most amiable offices of private friendship to blunt the sting of misery by a participation of our sorrows. But as friendship will seldom bear the test of adversity, and shrinks into nothing at the frown of fortune, so those who are most in need of its comforts, generally find themselves most destitute of its support; and are then privileged to make an appeal to the public. It is under this unfortunate sanction that the following pages are submitted to the reader. I boast no advantages that can render me equal to the task of writing for the press: I am unskilled in eloquence; the only merit of the following sheets is a strict adherence to truth. I lay claim to some indulgence for the style, and more to pity for the subject.

Elizabeth Sarah Villa-Real Gooch.

Fleet Prison,
  Jan. 1, 1788.

★★*The original and only copy of this* APPEAL *being destroyed by an inevitable accident, subsequent to the work being advertised, the indulgence of the Reader is requested to such inaccuracies as may have occured in the haste of composition, and will no doubt be granted, when the unmerited and melancholy situation of Mrs.* GOOCH *is considered.*

An APPEAL, &c.

I have lived long in hopes that I should not be forced thus publickly to lay open to the world the many injuries I have endured; after having borne them in silence for ten years, I would be still satisfied to do so, did not my situation and my embarrassments force me to complain, and to appeal to the laws of my country, and before the tribunal of Justice.

'Till the age of seventeen, the tender care of one Parent, made up to me, in some degree, my early loss of the other. Sole heiress to my father's fortune, I was educated with the idea that I was born to be perfectly and completely happy.

In the beginning of the year 1775, being just returned from school, I accompanied my mother on a visit to the late Lord *Ducie's* in Gloucester-shire, where we passed six weeks, and from thence to Bath. It was immediately reported that my fortune was much more considerable than it realy was, and it soon attracted me the attention of those many individuals drawn there by the hope of making a splendid establishment. It was my misfortune to give the preference to Mr. *Gooch,* and to tell him so. Proposals from his father and himself soon followed. My mother disapproved the connection; but not choosing herself to determine on so important a point, she brought me to London, to consult with my uncles, and my aunt, on the subject, and on the same day, all *Sir Thomas Gooch's* family arrived in Town also[.] The knowledge of my independence, and my infatuation, prevailed against the advice of all my own friends, and we were married at St. George's, Hanover-square, on the 13th of May following.

To excuse the hasty step I then took, I must be allowed to plead my youth, and total ignorance of the world, the artifices employed by Mr. *Gooch* to determine me on a speedy conclusion, and the childish ideas which filled my mind of being mistress of myself, and that I was going to shine with that splendour to which I thought myself intitled.

On the day of the marriage, we went to the house of my father in law at Hampton, with the intention of passing a few months. My mother accompanied, but soon left me there. A fortnight had not elapsed after her departure, before I began to feel heavily the weight of the yoke I had brought upon myself; and even now, at this distant period, my mind recoils at the remembrance of what I was doomed to suffer. My extreme inexperience could not shut my eyes: it was impossible for me to avoid perceiving the very great, the very improper intimacy that subsisted between my husband and another person under his father's roof, and that I was considered more as an incumbrance, than as an advantage to the family. From this moment, insults succeeded to indifference; the mask was thrown off, and I severely felt that I had been sacrificed to interest. Sorrow preyed upon my heart; I saw myself for the first time of my life, devested of all my natural friends, and surrounded only by strangers, who seemed to vie with each other, which most could distress me, and whose sole aim was to eradicate the first appearance of affection for me, which they might perceive likely to grow in the breast of him, to whom alone I could now look up for protection, and for whom I had sacrificed every worldly good!

A faithful woman-servant of my mother's, whom she had left with me, was now become my only confident: and from her, my mother, then in Yorkshire, became acquainted with my situation; the pressing letters I received from her to go there, and the express injunctions of my uncles, who declared my health to be in danger if I did not, determined Mr. *Gooch* on indulging this wish of my heart; and we left his father's house. I was received at my mother's with a tenderness which made me more than ever lament my sad separation from my own family.

Mr. *Gooch* took a house at York, where I laid in of my eldest son; and the year following, resided in a house belonging to Sir *William Milner*, at Nun-Appleton Park, where I laid in of my youngest. We lived in Yorkshire above two years. Mr. *Gooch* had cruelly deprived me of the maid mentioned, because he thought her a spy upon his actions, and those of his family; but it was the only mark of his unkindness I had to complain of, as we lived happily together, and should still have done so, had Mr. *Gooch* complied with my reasonable request, that of never more taking me amongst his own relations.

In the latter end of 1778, he insisted on my accompanying him to his father's house at Bath. In vain I urged every intreaty to dissuade him. I felt that such a step, would end, as it was proved, in utter ruin. We went there, leaving the children in Yorkshire, and, as I thought, with the resolution of soon returning.

But the period to[1] my happiness was now arrived. It was time to put in execution the black scheme formed against me, and nothing was left wanting to complete it, but a trivial pretence, which my own liveliness of disposition, and inexperience of the world soon furnished.

Various and unfortunate are the circumstances that have since occurred, and marked the train of events which have rapidly succeeded to each other; not one of which but has been a source of sorrow and disquiet to myself; I have been continually the dupe of treacherous lovers, false friends, and worthless acquaintance; those, who have appeared most zealous to serve me, have been almost constantly the first to deceive, and to betray! Of this number, I cannot avoid mentioning one person, as a caution to whoever puts confidence in the most plausible appearances of disinterested friendship.—A Mr. *Philip Ryan*, formerly a merchant, who now resides at Valenciennes, and with whom I [was] most unfortunately acquainted there, seemed to entertain for me the purest sentiments of pity and esteem; I placed in him that unlimited confidence, which should be the reward only of years of trial, but which it has ever been my misfortune to grant to every specious appearance. Mr. *Ryan* lent me a sum of money, in exchange for drafts for my quarterly payments, which were regularly paid. In the beginning of the year 1785, I was under many embarassments in London; I informed Mr. *Ryan* of them by letter, who returned me for answer, that his own affairs would have called him to England within a few months; but that the difficulties of mine, had determined him on setting out immediately, to assist me, as far as was in his power, with his purse, and his advice. He accordingly came; but the purity of his sentiments were soon converted from that disinterestedness I expected, and desired. He proposed to me a plan of life, which was by no means suitable to my inclinations, and my telling him so was productive of the most violent hate, succeeding to that sincere friendship which I thought I had found only in him.

Mr. *Ryan*, on his leaving England, told me, I was indebted to him 26l. and desired I would give him my note of hand for the money. I did so, after having given him previously an order on a Mr. *Stival*, a merchant at Dunkerque, who was keeping for me three trunks, containing all I had collected, and possessed, of any value in the world; I desired Mr. *Ryan* to take care of them 'till my return. Arriving at Dunkerque, I found he had placed them at the house of a Mr. *Greville*, a wine merchant, who resides there; and on my demanding them, I found to my great astonishment, that Mr. *Ryan* had stopt them for my note of hand; and although I have repeatedly offered him a fresh note, and security to have them again, I have never been able to recover them. These trunks contained a large collection of manuscript books and music, for which I would not have taken, in any moment of distress, two hundred pounds.

It was in that same year, that Mr. *Gooch* and Mr. *Woodcock*, both wrote to me; to inform me, that the education of my children becoming more expensive, Mr. *Gooch* had determined on taking off fifty pounds a year, from the two hundred I had till then enjoyed, and that he should continue to do so during four years, in which time he should have an estate in Norfolk belonging to himself, disengaged, and he would then return it to me. This alteration took place on the first of August, 1785; when, in drawing, as usual, a note on Mess. *Hoare*, for fifty pounds, I was answered, that I had henceforwards the privilege of demanding no more than thirty-seven pounds, ten shillings per quarter; this has continued ever since; and to embarrass my circumstances still more, I am not permitted to have any kind of security for the payment even of this, one day before it becomes due; notwithstanding that one hundred pounds per annum, is settled on me for pin money, by marriage articles. Mr. *Gooch* will not suffer the banker to accept, or even say that he will pay any draft of mine; in this, he has been perfectly seconded by Mess. *Hoare,* from their not chusing to give a satisfactory account of the certainty of my payments, to any person inclined to serve me, and who refers to them.

Thus is every stratagem employed to persecute me still farther, in hopes to obtain an excuse in the eyes of the world, for premeditated, for cruel injustice, and oppression! No pains have been spared to ruin, and crush me for ever; and sorry I am to say, that my family, if it has not laboured at my undoing, has of late years been silent on the subject of my unparalelled wrongs: How far Mr. *Gooch* can answer to this, I leave to the heart's best monitor, his own conscience, to determine. He has torn me from every tie; he has blackened me in the eyes of the world, and of my family, and thus for ever deprived me of their protection; he has divided me from my children, and robbed them of that tender care, a mother best can give; every tender connection, every social tie he has now dissolved; and in plunging me into sorrow, disgrace, and infamy, he has still left me, though surrounded by wretchedness, that triumph, which the consciousness of integrity bestows, and which it is not in the power of a whole host of foes to take away.

I have been accused as an unnatural daughter, and mother: Can my mother, can my children prove me to be so? That pure, that heartfelt affection I ever felt for the only remaining author of my being, has long since turned into the deepest of my wounds. Had I been in her situation, and she in mine, I would have renounced every worldly, every little consideration, and flown to the assistance of my child, to save her from destruction. Had my mother done this, when Mr. *Gooch* left me at Lille, my every pang had been spared; for where is there a heart, which although led away by the blandishments of pleasure, and transient gratification, could still be so lost, so irrecoverably bad, as to withstand a mother's pleadings, an only parent's tears?

My children may be deceived into a persuasion, that I am an unnatural mother; but have I been permitted to prove to them the contrary? From the year 1778, that I was forced from them, 'till the year 1782, it was out of my power to see them, and even to know where they were; at that time I learnt they were at a school at Walthamstowe. I went there and saw them. It is needless to dwell on the sensations which at that moment filled my eyes with tears, and my heart with the most unutterable anguish; sensations, which every bosom would feel under such circumstances, and in such a situation! But as I was totally ignorant what was their knowledge respecting myself, I thought it necessary to conceal from them who I was, 'till I had gained farther information. On questioning my eldest boy about his mother, he informed me, she was in France; I found they knew that I existed, and at our next interview, I determined to discover myself to them.

Their young minds were unconscious how much severer were the pangs I felt on thus seeing them, than those moments when first I wakened them into life! They saw me with a childish, and artless fondness, and wished for me to stay with them; I promised to return on the Sunday following; and when I did so, the mistress of the school told me with tears in her eyes, that Mr. *Gooch* had been there, and left absolute orders that I should see them no more; she kindly added, that the sincere interest she took in my situation, and the impatient desire my boys had expressed to see me again, had determined her on suffering it should be so; but I did not mean to injure her for her goodness, and after having affectionately kissed, and bid them adieu, I left them, with a promise to her that I would not return.

I patiently supported this instance of cruelty, in the hope, which has never forsaken me, that I shall at least once more before my last hour, press them to my breast, with all the transports of unrestrained maternal affection; should even this last looked for blessing be denied my heart, Nature will, I trust, when I am gone, plead powerfully in their's, and in a mother's cause.

'Till within the last eighteen months, the walls of a prison were still unknown to me; it was in 1786, that I was at Lille, in the utmost embarrassment. I wrote to intreat my family would advance me a sufficient sum of money to release me from the credit I found there, and so dearly paid; but all was ineffectual; not even letters sent to them from Lille, by some of the most respectable of its inhabitants, could induce them to relieve me; a long fit of illness, occasioned by real grief and disappointment, kept me confined above two months in bed, where I was without money, or resource of any kind. I had not gained strength sufficient to leave the house, when I was arrested for upwards of three hundred pounds, and conveyed to a prison, whose least horror was in its name.

It was in the month of October, and the season most rigorous, when I was taken out of a sick room, and placed in a garret, where there was no fire-place, and a miserable bed on a stone floor; in the anti-chamber, leading to it, there was a grate, and the furniture of it consisted of the different engines and implements made use of for the horrid purpose of the rack, and executions. The door of this anti-chamber, was double ironed, and barred, and was locked from five in the afternoon, till ten in the morning; during which length of time, it was impossible for me to see, or speak with any one; and the rooms were at the farther end of the house, out of the reach of assistance, or the hearing of any human beings, except the criminals, whose dungeons were the only prospect my double-barred chamber window commanded.

Thus was I confined upwards of two months, without any other society than a profusion of enormous rats, who came to plunder my miserable shelf. My family when apprized of my being there, ordered a Banker to pay me two guineas a week during the time of my confinement, but they never meant to release me, and I am to thank providence who sent a stranger to deliver me from a situation, the idea of which would be sufficient to melt with pity the most obdurate heart.

Since my return to England, a twelvemonth ago, I have been arrested for the same money, which relieved me from Lille; that, added to other debts I contracted several years ago in England, now detains me in the Fleet Prison; where, oppressed by Mr. *Gooch*, forsaken by my family, and destitute of friends, I am ignorant whether he is not answerable for my debts if I have no regular settlement, or if it is not fitting that I should have one to support me as a gentleman's daughter, and adequate to the fortune which I brought. Obliged as I have been, and still am, to make away with every thing on which I can raise a single shilling, without even the power of borrowing a few guineas on a future quarter; subject to every insult which the want of money seems to authorize; my health fallen a prey to my situation, without one single comfort the world can give; it is not to be wondered at that I have long and sincerely wished a happy release from every pang, convinced as I must be, that I have no farther happiness to expect on earth!—I am drawing near (and I rejoice at it) this period of all my woes! My family will perhaps, when it is too late, lament their unkindness—they will allow with all those who knew me, that a too great liberality of mind has been my undoing, and they will wish they had been less severe!

The justice I am now about to solicit from the laws of my country, is the effect of absolute necessity; and not, as may be supposed, that of a resentment which my heart never felt. I wish it was in my power to extricate myself without having recourse to those laws; but it is impossible. I have long and ineffectually tried if the picture of real woe could not influence my family to release me from a situation which must reflect dishonour on themselves: In the first two years of my separation, they endeavoured it; I was then blinded by my own folly, and the only aggressor. I am far from vindicating my subsequent conduct: it has been highly blameable and improper; its evil consequences, however, have been all my own; and though others have drawn down ruin on me, none can ascribe to me the diminution of their happiness. Thus have I been for several years tost on a tumultuous sea—driven by its storms from one kingdom to another, without even the hope of a calm, or a wish, but in death! My only consolation is derived from the consciousness that my misfortunes did not originate with myself. I have been compelled by the avarice of some, and the insidiousness of others, to act in opposition to the dictates of my own heart. But I harbour no resentment against the first authors of my unmerited sufferings; and hope to find that lenity from the world which I am inclined to extend to those by whose artifices I have been deprived of all the blessings attendant on birth, fortune, and innocence. I cannot conclude, without expressing a hope, that this address will remove some of those prejudices which ignorance and malignity have raised against me; and that my name may be remembered with pity, rather than with indignation, when I become an inhabitant of those realms "where the wicked cease from troubling, and the weary are at rest."[2]

Notes

1. End of.
2. The reference is to Job 3:17.

Hannah Robertson

1724–1806?

The Life of Mrs. Robertson, (A Tale of Truth as well as of Sorrow) who, though a Grand-Daughter of Charles II. has been reduced, by a variety of very uncommon events, from splendid Affluence to the greatest Poverty. And, after having buried nine children, is obliged, at the age of sixty-seven, to earn a scanty maintenance for herself and two orphan grand-children, by teaching embroidery, filligree, and the art of making artificial flowers. Derby: J. Drewry, 1791.

Hannah Robertson was born in Glasgow on 2 October 1724, one of six children born to her father and his second wife. Although her father had been given the surname Swan, he was in fact the illegitimate son of King Charles II of England and a woman whom Hannah identifies only as belonging to the "distinguished . . . D—— family" (1–2). Swan "perpetually" (3) reminded Hannah that she was "the grand daughter of a king," and the *Life* seldom allows the reader to forget this fact. Even at the age of six, Hannah was "too proud" (4) of her royal blood to attend the local school; instead she began to teach herself embroidery, drawing, flower-making, and other elegant pursuits that would later stand her in good stead. Within six months of her father's death in 1730, her mother married Alexander Christie. In 1736 the family relocated to Perth, where her stepfather established extensive linen manufactures. She returned to Glasgow in 1744, where she witnessed several "horrid scenes" (9) during the pro-Stuart rising of 1745. She became engaged to a Captain Johnstone, but later, believing that he had died in battle, she agreed to marry her brother's friend Mr. Robertson, and she went through with the ceremony even though Johnstone returned the day before the wedding.

After several years of prosperity, Robertson's business failed owing to his partner's incompetence. Hannah began to run a tavern in Aberdeen in order to pay her husband's debts. When the tavern was destroyed by fire, she returned to Perth and opened a school; it failed, and although she then turned to selling millinery, she was arrested for debt. In 1767 she published *The Young Ladies School of Arts,* a manual of "practical receipts" for domestic arts from filigree-making to clear starching. A second, revised edition appeared the same year, and she continued to revise the book up to its tenth and final edition of 1806. After her husband died in 1771, Robertson supported herself and her four surviving children in Edinburgh and later in London, York, and Birmingham. At one point she and her daughters opened London's first shop for the sale of ornamental or "fancy" work, and they taught the arts of fancy work to aristocratic young women. By 1791, however, Robertson's children had either died or departed, and she was left with three grandchildren to feed. Publishing the *Life* was one of her efforts to support her family. It takes the form of letters to one "Madam," and it seems to have been written at the suggestion of this unnamed patroness to help her make a case for a court pension for Robertson. It is not clear whether she succeeded. The *Life* was published by subscription in 1791 and thus raised money for Robertson's immediate needs, but the fact that in 1806 she was relying on sales of the *School of Arts* for "assistance in her present weakly situation" suggests that, at the age of eighty-two, she was still struggling to support herself.

TEXT: Hannah Robertson's *Life* first appeared in 1791. A second, revised version was published in 1806, as preface to the tenth edition of her *Young Ladies School of Arts*; it contains little new information. The selection (pp. 16–28 of the 1791 *Life*) details the economic trials of Robertson's married life.

☙ ❧

THUS, MADAM, did I exist thro' the first year of my married state—a mourning bride,[1] and a melancholy wife!—I was now preparing for a little stranger who was likely to encrease our family; one day as I sat musing alone, Capt. Johnstone[2] unexpectedly appeared, and falling upon one knee before me, he put into my hand a splendid coral, which he begg'd I would present to the young stranger, whom (he told me) his happiness required he should never behold: Captain Johnstone left the room before I had courage to reply; and although near fifty years have since passed away, I never from that fatal period have once enjoy'd the melancholy satisfaction of beholding capt. Johnstone more.—If my friend (for I dare no longer call him lover) be yet on earth, may he have regain'd that peace which I have so long outlived!—or, if in heaven—may he enjoy there the reward of his constancy, and of his virtues, unconscious of the woes which his fatal affection has entailed on this sad, sorrowing heart! With respect however, to what the world calls prosperity, you see me, Madam, at this time basking in the brightest sun-shine of my days. Every succeeding year added to our family, and to our comforts: altho' I was the grand-child of a king, and perhaps too much flattered by that dignity, yet never did I consider myself superior to the duties of a mother; my children indeed were my delight. I nursed[3] the infants, and presided over the education of my eldest daughter and son. The short intervals of leisure, which my duties allowed, were chiefly devoted to those favourite arts which I had ever cultivated with delight; I studied nature with a view to imitate her most elegant productions,—a new creation rose beneath my hands,—I formed flowers of art—I painted, and I embroidered; so that (like Penelope of old)[4] I charmed away with works of fancy, the tedious hours, during the absence of my lord. As for Mr. Robertson, if he had not before marriage succeeded in fixing my affections, at least his unremitted attentions afterwards excited my warmest gratitude; and the consistency of his conduct could not fail of fixing my esteem; I respected, if I did not love him; and my endeavours to make *him* happy, contributed in a great measure towards rendering *me* so likewise. My solicitudes and cares became transferred from myself to other objects; present comforts also softened the rigours of my former fate, and I began to contemplate our future prospects with hope, and with confidence. But, alas! I was deluded like an unskilful mariner, who puts his trust in the smooth (but deceitful) surface of the inconstant deep: in the mutability of life, as in the vicissitudes of the ocean, who can tell what to-morrow may bring forth! Let those who have gained the giddy heights of prosperity, remember that a precipice is near, and learn from my fatal experience to "tremble at the gulf that yawns below."[5] —With respect to myself, Madam, when I the least anticipated misfortune, behold me plunged into a "sea of troubles:"[6] and from henceforth you will see me only a wretched wanderer, thro' a vale of tears.

Sickness now began to visit us in its most hideous forms; our eldest and indeed (at that time) our only son, was seized with a dreadful and a mortal disease; the loss of this darling child prey'd upon my spirits, and being at time nurse to the youngest, my bodily strength was rapidly declining. One day as I sat musing with the infant in my arms, I was overspread (as it were) with a sudden and preternatural horror: I flew to my husband (who was sitting with a book in the garden) and throwing myself into his arms, I exclaim'd in an agony, "Oh! Mr. Robertson, I have lost my reason!" From that moment, Madam, I continued for two long years in a situation, which, if it were in my power, I would not describe: my imagination cannot bear to dwell upon the dismal scene, the bare recollection, even at this remote period, chills me with unutterable horror. My husband (who attended me with sincere affection) seemed to sink also under the weight of my affliction; he soothed me with his care, and watched over my sleeping hours; but his own health and spirits were inadequate to the burden of his misery; he became incapable of all exertion, and leaving his other concerns, devoted his time, his fortune, and all his cares to me alone. The business in which my husband was engaged, was now consigned to the care of an incompetent partner. My husband was partner with Mr. Brown, and their bills signed "Brown, Robertson, and Co." the house or business had long gone in that name, Provost Brown being grandfather to both.—I know not accurately (for I was incapable of knowing) the various complications of all those disastrous events which precipitated us into ruin; but a bankruptcy ensued, with all its attendant train of horrors; and the failure of a capital house at the same time, with which our's was connected in London, involved my unfortunate husband in the same melancholy fate. Thus began the sad series of our future sorrows, in the year 1756. I do really believe, Madam, that it was the sudden shock of this unexpected misfortune, that first roused me from the lethargy into which I was fallen. I gradually recovered; and thro' the kindness of my father, Mr. Robertson was put into the distillery business, which (with better health) he might have easily conducted; but his spirits were too much broken to enter into new cares; the undertaking did not succeed, and he was now thrown into prison for an old debt. It was now my turn to comfort the afflicted; I shared in all his sorrows—I watched by his side—and nothing should have separated me from my kind husband, tho' condemn'd to the dismal solitude of a dark jail, but the hope of releasing him by my industry. In a newspaper, which I had taken to amuse my husband in his confinement, I saw an advertisement for a proper person to conduct a new tavern which was building by the free masons,[7] next to their lodge in Aberdeen. I shew'd it to my husband, and begged his permission to undertake it; but he wisely foresaw how entirely I was unqualified for such a laborious office, accustomed as I had been to all the conveniences, and elegancies of life: and in truth, a lady of quality might have been considered as well qualified as myself to have become the mistress of an inn: I was however firm in my purpose, and extorted his reluctant consent. I hired a vessel to carry my furniture to Aberdeen, for his creditors took none of it from us, and I was supplied with more by my relations, and taking leave of the forlorn prisoner, I set out northward in 1762.

The difficulties, which crowded round me, inspired me with courage. At first I succeeded in this new undertaking, for my tavern was much frequented; and I had it soon in my power to discharge many of my husband's debts, and to release him from confinement, which more than compensated for every toil and every care. He joined me at Aberdeen, where we once more enjoyed a gleam of tranquility; tho' fallen, never to rise again to our former rank in life. I yet enjoyed some comforts in my humble station: it is one of the advantages of adversity, that it renders the mind susceptible of the affliction of others. I at least enjoyed in this situation, the luxury of doing some good: if I possessed not wealth to cloath the naked, I yet allow'd myself the pleasure of feeding the hungry, for nobody went empty away from my door; and to many a dependant heir have I administered his daily bread, who at this time is wanting only in the will to requite me.—How deceitful are human prospects!—a gentleman from Norway who lodged in our house, unhappily falling asleep as he was reading in bed, the curtains took fire, and the flames communicating with other parts of the furniture and buildings, a great share of our possessions were consumed. The unhappy stranger also, falling a sacrifice to his own imprudence, with all that belong'd to him, we were obliged to bear the expence of his funeral; which was however, but a very trifling addition to the weight of our other alarming and serious losses occasioned by this calamity; which was soon after succeeded by a second of the same kind. Another dreadful fire which happened in the neighbourhood shortly after, consuming the greatest part of our property which before had escaped, we again were reduced to the brink of destruction; and the proprietors, when I was re-established, by a series of oppressions finally compelled me to quit, having seized and sold my wines and furniture, though my debt to them was inconsiderable. We return'd to Perth, but alas! how fallen! I attempted to do something for my family, first by teaching school, for which charge however the distress of my mind finally disqualified me. Behold, Madam, the grand-child of a king, reduced to the painful necessity of relying for her support upon that class, with which she was formerly too proud to associate.

The school failing, I attempted to sell a few millinery articles: and in this situation, I became the instrument of some good to my sex. An infamous attorney (tho' I was a married woman) cast me into prison for a small debt.[8] My husband and myself were sitting peaceably at our frugal supper, when the ruffians rudely entered, and seized me.—I had then an infant which I could not leave:—so, taking the child in my arms, (with a kind of desperate resolution which misfortune inspires) I boldly promised to follow them. They led me into a damp and dismal dungeon; but I cannot say that it was *not inhabited;* for the place was occupied in every part by innumerable *rats,* the only creature that chills me with horror!

Some clean straw was strewed over the floor, to keep the wet from my feet; but my chief apprehension was on account of my innocent child that I nourished, left it should suffer from the noisome vapours that issued like smoke from the walls. In this situation I wrote my case:—the fifteen judges assembled, and awarding me 50£. as some compensation for the injury, they sentenced Mr. G. the attorney to infamy. Released from confinement, I continued my little business, oppressed with many a domestic care, and foreboding apprehension; among which, it was by no means the least, that my eldest daughter—my majestic Anna, was now rising as a beauty into fame. It is not without tears, Madam, that I yet recall to my remembrance her lovely image, at that time the emblem of innocence and every youthful charm: it was a general observation, that in my Anna's features might be distinctly traced those of our unfortunate family, for she was the living image of Mary, queen of Scots—equally distinguished for her beauty, and (as you will see hereafter, Madam) for her misfortunes! In such circumstances, it was only with sorrow that I could contemplate that beaming beauty, which, in our original sphere, might have nobly distinguished my daughter as the [great-]grand-child of a king.—My youngest girl (who was call'd Minia) was less beautiful, but her gentle and unoffending nature proved the consolation of my desponding heart. We had also two little sons, who divided our attention and our love. Thus, Madam, you see me oppressed with many cares, "but the winds are tempered to the shorn lamb."[9] Thro' every scene of sorrow, I had found an unfailing resource in my brother's sympathy and kind affection: he resided in Perth, and it was his kindness that consoled, his counsel that directed me; and his bounty that supplied my wants. It was also an additional comfort, that my sister resided within our reach: she had married a man in affluence, and they lived within a mile of Perth, in a large house that was the family seat of Lord Oliphant.

I was also still honoured with the friendship of the Dutchess of Athol, who often sent for me to visit her; but one of those visits had nearly put an end to my misery, and my life. It was in the depth of a severe winter, and the Dutchess had sent for me to spend a few days at Dunkeld. I return'd (with a maid servant and our youngest child, who had accompanied me) in the duke's carriage. The river Almond was frozen over with a thick ice, which we had crossed in safety a few days before; but as we were repassing the river on our way back to Perth, the ice burst with a terrible crash, and the horses and carriage were plunged into the stream. It was a shallow part of the river, yet I need not say with what difficulty we were extricated, nor in what situation we were drawn from the flood.

After spending some hours in a neighbouring cottage to recover, we again attempted to pursue our ride to Perth, which was not very distant: Yet in this short interval, we were attacked by a highwayman, and narrowly escaped with our lives. Thus, Madam, thro' life have I been pursued in every undertaking (whether great or small) by the impoisoned arrows of unrelenting fortune: but indeed had I died on this occasion, my death would have preserved me from many a future pang. Some advantages however accompany even adversity—if it scatters our associates, it distinguishes our friends: the supercilious contempt that I experienced from many who were once my inferiors, rendered my sensibility more acute to the instances of gratitude from those (who like the widow in the gospel) had only their mite to give. One unfortunate gentleman, Sir John S——, of G——ly, I shall ever remember, and the recollection has drawn from me many a tear of gratitude. I served him in my prosperity, when he stood in need of assistance, and now he sold his watch, and every valuable he possessed, sending me the small sum he had thus raised for my support, at a time when the few cloaths that covered me could scarcely be called my own. I did not consider it as a debt due to me, but as money given me out of charity, which at that time hurt my pride, and the method he took to raise it sensibly affected my feelings.

I now printed the *young ladies school of arts*, which, at the request of some female friends of distinction, I had composed at Aberdeen, and went over to Edinburgh to inspect the press. Here my eldest daughter, (whom I seldom left) became acquainted with Dr. Wilson, nephew to a physician of that name; a distinguished character: he had travelled thro' Europe and Asia—and in a visit to China, had been by a variety of strange accidents introduced to the empress, whom he cured of a dangerous disease. Young Dr. Wilson was heir to his uncle, who possessed a large fortune; and I appeal to you, Madam, as to a fond mother, whether I had not every apparent reason to rejoice in such a connection for my child; I consulted Mr. Robertson, (whom I had left in Perth) and I soon after married our beloved Anna, not only with her father's approbation, but to his delight. But alas! Madam, "we see here (indeed) as thro' a glass, darkly;"[10] and my accumulated misfortunes (or rather the various unexpected turns of my evil fortune) have at least taught me one act of wisdom—it is that of joining only in the Lacedæmonian prayer[11]—"Give us, Oh Lord! the things that are good for us, altho' we ask them not; and remove from us those that are evil, although we were to ask them!" so incompetent are we to foresee, or to judge of the future.

Notes

1. Perhaps a reference to William Congreve's 1697 tragedy of the same name.

2. The man to whom Robertson had once been contracted in marriage.

3. At this time many upper-class women hired wet nurses to breast-feed their children. By stating that she nursed her infants herself, Robertson is emphasizing her commitment to "the duties of a mother."

4. In Homer's *Odyssey*, the wife of Odysseus, who spends the ten years of his absence doing embroidery.

5. Source unidentified.

6. Shakespeare, *Hamlet* 3.1:58.

7. In this usage, "free" means superior. The Freemasons were skilled workers in stone, with secret signs and passwords by which they could recognize each other.

8. According to the principle of *feme covert* in common law, a married woman had no legal identity separate from her husband and therefore could not be sued for debt.

9. Spoken by the character Maria in Laurence Sterne's novel *A Sentimental Journey through France and Italy* (1768).

10. From Paul's epistle to the Corinthians (1 Cor. 13:12).

11. The phrase is obscure; since "Lacedæmonian" is another word for "Spartan," and "Spartan" means "laconic" when used of speech, Robertson may mean a prayer that is short and to the point.

Anna Maria Falconbridge

FL. 1790S

Narrative of Two Voyages to the River Sierra Leone, during the Years 1791–2-3, performed by A. M. Falconbridge. With a Succinct account of the Distresses and proceedings of that Settlement; a description of the Manners, Diversions, Arts, Commerce, Cultivation, Custom, Punishments, &c. And Every interesting Particular relating to the Sierra Leone Company. Also The present State of the Slave Trade in the West Indies, and the improbability of its total Abolition. 2d ed. London: L. I. Higham, 1802.

Anna Maria Falconbridge's *Narrative* is the source of the scant information available about her. By 1791 she had married ship's surgeon Alexander Falconbridge, "hastily" (9) and against her family's wishes. "Rather than be an incumbrance on them," she accompanied her husband to Sierra Leone in West Africa. This settlement, established by British abolitionists for ex-slaves, had a checkered career. The first group of freed slaves arrived in 1787 and built a village named Granville Town on land ceded by the local chief, King Tom. The village was razed in 1789 by order of Koya Temne chief King Jimmy, King Tom's successor. Hoping to rebuild the settlement, a group of abolitionists incorporated the hitherto private Sierra Leone Company under government charter and with a broad remit: "the Abolition of the Slave-Trade, the Civilization of Africa, and the Introduction of the Gospel there" (qtd. in J. Walker 103), by replacing the slave trade with legitimate trade in handicrafts and the like. In 1791 Alexander Falconbridge, the company's agent, journeyed to Sierra Leone with his wife to regroup the scattered settlers and begin rebuilding on a new site.

Anna Maria's account of this first stay often records her "astonishment" (32): at three hundred "wretched" slaves chained and eating from a trough; at a local queen wearing "*neither shoes nor stockings*" (44); at women drinking rum "as deliberately as I would water" (54); and—in an account that historians of Sierra Leone continue to dispute—at one woman's charge that the British government had inveigled her and other prostitutes into accompanying the 1787 settlers. By her second sojourn in Sierra Leone,

Anna Maria had become increasingly critical of the company that employed her husband. She felt its plan to enlarge the settlement with freed blacks from Nova Scotia was "premature, hair-brained, and ill digested" (125); she also found "preposterous" the company's effort to "imprint notions of Christianity" on the native peoples using "a language they do not understand" (199–200). Anna Maria's allegiances further shifted with her second marriage. "Constantly intoxicated" (169) after being replaced as the company's commercial agent, Alexander Falconbridge "gasp'd his last!!!" in December 1792; three weeks later she married Isaac Dubois, another company official, and soon thereafter they decided to leave the colony. On her return to England in October 1793 she badgered the company for monies owed to Alexander. Little more is known of her life.

TEXT: Anna Maria Falconbridge opened the 1794 edition of the *Narrative* by eschewing the "threadbare prevailing custom" (v) of claiming that her letters were not intended for publication: "on the contrary, she candidly confesses having some idea of the kind when writing them." The 1794 edition of the *Narrative* includes her two letters to Henry Thornton, member of Parliament and chair of the Sierra Leone Company, as a "vindication" both of her own conduct and of "present[ing] to the World" her wrongs. The book was reprinted in 1794 and 1795, and a new edition of this text appeared in 1999. Anna Maria published a revised version of her book in 1802, with added materials about Sierra Leone which further clarify her original intentions. The excerpt is from the second edition; covering her second sojourn in Sierra Leone (pp. 132–143), it well illustrates Falconbridge's position in and responses to the colony.

◌℘℘

LETTER VII.

Free Town, Sierra Leone
10th April, 1792.

My dear Madam,

Here I am, once more exposed to the influence of a Torrid Sun, near three thousand miles apart from my dearest friends, experiencing, not only, the inevitable hardships of Colonization, but wallowing in a multiplicity of trouble and confusion, very unnecessarily attached to the infant Colony.

We sailed from Falmouth the 19th of December [1791], and arrived at this place the 16th of February, when we found the Harpy, Wilson, a Company ship, that left England some time after us; but our voyage was prolonged, in consequence of being obliged to stop at Teneriff for a few pipes[1] of Wine.

Immediately on entering the river we were visited by Captain Wilson, and after the customary civilities, he told us, several Colonial Officers, a few soldiers, and some independant Settlers came passengers with him, who were greatly rejoiced at seeing the Amy;[2] for being all strangers, they were at a loss what to do, and wholly relied on Falconbridge to make good their landing.

In the course of conversation many sentences escaped Captain Wilson, importing a very unfavourable account of his passengers, but imagining they proceeded from some misunderstanding between them and him, neither Falconbridge or myself allowed what he said, to bias or prejudice us in any shape.

Captain Wilson having directed the most eligible spot for us to bring up, waited until our anchor was gone, and then returned to his ship: Falconbridge accompanied him to make his obeisance to the Ladies and Gentlemen on board.

In a short time, he was confirmed, our surmise, with regard to disagreements subsisting between the parties, was well grounded, for they were constantly snarling at each other; but it required very little penetration to arrive at the true source of their animosities, and before I proceed further I must acquaint you, the Directors have appointed eight persons to represent them, and conduct the management of their Colony, under the *dignified appellation of Superintendant and Council.*

It is a pity when making those appointments, they had not probed for characters of worth and respectability, as success in any enterprise greatly hinges on skilful, prudent conduct; qualities more especially requisite in an undertaking like this, laboring under a load of enemies, who will, no doubt, take advantage to blow the smallest spark of mal-conduct into a flame of error.

Perhaps the Directors imagine they were particularly circumspect in their choice of representatives, if so, they are grossly deceived, for never were characters worse adapted to manage any purpose of magnitude than some whom they have nominated.

Are men of little worth and much insignificance fit to be guardians and stewards of the immense property required, for erecting the fabric of a new Colony? Are Men, whose heads are too shallow to support a little vicissitude and unexpected *imaginary* aggrandizement, whose weak minds delude them with wrong notions of their nominal rank, and whose whole time is occupied with contemplating their fancied consequence, in place of attending to the real and interesting designs of their mission, calculated for the executors of a theory, which can only be put in practice by wise and judicious methods?

Certainly not; yet of this description are the greater part who guide and direct our Colony; a majority of whom came passengers in the Harpy, and who, intoxicated with false ideas of their authority, wished to assume the prerogative of controling Captain Wilson in managing and governing his ship; but the latter treated their arrogance with contempt, and consequently grew the dissentions alluded to, which have since been the cause of many disagreeable unpleasant occurrences.

Falconbridge soon returned with Captain and Mrs. Wilson, whom we had invited to dine with us; four Honorable Members of the Council, dressed *cap a pie*, in a uniform given them by the Directors to distinguish their rank, came with them, to make their bows to your humble servant, as the wife of their *superior*, Falconbridge being the eldest member of this *supreme* body.

A message was then sent to King Jemmy[3] (opposite to whose town the Amy lay) to announce our arrival to him and King Naimbana[4] (who was there at the time,) requesting they would come on board.

Naimbana, accompanied by Mr. Elliotte[5] and a number of attendants, soon complied with our request, but Jemmy would not be prevailed upon.

The old King was overjoyed at seeing me; being seated, Falconbridge shewed him the portrait of his son,[6] a present from the Directors.

The picture is an admirable likeness, and the poor Father burst into tears when he saw it.

He stayed with us five days; and, notwithstanding every courteous art was used to persuade King Jemmy to honor us with a visit, we could not effect it: He once consented on condition I remained in his town a hostage till he returned; this I agreed to, and went on shore for the intention; but his people dissuaded him just as he was going off.

You may remember I mentioned in a former letter, the ground where the *first Settlers* were driven from by King Jemmy, being the most desirable situation hereabouts for a settlement, but by the Palaver[7] it was objected to; however, with coaxing, and the irresistibility of presents, King Naimbana was prevailed upon to remove whatever objections there were, and on the 28th of February put us in quiet possession of the very spot; which is named *Free Town*, from the *principles* that gave rise to the establishment.[8]

The second day after our arrival, there was a grand Council held on board the Amy when their Secretary delivered Mr. Falconbridge new instructions from the directors, directly counter to those he received in London; subjecting him, in his commercial capacity, to the control of the Superintendant and Council, and acquainting him, Lieutenant Clarkson was appointed Superintendant.[9]

This has disconcerted Falconbridge vastly, and inclines him to construe their conduct to us in England, as juggle and chichane [i.e., chicanery], for the mere purpose of enticing him here, knowing he was the fittest, nay only person, to secure a footing for the Nova Scotia Emigrants; but I cannot think so harshly.

After been [sic] here a fortnight, Mr. Clarkson arrived, with the Blacks from America, a part of whom came some days before him.

When he left Nova Scotia they amounted to between eleven and twelve hundred, but during the voyage a malignant fever infested the Ships, and carried off great numbers.

Mr. Clarkson caught the fever, and miraculously escaped death, which would have been an irreparable loss to the Colony, being the only man calculated to govern the people who came with him, for by his winning manners, and mild, benign treatment, he has so gained [their] affections and attachment, that he can, by lifting up his finger (as he expresses it) do what he pleases with them.

They are in general, a religious temperate, good set of people; at present they are employed in building huts for their temporary residence, till the lands promised them can be surveyed; when that will be God only knows; the surveyor being a *Counsellor* and *Captain* of our *veteran host*, is of too much consequence to attend to the servile duty of surveying, notwithstanding he is paid for it.

Few of the Settlers have yet got huts erected, they are mostly encamped under tents made with sails from the different ships, and are very badly off for fresh provisions; indeed such is the case with us all, and what's worse, we have but half allowance of very indifferent salt provision, and bad worm eaten bread.[10]

Painfully do I say, nothing promises well.—Mr. Clarkson, as Superintendant, is so tied up, that he cannot do any thing without the approbation of his Council, and those opinionated upstarts thwart him in all his attempts.

He is an amiable man, void of pomp or ostentation, which his senatorial associates disapprove of exceedingly, from the ridiculous idea that their *dignity* is lessened by his frankness.

How truly contemptible it is to see men stickle in this way after foolish unbecoming consequence, blind to the interest of their employers, whereby, they must, without question, rise or fall.

Their absurd behaviour[11] make them the laughing stocks of the neighbouring Factories[12] and such masters of slave ships as have witnessed their conduct, who must certainly be highly gratified with the anarchy and chagrin that prevails through the Colony.

The Blacks are displeased that they have not their promised lands; and so little do they relish the obnoxious arrogance of their rulers, that I really believe, was it not for the influence of Mr. Clarkson, they would be apt to drive some of them into the sea.

The independant European Settlers are vastly disappointed, and heartily wish themselves back in their own country.

This is not to be wondered at, when in addition to the calamity of being in a new Colony, over-run with confusion, jealousy, and discordant sentiments, they are exposed to the oppression of wanting almost every necessary of life, having no shops where they might purchase, or any other medium of procuring them.

I have only one piece of pleasing intelligence to give you:—The Colony just now is tolerable healthy; very few deaths have occurred among the Blacks since their arrival, and but two among the Whites; the latter were Doctor B——, (our physician,) and the Harpy's gunner.

The gunner's death was occasioned by that of the former, who brought on his dissolution by inebriety and imprudence; being a member of the Magisterial body, he was buried with all the pomp and ceremony circumstances would admit of.

While the corpse moved on in solemn pace, attended by Members of Council, and others in procession, minute guns[13] were fired from the Harpy; in executing this, the gunner lost his arm, of which he died very shortly.

I yet live on ship board, for though the Directors had the goodness to send out a canvas house purposely for me, I have not the satisfaction of occupying it, our *men of might* having thought proper to appropriate it another way.

Mr. Gilbert, our clergyman, returns to England in the vessel I write by, a fast sailing schooner, Mr. Clarkson has purchased for the painful, but indispensible intention of sending the Directors information of our distracted, deplorable situation; at the same time exhorting them in their *wisdom* to make some immediate, efficacious change in our government, without which their Colony will, irrecoverably be stifled in its infancy.

Mr. Gilbert is a man of mild agreeable manners, truly religious, without the hypocritical shew of it; he is universally liked in the Colony, and I am sure his absence will be greatly regreted; but Mr. Clarkson's indisposition, rendering him unable to write so fully as he wishes, or necessity demands, has prevailed on him (Mr. Gilbert) to return to England, and represent to the Directors, by word of mouth, whatever he may neglect to do in writing.

A party of us will accompany him to the Banana Islands, about ten leagues from hence, where he is in hopes of procuring fresh stock, and other necessary sea stores, which are not to be had here for love or money.

I do not think it will be in my power to write you from the Banana's; shall, therefore, close this letter with sincere hopes my next may give you a more favourable account of things.

Farewel, &c. &c.

Notes

1. Casks for wine, each usually holding approximately 105 gallons.
2. The ship carrying the Falconbridges.
3. In 1789 King Jimmy had attacked the company's settlement at Granville Town, so the company was eager to conciliate him.
4. Overlord or paramount subchief of the Koya Temne kingdom.
5. Elliotte Griffiths, King Naimbana's secretary.
6. The first of his family transfered on canvas [Falconbridge]. Naimbana had sent his son to England to be educated by the Sierra Leone Company.
7. Falconbridge defines a palaver as a "Court House"; a palaver is also the meeting of such a court.
8. It is situated on a rising ground, fronting the sea; six miles above Cape Sierra Leone, and eighteen from Bance Island; separated from King Jemmy's town by a rivulet and thick wood, near half a mile through: before the town, is pretty good anchorage for shipping, but the landing places are generally bad in consequence of the shore being bound with iron rocks, and an ugly surge, most commonly breaking on them [Falconbridge].
9. John Clarkson, brother of the Rev. Thomas Clarkson (well-known abolitionist and a director of the Sierra Leone Company), had earlier recruited freed blacks from Nova Scotia for the reorganized Sierra Leone colony.
10. The James, of Bristol, being unfit to proceed her voyage, was condemned and sold at Bance Island about this time; from her a quantity of beans and other provisions were purchased which was a fortunate circumstance for the Colony, then in a starving state [Falconbridge].
11. Few days escaped without a quarrel, which sometimes came the length of blows: Members of Council were daily ordering goods from the ships, not wanted, and inevitably to be destroyed, merely for the purpose of shewing their authority [Falconbridge].
12. Establishment for traders doing business in a foreign country, or a merchant company's trading station.
13. Guns fired at one-minute intervals as a sign of mourning or distress.

Mary Eleanor Bowes

COUNTESS OF STRATHMORE

1749–1800

The Confessions of the Countess of Strathmore; written by herself. Carefully copied from the original, lodged in Doctor's Commons. London: W. Locke, 1793.

Mary Eleanor Bowes was born on 24 February 1749 into a wealthy coal-owning family. Her father, George Bowes, was a member of Parliament and lobbyist for the coal interests. She could read by the age of four, and her father ensured that she was educated "in every kind of learning" (49) but not, she later felt, in such moral virtues as "chastity, patience, and forgiveness of injuries" (52). As an only child, she was a substantial heiress: in addition to a £600,000 estate from her father, she inherited a great deal of property from her mother. Much courted, she eventually accepted a proposal from John Lyon, earl of Strathmore, and against her mother's advice married him on 24 February 1767. During their nine-year marriage, Bowes had five children, pursued her botanical studies, and wrote *The Siege of Jerusalem*, a dramatic poem privately printed in 1774. Lord Strathmore died at sea on 7 March 1776, and Bowes engaged herself "most solemnly" (7) to George Grey, with whom she was having an affair. But she was industriously pursued by Andrew Robinson Stoney, whom she met in August or September of 1776, and she married him in January 1777. Enraged, Grey threatened a breach-of-promise suit but was eventually bought off. At this point Bowes seemed to have the upper hand with her husband as well: by the terms of her father's will he was required to take her name, and she had set up an antenuptial trust so that he would have no control over her property. Within four months of the wedding, however, he had broken the trust, using physical violence to force her to revoke the deeds. The same sense of her being alternately controller and controlled emerges in her *Confessions*, written early in 1778: it is unclear whether her husband demanded that she record her "crimes" (5) and "imprudencies" (7), or whether she negotiated this solution to some domestic contretemps; she admits her own faults but also criticizes her husband's; while she produces an exhaustive list of misdeeds, this very minuteness hints a parody of confession, and one biographer finds several "deliberate suppressions and falsehoods" in the account (Arnold 84).

Bowes's life with her husband over the next ten years was tempestuous. In 1781 Thomas Lyon, her former brother-in-law, succeeded in having her children by Lord Strathmore declared wards in chancery. In May 1784 the Boweses kidnapped one daughter from her school but in December returned her. In February 1785 Bowes obtained Articles of Peace, a sort of restraining order, against her husband, and began legal proceedings to regain control of her property and to divorce him on the grounds of adultery and cruelty—"beating, scratching, biting, pinching, whipping, kicking, imprisoning, insulting, provoking, tormenting, mortifying, degrading, tyrannizing, cajoling, deceiving, lying, starving, forcing, compelling, and wringing of the heart" (qtd. in Arnold 105). He countered first by publishing the *Confessions* as a pamphlet, then with an elaborate scam that culminated in his abducting his wife to compel her to drop the divorce suit. After she was rescued and he was imprisoned, he bought an interest in the *Universal Register* newspaper and wrote letters to it alternately attacking and defending the case against himself. Despite a number of cross-suits and appeals, she was finally granted a divorce on 2 March 1789. Bowes then lived fairly calmly and in harmony with her children until her death on 28 April 1800. She is buried in Westminster Abbey.

TEXT: Mary Eleanor Bowes wrote her *Confessions* in 1778 and asked her husband "as a favour" (47) to burn it after her death. Instead, it became an exhibit in her divorce case and a public scandal when he published it as a pamphlet in 1788 and again in 1789. The excerpt (pp. 66–100) covers her first marriage, her affair with George Grey, and various other peccadilloes. It exhibits the alternation between testy and hangdog that characterizes the narrative's tone.

 C& ℬ

I INTENDED CANDIDLY, and in the fullest manner, to lay before you every action of my life, relative to the least imprudence I ever was guilty of: I have written a good deal; but as you are impatient, and perceiving I labour under a load of imputations, yet unknown to me, though credited by you, many of which, I dare say, are false; I shall, till after this is finished, leave the trifling things, which were only inadvertencies any girl might be and is guilty of; and hasten to tell you, in as few words as possible, every imprudence, and every crime, I have been guilty of, since my marriage with Lord Strathmore, which is as far back as I imagine you are immediately anxious to know.

I had by him all my five children; and during that time, never had one thought, did one action, or said one word, which Heaven might not know without blaming me, or indeed himself; except the dislike I had but too much cause to entertain for Mr. Lyon.[1] Before I had been many months married, however, I put up with that, and the disagreeable behaviour of the rest of the family, and concealed it as much as possible from the world, till he publicly, and causelessly, as many can witness, insulted me in the public rooms at Edinburgh, where I was with him and Mrs. Lyon, who was just married, all the race-week without Lord Strathmore; during which time, he behaved in such a manner, as scandalized the whole town of Edinburgh; who, at that time, hated him as much as they liked and pitied me. I complained mildly to Lord Strathmore about his brother; but it was an unfortunate and most prejudiced rule with him, that Mr. Lyon could not err; so I got no other redress than his saying, that though he was hasty, he had a good heart, and never meant to offend. I never complained to my mother on any occasion of Lord S. or his family; but on the contrary, expressed an uncommon regard for both, of which she was jealous, and made her believe they used me extremely well: for as I had married him against her advice, my pride would not let me complain, had they used me ten times worse.

The year before this, Mr. Robert Graham, of Fuitry, took all opportunities to be in my company, and to express, though not improperly, his regard and attention to me. He once told me so positively, and received such an answer as was proper, and which, from my foolish flirting with him, I dare say he did not expect. He went from Glames[2] in a pet, and being a man of violent resentments (which in all instances have turned out against himself), he directly proposed to Miss Peggy Mylne, who always had a penchant for him; but whom he had taken every opportunity, both in public and private, to abuse in a most groundless and violent manner; and to profess, that he would rather die than marry her: yet she consented—they were married suddenly without his parents consent.

The year before, when I was on a visit to his mother, I saw for the first time, and not again for two years, his youngest brother, James; he was quite a boy, but a very extraordinary one, and I must confess, much too forward for his years, and too conscious of those shining talents, which no heart can, in some degree without difficulty, be proof against, when he chose to exert his art. I have the greatest reason to think, he, from that time, formed a design of enjoying my affections: he made many attempts to come with his other brothers to Glamis; but they constantly, as Miss Graham told me, refused to bring him: and he introduced himself, or rather in a manner forced himself in, to come to Glamis one day with his sister; when she walked to Bridge Town, scarce three miles from Glamis, where she, and indeed myself, often used to go, to see an amiable and elegant woman, one Mrs. Douglas, wife to my dear Emilia's brother; where he sometimes, and particularly at that time, was staying. He, as I afterwards found, offered to set her home to Glamis, when she was staying with me, but she would not let him; upon which he told her, there were droves of horned cattle on the road, as it was the high road to Forfar, where he told her it was market-day; and knowing her extreme timidity in that respect, he was sure she would not refuse him. She did not, and as he has a consummate assurance and high opinion of himself, though he sometimes affects modesty, he introduced himself to Lord S. and me; and under one pretence or other, contrived to stay a fortnight at Glamis; during which time, he did every thing to ingratiate himself, and succeeded so well, that he could not help perceiving the progress he had made: and indeed, when he pressed me to it, I partly confessed it. Luckily his sister was staying with me; so we never were alone, but us three walking a whole morning, to the amount of several miles measured, in the great hall at Glamis; every turn he marked with a pencil. I had my hand on a piece of paper he pinned up at the end of the hall, which paper and pencil, unluckily a very remarkable one, he told me he would preserve as his life; but I hope he has lost it. I am not sure, but I have reason to think, he got some of my hair from his sister. He was ordered to London to join his regiment.

Mr. Graham, of Fuitry, did not know of my liking for his brother; but as his assistance was absolutely necessary in getting the money conveyed to London, which I was bent on sending him as from an unknown; Miss G. told him that, out of friendship for her, and thinking her brother James a very promising young man, I meant to send him some money to spend in London: accordingly, he assisted her in forwarding it to him. Miss Graham contrived a way for us to correspond, which, though the letters were intercepted, nothing could be discovered, as we fixed initials quite different from the real names; by which we signified ourselves, and the people we had oftenest occasion to mention: and when I meant to tell her any thing, or she to me, always said C. L. bid me tell A. B. so and so. I burnt all her letters as I received them, which I am now sorry I did, and I demanded the same of her; but she begged of me earnestly to let her keep, for her perusal and entertainment, sometimes those parts of my letters which did not concern her brother:—that, I would not refuse her, promising me she would burn or deface every word concerning him, and shewing me a letter for an example of what she said.

I saw Mr. James Graham in London after he left Scotland, just before he sailed for Minorca; but found him much altered towards me, and therefore my pride made me treat him with the indifference I ought, though it almost broke my heart. This is all, and far too much, of this foolish affair.

I had almost forgotten to mention, that Miss Graham told me, the second of her three brothers (David) was a great admirer of mine, and perpetually talking of me; and that when he did, his eyes used to dart fire, and sparkle like diamonds (these were her very words) but I had only her word for thinking he had any partiality for me. He was still handsomer than either of his brothers (my favourite was the least so) but before I was scarce acquainted with David, I was so taken up with James, that I paid no attention to him. James has or had a picture of me, which he drew himself from memory; and I am told by the few who saw it, that it resembles me more than any picture which was ever taken of me. I ought to tell you, why I said Mrs. G. was not good and virtuous: I am convinced, she did Miss Douglas's (Emelia) memory a great injustice, and in a most treacherous manner; for I am sure it sprang from her. She then quarrelled with Mrs. Mylne, an amiable woman, and universally respected, because her eldest brother married her second daughter; an agreeable good girl, but with no fortune: and before this, she used to profess just the same friendship and disinterested friendship she afterwards did for me; which had she been a man, was seemingly so violent, I should have called it love. She was very deceitful and cunning, and, I believe, had an intrigue with Mr. Dempster: she would with Mr. Nairn, had he chosen.

I asked Mr. and Mrs. Stephens,[3] at the same time, for some of their hair (I think they were together, but of that cannot be positive) when I asked them. I asked also, Mr. Matra for a lock of his. Mr. Stephens had a ring composed, half of Mrs. Stephens's hair and half of mine; it is quite plain, not set round with any thing: I cannot be certain whether I gave it him, or whether he got it himself—I think I gave it him myself; it was immediately after his marriage: but what puzzles my positive recollection is, that I know about that time, Mrs. Stephens asked me for some of my hair, which I gave her. She told me, soon after, that she intended giving George Walker some present, for the trouble he had about Mr.——— and her letters;[4] and that she intended giving him a breast locket, with her own hair set in one part of it, and a bit of mine with it, and that she had some of it by her; which, as she could not afford to make him a great present of intrinsic value, she thought nothing could be more acceptable to so faithful a servant. I told her, as I then thought, that he certainly was so, and had been of great use to Mr. G. and me; but, that I thought it an odd present, these were my very words; and as I said no more, she bespoke it, and when it was finished, the addition of the piece of hair, which was very small and covered with glass, prevented its fastening: so it was returned, and Mrs. Stephens got one ready made at a pawnbroker's shop, one day when she and me walked into the city, out of curiosity to see those kind of shops, and called at a great number: at one of them, I bought a watch which I gave George.—I gave George, about this time, some very old horse furniture; which, though quite spoilt, besides being infinitely too antiquated for use, contained so much silver, that if I do not mistake, it sold for upwards of 20£: Mrs. Parish had displeased me so much, and, apt as I am to be imposed on, had shewn such proofs of a dirty interestedness, that I determined to part with her; but, as she had lived with, and partly educated me so many years, was resolved it should be on good terms; therefore, I resolved to raise 2000£. by any means, the first money I expended. This, I thought, would be sufficient to make her easy in circumstances, if she was interested as I thought her, or, if it was possible I had been mistaken in her character, convince me by her still remaining with me, that I had done her injustice. This I concealed from my mother, till I put it in execution, being greatly displeased at her offer of lending me 500£. when she knew, what distress I was in, and that such a sum would do nothing for me. I even denied to my mother, when I gave Mrs. Parish the 2000£ (which I did at Paul's Walden,[5] borrowing it of Mr. Peele,[6] when he came there after Lord S.'s death, some time before I returned to town) and my mother believed I did not entertain the most distant thought that she would leave me, except by marrying.

As Mrs. Parish's conduct to me, has been, her sister's excepted, the most vile, ungrateful, and pernicious, that ever was heard of; I shall say nothing about it here, as, during the whole, I cannot tax myself with doing any thing wrong; and this paper is only meant as a confession of my crimes and faults. But, if you please, I will tell you every circumstance relating to her behaviour, and to the strange manner she behaved to Mr. G. when, at his earnest request, he thinking she might be of use to me, I consented to his talking to her, and attempting to persuade her to stay with me, as from himself.

Just before she left me, I went to Paul's Walden, to tell my mother I was married, that I might get the start of Mrs. Parish, who, I was sure, would write to tell her the very day after our parting was agreed on; and who, I believe, had it not been for interested motives, and the fear of displeasing my mother, would have told her long before, which I have many reasons to be certain she did not. I did not intend to declare my marriage till April, just before we left England, or to be married actually till we were abroad, a short time before I laid in; and I proposed to stay three or four years to visit France, Italy, Hungary, and Bohemia, and perhaps Spain and Portugal: I did not tell even Mr. Gray, positively, my designs about marriage.

But I had almost forgotten, that the reason why I mentioned the 2000£ and Mrs. Parish, was, that I might tell you, soon after I came out of town after Lord S.'s death, I was perpetually sending George backwards and forwards to London, to raise the 2000£. After I applied to Mr. Mayne, (who said, he could not lend me that sum without his partner's concurrence), I then applied to Fernandez, and a number of other Jews, who did not know me, and I did not sign my name to the letter; but they would not lend me on any other terms than annuities, which I would not think of, and they were dreadfully unreasonable ones. If I could, I would have raised three thousand pounds, to have had one thousand pounds in hand. When George went backwards and forwards to these Jews, I used always to write to, and hear from Mr. G. who stayed just about that time after me in town. When I was at Paul's Walden, and he in Scotland, all his letters to me came under cover to George, and he always directed mine to him; and under some pretence or other, went to Welwyn, Stephenage, Hitchin, or Hatfield, and put them in himself.

When I came occasionally to Paul's Walden, for a week or a few days, once or twice a fortnight, after I was settled in town, I used to enclose my letters often, under cover to George, (whom, on that account, I generally left in town) and with it, directions sometimes to him, to send messages, or deliver notes about plays, operas, dinings, tea-drinking, &c. and often inclosed directions to the housekeeper of affairs relating to the house, &c. and sometimes I enclosed to George under the frank to her, and bid her give it once or twice. I remember, that having enclosed a number of letters and notes to be delivered out, I said, Go and tell Mr. G. I have no time to write now, but shall be in Grosvenor-square, and expect him at such an hour. When Mrs. Stephens eloped, and I came to Paul's Walden, I left George in town to receive the Planta family,[7] and send me a constant account of their motions; which he did: I wish I had kept them, as you might have liked to see them; but being, as I thought, of no consequence after she returned and knew the accounts, I burnt them.

Mr. Mylne, whose sister married Mr. G. only lent Lord S. 10,000£ the half of what he is worth; and though the physicians declared her life was in danger, if she did not go to Italy for her health directly (where I believe she now is) he was threatened to be stopped by Lord S.'s creditors, who would come upon him. In this situation, he desired Mr. G. when he saw him in Scotland, and who he knew had long been an acquaintance of mine, to write to me, and beg I would allow him to use my name, and say, I would see the money should be paid out of the Scotch estates, and the first debt discharged. Mr. G. told him, he could not possibly take such a liberty with me; especially as he had not written to me even a letter of condolence, as civility required, since Lord S.'s death. But Mr. Mylne pressed him so much, and conjured him, as he regarded his sister's life; that, not to make it appear suspicious by too positive refusing, he wrote me a formal letter, and, at the same time a private one, (both of which I am pretty sure are returned, and I can shew you) and I answered him in the same way: to Mr. Mylne I wrote a civil letter, telling him Mr. G. had informed me of his wishes; that I was sorry it was not in my power to see his money paid which was due to him, as I had refused taking administration; but that if it was absolutely necessary, my regard for Mrs. Mylne, who is indeed an amiable woman, would induce me to join with him in being security to his creditors: however, he never, after writing me a letter of thanks, claimed any offer, and got abroad very well without it.

I confess, I should not have thought it necessary, or any part of my agreement, to tell you the reason why I saw Mr. G. only every other night, had you not desired I would: it was so agreed on between us, that by the intervention of one night, we might meet the next with more pleasure, and have the less chance of being tired of each other. Not to mention, that as it was often four or five in the morning before he went away, a night of sleep was absolutely necessary: as our conversation was to be lasting, and I generally went to my room at eleven o'clock the night he came, which I thought would look odd, and sometimes put me to difficulties if I was at the Opera in a great croud, had company supped with me, or any other hindrance; and I always contrived that should not be the case the nights he came: I saw him some part of every day, or when I did not by any accident, he never failed writing.

A black inky kind of medicine (which I have mentioned before) occasioned two of my miscarriages: the third, after trying the black medicine without effect, was occasioned by a vomit of emetic; eating much pepper, and drinking a wine-glass of brandy. I am ashamed to say, I tried all these things the fourth time, without the smallest effect.

I do assure you, that no man ever took the smallest liberty with me (Lord S. yourself, and Mr. G. excepted) except three or four times that Mr. Stephens kissed me, under one pretence or other; and once or twice that Mr. G. S. as we were standing by the fire-side, put his arm round my waist. Once, also, as I was admiring some very scarce and valuable plants at Hammersmith, Mr. Lee told me, if I would allow him the honour to salute a Countess, he would give me the most curious; which I did, and had the plant. I recollect once, that Mrs. Stephens sitting on one of her husband's knees, I sat on the other.

Mr. G. S. I know, was free in his way of thinking and acting; but his brother, I thought a different man, from some things I had heard him say; and which Mrs. Matra told me. Two or three times Mr. Stephens has come into my room, when my maid was dressing my hair, and I took him into my bed-room, out of the drawing-room, where Mr. G. M. was to speak about going off with Mrs. Stephens.

Many of the things these papers contain, I have had an opportunity of telling you since I began to write them, which I did not intend to do, till you read them here: other things you have, in the course of the same time, told me you was thoroughly acquainted with: however I would not alter, and I give you my thoughts exactly, as they first presented themselves to me, as you will easily perceive I wrote no rough copy.

My almost starving myself to death at Glamis; my taking, in anger, almost a whole bottle of that black medicine; my foolish behaviour about the cloaths and favours I bespoke for Mr. Stephens's wedding; the dancings on that occasion; my allowing Mr. Stephens to call me his own wife; my worse than foolishness in going to St. Paul's with Mrs. Stephens and Mr. Pennick; and my making an excuse (with the last desert [sic] of christening some kittens) to have company to dine with me that day: all this knowing you are thoroughly informed of; I do not give more minutely than thus, on that account, nor should I have named them at all, had it not been for the oath's sake, which I could not satisfy my conscience in taking, if I omitted, at least, mentioning, any one of even the most trifling imprudencies I committed.

I have told you of Mr. C. W. having my hair and I his; and you know what a silly, though short refusal, I wrote to Mr. Mac Callaster, the autumn (I think it was) before my marriage—To his last, I gave him no answer.

I have now fully performed my promise, and I rely on your's to excuse all my faults, except want of veracity, which I am certain you cannot find here, and never shall again, even in the most trifling matter: as I will always rather prefer incurring your more than usual share of dislike to me, than say what is not true.

You saw a bit of these papers last night, when you came into my dressing-room, though I begged you would not look, and was angry at my minuteness, and telling you such trifles: if I had done otherwise, (besides my oath) might you not with justice, and would you not have said, I ordered you to be exact, minute, and scrupulous; so as to declare every thought that you had; were not these your own words? And how did you know what I should esteem trifling? Therefore, my dearest, you should excuse this minuteness, and whatever manner I may mention the facts in, so they be but facts!

God bless you, and forgive me all my sins and faults.

February 3d, 1778. Tuesday morning.

I have had, you know, the paper you gave me in my pocket-book these three or four days; but, according to your orders, never looked at it till now. In consequence of what you there say, I find myself obliged to say something more about my fits, to which I did not intend, otherwise, to have added any thing. If I were to say, as you seem to require of me, that I ever could prevent or shorten them, and did not, except the one time I have mentioned, I should take my oath of a lie.

When I was a girl, I had two or three times obstructions, and then I took, as it were, common hysteric fits; but I never had them so violent, or any thing like convulsions, till four months that I had an obstruction after my second or third child, I forget which. And though my mind was perfectly easy at that time, I being in Scotland, and had always company that I liked, yet I suffered incredibly from these fits, both in health and looks; being exceedingly reduced and weakened. I really believe it was owing to Dr. Ferguson's prescriptions, and to the easy state of my mind and good spirits, that I recovered; but I have been subject to them ever since. Dr. Hunter knows, about three years ago or four, how much I suffered in my looks from them; when he was sent for to me the day after I had been in one very bad, (no affectation) had you seen me after, you would have been convinced, would have affected a person both at the same time and afterwards, as it has often done me. Sometimes when I have had warning, which is not often, I have stopped the fit, by plunging my hands into cold water, and sometimes by drinking hot water or camomile tea. The time you went to Newcastle; after that, when on your return you found me so ill, I felt myself going to be ill; and having warning enough to drink a bason of warm water, and plunging my hands in cold water, I prevented the fit coming on; but I never durst mention it till now, lest you should say it was an affectation or air that I gave myself.

What you say Dr. Scott told you about my fits being pretended, and not a natural complaint, was as false, as I dare say his saying my miscarrying was, when I had that flooding, the first time of my being regular after my lying-in; for you always took (at least I never perceived you did in the least otherwise) a most certain precaution. I remember Dr. Scott asked me once, if not twice, whether I did not think I might have miscarried; I said, I could not tell, but thought only a flooding; for you may be sure, I would not hint, or even have him suspect, that there was any reason why I could not have miscarried. To the best of my recollection, he questioned me on this subject, one day when you brought him into the bed-room, and slipped yourself into the dressing-room for a minute, and not the moment I conclude you mean; that is, when he saying you sent him, which you was angry at that time; upon the maturest recollection, I can venture to say, he did not ask me that question, or any other about my health, except in general terms, how I did; something about my dinner, and mentioned the weather, or some such subject: you wanted an explanation, or should not have written this.

N.B. Though I do not recollect, I declare upon oath, Mr. Stephens kissing me oftener than I have mentioned; my sitting on his knee oftener; or Mr. G. S. putting his arms oftener around my waist, and that was by accident; yet I have such a dread of the possibility of perjuring myself, that I will not take my oath without a proviso, I really believe a needless one, that they may have repeated these liberties oftener, but never any others; except Mr. Stephens shaking me by the hand.

May I never feel happiness in this world, or the world to come; and may my children meet every hour of their lives unparalleled misery, if I have, either directly or indirectly, told one or more falsehoods in these narratives; or if I have kept any thing a secret, that even Mr. Bowes could esteem a fault.

This I give under my hand, and shall never plead forgetfulness, or any thing else, for the truth of one tittle of it. And I do further swear the truth of it upon the Holy Bible: and as a declaration of my sincerity, shall take the Holy Sacrament upon it the next time I go to church, when there is one.

Gibside, Feb. 3, 1778.

Examined with the Exhibit, contained in the Process transmitted from the Arches Court of Canterbury, this Fourth Day of October, 1788. By me, T. Dodd, Clerk to Mr. Morley, Proctor, Doctor's Commons.

Notes

1. Thomas Lyon, a brother of Lord Strathmore.

2. Lord Strathmore's estate, where Graham was gamekeeper; spelled both "Glames" and "Glamis" by Bowes.

3. Henry and Eliza Stephens, along with Mr. Matra in the next sentence, belonged to the circle of friends introduced to Bowes by the Mrs. Parish mentioned later in the paragraph. Mrs. Parish, Eliza Stephens's sister, had been Bowes's governess and later became her companion and governess to her children.

4. George Walker is Bowes's footman; Mr.——— is George Grey, with whom Bowes began an affair in February 1776. Walker and Mrs. Stephens acted as conduits for letters between Grey and Bowes.

5. A property owned by Bowes's mother; Bowes was married there, and later inherited the estate.

6. Bowes's solicitor.

7. Joseph and Eliza Planta, Mrs. Parish's brother and sister; Eliza married Henry Stephens (see note 3).

Margaret Coghlan

1762?–1787

The Memoirs of Mrs. Coghlan, (Daughter of the late Major Moncrieffe,) written by herself, and Dedicated to the British Nation; being interspersed with anecdotes of the late American and present French War, with remarks moral and political. 2 vols. London: C. and G. Kearsley, 1794.

Margaret Moncrieffe's parents were Scots, but she was born in America, probably in 1762; her mother, Margaret, died three years later. At that time her father, Thomas Moncrieffe, was a major of brigade under General Thomas Gage, commander in chief of the British army in North America, and Margaret and her brother, Edward, were taken in by the general and his wife. Margaret was educated in Dublin. Her father remarried twice, both times to American women, and in 1772 she was sent to New York. By 1775, after the death of her second stepmother, Margaret was under the care of her stepbrother, Frederick Jay; this is the year of the encounter with George Washington recorded in her *Memoirs*. In 1776 John Coghlan, a British lieutenant, "demanded me in marriage" (1:66), and on 28 February 1777, at the age of fourteen, she was joined to him in "honorable prostitution" (1:71). Soon thereafter they sailed for England; during the journey her husband subjected her to "barbarous treatment" (1:79), and after they docked he abandoned her for two weeks. Margaret wrote for help to Lord Thomas Clinton, later Lord Lincoln, whom she had known in New York, and was soon his mistress. Discovered in this situation by General Gage and her father-in-law, she took their advice and left for France. When Lord Lincoln found her there she returned to England, lodging with friends of General Gage, but continuing to see Lord Lincoln. Two years later she met Charles James Fox, and although the *Memoirs* are impenetrably coy on the subject, seems to have had an affair with him. In 1779 she decided to follow her "natural inclination for the stage" (1:116), but there is no record of her acting under her maiden or married name. Several long-term affairs followed—four years and one daughter with a Mr. Fazakerly, several years and two sons with a Captain

B——, as well as liaisons with Sir Robert Harland, the duke of York, and others.

Margaret Coghlan died suddenly in 1787, but volume two of the *Memoirs* continues beyond that year, and the preface is dated 7 December 1793. Possibly the manuscript was completed and published to capitalize on the fashion for *mémoires scandaleuses*: volume two conforms to the genre in its records of debts, arrests, and quarrels with family, and it includes the standard warnings to "the giddy, dissipated fair ones of my sex" (2:81). But volume two is unlike most *mémoires scandaleuses* in its explicitly revolutionary politics. The "nocturnal orgies" (2:5) of prerevolutionary France are contrasted with the "stern, inexorable Republican virtue" of 1794; "mercenary, corrupt, vindictive Lawyers" (2:94) must be purged from an England whose constitution's "leading principle" is liberty; even the standard appeal to "the Liberality of the British Nation!" (2:154) is accompanied by a thinly veiled warning that "the gay, thoughtless Inhabitants" (2:161) of Versailles might have avoided the tumbrels had they "shewn more attention to private or public woe." Even if Coghlan's *Memoirs* is in some sense inauthentic, then, it remains an interesting example of generic innovation.

TEXT: *The Memoirs of Mrs. Coghlan* was first published in 1794 and by the following year had gone into two American and three British editions. Although Coghlan did not write the preface or the excerpt from volume two (pp. 8–43), they are included to suggest the radicalism *scandaleuse*, political as well as sexual, to which a public woman's *mémoire* might appeal. The excerpt from volume one (pp. 28–38), written by Coghlan, takes up her early years in New York during the Revolutionary War (it appears between the two other excerpts).

☙ ❧

PREFACE

Amidst the Tempest that now rages in the Political World, the Cabals of Faction, and the Terrors of Revolution,[1] the private Sorrows of an Individual pass unregarded: The most splendid Contributions are raised for Support of Foreign Refugees; Loans and Benevolencies, to an amazing Extent, are piously, if not constitutionally, furnished, to supply the Wants of our suffering Troops; and all the Passions inherent in the Human Breast, are awakened and set in Motion, to give a pompous Display to the Humility and Meekness of tender-hearted Charity.—

We read of Titled Individuals bestowing Hundreds in Behalf of Emigrant POPISH PRIESTS, while ONE SOLITARY GUINEA is prefixed to the same Names in Support of their own Countrymen, poor, industrious, famished Manufacturers![2]

Our Streets swarm with Beggars, our Looms are deserted;—Poverty every where raises her haggard Mien amongst us; at the same Time that National Treasures are indiscriminately lavished with Profusion upon Foreigners, and expended in the further Prosecution of a most disastrous War; whereby the Fund of Wretchedness is daily augmented; and the Spectacles of Misery that torture the Sight in all our Streets, proclaim the fatal Consequences it has already produced, and the absolute Necessity of putting a Period to the Evil.

The baneful Effects attending this Calamity, fall principally on the poor, and industrious Classes of Society; They extend themselves even unto Myself: The Luxuries of the Great will easily admit of Curtailment, but the Wants of the Poor call aloud for Redress. Yet, as the Former find themselves in some Measure, called on to reduce the Number of their Superfluities from the many Claims which the Exigency of public Affairs has upon them, so are they less disposed to follow the Dictates of Charity in relieving the Pangs of Domestic Woe.

There exists another Description of the Great, who thrive on the Misfortunes which the present System creates, without directing a Thought to their Alleviation; I allude to the vast additional number of Contractors, Commissaries, Pensioners, and Human Locusts of every kind, preying on the decayed Vitals of their Country. These Men drain immense Fortunes from the Increase of Public Burthens, and in every new Tax, originates a new Place,[3] whereby the Scale of Influence is alarmingly increased.

Hence Princes and their Ministers are apt to delight in War: It furnishes them with a Pretext for adding to their Military Establishments; the Splendour of the Throne shines brighter, and they conceive that they enjoy a more perfect State of Security, from the immense Armies they retain in their pay.

Wretched, however, is the Prince, who rests his Hope on such Foundation; the NORTHERN DESPOTS of Europe can have no other Basis than Military Force, on which to depend for the Preservation of their Tyranny; but the KING of a FREE Country, should look to other Principles: He should depend for the Preservation of HIS Power on the Peace, Happiness, Choice, and Affections of an united People.

While the Bulk of a Nation is distressed, a virtuous Prince can never enjoy a Moment's content; he cannot depart from his Threshold, that he does not meet some Object of Calamity, to strew Thorns in his way, He must reflect on the enormous Salary that he himself receives, the Magnificence and Waste by which he is surrounded, while so many forlorn Wretches are perishing through Want of the smallest Part of those Superfluities, daily consumed within his own Palace.

The Writer of the following Sheets, nursed in the Lap of tenderest Indulgence, sprung from a Father whose Attachment to a KING even superseded the Duties he owned to HIS COUNTRY; she who once basked in the Sunshine of Fortune, has lately herself struggled with all the Miseries she has endeavoured to describe.

Affliction cuts the deeper from a Recollection of former Enjoyments: The Memory of past Joys sharpens the Sense of her present Sufferings: She once little dreamed of those Scenes of Horror, through which she has passed; She little anticipated that whenever she should have Occasion for the WORLD'S assistance, the World would with-hold it from her. She had fondly imagined, that every one was her FRIEND; nor was the Veil of Deception withdrawn, till, alas! she had Occasion for its Friendship. Then the very Persons who had been most anxious to court her Smiles, who had beguiled her with their delusive Flatteries, who had encouraged her Errors, and soothed her Vices, were the first to keep aloof, and shun the Wretchedness they had helped to accomplish.—They who had been the bosom Friends of her Father, refused even to hear the hapless Tale of his ill-fated Child: Nor did his unshaken Zeal in the Cause of HIS SOVEREIGN, ever produce to his Daughter the Recompence of a Shilling from the English Government.

These are the Reflections of one, undisturbed by the Frenzy of Party Conflicts, and only zealous in the general Cause of Humanity.—They are the Reflections of a Woman, chastened in Affliction's School, restored to Reason by the wholesome Lessons she has received from that most instructive of all Monitors,—Adversity!

"Want, worldly Want, that hungry meagre Fiend,
"Is at her Heels and chases her in view."[4]

To drive off this Fiend, alas! she has no other Hope, than from the Advantage she may derive from this faint Production of her Pen; The Perspective which the World now presents to her View, is gloomy indeed: Nevertheless, it would be greatly brightened, if, she conceived that her Example might serve as a Beacon to others of her Sex.

Oh! may the generous Character of the British Nation, which has so often shone resplendent in Acts of amiable Benevolence, long preserve its Lustre; May it wipe off those Tears, calculated to fade the Cheek of

Beauty! May no Political Discord, no Party Rage ever obscure it, and while GALLIA's [i.e., France's] Refractory Sons are revelling on the Fruits of British Benevolence, let it not be said that Britania's own Legitimate Children ever sighed or wept in vain!

I applied for protection[5] to Mr. William Livingston, (my first step mother's brother,) who was the governor of New Jersey: He behaved to me with harshness, and even added insult to his reproaches. Thus destitute of friends, I wrote to General Putnam,[6] who instantly answered my letter by a very kind invitation to his house, assuring me, that he respected my father, and was only his enemy in the field of battle; but that in private life, he himself, or any part of his family, might always command his services. On the next day, he sent Colonel Webb, one of his aid de camps, to conduct me to New York. When I arrived in the Broad Way (a street so called), where General Putnam resided, I was received with the greatest tenderness both by Mrs. Putnam and her daughters, and on the following day, I was introduced by them to General, and Mrs. Washington, who likewise made it their study to shew me every mark of regard; but I seldom was allowed to be alone, although sometimes indeed, I found an opportunity to escape to the gallery on the top of the house,[7] where my chief delight was to view with a telescope, our fleet and army at Staten Island. My amusements were few, the good Mrs. Putnam employed me and her daughters constantly to spin flax, for shirts for the American soldiery: Indolence in America being totally discouraged; and I likewise worked some for General Putnam, who, though not an accomplished *Muscadin*, like our Dilletantis of St. James's street,[8] was certainly one of the best characters in the world; his heart being composed of those noble materials, which equally command respect and admiration. One day after dinner, the congress was the toast; General Washington viewed me very attentively, and sarcastically said, "Miss Moncrieff, you don't drink your wine." Embarrassed by this reproof, I knew not how to act; at last, as if by a secret impulse, I addressed myself to the American commander, and taking the wine I said, General Howe *is* the toast.—Vexed at my temerity, the whole company, especially General Washington, censured me; when my good friend, General Putnam, as usual, apologised and assured them, I did not mean to offend; besides, replied he, "every thing said or done by such a child, ought rather to amuse than affront you"—General Washington, piqued at this observation, then said, "Well Miss,—I will overlook your indiscretion, on condition that you drink my health, or General Putnam's, the first time you dine at Sir William Howe's table, on the other side of the water."

These words conveyed to me a flattering hope, that I should once more see my father; and, I promised General Washington, to do any thing which he required, provided he would permit me to return to him.

Not long after this circumstance, a flag of truce arrived from Staten-Island, with letters from Major Moncrieff,[9] demanding me, for he now considered me as a prisoner. General Washington would not acquiesce in this demand, saying, "that I should remain a hostage for my father's good behaviour." I must here observe, that when General Washington refused to deliver me up, the noble minded Putnam, as if it were by instinct, laid his hand on his sword, and with a violent oath swore, "that my father's request *should* be granted." The commander in chief, whose influence governed the Congress, soon prevailed on them to consider me as a person whose situation required their strict attention;[10] and, that I might not escape, they ordered me to [the encampment at] Kings Bridge, where, in justice, I must say, that I was treated with the utmost tenderness; . . .

To resume the thread of my narrative—About the latter end of July, 1788, a Mr. Beckett, with whom I became acquainted, and for which acquaintance I am indebted to my old friend Colonel Freemantle, *came to Paris*— He lived in the same Hotel with myself, in the greatest splendour; his table was continually crouded by persons of the highest rank, amongst whom were the late unfortunate duc d'Orleans, the Ducs de Monmorency, Pienne, Prince Louis d'Aremberg, Marquis de Bouille, &c. &c. &c.—Amidst my manifold misfortunes, I consider it some consolation that the persons with whom I have been acquainted, were the most part distinguished for genius and talents, and this young man was remarkably so:— Mr. Beckett flattered me by his addresses, at a time when all the Parisian beauties were emulous with each other for his affections; whether it were vanity, affection, preference, or any sentiment bordering on self-love, I will not say; but, living in the same Hotel with him, he continually made choice of me as the Sultana to preside at his table, and I had the direction of all his entertainments. At the end of four months, after various oblique and fruitless hints, Madame Lafar[11] became clamorous for payment of her bill, which amounted to the *small sum* of five hundred pounds. He drew bills upon his father for fifteen hundred pounds, which were the amount of his whole debts.—A special Courier was dispatched to England, and as the father would not, or could not, pay the extravagant demands of his son, the bills returned to Paris *protested.*—In this situation I advised him to consult his own Countrymen, then in Paris: He was at that time intimately acquainted with Lord Gillford, son of Lord Clanwilliam.—This young nobleman, assured him that he had only a few hours to determine on his escape, as he had private information, that Madame Lafar meant to arrest him.—I must do Mr. Beckett the justice to say, that it was with the utmost reluctance that he pursued the advice of his friends, as he expressed strong apprehensions for my safety; however, touched with his generosity, I became entirely regardless of myself, and positively *insisted on his flight,*— and he yielded obedience.—He had not departed many hours, before all his creditors were in an uproar, the hue and cry was raised, that an Englishman had run away for his debts: The police officers were sent after him, but returned with sorrowful countenances, their mission unaccomplished.—

Madame Lafar, *who, poor dear woman!* was the principal sufferer, now turned all her vengeance against me, knowing that I had a travelling Post Chaise and a Chariot, together with several valuable effects, on these articles she fixed *her attention,* determined to plunder me.

Two days after Mr. Beckett left Paris, I was, while on a visit at Madame Smith's, informed by Mr. Robert Knight (another of the few good men I have found in the world) that his carriage had just been surrounded by a party of armed ruffians, inquiring for me, and he had scarcely uttered the words when the house of Madame Smith was beset by at least an hundred men, preceded by Mr. de Lomprey, Exempt de Police.[12] *My friends,* alarmed for my situation (for I was then seven months advanced in pregnancy) intreated the Exempt to dismiss his followers.—Mr. Knight kindly pledging himself to be responsible for any complaint which they had to make against me.—Mr. de Lomprey replied, "that he had a *Lettre de Cachet* from *the King,* ordering me to close confinement in the *Hotel de la Force.*" My valuable *friend,* who was a young man of very independant fortune, would not suffer this arbitrary act *of power* to be exercised against an helpless woman, without first demanding that satisfaction to which he thought me entitled.—He, therefore, at *that late hour,* went to the Duke of Dorset, *the English* Ambassador: His Grace was from home; thus I was obliged to go, at two o'clock in the morning, to that mansion of slavery, the Hotel de la Force: I had with me my infant son, then only two years old. The innocence of this tender lamb—who seemed sensible that some misfortune had happened, overcame what resolution I possessed, he held *up his little hands* and cried out, "Oh! you shall not hurt *my Mother!*" Mr. Knight, however, comforted me by every assurance of protecting the child, and carried him away in his carriage, having first attended me himself to the wretched apartment destined for me—a miserable *Bed of Straw,* with one wretched blanket was all the furniture in the room,—and the floor was completely covered with vermin.—'Till this moment, I was a stranger to prisons; therefore, perhaps, my mind was more sensible to the *shock*, but even now that I have been habituated to the horrors of confinement, I cannot conceive such a dreadful epitome of wretchedness as this vile dungeon, on mature reflection, still appears to be;—and, for the sake of humanity, I fervently pray, that if it be not already done, the new government of France, may utterly destroy similar *abominations*.

—My woman, the faithful partner of all my misfortunes, accompanied me, nor could even this spectacle of horror induce her to forsake her Mistress.—We passed the few remaining hours, conversing on the sudden transition *of fortune*—I wished to convince her of the mutability of human happiness.—In three days I was reduced from scenes of pleasure and tranquility, to my present wretched condition!—As soon as day approached, we examined our sad habitation;—the first object that struck my eye, was a huge tremendous padlock, projecting from the Cieling, and to which was fastened an immense *iron* Collar—We could not, at first, imagine the use of this frightful instrument, but my poor, faithful attendant soon guessed it, and exclaimed, "O, Madam! it is to fasten us up at night!" She had scarce uttered these words, when the Goalor [i.e., jailer] appeared (for, in France, it is the duty exacted from the keeper of such a place to pay personal attendance to the unfortunate *in his power*); he had a great bunch of Keys in his hand—he walked up to me, and immediately cried out, "*Oh, Ciel! quel dommage!*"[13] adding, that he had received orders from the Government to treat me with the greatest respect—This civil Frenchman ended his harangue by requesting me to give him permission to order my breakfast.—I thanked him for his politeness, but declined receiving any refreshment until my friends came to me.—At a very early hour (before noon,) Mr. Knight, accompanied by Mr. Western, the present Member [of Parliament] for Malden, paid me a visit.—These gentlemen, in concert with Captain Winder, of the Guards, were for ever employed to obtain my liberty, availing themselves of a most necessary and humane law that exists in France, prohibiting the imprisonment of pregnant women for debt.—If such laws were in full force under the most Despotic Government of Europe, how much more consistent were it in force under that which calls itself the most free? Aged persons were also exempt from this penalty, but here [in England] our ears are for ever stunned with the sound of Liberty, and Humanity: Women in the pangs of Child-bed, Men in the agonies of Death, (such instances have occurred) in virtue of a Sheriff's Writ, may be dragged to the most *loathsome Goal* [i.e., jail]; Were it not then devoutly to be wished, that our Legislators, instead of empty Panegyric, would afford us a little of the Substance?—In my own opinion, who have had some experience in these cases, the reason why such horrible laws are suffered to exist, is under the supposition of their being seldom or ever executed; the fact, however, is notoriously otherwise; at all events, Policy, as well as Mercy, requires,—*the* national character demands,—that the life of Freemen should not be exposed to the discretion, or depend on the pity, of a Sheriff's Officer.

Madame Lafar, alarmed least I should escape out of the snare she had laid, endeavoured to persuade my friends, I was not in the predicament described; but all her projects failed, as they insisted on a consultation of the Faculty,[14] who ascertained my pregnancy; at the same time, expressing apprehensions of immediate labour from the sudden revolution I had undergone. In this situation, a female of my acquaintance, (although by no means a lady of rigid virtue, not therefore less susceptible of generosity and compassion,) immediately repaired to Monsieur Pacquet, then first President of the Parliament of Paris, relating the circumstance, and at the same time, giving a Miniature picture of me. This gentleman went the following day to Versailles, and informing Monsieur, and the Comte d'Artois, *the late king's* Brothers of my misfortune; they, with a generous sympathy, rarely to be found in Princes, and which causes me to lament most bitterly their sad reverse of fortune, took pity on my situation and became my advocates; and in a few hours I received his Majesty's order for my release.—The Comte d'Artois, in particular, entered into the hardships of my case, and on delivering the king's signature, cancelling the Letter de Cachet, advised that I should put myself under the protection of his Palace,[15] signifying that Mr. Beckett's creditors, might then proceed against me in a Court of Law.—The instant I returned from prison, I went accordingly to the Place du Temple, where I had not remained many hours, before I received a visit from the Duc de F——, another nobleman who also boasts of Royal Blood in his veins, but whose actions unfortunately were not calculated to efface those unfavorable prepossessions, with which I had been inspired by a similar conduct in *a truly* Royal Duke, who now makes such a capital figure on the theatre of European Politics. The familiar epithet applied to the ci devant[16] Duc de F—— in Paris, (that loyal and renowned Emigrant) was an *Escroc*, (in English, signifying Sharper or Greek.) All I can say is, that I have no reason to dispute the propriety of the application.

In my new abode I had soon the mortification to learn from my servants, that my two Carriages, together with all my Cloaths and Jewels, were seized by Mr. Beckett's Creditors, so that I was, in an instant, stripped of every necessary, in a country where I had no connections, but such as had been formed on the principles of interest.—Thus circumstanced, a young Irish Nobleman, in whose favor I had made an exception, and from my general opinion of his friendship I had confidence, I frankly communicated what had befallen me, and received from his Lordship every assurance *of protection*; but his fortune not being adequate to his generosity, he immediately proposed a subscription amongst my friends then in Paris, and in the course of twenty-four hours, I found myself, through their exertions, in possession of two hundred and fifty Louis d'Or's.[17]

I have before observed, that adversity is the true criterion of friendship, and I am bound in gratitude, to render justice to that virtue in the French Nation.

In France I ever met with the greatest humanity, tempered with delicacy and politeness; and if my misfortunes, during the latter part of my residence in that country, called for the aid of others, I also received it: at the same time, it was always conveyed in a manner which reflected honor on the generous donors, ever unaccompanied with those disgusting marks of ostentation, which too frequently attend acts of pecuniary relief.

I remained six months in the Temple, and returned to England ten days before that *glorious* Epoch, the 14th of July, 1789, when Frenchmen threw off for ever, THE YOKE OF SLAVERY.—Oh! may that day yield an awful and impressive lesson!—It forms an æra replete with events, still in the womb of time to produce. It threatens destruction to long established systems—to long established orders. It presages Revolution, and strikes at those antique Governments, in defence of which, so many of my Ancestors have bled.

Should they have bled in vain, and if a new order of things be destined to succeed, may humanity still profit by the change!—may a more equal distribution of sublunary enjoyments, banish from the face of the earth, those scenes of horror that have so long tortured the sight, and disgraced the policy of social institutions!—Perhaps the Millenium, so long and so anxiously anticipated, is at hand, when nations will be linked in one fraternal bond—when civil discord and foreign wars shall cease to desolate the world.—Which ever party may prevail in this tremendous crisis, my only prayer is, that it may terminate to the advantage and improvement of the human race!—The reader will pardon these frequent digressions; they arise naturally from the subject, and are the spontaneous emanations of a soul, fraught with sensibility and glowing with zeal, for the general happiness and improvement of mankind.—I have formerly experienced from Frenchmen, compassion and generosity; and I have sometimes found those virtues in the English.—Born in America, and resident many years in England, I feel no local partialities, no prepossessions or disgusts; My Country is the World! and whatever the Political sentiments of others may be, I consider it the duty of Citizens to yield implicit submission to the Laws of that Government under which they live.

Passing eighteen months in France, under her ancient Monarchy, I had the opportunity of manifesting my respect to the Laws which then existed, and if I were at present in that nation, now that it has judged proper to adopt the Republican form of Government, I should hold myself equally bound, faithfully to obey the laws of that Republic.

Such are my opinions, which I believe are founded in truth and justice, and I should be ever emulous to preserve the character of a *peaceful*, and, I hope, in future, to add, of a *virtuous* Citizen.

Notes

1. The French Revolution; England had been at war with the Republic of France since 1791.

2. A Subscription now on foot for the Benefit of the Spitalfields Weavers [Coghlan]. "Manufacturers" are laborers (such as weavers) who work with their hands.

3. A position as tax collector; such "places" were often used as bribes or rewards.

4. Venice Preserved [Coghlan]. Thomas Otway's 1682 blank-verse tragedy.

5. Coghlan is alone in Elizabethtown, where the American forces are under attack by General Howe's army.

6. Israel Putnam (1718–1790), major general in the Continental Army.

7. Almost every gentleman's house in New York, has a gallery, with a summer house on the top [Coghlan].

8. "*Muscadin*," French term for a dandy very meticulous about his dress; while "dilettante" usually means a dabbler in the fine arts, Coghlan is apparently using it as the British equivalent of *muscadin*.

9. Coghlan's father.

10. My father's knowledge of the country, induced General Washington to use every expedient in order to seduce him from the Royal cause, and he knew there was none more likely to succeed than that of attacking his parental feelings [Coghlan].

11. The landlady.

12. Officer of police (Fr).

13. Oh, heaven! what a shame! (Fr.).

14. Members of a profession regarded as one body; here, medical men.

15. The Temple at Paris where Louis the XVI, and the Royal Family were confined, was formerly a palace occupied by the Comte d'Artois, and its environs afforded protection to unhappy insolvent debtors [Coghlan].

16. Former or past (Fr.).

17. Literally, "gold Louis"; gold coin in use from the reign of Louis XIII to that of Louis XVI.

Ann Radcliffe

1764–1823

A Journey made in the Summer of 1794, through Holland and the Western Frontier of Germany, with a return down the Rhine: to which are added Observations during a Tour to the Lakes of Lancashire, Westmoreland, and Cumberland. London: G. G. and J. Robinson, 1795.

Ann Ward was born in London on 9 July 1764 into a family with connections to the landed gentry. Although her father was first a haberdasher and later a sales representative for Wedgwood pottery, on her visits to her uncle Thomas Bentley she was introduced to an intellectual and literary elite. In 1787 she married William Radcliffe, a journalist who later owned and edited the *English Chronicle.* Her first novel, *The Castles of Athlyn and Dunblayne,* was published in 1789; it was followed by *A Sicilian Romance* in 1790, *The Romance of the Forest* in 1791, and the phenomenally successful *Mysteries of Udolpho* in 1794. Just as these Gothic novels caught and fed a popular interest in the outré, so her travel book tapped interest in a new kind of tourism: not the eighteenth-century Grand Tour that focused on high culture but the Romantic journey that emphasized personal responses to sublime nature. She asks, for example, "who can pause to admire the elegancies of art, when surrounded by the wonders of nature?" And just as Radcliffe's Gothic novels explained their supernatural elements, so her *Journey* domesticated the unfamiliar. Radcliffe often uses particular observations as lead-ins to universal conclusions. Similarly, she defends the "apparent nationality" of her repeated references to England as a technique for representing the unknown in terms of the known, although she does admit that "the love of our own country [was] greatly enhanced by all that had been seen of others" (359). Radcliffe traveled with her husband and carefully acknowledged his contribution to the *Journey's* sections on "œconomical and political conditions." He had long been a strong supporter of her writing, and perhaps his illness in 1798 slowed her productivity; in any event, except for posthumous publications, *The Italian* (1797) was her last novel. During the remaining twenty-five years of her life

Radcliffe suffered from severe respiratory and digestive problems, and she seems to have become somewhat reclusive. She died in London on 7 February 1823.

TEXT: Published in 1795, Ann Radcliffe's *Journey* was perhaps intended as a leisure commodity; the first edition, with its large print and wide margins, is far too substantial to be a guidebook, and the text is generally more reflective than descriptive. The excerpt, the Cologne segment of the Germany section (pp. 99–116), demonstrates that reflectiveness, as well as her characteristic antiwar sentiments and an interest in politics and government presumably shared by her intended audience.

⊂⊘ ℬↄ

THE APPEARANCE OF COLOGNE, at the distance of one, or two miles, is not inferior to the conception, which a traveller may have already formed of one of the capitals of Germany, should his mind have obeyed that almost universal illusion of fancy, which dresses up the images of places unseen, as soon as much expectation, or attention is directed towards them. The air above is crowded with the towers and spires of churches and convents, among which the cathedral, with its huge, unfinished mass, has a striking appearance. The walls are also high enough to be observed, and their whole inclosure seems, at a distance, to be thickly filled with buildings.

We should have known ourselves to be in the neighbourhood of some place larger than usual, from the sight of two, or three carriages, at once, on the road; nearly the first we had seen in Germany. There is besides some shew of labour in the adjoining villages; but the sallow countenances and miserable air of the people prove, that it is not a labour beneficial to them. The houses are only the desolated homes of these villagers; for there is not one that can be supposed to belong to any prosperous inhabitant of the city, or to afford the coveted stillness, in which the active find an occasional reward, and the idle a perpetual misery.

A bridge over a dry fossé leads to the northern gate, on each side of which a small modern battery defends the ancient walls. The city is not fortified, according to any present sense of the term, but is surrounded by these walls and by a ditch, of which the latter, near the northern gate, serves as a sort of kitchen garden to the inhabitants.

Before passing the inner gate, a soldier demanded our names, and we shewed our passport, for the first time; but, as the inquisitor did not understand French, in which language passports from England are written, it was handed to his comrades, who formed a circle about our chaise, and began, with leaden looks, to spell over the paper. Some talked, in the mean time, of examining the baggage; and the money, which we gave to prevent this, being in various pieces and in Prussian coin, which is not perfectly understood here, the whole party turned from the passport, counting and estimating the money in the hand of their collector, as openly as if it had been a legal tribute. When this was done and they had heard, with surprise, that we had not determined where to lodge, being inclined to take the pleasantest inn, we wrote our names in the corporal's dirty book, and were allowed to drive, under a dark tower, into the city.

Instantly, the narrow street, gloomy houses, stagnant kennels[1] and wretchedly looking people reminded us of the horrors of Neuss.[2] The lower windows of these prison-like houses are so strongly barricadoed [i.e., barricaded], that we had supposed the first two, or three, to be really parts of a gaol; but it soon appeared, that this profusion of heavy iron work was intended to exclude, not to confine, robbers. A succession of narrow streets, in which the largest houses were not less disgusting than the others for the filthiness of their windows, doorways and massy [i.e., massive] walls, continued through half the city. In one of these streets, or lanes, the postillion stopped at the door of an inn, which he said was the best; but the suffocating air of the street rendered it unnecessary to enquire, whether, contrary to appearances, there could be any accommodation within, and, as we had read of many squares, or market-places, he was desired to stop at an inn, situated in one of these. Thus we came to the Hotel de Prague, a large straggling building, said to be not worse than the others, for wanting half its furniture, and probably superior to them, by having a landlord of better than German civility.

Having counted from our windows the spires of ten, or twelve churches, or convents, we were at leisure to walk further into the city, and to look for the spacious squares, neat streets, noble public buildings and handsome houses, which there could be no doubt must be found in an Imperial and Electoral city,[3] seated on the Rhine, at a point where the chief roads from Holland and Flanders join those of Germany, treated by all writers as a considerable place, and evidently by its situation capable of becoming a sort of *emporium* for the three countries. The spot, into which our inn opened, though a parallelogram of considerable extent, bordered by lime trees, we passed quickly through, perceiving, that the houses on all its sides were mean[4] buildings, and therefore such as could not deserve the attention in the Imperial and Electoral city of Cologne. There are streets from each angle of this place, and we pursued them all in their turn, narrow, winding and dirty as they are, pestilent with kennels, gloomy from the height and blackness of the houses, unadorned by any public buildings, except the churches, that were grand, or by one private dwelling, that appeared to be clean, with little shew of traffic and less of passengers, either busy, or gay, till we saw them ending in other streets still worse, or concluded by the gates of the city. One of them, indeed, led through a market-place, in which the air is free from the feculence of the streets, but which is inferior to the other opening in space, and not better surrounded by buildings.

"These diminutive observations seem to take away something from the dignity of writing, and therefore are never communicated, but with hesitation, and a little fear of abasement and contempt."[5] And it is not only because they take away something from the dignity of writing, that such observations are withheld. To be thought capable of commanding more pleasures and preventing more inconveniences than others is a too general passport to respect; and, in the ordinary affairs of life, for one, that will shew somewhat less prosperity than he has, in order to try who will really respect him, thousands exert themselves to assume an appearance of more, which they might know can procure only the mockery of esteem for themselves, and the reality of it for their supposed conditions. Authors are not always free from a willingness to receive the fallacious sort of respect, that attaches to accidental circumstances, for the real sort, of which it would be more reasonable to be proud. A man, relating part of the history of his life, which is always necessarily done by a writer of travels, does not choose to shew that his course could lie through any scenes deficient of delights; or that, if it did, he was not enough elevated by his friends, importance, fortune, fame, or business, to be incapable of observing them minutely. The curiosities of cabinets[6] and of courts are, therefore, exactly described, and as much of every occurrence as does not shew the relater moving in any of the plainer walks of life; but the difference between the stock of physical comforts in different countries, the character of conditions, if the phrase may be used, such as it appears in the ordinary circumstances of residence, dress, food, cleanliness, opportunities of relaxation; in short, the information, which all may gain, is sometimes left to be gained by all, not from the book, but from travel. A writer, issuing into the world, makes up what he mistakes for his best appearance, and is continually telling his happiness, or shewing his good-humour, as people in a promenade always smile, and always look round to observe whether they are seen smiling. The politest salutation of the Chinese, when they meet, is, "Sir, prosperity is painted on your countenance;" or, "your whole air announces your felicity;" and the writers of travels, especially since the censure thrown upon SMOLLETT,[7] seem to provide, that their prosperity shall be painted on their volumes, and all their observations announce their felicity.

Cologne, though it bears the name of the Electorate, by which it is surrounded, is an imperial city; and the Elector, as to temporal affairs, has very little jurisdiction within it. The government has an affectation of being formed upon the model of Republican Rome; a form certainly not worthy of imitation, but which is as much disgraced by this burlesque of it, as ancient statues are by the gilding and the wigs, with which they are said to be sometimes arrayed by modern hands. There is a senate of forty-nine persons, who, being returned at different times of the year, are partly nominated by the remaining members, and partly chosen by twenty-two tribes of burgesses, or rather by so many companies of traders. Of six burgomasters,[8] two are in office every third year, and, when these appear in public, they are preceded by LICTORS, bearing *fasces*,[9] surmounted by their *own arms!* Each of the tribes, or companies, has a President, and the twenty-two Presidents form a Council, which is authorised to enquire into the conduct of the Senate: but the humbleness of the burgesses in their individual condition has virtually abolished all this scheme of a political constitution. Without some of the intelligence and personal independence, which are but little consistent with the general poverty and indolence of German traders, nothing but the forms of any constitution can be preserved, long after the virtual destruction of it has been meditated by those in a better condition. The greater part of these companies of traders having, in fact, no trade which can place them much above the rank of menial servants to their rich customers, the design, that their Council shall check the Senate, and the Senate direct the Burgomasters, has now, of course, little effect. And this, or a still humbler condition, is that of several cities in Germany, called free and independent, in which the neighbouring sovereigns have scarcely less authority, though with something more of circumstance, than in their own dominions.

The constitution of Cologne permits, indeed, some direct interference of the Elector; for the Tribunal of Appeal, which is the supreme court of law, is nominated by him: he has otherwise no direct power within the city; and, being forbidden to reside there more than three days successively, he does not even retain a palace, but is contented with a suite of apartments, reserved for his use at an inn. That this exclusion is no punishment, those, who have ever passed two days at Cologne, will admit; and it can tend very little to lessen his influence, for the greatest part of his personal expenditure must reach the merchants of the place; and the officers of several of his territorial jurisdictions make part of the inhabitants. His residences, with which he is remarkably well provided, are at Bonn; at Bruhl, a palace between Cologne and that place; at Poppelsdorff, which is beyond it; at Herzogs Freud, an hunting seat; and in Munster, of which he is the Bishop.

The duties of customs and excise are imposed by the magistrates of the city, and these enable them to pay their contributions to the Germanic fund; for, though such cities are formally independent of the neighbouring princes and nobility, they are not so of the general laws or expences of the empire, in the Diet of which they have some small share, forty-nine cities being allowed to send two representatives, and thus to have two votes out of an hundred and thirty-six. These duties, of both sorts, are very high at Cologne; and the first form a considerable part of the inter-ruptions, which all the States upon the Rhine give to the commerce of that river. Here also commodities, intended to be carried beyond the city by water, must be re-shipped; for, in order to provide cargoes for the boatmen of the place, vessels from the lower parts of the Rhine are not allowed to ascend beyond Cologne, and those from the higher parts can-not descend it farther. They may, indeed, reload with other cargoes for their return; and, as they constantly do so, the Cologne boatmen are not much benefited by the regulation; but the transfer of the goods employs some hands, subjects them better to the inspection of the customhouse officers, and makes it necessary for the merchants of places, on both sides, trading with each other, to have intermediate correspondents here. Yet, notwithstanding all this aggression upon the freedom of trade, Cologne is less considerable as a port, than some Dutch towns, never mentioned in a book, and is inferior, perhaps, to half the minor seaports in England. We could not find more than thirty vessels of burthen against the quay, all mean and ill-built, except the Dutch, which are very large, and, being constructed purposely for a tedious navigation, contain apartments upon the deck for the family of the skipper, well furnished, and so commodious as to have four or five sashed windows on each side, generally gay with flower-pots. Little flower-gardens, too, sometimes formed upon the roof of the cabin, increase the domestic comforts of the skipper; and the neat-ness of his vessel can, perhaps, be equalled only by that of a Dutch house. In a time of perfect peace, there is no doubt more traffic; but, from what we saw of the general means and occasions of commerce in Germany, we cannot suppose it to be much reduced by war. Wealthy and commercial countries may be injured immensely by making war either for Germany or against it; by too much friendship or too much enmity; but Germany itself cannot be proportionately injured with them, except when it is the scene of actual violence. Englishmen, who feel, as they always must, the love of their own country much increased by the view of others, should be induced, at every step, to wish, that there may be as little political intercourse as possible, either of friendship or enmity, between the blessings of their Island and the wretchedness of the Continent.

Our inn had formerly been a convent, and was in a part of the town where such societies are more numerous than elsewhere. At five o'clock, on the Sunday after our arrival, the bells of churches and convents began to sound on all sides, and there was scarcely any entire intermission of them till evening. The places of public amusement, chiefly a sort of tea-gardens, were then set open, and, in many streets, the sound of music and dancing was heard almost as plainly as that of the bells had been before; a disgusting excess of licentiousness, which appeared in other instances, for we heard, at the same time, the voices of a choir on one side of the street, and the noise of a billiard table on the other. Near the inn, this contrast was more observable. While the strains of revelry arose from an adjoining garden, into which our windows opened, a pause in the music allowed us to catch some notes of the vesper service, performing in a convent of the order of Clarisse, only three or four doors beyond. Of the severe rules of this society we had been told in the morning. The members take a vow, not only to renounce the world, but their dearest friends, and are never after permitted to see even their fathers or mothers, though they may sometimes converse with the latter from behind a curtain. And, lest some lingering remains of filial affection should tempt an unhappy nun to lift the veil of separation between herself and her mother, she is not allowed to speak even with her, but in the presence of the abbess. Accounts of such horrible perversions of human reason make the blood thrill and the teeth chatter. Their fathers they can never speak to, for no man is suffered to be in any part of the convent used by the sisterhood, nor, indeed, is admitted beyond the gate, except when there is a necessity for repairs, when all the votaries of the order are previously secluded. It is not easily, that a cautious mind becomes convinced of the existence of such severe orders; when it does, astonishment at the artificial miseries, which the ingenuity of human beings forms for themselves by seclusion, is as boundless as at the other miseries, with which the most trivial vanity and envy so frequently pollute the intercourses of social life. The poor nuns, thus nearly entombed during their lives, are, after death, tied upon a board, in the clothes they die in, and, with only their veils thrown over the face, are buried in the garden of the convent.

During this day, Trinity Sunday, processions were passing on all sides, most of them attended by some sort of martial music. Many of the parishes, of which there are nineteen, paraded with their officers; and the burgesses, who are distributed into eight corps, under a supposition that they could and would defend the city, if it was attacked, presented their captains at the churches. The host accompanied all these processions. A party of the city guards followed, and forty or fifty persons out of uniform, the representatives probably of the burgesses, who are about six thousand, succeeded. Besides the guards, there was only one man in uniform, who, in the burlesque dress of a drum-major, entertained the populace by a kind of extravagant marching dance, in the middle of the procession. Our companion would not tell us that this was the captain.

The cathedral, though unfinished, is conspicuous, amongst a great number of churches, for the dignity of some detached features, that shew part of the vast design formed for the whole. It was begun, in 1248, by the Elector Conrad, who is related, in an hexameter inscription over a gate, to have laid the first stone himself. In 1320, the choir was finished, and the workmen continued to be employed upon the other parts in 1499, when of two towers, destined to be 580 feet above the roof, one had risen 21 feet, and the other 150 feet, according to the measurement mentioned in a printed description. We did not learn at what period the design of completing the edifice was abandoned; but the original founder lived to see all the treasures expended, which he had collected for the purpose. In its present state, the inequality of its vast towers renders it a striking object at a considerable distance; and, from the large unfilled area around it, the magnificence of its Gothic architecture, especially of some parts, which have not been joined to the rest, and appear to be the ruined remains, rather than the commencement of a work, is viewed with awful [i.e., awestruck] delight.

In the interior of the cathedral, a fine choir leads to an altar of black marble, raised above several steps, which, being free from the incongruous ornaments usual in Romish[10] churches, is left to impress the mind by its majestic plainness. The tall pointed windows above, of which there are six, are superior in richness of colouring and design to any we ever saw; beyond even those in the Chapter-house at York,[11] and most resembling the very fine ones in the cathedral of Canterbury. The nave is deformed by a low wooden roof, which appears to have been intended only as a temporary covering, and should certainly be succeeded by one of equal dignity to the vast columns placed for its support, whether the other parts of the original design can ever be completed or not.

By some accident we did not see the tomb of the three kings of Jerusalem, whose bodies are affirmed to have been brought here from Milan in 1162, when the latter city was destroyed by the Emperor Frederic Barbarossa. Their boasted treasures of golden crowns and diamonds pass, of course, without our estimation.

A description of the churches in Cologne, set out with good antiquarian minuteness, would fill volumes. The whole number of churches, chapters and chapels, which last are by far the most numerous, is not less than eighty, and none are without an history of two or three centuries. They are all opened on Sundays; and we can believe, that the city may contain, as is asserted, 40,000 souls, for nearly all that we saw were well attended. In one, indeed, the congregation consisted only of two or three females, kneeling at a great distance from the altar, with an appearance of the utmost intentness upon the service, and abstraction from the noise of the processions, that could be easily heard within. They were entirely covered with a loose black drapery; whether for penance, or not, we did not hear. In the cathedral, a figure in the same attitude was rendered more interesting by her situation beneath the broken arches and shattered fret-work of a painted window, through which the rays of the sun scarcely penetrated to break the shade she had chosen.

Several of the chapels are not much larger than an ordinary apartment, but they are higher, that the nuns of some adjoining convent may have a gallery, where, veiled from observation by a lawn curtain, their voices often mingle sweetly with the choir. There are thirty-nine convents of women and nineteen of men, which are supposed to contain about fifteen hundred persons. The chapters, of which some are noble and extremely opulent, support nearly four hundred more; and there are said to be, upon the whole, between two and three thousand persons, under religious denominations, in Cologne. Walls of convents and their gardens appear in every street, but do not attract notice, unless, as frequently happens, their bell sounds while you are passing. Some of their female inhabitants may be seen in various parts of the city, for there is an order, the members of which are employed, by rotation, in teaching children and attending the sick. Those of the noble chapters are little more confined than if they were with their own families, being permitted to visit their friends, to appear at balls and promenades, to wear what dresses they please, except when they chaunt in the choir, and to quit the chapter, if the offer of an acceptable marriage induces their families to authorise it; but their own admission into the chapter proves them to be noble by sixteen quarterings, or four generations, and the offer must be from a person of equal rank, or their descendants could not be received into similar chapters; an important circumstance in the affairs of the German noblesse.

Some of these ladies we saw in the church of their convent. Their habits were remarkably graceful; robes of lawn and black silk flowed from the shoulder, whence a quilled ruff, somewhat resembling that of Queen Elizabeth's time, spread round the neck. The hair was in curls, without powder, and in the English fashion. Their voices were peculiarly sweet, and they sung the responses with a kind of plaintive tenderness, that was extremely interesting.

The Jesuits' church is one of the grandest in Cologne, and has the greatest display of paintings over its numerous altars, as well as of marble pillars. The churches of the chapters are, for the most part, very large, and endowed with the richest ornaments, which are, however, not shewn to the public, except upon days of fête. We do not remember to have seen that of the chapter of St. Ursula, where heads and other relics are said to be handed to you from shelves, like books in a library; nor that of the convent of Jacobins, where some MSS. and other effects of Albert the Great, bishop of Ratisbon, are among the treasures of the monks.

Opposite to the Jesuits' church was an hospital for wounded soldiers, several of whom were walking in the court yard before it, half-cloathed in dirty woollen, through which the bare arms of many appeared. Sickness and neglect had subdued all the symptoms of a soldier; and it was impossible to distinguish the wounded French from the others, though we were assured that several of that nation were in the crowd. The windows of the hospital were filled with figures still more wretched. There was a large assemblage of spectators, who looked as if they were astonished to see, that war is compounded of something else, besides the glories, of which it is so easy to be informed.

The soldiery of Cologne are under the command of the magistrates, and are employed only within the gates of the city. The whole body does not exceed an hundred and fifty, whom we saw reviewed by their colonel, in the place before the Hotel de Prague. The uniform is red, faced with white. The men wear whiskers, and affect an air of ferocity, but appear to be mostly invalids, who have grown old in their guard-houses.

Protestants, though protected in their persons, are not allowed the exercise of their religion within the walls of the city, but have a chapel in a village on the other side of the Rhine. As some of the chief merchants, and those who are most useful to the inhabitants, are of the reformed church, they ventured lately to request that they might have a place of worship within the city; but they received the common answer, which opposes all sort of improvement, religious or civil, that, though the privilege in itself might be justly required, it could not be granted, because they would then think of asking something more.

The government of Cologne in ecclesiastical affairs is with the Elector, as archbishop, and the Chapter as his council. In civil matters, though the city constitution is of little effect, the real power is not so constantly with him as might be supposed; those, who have influence, being sometimes out of his interest. Conversation, as we were told, was scarcely less free than in Holland, where there is justly no opposition to any opinion, however improper, or absurd, except from the reason of those, who hear it. On that account, and because of its easy intercourse with Brussels and Spa, this city is somewhat the resort of strangers, by whom such conversation is, perhaps, chiefly carried on; but those must come from very wretched countries, who can find pleasure in a residence at Cologne.

Amongst the public buildings must be reckoned the Theatre, of which we did not see the inside, there being no performance, during our stay, except on Sunday. This, it seems, may be opened, without offence to the Magistrates, though a protestant church may not. It stands in a row of small houses, from which it is distinguished only by a painted front, once tawdry and now dirty, with the inscription, "*Musis Gratiisque decentibus.*"[12] The Town-house is an awkward and irregular stone building. The arsenal, which is in one of the narrowest streets, we should have passed, without notice, if it had not been pointed out to us. As a building, it is nothing more than such as might be formed out of four or five of the plainest houses laid into one. Its contents are said to be chiefly antient arms, of various fashions and sizes, not very proper for modern use.

Notes

1. Gutters into which waste of every sort was thrown.
2. There Radcliffe had seen "haggard" (96) and "gaunt" men and women with, "at first, more fear than pity" (97).
3. Cologne was an Electoral city because its bishop was entitled to cast a vote for king.
4. Shabby or inferior.
5. From *Journey to the Western Islands of Scotland* (1775), by Samuel Johnson (1709–1784), highly regarded essayist, biographer, lexicographer, and talker.
6. A room for the display of "curiosities," or objects of interest.
7. Tobias Smollett's *Travels through France and Italy* (1766) was censured by some

contemporaries for its often ill-tempered tone; the crotchety Dr. Smelfungus of Laurence Sterne's *Sentimental Journey through France and Italy* (1768), for example, is a parody of Smollett.

8. Chief magistrates.

9. "Lictors," officers who attend on magistrates and execute their sentences. "Fasces," a bundle of rods bound up around an ax with its head projecting, is the lictor's emblem of authority.

10. Roman Catholic.

11. Building where a chapter (canons or resident ecclesiastical dignitaries) meets to manage a cathedral's affairs.

12. Fitting for the Muses and the Graces (L.).

Mary Ann Parker

1760?–AFTER 1795

A Voyage round the World, in the Gorgon man of war: Captain John Parker. Performed and written by his widow; for the advantage of a numerous family. London: John Nichols, 1795.

The eighteen months described in *A Voyage round the World* is the only period of Mary Ann Parker's life about which much is known. Before her marriage she traveled extensively with her mother in Europe, and when she was very young they lived for more than three years in Spain. By 1791 she was married to Captain John Parker and the mother of two young children; that year she left the children with her mother and accompanied her husband to New South Wales, the convict settlement in what is now Australia. Captain Parker's mission was to transport sorely needed supplies to the colony and to bring returning colonists back to England. What was certainly a long journey, and potentially a grueling one, becomes in Mary Ann Parker's account almost a lark. Although she records storms and her own fears, she seems genuinely to have discounted the various "little difficulties" (32) of travel. The ship reached the Cape of Good Hope on 21 June 1791 and New South Wales some three months later.

As she describes Cape Town, Sidney Cove, Parramatta, and various excursions, Parker apologizes for the "slender remarks" (45) that do not measure up to works by "authors of knowledge and taste" (44). Yet her narrative evinces an attractive good humor and delight in her surroundings, and it also records contemporary debates about the future of Australia: the need to alter a system of transporting convicts that produced such "dreadful mortality" (72); the possibility of establishing a whale fishery as "an encouragement to settlers" (80). The text is particularly compelling as a record of "irreparable loss" (38). While commanding HMS *Woolwich*, Captain Parker died suddenly of yellow fever on 4 August 1794; because the book's title, its preface, and scattered remarks foreshadow his death, the reader repeatedly contrasts Parker's pleasures as a traveler with the coming grief for a "beloved husband, the tender partner of my life, and my only support in the time of trouble and affliction." The Parkers returned to England in June 1792, where she learned that her son had died. Within a few weeks she bore another child, and the narrative concludes with a plea on behalf of this "infant of *seven* months, who has chiefly been on my left arm, whilst the right was employed in bringing once more to my recollection the pleasing occurrences of *fifteen* months" (148).

TEXT: Mary Ann Parker's *A Voyage round the World* appeared in 1795. It was published by subscription, a method whereby donors (258 of them in Parker's case) defrayed the expenses of publication (with the balance of the contributions going to the author). Modern editions were published in 1991 and 1999. Excerpted from the 1795 text are chapter one, very characteristic of Parker's cheerful openness as a traveler, and chapter eight, of interest for its reflections on Australian aboriginals and on the slave trade.

&

CHAP. I.

Reasons for undertaking the voyage—set out for Portsmouth—passengers on board—sail from Spithead—arrive at the island of Teneriffe—pay a visit to the Governor—description of the town of Santa Cruz—an excursion to Puerto Oratava—a laughable occurrence—Lieutenant Rye—another excursion—return to the ship—and set sail.

On the *first* day of January 1791, my late husband, Captain John Parker, was appointed by the Right Honourable the Lords Commissioners of the Admiralty to the command of His Majesty's ship the Gorgon.—On the *second* he received his commission. The ship was then lying at her moorings off Common-hand in Portsmouth harbour, refitting for her intended voyage to New South Wales, and exchanging the provisions she then had, for the newest and best in store.

There were embarked for their passage to the aforenamed colony, a part of the new corps that had been raised for that place, commanded by Major Grose.[1] By the last day of January the ship was ready for sea; and on the *first* day of February the pilot came on board, in order to conduct her out of the harbour to Spithead.

When things were in this state of forwardness, it was proposed to me to accompany Captain Parker in the intended expedition to New Holland.[2] A fortnight was allowed me for my decision. An indulgent husband waited my answer at Portsmouth: I did not therefore take a minute's consideration; but, by return of post, forwarded one perfectly consonant to his request, and my most sanguine wishes—that of going with *him* to the remotest parts of the globe; although my considerate readers will naturally suppose that my feelings were somewhat wounded at the thoughts of being so long absent from two dear children, and a mother, with whom I had travelled into France, Italy, and Spain; and from whom I had never been separated a fortnight at one time during the whole course of my life.

Attended by an intimate friend, I repaired to the West end of the town, and set off for Portsmouth the next morning. We remained at Spithead until the12th of March. In the interim orders had arrived to receive on board Captain Gidley King, of the Royal Navy, the intended Lieutenant Governor of Norfolk Island[3] in the Pacific Ocean, together with Mrs. King and their family; also to disembark Major Grose, and such part of the corps as were on board, except Mr. Burton a botanist, Mr. Baines the chaplain, and Mr. Grimes, who, with their attendants, were directed to be continued on board, and to take their passage for the new settlement.

On Tuesday, the 15th of March, we sailed from Spithead, by way of St. Helens; and, after a fortnight's seasoning and buffeting in the channel, I began to enjoy the voyage I had undertaken; and with the polite attention of the officers on board, and my amiable companion Mrs. King, we glided over many a watery grave with peace of mind, and uninterrupted happiness; although many calms tended to render our passage to the island of *Teneriffe*[4] somewhat tedious.

We arrived, however, safe in the bay of *Santa Cruz* on the *fifteenth* of April; and captain Parker sent the second lieutenant on shore, to acquaint the Governor of our having put into that port for refreshment, and offered to exchange salutes, provided his Excellency would assure him the return of an equal number of guns from the garrison; at the same time informing him that he should have the honour, together with the officers, of waiting on him the ensuing day; and that lieutenant governor King of Norfolk Island was a passenger, and also intended to do himself the honour of paying his respects to his Excellency.

The officer returned with the Governor's answer, that whatever the ship stood in need of, she might have; and that an officer should be sent on-board, to signify the time when it would be most convenient for His Excellency to receive the compliments we had been so polite as to offer, of waiting on him; but that he had orders from his Court not to return any salute to a foreign Ship of War.

About half an hour after the return of the officer, one of the Governor's Aid-de-Camps came on board: he congratulated us, in his Excellency's name, on our safe arrival, and informed us that the Governor would be happy to see us, and requested that we would favour him with our company to dine with him on the ensuing day.

The invitation was accepted. Our party consisted of Lieutenant Governor King, his lady, our officers, together with Mr. Grimes, and Mr. Baines. The company at Don Antonio di Gutierez (that was the name of the Governor) were; the former Governor the Marquis di Branciforti, the Lieutenant Governor and his lady, with several other officers and their ladies.

The reception we met with, and particularly the compliments *di los manos,*[5] would have struck me by their singularity, had I not resided when very young upwards of three years in Spain; during which time I had every reason to believe them particularly attentive to the *English ladies:* and I hope it will be allowed me to remark the great satisfaction which they expressed at my being capable of conversing in their own language— a pleasure which I could not help participating with them, from having it in my power to be of some service, as *Interpreter General* to the party with whom I had the satisfaction of sailing.

It being Passion-week, the dinner, although sumptuous, consisted of many dishes dressed with oil.—After having, from hunger and politeness, ate more than we wished of the least rancid dishes, not expecting any plain ones to make their appearance; we were quite surprized when a large roasted Turkey, dressed quite in the English fashion, was brought on the table:—had it made an earlier entrance, it would have been well finished, but, unfortunately, it came so unexpectedly, that our appetites had been satisfied, with a previous course of rancid plenty.

After dinner our formidable party paraded the town, which I suppose to be very near a mile in length, and about half a mile in breadth. There are several neat churches in it, but only one good street, which is remarkably broad:—the rest are generally very narrow, and abound in beggars, who are extremely troublesome to travellers.

At sun-set we returned on board, well satisfied with the reception we had met with; and on the following day, the same party dined at Mr. Rooney's, a Gentleman in partnership with the English house of Mess. Little and Co. and to whom Captain Parker had been introduced by means of a letter from Sir Andrew Hammond. From a desire of making me acquainted with some Spanish ladies, Mr. Rooney engaged us in an afternoon's walk to visit Captain Adams, the Captain of the Port, and there I had the pleasure of meeting with several females. They seemed highly delighted with my hat and dress, and took singular satisfaction in repeatedly taking off the former, and in examining my coat, which was half uniform. My having formerly travelled in Spain, and consequently having acquired a tolerable knowledge of their language procured me unusual attention, such as I shall ever remember with pleasure, though mingled with a degree of regret, arising from the improbability of my ever revisiting a country, in which I had the happiness to meet with unlimited kindness.

The next morning we were presented with sallads, fruits, lemons, &c. from different inhabitants of the town, who seemed to vie with each other in presenting us with those salutary refreshments.

The following day was fixed for an excursion to *Puerto Oratava*. Accompanied by Governor King, his lady, our first Lieutenant, and a young gentleman belonging to Mess. Little and Co. we went on shore at daybreak, and after breakfasting mounted our buricos or donkeys. The roads (hardly deserving that appellation) were rugged indeed; in some places the stones were sufficiently out of the ground to afford us seats, but the good humour which reigned amongst our party made ample amends for any trifling difficulty of that nature—and indeed little difficulties make social excursions more interesting.

Our first halting-place was a small hut, where Mr. Malcolme, a gentleman belonging to the same house, had taken care to provide us with biscuits, wine, &c. Having refreshed ourselves we continued our ride until *meridian* [i.e., noon], when it was judged prudent for us to tarry during the heat of the day. Here Mr. Malcolme had also procured a cold collation, or a first dinner.—Two sultry hours having passed away very cheerfully, we again mounted our buricos, and, upon my making use of the Spanish method of quickening their pace, my animal set off on full speed, left the muleteer staring with astonishment, and poor me rolling down a steep hill; but perceiving the party, who had not got up with us, coming rapidly to my assistance, fearful lest they should gallop over me, I arose as quickly as possible, and scrambling to a stone sat myself down upon it, and laughed as heartily as I ever recollected to have done in my life. This little accident let my muleteer into the secret of my having understood the chief of his conversation with the other, who had the honour of attending my companion Mrs. King, which was "his inclination to stop at all the *posadoes*, or public houses, we had passed by."

At a short distance from this laughable scene, we were met by Mr. Little, who very politely conducted us to his town residence, where he had prepared a most splendid entertainment replete with every delicacy of the season. The fruits and vegetables were luxuries indeed to us, who had been accustomed to little choice during our passage.

From this town, on the same evening, one of our officers, Lieutenant Rye, accompanied by Mr. Burton the botanist, took his departure for the Peak of Teneriffe, in which enterprize, notwithstanding the great danger pointed out to him at that season of the year, he was fortunate enough to succeed, and arrived at its summit.

On his return to England, his excursion was published;[6] and I recommend it to the perusal of my readers; yet must at the same time take the liberty of observing, that although he has been minute as to particulars that tend to the information and benefit of such as may hereafter wish to visit the Peak, he has been too diffident in mentioning the extreme fatigues and difficulties which he underwent in the accomplishment of his wishes. The inhabitants spoke of his courage in terms of astonishment—too much cannot be said in praise of his perseverance, it is sufficient of itself to convince us that no difficulties are insuperable to the prudent and brave, and at the same time brings to my remembrance the following lines of Mr. Rowe:

"The wise and prudent conquer difficulties
"By daring to attempt them: Sloth and folly
"Shiver and shrink at sight of toil and hazard,
"And make th' impossibility they fear."[7]

We were the next morning regaled with a breakfast equally profuse and delicate as the preceding meals. The greater part of that day being too sultry to walk, we were much indebted to the polite and respectful attention of the aforementioned gentlemen, who, studying our amusement, proposed an evening excursion to their country residence, situated at a short distance from the town. It is a small neat house, standing upon a hill, commanding an extensive view of the Bay of Santa-Cruz; the garden is enclosed with myrtle hedges, the walks were shaded with vines, and lofty lemon trees, and the parterre[8] before the door arranged with pots of most beautiful carnations.

Having comfortably regaled ourselves, we returned back to tea and supper; retired early, and arose at four the next morning. After breakfasting we set out upon our return; at *eleven* we stopped to partake of some refreshments, and then proceeded *two* leagues farther, when we again alighted to avoid the intense heat; during which time Mrs. King and myself strolled to several little huts. The inhabitants were surprized at seeing strangers of our sex alone; but their astonishment soon subsided when I spoke a few words to them in Spanish;—from this moment pleasure was visible in every countenance; in proof of which, although their spot of ground was small, their kindness induced them to present us with some sage, and an egg apiece—the *little* all they had to proffer us; and I make no doubt but we were remembered by them the remainder of the day; nay I will even think they have not yet forgotten us.

Returning to our party, and finding all ready, we remounted, and after riding a few miles our English friends took leave of us. Their uniform attention has induced me to name them so often in this narrative—the only return I shall ever have it in my power to make them.

It may afford a smile to my readers to add, that, after it was found out that I could speak Spanish, I entered into conversation with my muleteer, which made him so proud of his charge, that, previous to our entering any town or village, he, with great form, requested me to sit upright, and then spread my hair very curiously over my shoulders.—Poor fellow! could I be displeased with his request; since it arose, without doubt, from a desire of making me appear to the greatest advantage?

Thus, by the favour of a serene evening, we returned to Mr. Rooney's, who wished us to sleep on shore, as the wind began to blow fresh, and the surf rendered it very unpleasant for us to go on-board; but having resolved prior to my leaving England, to bear every difficulty, if possible, and determined to start none, I, with my good friends, took leave; and, after a few lifts over a heavy sea, we reached the wished-for vessel.

The next morning we paid a visit to the Spanish Lieutenant Governor's Lady, who introduced us to several ladies. The following day Mr. Rooney and Mr. Malcolme favoured us with their company on-board. After dinner they took leave of us, and shortly after we received from them a present of some lemons, and such other fruit as they deemed most acceptable for our intended voyage.

On the 24th of April we attempted to sail; but unfortunately the anchor of our vessel hooked the cable of a Spanish brig, owing to a strong tide; which broke the window, and carried away part of our quarter gallery. This accident detained us until the following day, when we sailed with a fresh and favourable breeze, and saw the Peak many leagues distant.

CHAP. VIII.

Description of the inhabitants of New South Wales—their huts—their extraordi-
nary honesty—account of Banalong—an instance of his sensibility—observa-
tions on the Slave Trade.

The Inhabitants of New South Wales, both male and female, go without apparel. Their colour is of a dingy copper; their nose is broad and flat, their lips wide and thick, and their eyes circular. From a disagreeable practice they have of rubbing themselves with fish-oil, they smell so loathsome, that it is almost impossible to approach them without disgust.

The men in general appeared to be from five feet six to five feet nine inches high, are rather slender, but straight and well made: they have bushy beards, and the hair on their heads is stuck full with the teeth of fish, and bits of shells: they also ornament themselves with a fish-bone fastened in the gristle of the nose, which makes them appear really frightful; and are generally armed with a stick about a yard long, and a lance which they throw with considerable velocity.

The stature of the women is somewhat less than that of the men—their noses are broad, their mouths wide, and their lips thick. They are extremely negligent of their persons, and are filthy to a degree scarcely credible: their faces and bodies are besmeared with the fat of animals, and the salutary custom of washing seems entirely unknown to them.

Their huts or habitations are constructed in the most rude and barbarous manner: they consist of pieces of bark laid together somewhat in the form of an oven, with a small entrance at one end. Their sole residence, however, is not in these huts; on the contrary, they depend less on them for shelter than on the numerous excavations which are formed in the rocks by the washing of the sea; and it is no uncommon thing to see fifty or sixty of them comfortably lodged in one of these caves.

Notwithstanding the general appearance of the natives, I never felt the least fear when in their company, being always with a party more than sufficient for my protection. I have been seated in the woods with twelve or fourteen of them, men, women, and children. Had I objected, or shewn any disgust at their appearance, it would have given them some reason to suppose that I was not what they term their *damely*, or friend; and would have rendered my being in their company not only unpleasant, but unsafe.

Before I conclude my description of the natives, it is but justice to remark, that, in comparison with the inhabitants of most of the South-Sea Islands, they appear very little given to thieving; and their confidence in the honesty of one another is so great, that they will leave their spears and other implements on the sea-shore, in full and perfect security of their remaining untouched.

From the treatment which I invariably experienced, I am inclined to think favourably of them; and fully believe that they would never injure our people, were they not first offended by them.

I cannot help observing that one of the men had a most engaging deportment; his countenance was pleasing, and his manners far beyond what I could possibly have expected. He was pleased to seat himself by me, [ex]changed names with Captain Parker, and took particular notice of the travelling knife and fork with which I was eating, and which I did myself the satisfaction to give him: he paid us a visit on-board the ensuing day, and shewed me that he had not lost my present, but made use of it, though somewhat aukwardly, whilst he demolished *two* or *three* pounds of the ship's pork.

The natives very frequently surrounded our vessel with their canoes. The women often held up their little ones, as if anxious to have them noticed by us. Sometimes, for the sake of amusement, I have thrown them ribbands [i.e., ribbons] and other trifles, which they would as frequently tye round their toes as any other part of their person.

Since my return to England, Banalong, one of the natives brought hither by Governor Phillip,[9] came to see me. To describe the pleasure that overspread this poor fellow's countenance when my little girl presented to him the picture of her dear father, is impossible; it was then that the tear of sensibility trickled down his cheeks; he immediately recognized those features which will never be obliterated from my memory, and spoke, with all the energy of Nature, of the pleasing excursion which they had made together up the country. The above is one amongst many instances which I could relate of the natural goodness of their hearts; and I flatter myself that the time is hastening when they will no longer be considered as mere savages;—and wherefore should they?

> "Fleecy locks, and black complexion,
>   "Cannot forfeit Nature's claim:
> "Skins may differ, but affection
>   "Dwells in white and black the same."[10]

Notes

1. Francis Grose (1758?–1814), lieutenant governor of New South Wales December 1792–December 1794.

2. Dutch name for what is now Australia; at this time used interchangeably with New South Wales.

3. A convict settlement notorious for the severity with which prisoners there were treated.

4. Located off the northwest coast of Africa.

5. A compliment paid in Spain by the ladies to each other on entering a room. The last comer just touches the hand of every lady, at the same time curtseying and repeating continually *"di los manos"* [Parker].

6. *An Excursion to the Peak of Teneriffe, in 1791* (London: R. Faulder, 1793).

7. Slightly misquoted from a speech by Mirza in act 1, scene 1, of Nicholas Rowe's tragedy *The Ambitious Step-Mother* (1700).

8. Level space in a formal garden for ornamental flower beds.

9. "Banalong," also spelled Bennelong; one of the "two aboriginal friends, or specimens" (Hughes 108), whom Governor Arthur Phillip took back to England in 1792.

10. From William Cowper's poem "The Negro's Complaint," very popular with opponents of the slave trade.

Mary Wollstonecraft

1759–1797

Letters Written during a Short Residence in Sweden, Norway, and Denmark.
London: J. Johnson, 1796.

Mary Wollstonecraft was born near London in 1759. When her mother
died she and her two sisters left the home of their abusive father. After
directing a school with one of her sisters and serving as a governess, Wollstonecraft became a reader and translator for a London publisher. It was
at this time that she met William Godwin, a radical political philosopher
and author who, like Wollstonecraft, wrote and spoke in favor of the
French Revolution. In 1792 she went to Paris for the purpose of writing
a firsthand account of the conflict. From 1793 to 1795 she lived in Paris
with her lover, Gilbert Imlay, an American adventurer. In 1794 their child,
Fanny, was born, the same year that she published her *History and Moral
View of the Origin and Progress of the French Revolution.* In 1795 she returned
to England. Suicidal over fears that Imlay would abandon her, Wollstonecraft agreed, at Imlay's insistence, to serve as representative for his shipping
interests in Sweden, Norway, and Denmark. Imlay hoped that he could
extricate himself from Wollstonecraft while she was away and that the trip
would relieve some of her depression and restore her health.

The twenty-five letters are an epistolary journal of Wollstonecraft's travels through the three Scandinavian countries. Meant for publication from
the outset, they reflect a thorough knowledge of the conventions of
eighteenth-century travel literature. "In writing these desultory letters, I
found I could not avoid being continually the first person—'the little hero
of each tale.' I tried to correct this fault, if it be one, for they were designed
for publication," but the letters became "stiff and affected," and she "determined to let my remarks and reflections flow unrestrained" ("Advertisement"). Thus the *Letters* not only departs from typical travel narratives
in its descriptions of what she saw "and the effect different objects had
produced on my mind and feelings"; it also calls for a superior form of
travel writing, which Wollstonecraft herself attempts. She gives advice to

Mary Godwin (née Mary Wollstonecraft), by John Opie, 1797. Courtesy of the National Portrait Gallery, London.

would-be travelers and criticizes the universalizing tendencies of travel writers in general. To avoid mindless characterizations of other peoples and nations, she seeks to "discriminate natural and acquired differences" in individuals and nations "by promoting inquiry and discussion" (Letter V). Even as she smothers in the coffinlike beds stuffed with down mattresses and coverlets, decries the unhealthy practices of bundling children in heavy layers of clothing, and bemoans the poor diets that turn young women old much too soon, she, in the spirit of inquiry she has recommended, questions why the practices have prevailed and finds answers in the current state of societies where health improvements are not available. As she observes the poverty and indolence around her and the unsavory business practices of many, she comes to realize that these behaviors cannot be corrected until progress and economic development make their appearances.

Wollstonecraft's remarks are not surprising; this is the Wollstonecraft with whom we are familiar, the woman who tells us that her "favourite subject of contemplation [is] the future improvement of the world" (Letter XXII) and whose treatise *A Vindication of the Rights of Woman* (1792) has made her political and literary reputation. It is the epistolary journal, however, that seems to be "the perfect literary mode for Wollstonecraft's strengths as a writer and thinker, for in a journal an almost random movement from subject to subject is acceptable" (Poston xi–xii). Wollstonecraft excels at life-writing, and in taking up this form of discourse she is able to give full play to her many voices and varied concerns. Her political voice is juxtaposed to her artistic descriptions of the "primitive" characters she encounters. Her calls for progress in education and economic development give way to her concerns for the environment. Her impatient traveler voice is offset by her respectful observations of the rude circumstances the Scandinavians must endure. Her philosophical discussions of aesthetics and the sublime and the beautiful are tied to her terrifying fear of death: "I cannot bear to think of being no more—of losing myself— though existence is often but a painful consciousness of misery" (Letter VIII). Her professional voice that "asks men's questions" becomes a feminist voice that expresses severe distaste for Imlay's business affairs: "you— yourself, are strangely altered, since you have entered deeply into commerce—more than you are aware of—never allowing yourself to reflect, and keeping your mind, or rather passions, in a continual state of agitation" (Letter XXIII). Her maternal voice, with its tender care for her "Fanni-kin," is clouded by her unrequited lover voice as she longs to be rejoined with Imlay. And throughout the *Letters*, her moving, poetic voice responds with reverence to the healing powers of the natural world.

The three letters excerpted here were chosen because they detail her journey in miniature—from Sweden to Norway to Denmark—and they bring the full range of Wollstonecraft's voices to the reader. Wollstonecraft is most poetic in Letter V (from Sweden), as she paints word pictures of the natural beauty of the Scandinavian mountains, lakes, and woods. Letter VI (from Norway) begins with the words of the tired, lonely traveler who grieves for her absent daughter and closes with a meditation on nature as the "nurse of sentiment." In Letter VII (from Denmark) the voices of the social and political critics, with which we are more familiar, are joined by her philosophical and poetic voices and the voice of the sorrowing lover.

Wollstonecraft separated from Imlay in 1796 and resumed her literary career in London. She was reunited with Godwin, and they were married in 1797. Their child, Mary, was born five months later. Wollstonecraft died the following month, September 1797.

TEXT: The excerpt is from Mary Wollstonecraft's original 1796 edition of the *Letters* published by Joseph Johnson (pp. 42–92). A facsimile edition introduced by Sylvia Norman (Fontwell, Sussex: Centaur Press, 1970) and an edition introduced and edited by Carol H. Poston (Lincoln and London: University of Nebraska Press, 1976) are currently available.

ᘓ ᗷ

LETTER V.

Had I determined to travel in Sweden merely for pleasure, I should probably have chosen the road to Stockholm, though convinced, by repeated observation, that the manners of a people are best discriminated in the country. The inhabitants of the capital are all of the same genus; for the varieties in the species we must, therefore, search where the habitations of men are so separated as to allow the difference of climate to have its natural effect. And with this difference we are, perhaps, most forcibly struck at the first view, just as we form an estimate of the leading traits of a character at the first glance, of which intimacy afterwards makes us almost lose sight.

As my affairs called me to Stromstad (the frontier town of Sweden) in my way to Norway, I was to pass over, I heard, the most uncultivated part of the country. Still I believe that the grand features of Sweden are the same every where, and it is only the grand features that admit of description. There is an individuality in every prospect, which remains in the memory as forcibly depicted as the particular features that have arrested our attention; yet we cannot find words to discriminate that individuality so as to enable a stranger to say, this is the face, that the view. We may amuse by setting the imagination to work; but we cannot store the memory with a fact.

As I wish to give you a general idea of this country, I shall continue in my desultory manner to make such observations and reflections as the circumstances draw forth, without losing time, by endeavouring to arrange them.

Travelling in Sweden is very cheap, and even commodious, if you make but the proper arrangements. Here, as in other parts of the continent, it is necessary to have your own carriage, and to have a servant who can speak the language, if you are unacquainted with it. Sometimes a servant who can drive would be found very useful, which was our case, for I travelled in company with two gentlemen, one of whom had a german servant who drove very well. This was all the party; for not intending to make a long stay, I left my little girl[1] behind me.

As the roads are not much frequented, to avoid waiting three or four hours for horses, we sent, as is the constant custom, an *avant courier* [i.e., messenger] the night before, to order them at every post, and we constantly found them ready. Our first set I jokingly termed *requisition* horses;[2] but afterwards we had almost always little spirited animals that went on at a round pace.

The roads, making allowance for the ups and downs, are uncommonly good and pleasant. The expence, including the postillions and other incidental things, does not amount to more than a shilling the swedish mile.[3]

The inns are tolerable; but not liking the rye bread, I found it necessary to furnish myself with some wheaten before I set out. The beds too were particularly disagreeable to me. It seemed to me that I was sinking into a grave when I entered them; for, immersed in down placed in a sort of box, I expected to be suffocated before morning. The sleeping between two down beds, they do so even in summer, must be very unwholesome during any season; and I cannot conceive how the people can bear it, especially as the summers are very warm. But warmth they seem not to feel; and, I should think, were afraid of the air, by always keeping their windows shut. In the winter, I am persuaded, I could not exist in rooms thus closed up, with stoves heated in their manner, for they only put wood into them twice a day; and, when the stove is thoroughly heated, they shut the flue, not admitting any air to renew its elasticity, even when the rooms are crowded with company. These stoves are made of earthenware, and often in a form that ornaments an apartment, which is never the case with the heavy iron ones I have seen elsewhere. Stoves may be economical; but I like a fire, a wood one, in preference; and I am convinced that the current of air which it attracts renders this the best mode of warming rooms.

We arrived early the second evening at a little village called Quistram, where we had determined to pass the night; having been informed that we should not afterwards find a tolerable inn until we reached Stromstad.

Advancing towards Quistram, as the sun was beginning to decline, I was particularly impressed by the beauty of the situation. The road was on the declivity of a rocky mountain, slightly covered with a mossy herbage and vagrant firs. At the bottom, a river, straggling amongst the recesses of stone, was hastening forward to the ocean and its grey rocks, of which we had a prospect on the left, whilst on the right it stole peacefully forward into the meadows, losing itself in a thickly wooded rising ground. As we drew near, the loveliest banks of wild flowers variegated the prospect, and promised to exhale odours to add to the sweetness of the air, the purity of which you could almost see, alas! not smell, for the putrifying herrings, which they use as manure, after the oil has been extracted, spread over the patches of earth, claimed by cultivation, destroyed every other.

It was intolerable, and entered with us into the inn, which was in other respects a charming retreat.

Whilst supper was preparing I crossed the bridge, and strolled by the river, listening to its murmurs. Approaching the bank, the beauty of which had attracted my attention in the carriage, I recognized many of my old acquaintance growing with great luxuriancy.[4]

Seated on it, I could not avoid noting an obvious remark. Sweden appeared to me the country in the world most proper to form the botanist and natural historian: every object seemed to remind me of the creation of things, of the first efforts of sportive nature. When a country arrives at a certain state of perfection, it looks as if it were made so; and curiosity is not excited. Besides, in social life too many objects occur for any to be distinctly observed by the generality of mankind; yet a contemplative man, or poet, in the country, I do not mean the country adjacent to cities, feels and sees what would escape vulgar eyes, and draws suitable inferences. This train of reflections might have led me further, in every sense of the word; but I could not escape from the detestable evaporation of the herrings, which poisoned all my pleasure.

After making a tolerable supper, for it is not easy to get fresh provisions on the road, I retired, to be lulled to sleep by the murmuring of a stream, of which I with great difficulty obtained sufficient to perform my daily ablutions.

The last battle between the Danes and Swedes,[5] which gave new life to their ancient enmity, was fought at this place 1788; only seventeen or eighteen were killed; for the great superiority of the Danes and Norwegians obliged the Swedes to submit; but sickness, and a scarcity of provisions, proved very fatal to their opponents, on their return.

It would be very easy to search for the particulars of this engagement in the publications of the day; but as this manner of filling my pages does not come within my plan, I probably should not have remarked that the battle was fought here, were it not to relate an anecdote which I had from good authority.

I noticed, when I first mentioned this place to you, that we descended a steep before we came to the inn; an immense ridge of rocks stretching out on one side. The inn was sheltered under them; and about a hundred yards from it was a bridge that crossed the river, whose murmurs I have celebrated; it was not fordable. The swedish general received orders to stop at the bridge, and dispute the passage; a most advantageous post for an army so much inferior in force: but the influence of beauty is not confined to courts. The mistress of the inn was handsome: when I saw her there were still some remains of beauty; and, to preserve her house, the general gave up the only tenable station. He was afterwards broke for contempt of orders.

Approaching the frontiers, consequently the sea, nature resumed an aspect ruder and ruder, or rather seemed the bones of the world waiting to be clothed with every thing necessary to give life and beauty. Still it was sublime.

The clouds caught their hue of the rocks that menaced them. The sun appeared afraid to shine, the birds ceased to sing, and the flowers to bloom; but the eagle fixed his nest high amongst the rocks, and the vulture hovered over this abode of desolation. The farm houses, in which only poverty resided, were formed of logs scarcely keeping off the cold and drifting snow; out of them the inhabitants seldom peeped, and the sports or prattling of children was neither seen nor heard. The current of life seemed congealed at the source: all were not frozen; for it was summer, you remember; but every thing appeared so dull, that I waited to see ice, in order to reconcile me to the absence of gaiety.

The day before, my attention had frequently been attracted by the wild beauties of the country we passed through.

The rocks which tossed their fantastic heads so high were often covered with pines and firs, varied in the most picturesque manner. Little woods filled up the recesses, when forests did not darken the scene; and vallies and glens, cleared of the trees, displayed a dazzling verdure which contrasted with the gloom of the shading pines. The eye stole into many a covert where tranquillity seemed to have taken up her abode, and the number of little lakes that continually presented themselves added to the peaceful composure of the scenery. The little cultivation which appeared did not break the enchantment, nor did castles rear their turrets aloft to crush the cottages, and prove that man is more savage than the natives of the woods. I heard of the bears, but never saw them stalk forth, which I was sorry for; I wished to have seen one in its wild state. In the winter, I am told, they sometimes catch a stray cow, which is a heavy loss to the owner.

The farms are small. Indeed most of the houses we saw on the road indicated poverty, or rather that the people could just live. Towards the frontiers they grew worse and worse in their appearance, as if not willing to put sterility itself out of countenance. No gardens smiled round the habitations, not a potatoe or cabbage to eat with the fish drying on a stick near the door. A little grain here and there appeared, the long stalks of which you might almost reckon. The day was gloomy when we passed over this rejected spot, the wind bleak, and winter seemed to be contending with nature, faintly struggling to change the season. Surely, thought I, if the sun ever shines here, it cannot warm these stones; moss only cleaves to them, partaking of their hardness; and nothing like vegetable life appears to chear with hope the heart.

So far from thinking that the primitive inhabitants of the world lived in a southern climate, where Paradise spontaneously arose, I am led to infer, from various circumstances, that the first dwelling of man happened to be a spot like this which led him to adore a sun so seldom seen; for this worship, which probably preceded that of demons or demi-gods, certainly never began in a southern climate, where the continual presence of the sun prevented its being considered as a good [god?]; or rather the want of it never being felt, this glorious luminary would carelessly have diffused its blessings without being hailed as a benefactor. Man must therefore have been placed in the north, to tempt him to run after the sun, in order that the different parts of the earth might be peopled.[6] Nor do I wonder that the hordes of barbarians always poured out of these regions to seek for milder climes, when nothing like cultivation attached them to the soil; especially when we take into the view that the adventuring spirit, common to man, is naturally stronger and more general during the infancy of society. The conduct of the followers of Mahomet,[7] and the crusaders, will sufficiently corroborate my assertion.

Approaching nearer to Stromstad, the appearance of the town proved to be quite in character with the country we had just passed through. I hesitated to use the word country, yet could not find another; still it would sound absurd to talk of fields of rocks.

The town was built on, and under them. Three or four weather-beaten trees were shrinking from the wind; and the grass grew so sparingly, that I could not avoid thinking Dr. Johnson's hyperbolical assertion "that the man merited well of his country who made a few blades of grass grow where they never grew before," might here have been uttered with strict propriety.[8] The steeple likewise towered aloft; for what is a church, even amongst the Lutherans, without a steeple? But to prevent mischief in such an exposed situation, it is wisely placed on a rock at some distance, not to endanger the roof of the church.

Rambling about, I saw the door open, and entered, when to my great surprise I found the clergyman reading prayers, with only the clerk attending. I instantly thought of Swift's "Dearly beloved Roger;"[9] but on enquiry I learnt that some one had died that morning, and in Sweden it is customary to pray for the dead.

The sun, who I suspected never dared to shine, began now to convince me that he came forth only to torment; for though the wind was still cutting, the rocks became intolerably warm under my feet; whilst the herring effluvia, which I before found so very offensive, once more assailed me. I hastened back to the house of a merchant, the little sovereign of the place, because he was by far the richest, though not the mayor.

Here we were most hospitably received, and introduced to a very fine and numerous family. I have before mentioned to you the lillies of the north, I might have added, water lillies, for the complexion of many, even of the young women seem to be bleached on the bosom of snow. But in this youthful circle the roses bloomed with all their wonted freshness, and I wondered from whence the fire was stolen which sparkled in their fine blue eyes.

Here we slept; and I rose early in the morning to prepare for my little voyage to Norway. I had determined to go by water, and was to leave my companions behind; but not getting a boat immediately, and the wind being high and unfavourable, I was told that it was not safe to go to sea during such boisterous weather; I was therefore obliged to wait for the morrow, and had the present day on my hands; which I feared would be irksome, because the family, who possessed about a dozen french words amongst them, and not an english phrase, were anxious to amuse me, and would not let me remain alone in my room. The town we had already walked round and round; and if we advanced farther on the coast, it was still to view the same unvaried immensity of water, surrounded by barrenness.

The gentleman wishing to peep into Norway, proposed going to Fredericshall, the first town, the distance was only three swedish miles. There, and back again, was but a day's journey, and would not, I thought, interfere with my voyage. I agreed, and invited the eldest and prettiest of the girls to accompany us. I invited her, because I liked to see a beautiful face animated by pleasure, and to have an opportunity of regarding the country, whilst the gentlemen were amusing themselves with her.

I did not know, for I had not thought of it, that we were to scale some of the most mountainous cliffs of Sweden, in our way to the ferry which separates the two countries.

Entering amongst the cliffs, we were sheltered from the wind; warm sun-beams began to play, streams to flow, and groves of pines diversified the rocks. Sometimes they became suddenly bare and sublime. Once, in particular, after mounting the most terrific precipice, we had to pass through a tremendous defile, where the closing chasm seemed to threaten us with instant destruction, when turning quickly, verdant meadows and a beautiful lake relieved and charmed my eyes.

I have never travelled through Switzerland; but one of my companions assured me, that I should not there find any thing superior, if equal to the wild grandeur of these views.

As we had not taken this excursion into our plan, the horses had not been previously ordered, which obliged us to wait two hours at the first post. The day was wearing away. The road was so bad, that walking up the precipices consumed the time insensibly. But as we desired horses at each post ready at a certain hour, we reckoned on returning more speedily.

We stopt to dine at a tolerable farm. They brought us out ham, butter, cheese, and milk; and the charge was so moderate, that I scattered a little money amongst the children who were peeping at us, in order to pay them for their trouble.

Arrived at the ferry, we were still detained; for the people who attend at the ferries have a stupid kind of sluggishness in their manner, which is very provoking when you are in haste. At present I did not feel it; for scrambling up the cliffs, my eye followed the river as it rolled between the grand rocky banks; and to complete the scenery, they were covered with firs and pines, through which the wind rustled, as if it were lulling itself to sleep with the declining sun.

Behold us now in Norway; and I could not avoid feeling surprise at observing the difference in the manners of the inhabitants of the two sides of the river; for every thing shews that the norwegians are more indus- trious and more opulent. The Swedes, for neighbours are seldom the best friends, accuse the norwegians of knavery, and they retaliate by bringing a charge of hypocrisy against the Swedes. Local circumstances probably render both unjust, speaking from their feelings, rather than reason: and is this astonishing when we consider that most writers of travels have done the same, whose works have served as materials for the compilers of universal histories. All are eager to give a national character; which is rarely just, because they do not discriminate the natural from the acquired difference. The natural, I believe, on due consideration, will be found to consist merely in the degree of vivacity or thoughtfulness, pleasure, or pain, inspired by the climate, whilst the varieties which the forms of government, including religion, produce, are much more numerous and unstable.

A people have been characterized as stupid by nature; what a paradox! because they did not consider that slaves, having no object to stimulate industry, have not their faculties sharpened by the only thing that can exercise them, self-interest. Others have been brought forward as brutes, having no aptitude for the arts and sciences, only because the progress of improvement had not reached that stage which produces them.

Those writers who have considered the history of man, or of the human mind, on a more enlarged scale, have fallen into similar errors, not reflecting that the passions are weak where the necessaries of life are too hardly or too easily obtained.

Travellers who require that every nation should resemble their native country, had better stay at home. It is, for example, absurd to blame a people for not having that degree of personal cleanliness and elegance of manners which only refinement of taste produces, and will produce every where in proportion as society attains a general polish. The most essential service, I presume, that authors could render to society, would be to promote inquiry and discussion, instead of making those dogmatical assertions which only appear calculated to gird the human mind round with imaginary circles, like the paper globe which represents the one he inhabits.

This spirit of inquiry is the characteristic of the present century, from which the succeeding will, I am persuaded, receive a great accumulation of knowledge; and doubtless its diffusion will in a great measure destroy the factitious national characters which have been supposed permanent, though only rendered so by the permanency of ignorance.

Arriving at Fredericshall, at the siege of which Charles XII.[10] lost his life, we had only time to take a transient view of it, whilst they were preparing us some refreshment.

Poor Charles! I thought of him with respect. I have always felt the same for Alexander;[11] with whom he has been classed as a madman, by several writers, who have reasoned superficially, confounding the morals of the day with the few grand principles on which unchangeable morality rests. Making no allowance for the ignorance and prejudices of the period, they do not perceive how much they themselves are indebted to general improvement for the acquirements, and even the virtues, which they would not have had the force of mind to attain, by their individual exertions in a less advanced state of society.

The evening was fine, as is usual at this season; and the refreshing odour of the pine woods became more perceptible; for it was nine o'clock when we left Fredericshall. At the ferry we were detained by a dispute relative to our swedish passport, which we did not think of getting countersigned in Norway. Midnight was coming on; yet it might with such propriety have been termed the noon of night, that had Young[12] ever travelled towards the north, I should not have wondered at his becoming enamoured of the moon. But it is not the queen of night alone who reigns here in all her splendor, though the sun, loitering just below the horizon, decks her with a golden tinge from his car, illuminating the cliffs that hide him; the heavens also, of a clear softened blue, throw her forward, and the evening star appears a lesser moon to the naked eye. The huge shadows of the rocks, fringed with firs, concentrating the views, without darkening them, excited that tender melancholy which, sublimating the imagination, exalts, rather than depresses the mind.

My companions fell asleep:—fortunately they did not snore; and I contemplated, fearless of idle questions, a night such as I had never before seen or felt to charm the senses, and calm the heart. The very air was balmy, as it freshened into morn, producing the most voluptuous sensations. A vague pleasurable sentiment absorbed me, as I opened my bosom to the embraces of nature; and my soul rose to its author, with the chirping of the solitary birds, which began to feel, rather than see, advancing day. I had leisure to mark its progress. The grey morn, streaked with silvery rays, ushered in the orient beams,—how beautifully varying into purple!—yet, I was sorry to lose the soft watry clouds which preceded them, exciting a kind of expectation that made me almost afraid to breathe, lest I should break the charm. I saw the sun—and sighed.

One of my companions, now awake, perceiving that the postillion had mistaken the road, began to swear at him, and roused the other two, who reluctantly shook off sleep.

We had immediately to measure back our steps, and did not reach Stromstad before five in the morning.

The wind had changed in the night, and my boat was ready.

A dish of coffee, and fresh linen [i.e., undergarments], recruited my spirits; and I directly set out again for Norway; purposing to land much higher up the coast.

Wrapping my great coat round me, I lay down on some sails at the bottom of the boat, its motion rocking me to rest, till a discourteous wave interrupted my slumbers, and obliged me to rise and feel a solitariness which was not so soothing as that of the past night.

Adieu!

LETTER VI.

The sea was boisterous; but, as I had an experienced pilot, I did not apprehend any danger. Sometimes I was told, boats are driven far out and lost. However, I seldom calculate chances so nicely—sufficient for the day is the obvious evil!

We had to steer amongst islands and huge rocks, rarely losing sight of the shore, though it now and then appeared only a mist that bordered the water's edge. The pilot assured me that the numerous harbours on the Norway coast were very safe, and the pilot-boats were always on the watch. The Swedish side is very dangerous, I am also informed; and the help of experience is not often at hand, to enable strange vessels to steer clear of the rocks, which lurk below the water, close to the shore.

There are no tides here, nor in the cattegate;[13] and, what appeared to me a consequence, no sandy beach. Perhaps this observation has been made before; but it did not occur to me till I saw the waves continually beating against the bare rocks, without ever receding to leave a sediment to harden.

The wind was fair, till we had to tack about in order to enter Laurvig, where we arrived towards three o'clock in the afternoon. It is a clean, pleasant town, with a considerable iron-work, which gives life to it.

As the norwegians do not frequently see travellers, they are very curious to know their business, and who they are—so curious that I was half tempted to adopt Dr. Franklin's[14] plan, when travelling in America, where they are equally prying, which was to write on a paper, for public inspection, my name, from whence I came, where I was going, and what was my business. But if I were importuned by their curiosity, their friendly gestures gratified me. A woman, coming alone, interested them. And I know not whether my weariness gave me a look of peculiar delicacy; but they approached to assist me, and enquire after my wants, as if they were afraid to hurt, and wished to protect me. The sympathy I inspired, thus dropping down from the clouds in a strange land, affected me more than it would have done, had not my spirits been harrassed by various causes— by much thinking—musing almost to madness—and even by a sort of weak melancholy that hung about my heart at parting with my daughter for the first time.

You know that as a female I am particularly attached to her—I feel more than a mother's fondness and anxiety, when I reflect on the dependent and oppressed state of her sex. I dread lest she should be forced to sacrifice her heart to her principles, or principles to her heart. With trembling hand I shall cultivate sensibility, and cherish delicacy of sentiment, lest, whilst I lend fresh blushes to the rose, I sharpen the thorns that will wound the breast I would fain guard—I dread to unfold her mind, lest it should render her unfit for the world she is to inhabit—Hapless woman! what a fate is thine!

But whither am I wandering? I only meant to tell you that the impression the kindness of the simple people made visible on my countenance increased my sensibility to a painful degree. I wished to have had a room to myself; for their attention, and rather distressing observation, embarrassed me extremely. Yet, as they would bring me eggs, and make my coffee, I found I could not leave them without hurting their feelings of hospitality.

It is customary here for the host and hostess to welcome their guests as master and mistress of the house.

My clothes, in their turn, attracted the attention of the females; and I could not help thinking of the foolish vanity which makes many women so proud of the observation of strangers as to take wonder very gratuitously for admiration. This error they are very apt to fall into; when arrived in a foreign country, the populace stare at them as they pass: yet the make of a cap, or the singularity of a gown, is often the cause of the flattering attention, which afterwards supports a fantastic superstructure of self-conceit.

Not having brought a carriage over with me, expecting to have met a person where I landed, who was immediately to have procured me one, I was detained whilst the good people of the inn sent round to all their acquaintance to search for a vehicle. A rude sort of *cabriole* [i.e., cabriolet] was at last found, and a driver half drunk, who was not less eager to make a good bargain on that account. I had a danish captain of a ship and his mate with me: the former was to ride on horseback, at which he was not very expert, and the latter to partake of my seat. The driver mounted behind to guide the horses, and flourish the whip over our shoulders; he would not suffer the reins out of his own hands. There was something so grotesque in our appearance, that I could not avoid shrinking into myself when I saw a gentleman-like man in the group which crowded round the door to observe us. I could have broken the driver's whip for cracking to call the women and children together; but seeing a significant smile on the face, I had before remarked, I burst into a laugh, to allow him to do so too,—and away we flew. This is not a flourish of the pen; for we actually went on full gallop a long time, the horses being very good; indeed I have never met with better, if so good, post-horses, as in Norway; they are of a stouter make than the english horses, appear to be well fed, and are not easily tired.

I had to pass over, I was informed, the most fertile and best cultivated tract of country in Norway. The distance was three norwegian miles, which are longer than the swedish. The roads were very good; the farmers are obliged to repair them; and we scampered through a great extent of country in a more improved state than any I had viewed since I left England. Still there was sufficient of hills, dales, and rocks, to prevent the idea of a plain from entering the head, or even of such scenery as England and France afford. The prospects were also embellished by water, rivers, and lakes, before the sea proudly claimed my regard; and the road running frequently through lofty groves, rendered the landscapes beautiful, though they were not so romantic as those I had lately seen with such delight.

It was late when I reached Tonsberg; and I was glad to go to bed at a decent inn. The next morning, the 17th of July, conversing with the gentleman with whom I had business to transact, I found that I should be detained at Tonsberg three weeks; and I lamented that I had not brought my child with me.

The inn was quiet, and my room so pleasant, commanding a view of the sea, confined by an amphitheatre of hanging woods, that I wished to remain there, though no one in the house could speak english or french. The mayor, my friend, however, sent a young woman to me who spoke a little english, and she agreed to call on me twice a day, to receive my orders, and translate them to my hostess.

My not understanding the language was an excellent pretext for dining alone, which I prevailed on them to let me do at a late hour; for the early dinners in Sweden had entirely deranged my day. I could not alter it there, without disturbing the economy of a family where I was a visitor; necessity having forced me to accept of an invitation from a private family, the lodgings were so incommodious.

Amongst the norwegians I had the arrangement of my own time; and I determined to regulate it in such a manner, that I might enjoy as much of their sweet summer as I possibly could;—short, it is true; but "passing sweet."[15]

I never endured a winter in this rude clime; consequently it was not the contrast, but the real beauty of the season which made the present summer appear to me the finest I had ever seen. Sheltered from the north and eastern winds, nothing can exceed the salubrity, the soft freshness of the western gales. In the evening they also die away; the aspen leaves tremble into stillness, and reposing nature seems to be warmed by the moon, which here assumes a genial aspect: and if a light shower has chanced to fall with the sun, the juniper the underwood of the forest, exhales a wild perfume, mixed with a thousand nameless sweets, that, soothing the heart, leave images in the memory which the imagination will ever hold dear.

Nature is the nurse of sentiment,—the true source of taste;—yet what misery, as well as rapture, is produced by a quick perception of the beautiful and sublime, when it is exercised in observing animated nature, when every beauteous feeling and emotion excites responsive sympathy, and the harmonized soul sinks into melancholy, or rises to extasy, just as the chords are touched, like the æolian harp agitated by the changing wind. But how dangerous is it to foster these sentiments in such an imperfect state of existence; and how difficult to eradicate them when an affection for mankind, a passion for an individual, is but the unfolding of that love which embraces all that is great and beautiful.

When a warm heart has received strong impressions, they are not to be effaced. Emotions become sentiments; and the imagination renders even transient sensations permanent, by fondly retracing them. I cannot, without a thrill of delight, recollect views I have seen, which are not to be forgotten,—nor looks I have felt in every nerve which I shall never more meet. The grave has closed over a dear friend, the friend of my youth;[16] still she is present with me, and I hear her soft voice warbling as I stray over the heath. Fate has separated me from another, the fire of whose eyes, tempered by infantine tenderness, still warms my breast; even when gazing on these tremendous cliffs, sublime emotions absorb my soul. And, smile not, if I add, that the rosy tint of morning reminds me of a suffusion, which will never more charm my senses, unless it reappears on the cheeks of my child. Her sweet blushes I may yet hide in my bosom, and she is still to young to ask why starts the tear, so near akin to pleasure and pain?

I cannot write any more at present. Tomorrow we will talk of Tonsberg.

LETTER VII.

Though the king of Denmark be an absolute monarch, yet the norwegians appear to enjoy all the blessings of freedom. Norway may be termed a sister kingdom; but the people have no viceroy to lord it over them, and fatten his dependants with the fruit of their labour.

There are only two counts in the whole country, who have estates, and exact some feudal observances from their tenantry. All the rest of the country is divided into small farms, which belong to the cultivator. It is true, some few, appertaining to the church, are let; but always on a lease for life, generally renewed in favour of the eldest son, who has this advantage, as well as a right to a double portion of the property. But the value of the farm is estimated; and after his portion is assigned to him, he must be answerable for the residue to the remaining part of the family.

Every farmer, for ten years, is obliged to attend annually about twelve days, to learn the military exercise; but it is always at a small distance from his dwelling, and does not lead him into any new habits of life.

There are about six thousand regulars also, garrisoned at Christiania and Fredericshall, which are equally reserved, with the militia, for the defence of their own country. So that when the prince royal[17] passed into Sweden, in 1788, he was obliged to request, not command, them to accompany him on this expedition.

These corps are mostly composed of the sons of the cottagers, who being labourers on the farms, are allowed a few acres to cultivate for themselves. These men voluntarily enlist; but it is only for a limited period, (six years) at the expiration of which they have the liberty of retiring. The pay is only two-pence a day, and bread; still, considering the cheapness of the country, it is more than sixpence in England.

The distribution of landed property into small farms, produces a degree of equality which I have seldom seen elsewhere; and the rich being all merchants, who are obliged to divide their personal fortune amongst their children, the boys always receiving twice as much as the girls, property has not a chance of accumulating till overgrown wealth destroys the balance of liberty.

You will be surprised to hear me talk of liberty; yet the norwegians appear to me to be the most free community I have ever observed.

The mayor of each town or district, and the judges in the country, exercise an authority almost patriarchal. They can do much good, but little harm, as every individual can appeal from their judgment: and as they may always be forced to give a reason for their conduct, it is generally regulated by prudence. 'They have not time to learn to be tyrants,' said a gentleman to me, with whom I discussed the subject.

The farmers not fearing to be turned out of their farms, should they displease a man in power, and having no vote to be commanded at an election for a mock representative, are a manly race; for not being obliged to submit to any debasing tenure, in order to live, or advance themselves in the world, they act with an independent spirit. I never yet have heard of any thing like domineering, or oppression, excepting such as has arisen from natural causes. The freedom the people enjoy may, perhaps, render them a little litigious, and subject them to the impositions of cunning practitioners of the law; but the authority of office is bounded, and the emoluments of it do not destroy its utility.

Last year a man, who had abused his power, was cashiered, on the representation of the people to the bailiff of the district.

There are four in Norway, who might with propriety be termed sheriffs; and, from their sentence, an appeal, by either party, may be made to Copenhagen.

Near most of the towns are commons, on which the cows of all the inhabitants, indiscriminately, are allowed to graze. The poor, to whom a cow is necessary, are almost supported by it. Besides, to render living more easy, they all go out to fish in their own boats; and fish is their principal food.

The lower class of people in the towns are in general sailors; and the industrious have usually little ventures of their own that serve to render the winter comfortable.[18]

With respect to the country at large, the importation is considerably in favour of Norway.

They are forbidden, at present, to export corn or rye, on account of the advanced price.

The restriction which most resembles the painful subordination of Ireland, is that vessels, trading to the West Indies, are obliged to pass by their own ports, and unload their cargoes at Copenhagen, which they afterwards re-ship. The duty [i.e., tax] is indeed inconsiderable; but the navigation being dangerous, they run a double risk.

There is an excise on all articles of consumption brought to the towns; but the officers are not strict; and it would be reckoned invidious to enter a house to search, as in England.

The norwegians appear to me a sensible, shrewd people, with little scientific knowledge, and still less taste for literature: but they are arriving at the epoch which precedes the introduction of the arts and sciences.

Most of the towns are sea-ports, and sea-ports are not favourable to improvement. The captains acquire a little superficial knowledge by travelling, which their indefatigable attention to the making of money prevents their digesting; and the fortune that they thus laboriously acquire, is spent, as it usually is in towns of this description, in shew and good living. They love their country, but have not much public spirit.[19] Their exertions are, generally speaking, only for their families; which I conceive will always be the case, till politics, becoming a subject of discussion, enlarges the heart by opening the understanding. The french revolution will have this effect. They sing at present, with great glee, many republican songs, and seem earnestly to wish that the republic may stand; yet they appear very much attached to their prince royal; and, as far as rumour can give an idea of a character, he appears to merit their attachment. When I am at Copenhagen, I shall be able to ascertain on what foundation their good opinion is built; at present I am only the echo of it.

In the year 1788 he traveled through Norway; and acts of mercy gave dignity to the parade, and interest to the joy, his presence inspired. At this town he pardoned a girl condemned to die for murdering an illegitimate child, a crime seldom committed in this country. She is since married, and become the careful mother of a family. This might be given as an instance, that a desperate act is not always a proof of an incorrigible depravity of character; the only plausible excuse that has been brought forward to justify the infliction of capital punishments.

I will relate two or three other anecdotes to you; for the truth of which I will not vouch, because the facts were not of sufficient consequence for me to take much pains to ascertain them; and, true or false, they evince that the people like to make a kind of mistress of their prince.

An officer, mortally wounded at the ill-advised battle of Quistram,[20] desired to speak with the prince; and, with his dying breath, earnestly recommended to his care a young woman of Christiania, to whom he was engaged. When the prince returned there, a ball was given by the chief inhabitants. He inquired whether this unfortunate girl was invited, and requested that she might, though of the second class. The girl came; she was pretty; and finding herself amongst her superiors, bashfully sat down as near the door as possible, nobody taking notice of her. Shortly after, the prince entering, immediately inquired for her, and asked her to dance, to the mortification of the rich dames. After it was over he handed her to the top of the room, and placing himself by her, spoke of the loss she had sustained, with tenderness, promising to provide for any one she should marry,—as the story goes. She is since married, and he has not forgotten his promise.

A little girl, during the same expedition, in Sweden, who informed him that the logs of a bridge were cut underneath, was taken by his orders to Christiania, and put to school at his expence.

Before I retail other beneficial effects of his journey, it is necessary to inform you that the laws here are mild, and do not punish capitally for any crime but murder, which seldom occurs. Every other offence merely subjects the delinquent to imprisonment and labour in the castle, or rather arsenal, at Christiania, and the fortress at Fredericshall. The first and second conviction produces a sentence for a limited number of years,—two, three, five, or seven, proportioned to the atrocity of the crime. After the third he is whipped, branded in the forehead, and condemned to perpetual slavery. This is the ordinary march of justice. For some flagrant breaches of trust, or acts of wanton cruelty, criminals have been condemned to slavery for life, the first time of conviction, but not frequently. The number of these slaves do not, I am informed, amount to more than an hundred, which is not considerable, compared with the population, upwards of eight hundred thousand. Should I pass through Christiania, on my return to Gothenburg, I shall probably have an opportunity of learning other particulars.

There is also a house of correction at Christiania for trifling misdemeanors, where the women are confined to labour and imprisonment even for life. The state of the prisoners was represented to the prince; in consequence of which, he visited the arsenal and house of correction. The slaves at the arsenal were loaded with irons of a great weight; he ordered them to be lightened as much as possible.

The people in the house of correction were commanded not to speak to him; but four women, condemned to remain there for life, got into the passage, and fell at his feet. He granted them a pardon; and inquiring respecting the treatment of the prisoners, he was informed that they were frequently whipt going in, and coming out; and for any fault, at the discretion of the inspectors. This custom he humanely abolished; though some of the principal inhabitants, whose situation in life had raised them above the temptation of stealing, were of opinion that these chastisements were necessary and wholesome.

In short, every thing seems to announce that the prince really cherishes the laudable ambition of fulfilling the duties of his station. This ambition is cherished and directed by the count Bernstorf, the prime minister of Denmark, who is universally celebrated for his abilities and virtue. The happiness of the people is a substantial eulogium; and, from all I can gather, the inhabitants of Denmark and Norway are the least oppressed people of Europe. The press is free. They translate any of the french publications of the day, deliver their opinion on the subject, and discuss those it leads to with great freedom, and without fearing to displease the government.

On the subject of religion they are likewise becoming tolerant, at least, and perhaps have advanced a step further in free-thinking. One writer has ventured to deny the divinity of Jesus Christ, and to question the necessity or utility of the christian system, without being considered universally as a monster, which would have been the case a few years ago. They have translated many german works on education; and though they have not adopted any of their plans, it is become a subject of discussion. There are some grammar and free schools; but, from what I hear, not very good ones. All the children learn to read, write, and cast accounts, for the purposes of common life. They have no university; and nothing that deserves the name of science is taught; nor do individuals, by pursuing any branch of knowledge, excite a degree of curiosity which is the forerunner of improvement. Knowledge is not absolutely necessary to enable a considerable portion of the community to live; and, till it is, I fear, it never becomes general.

In this country, where minerals abound, there is not one collection: and, in all probability, I venture a conjecture, the want of mechanical and chemical knowledge renders the silver mines unproductive; for the quantity of silver obtained every year is not sufficient to defray the expences. It has been urged, that the employment of such a number of hands is very beneficial. But a positive loss is never to be done away; and the men, thus employed, would naturally find some other means of living, instead of being thus a dead weight on government, or rather on the community from whom its revenue is drawn.

About three english miles from Tonsberg there is a salt work, belonging, like all their establishments, to government, in which they employ above an hundred and fifty men, and maintain nearly five hundred people, who earn their living. The clear profit, an increasing one, amounts to two thousand pounds sterling. And as the eldest son of the inspector, an ingenious young man, has been sent by the government to travel, and acquire some mathematical and chemical knowledge in Germany, it has a chance of being improved. He is the only person I have met with here, who appears to have a scientific turn of mind. I do not mean to assert that I have not met with others, who have a spirit of inquiry.

The salt-works at St. Ubes are basons in the sand, and the sun produces the evaporation: but here there is no beach. Besides, the heat of summer is so short-lived, that it would be idle to contrive machines for such an inconsiderable portion of the year. They therefore always use fires; and the whole establishment appears to be regulated with judgment.

The situation is well chosen and beautiful. I do not find, from the observation of a person who has resided here for forty years, that the sea advances or recedes on this coast.

I have already remarked, that little attention is paid to education, excepting reading, writing, and the rudiments of arithmetic; I ought to have added, that a catechism is carefully taught, and the children obliged to read in the churches, before the congregation, to prove that they are not neglected.

Degrees, to enable any one to practise any profession, must be taken at Copenhagen; and the people of this country, having the good sense to perceive that men who are to live in a community should at least acquire the elements of their knowledge, and form their youthful attachments there, are seriously endeavouring to establish an university in Norway. And Tonsberg, as a centrical place in the best part of the country, had the most suffrages; for, experiencing the bad effects of a metropolis, they have determined not to have it in or near Christiania. Should such an establishment take place, it will promote inquiry throughout the country, and give a new face to society. Premiums have been offered, and prize questions written, which I am told have merit. The building college-halls, and other appendages of the seat of science, might enable Tonsberg to recover its pristine consequence; for it is one of the most ancient towns of Norway, and once contained nine churches. At present there are only two. One is a very old structure, and has a gothic respectability about it, which scarcely amounts to grandeur, because, to render a gothic pile grand, it must have a huge unwieldiness of appearance. The chapel of Windsor may be an exception to this rule; I mean before it was in its present *nice, clean* state. When I first saw it, the pillars within had acquired, by time, a sombre hue, which accorded with the architecture; and the gloom increased its dimensions to the eye by hiding its parts; but now it all bursts on the view at once; and the sublimity has vanished before the brush and broom; for it has been white-washed and scraped till it is become as bright and neat as the pots and pans in a notable house-wife's kitchen—yes; the very spurs on the recumbent knights were deprived of their venerable rust, to give a striking proof that a love of order in trifles, and taste for proportion and arrangement, are very distinct. The glare of light thus introduced, entirely destroys the sentiment these piles are calculated to inspire; so that, when I heard something like a jig from the organ-loft, I thought it an excellent hall for dancing or feasting. The measured pace of thought with which I had entered the cathedral, changed into a trip; and I bounded on the terrace, to see the royal family, with a number of ridiculous images in my head, that I shall not now recall.

The norwegians are fond of music; and every little church has an organ. In the church I have mentioned, there is an inscription importing that a king,[21] James the sixth, of Scotland, and first of England, who came with more than princely gallantry, to escort his bride home, stood there, and heard divine service.

There is a little recess full of coffins, which contains bodies embalmed long since—so long, that there is not even a tradition to lead to a guess at their names.

A desire of preserving the body seems to have prevailed in most countries of the world, futile as it is to term it a preservation, when the noblest parts are immediately sacrificed merely to save the muscles, skin and bone from rottenness. When I was shewn these human petrifactions, I shrunk back with disgust and horror. "Ashes to ashes!" thought I—"Dust to dust!"—If this be not dissolution, it is something worse than natural decay—It is treason against humanity, thus to lift up the awful veil which would fain hide its weakness. The grandeur of the active principle is never more strongly felt than at such a sight; for nothing is so ugly as the human form when deprived of life, and thus dried into stone, merely to preserve the most disgusting image of death. The contemplation of noble ruins produces a melancholy that exalts the mind.—We take a retrospect of the exertions of man, the fate of empires and their rulers; and marking the grand destruction of ages, it seems the necessary change of time leading to improvement.—Our very soul expands, and we forget our littleness; how painfully brought to our recollection by such vain attempts to snatch from decay what is destined so soon to perish. Life, what art thou? Where goes this breath? this *I*, so much alive? In what element will it mix, giving or receiving fresh energy?—What will break the enchantment of animation?—For worlds, I would not see a form I loved—embalmed in my heart—thus sacrilegiously handled! Pugh! my stomach turns.—Is this all the distinction of the rich in the grave?—They had better quietly allow the scythe of equality to mow them down with the common mass, than struggle to become a monument of the instability of human greatness.

The teeth, nails and skin were whole, without appearing black like the Egyptian mummies; and some silk, in which they had been wrapt, still preserved its colour, pink, with tolerable freshness.

I could not learn how long the bodies had been in this state, in which they bid fair to remain till the day of judgment, if there is to be such a day; and before that time, it will require some trouble to make them fit to appear in company with angels, without disgracing humanity.—God bless you! I feel a conviction that we have some perfectible principle in our present vestment, which will not be destroyed just as we begin to be sensible of improvement; and I care not what habit it next puts on, sure that it will be wisely formed to suit a higher state of existence. Thinking of death makes us tenderly cling to our affections—with more than usual tenderness, I therefore assure you that I am your's, wishing that the temporary death of absence may not endure longer than is absolutely necessary.

Notes

1. Fanny Imlay.

2. Large horses like those requisitioned for battle were generally unsuitable for drawing a carriage.

3. A swedish mile is nearly six English miles [Wollstonecraft].

4. The wild pansies, commonly called "heart's ease," which Wollstonecraft first mentioned in Letter I.

5. The two countries had been warring as members of various alliances off and on for many years. They signed an armistice in August 1788.

6. Poston notes that Wollstonecraft is here speculating on the origin of civilization based on sun worship, which Wollstonecraft claims preceded worship of the gods (44).

7. Muhammad (ca. 570–632), Arabian prophet and founder of the Moslem religion.

8. Samuel Johnson (1709–1784), English essayist, letter writer, and poet.

9. Jonathan Swift (1667–1745), English clergyman, poet, political writer, and satirist. Roger was at one time Swift's clerk.

10. Ruled Sweden from 1697 to 1718.

11. Alexander the Great (356–323 B.C.), king of Macedonia; military conqueror who forcibly spread Greek culture from Asia Minor to Egypt and India.

12. Edward Young (1683–1765), English poet; *The Complaint; or, Night Thoughts on Life, Death and Immortality* (1742–1746) is his best-known work.

13. Kattegat, the channel or inlet between Sweden and Denmark.

14. Benjamin Franklin (1706–1790), American diplomat, inventor, and author.

15. Allusion to William Cowper's poem "Retirement."

16. Fanny Blood, Wollstonecraft's dear friend from youth who died in childbirth in 1785.

17. The crown prince, future Frederick VI (1768–1839).

18 As Wollstonecraft suggests in Letter I, smuggling may have been among the sailors' other "ventures."

19. The grand virtues of the heart particularly the enlarged humanity which extends to the whole human race, depend more on the understanding, I believe, than is generally imagined [Wollstonecraft].

20. See note 5.

21. "Anno 1589, St. Martin's Day, which was the 11th Day of November, on a Tuesday, came the high-born Prince and Lord Jacob Stuart, King in Scotland, to this Town, and the 25th Sunday after Trinity (Sunday:) which was the 16th Day of November, stood his Grace in this Pew, and heard Scotch Preaching from the 23d Psalm, 'The Lord is my Shepherd,' &c. which M. David Lentz, Preacher in Lith, then preached between 10 and 12."

The above is an inscription which stands in St. Mary's church, in Tonsberg.

It is known that king James the sixth went to Norway, to marry princess Anna, the daughter of Frederick the second, and sister to Christian the fourth; and that the wedding was performed at Opslo (now Christiania), where the princess, by contrary winds, was detained; but that the king, during this voyage, was at Tonsberg, nobody would have known, if an inscription, in remembrance of it, had not been placed in this church [Wollstonecraft].

Mary Robinson

1758–1800

Memoirs of the Late Mrs. Robinson, written by herself. With some posthumous pieces. 4 vols. London: R. Philips, 1801.

Mary Darby Robinson first opened her eyes to "a world of duplicity and sorrow" in a gloomy mansion on College-Green, Bristol, 27 November 1758. Her mother, Hester, was the grandchild of Catherine Seys, co-heiress of Richard Seys, Esq., of Boverton Castle in Glamorganshire. Family ties on her mother's side also included John Locke and a grandmother who was a botanist and village "doctress."

Her father, Nicholas Darby, born in America of Irish descent, was a prosperous merchant in Bristol who threw caution aside and left his family to sail for America, establish a whale fishery on the coast of Labrador, "civilize" the Eskimo Indians, and employ them in the fishery. Darby's schemes failed. The Indians engaged in a bloody uprising, and he lost all his fortune. He sold the family residence and forced his wife and children to exchange a comfortable existence for near poverty. For Hester Darby the losses were compounded: shortly after learning that her husband was living with a mistress in America, she lost her six-year-old son to a deadly case of the measles. Despite Darby's demand—on taking leave of his family for America once again—that his wife "Take care that no dishonour falls upon my daughter," Mary became interested in the theater, a profession in which the public perceived actresses in the same light as prostitutes. Encouraged by Mrs. Hervey, her governess, and Mr. Hussey, her ballet master, she was presented to Thomas Hull, a Covent Garden actor and writer, and David Garrick, an actor and playwright and the manager of Drury Lane Theatre. Garrick was so impressed with the young woman's talent that he agreed to play opposite her when she debuted. In the whirl of preparing for a theater career, Mary met Thomas Robinson, who, though he wished to marry her, objected to her appearing on the stage—out of fear, he said, for her reputation. Mary's theatrical debut was put off indefinitely, and the two were married in 1773, when she was only sixteen.

Their first daughter, Maria, was born a year and a half later. Thomas Robinson had won Mary under false pretences. She soon discovered that he was the illegitimate son of the man he claimed was his uncle and that he was deeply in debt. When the "handsome fortune" that he was awaiting failed to materialize, Robinson was remanded to Fleet Prison for failure to pay his debts. Mary stayed with him for the duration. It was during this time that she determined to support her family by taking up the acting career she had earlier abandoned.

By this time Robinson had no objection to her supporting him, and Mary entered upon a successful stage career, performing more than twenty-five different character roles, including Statira in Nathaniel Lee's *Alexander the Great,* Amanda in Richard Brinsley Sheridan's *A Trip to Scarborough,* Fanny in George Colman and David Garrick's *The Clandestine Marriage,* and the ill-fated performance of Perdita in *The Winter's Tale.* It was at this time that the Prince of Wales, the eldest son of King George III and one of her many admirers, became enamored of her and proposed that she become his mistress. They exchanged passionate letters in the guise of Perdita and Florizel, the betrothed *Winter's Tale* lovers, and the brief, yearlong affair began.

Having divorced her husband and given up a successful acting career, Mary was devastated when the prince ended their affair. Furthermore, although she had expected a settlement from him when she became the royal mistress, only after repeated appeals did she receive a payment of £5000 in 1781. This affair and its breakup are the matter of the following excerpt. This is the episode in her life for which Robinson is most ill-famed.

While Robinson left readers of the *Memoirs* with a picture of herself as victim, and "the portrayal of Robinson by the press ranged from idolatrous to vicious, she seems always to have situated herself at the center of a stable circle of friends" (Pascoe, "Spectacular" 167–168). The philosopher William Godwin, feminist Mary Wollstonecraft, playwright Richard Brinsley Sheridan, novelist Eliza Fenwick, poets Robert Southey and Samuel Taylor Coleridge, political writer Edmund Burke, and numerous other major and minor literary and political figures were her correspondents and intimates. She maintained a high profile in London society; dressed in "a blue great coat prettily trimmed with silver, a plume of feathers" gracing her hat, she traveled the city in an impressive carriage, the keeping of which cost her £200 of her annual income of £500 (Pascoe 167). She was painted by leading artists Sir Joshua Reynolds, George Romney, and

Mary Robinson, painting by Sir Joshua Reynolds, 1784. By permission of the British Library.

Thomas Gainsborough, and she was known to have had affairs with political figures Lord Malden, Charles James Fox, and Banastre Tarleton. Wordsworth saw her as "mark'd by unexampled grace," "unsoiled" by her "public notice" (qtd. in Kramer 625). She was labeled "tragic actress," "beautiful whore," "transcendent muse," and, finally, "novelist of sensibility" (Ty, "Engendering" 412).

The image of the "beautiful whore" kept Robinson's *Memoirs* in wide circulation; the "novelist of sensibility" designation has been brought to the fore in more recent scholarship. She published her first book, *Poems by Mrs. Robinson,* in 1775, and in the twenty years following her affair with the prince she wrote six volumes of poetry, eight novels, two plays, and a pamphlet on women's rights. Robinson was extremely productive the last few years of her life. Her poem "Sappho and Phaon" (1796) is now considered "a central document in the poetry of sensibility" (McGann 55); her *Letter to the Women of England, on the Injustice of Mental Subordination* (1799) "represents a significant step toward the compilation of a women's literary history, an alternative form of legitimatizing identification" (Setzer, "Romancing" 531); and her articles in the *Monthly Magazine* and the *Morning Post* somewhat rescued her reputation from the stings of cartoon, caricature, satire, and gossip (see Ty, "Engendering" 426–427).

One of her last works, written for the *Post* in 1799–1800, was *The Sylphid*, a collection of fourteen editorial pieces that were later republished as volume three of the first edition of the *Memoirs*. *The Sylphid* relates Robinson's "most searing anecdotes and observations not as particular episodes within the narrative of her own life, but as generalized, satiric sketches drawn from the elevated perspective of a fictitious aerial being." They are "clearly in keeping with Robinson's original title for the *Memoirs:* 'Anecdotes of Distinguished Personages and Observations on Society and Manners during her Travels on the Continent and in England' " (Setzer, "Sylphid" 502).

These *chroniques scandaleuses,* or scandalous memoirs, as Robinson's *Memoirs* is often labeled, then, contain scandals other than her own, give readers a firsthand account of late eighteenth-century London society, and offer insight into her many talents as a writer. Robinson died the day after Christmas in 1800 and was buried at Old Windsor.

TEXT: Mary Robinson's *Memoirs* was first published in four volumes by R. Philips in 1801. It was edited by Robinson's daughter, Maria Elizabeth Robinson, who added some of her mother's poems to the second volume. There is disagreement as to who decided to include *The Sylphid* in the *Memoirs*. M. J. Levy, the most recent editor of the Robinson *Memoirs* (London and Chester Springs, Penn: Peter Owen Dufour, 1994) attributes the decision to the daughter; Setzer argues that Robinson herself made the decision ("Sylphid" 502). We are indebted to the University of Delaware for making this text available. The excerpt is from volume two, pages 59–85.

AT LENGTH an evening was fixed for this long dreaded interview. Lord Malden[1] and myself dined at the inn on the island between Kew and Brentford. We waited the signal for crossing the river in a boat which had been engaged for the purpose. Heaven can witness how many conflicts my agitated heart endured at this most important moment! I admired the Prince; I felt grateful for his affection. He was the most engaging of created beings. I had corresponded with him during many months, and his eloquent letters, the exquisite sensibility which breathed through every line, his ardent professions of adoration, had combined to shake my feeble resolution. The handkerchief was waved on the opposite shore; but the signal was, by the dusk of the evening, rendered almost imperceptible. Lord Malden took my hand, I stepped into the boat, and in a few minutes we landed before the iron gates of old Kew palace.[2] This interview was but of a moment. The Prince of Wales and the Duke of York[3] (then Bishop of Osnaburg) were walking down the avenue. They hastened to meet us. A few words, and those scarcely articulate, were uttered by the Prince, when a noise of people approaching from the palace startled us. The moon was now rising; and the idea of being overheard, or of his Royal Highness being seen out at so unusual an hour terrified the whole group. After a few more words of the most affectionate nature uttered by the Prince, we parted, and Lord Malden and myself returned to the island. The Prince never quitted the avenue, nor the presence of the Duke of York, during the whole of this short meeting. Alas! my friend, if my mind was before influenced by esteem, it was now awakened to the most enthusiastic admiration. The rank of the Prince no longer chilled into awe that being, who now considered him as the lover and the friend. The graces of his person, the irresistible sweetness of his smile, the tenderness of his melodious yet manly voice, will be remembered by me till every vision of this changing scene shall be forgotten.

Many and frequent were the interviews which afterwards took place at this romantic spot; our walks sometimes continued till past midnight, the Duke of York and Lord Malden were always of the party,[4] our conversation was composed of general topics. The Prince, had from his infancy been wholly secluded, and naturally took much pleasure in conversing about the busy world, its manners and pursuits, characters and scenery. Nothing could be more delightful or more rational than our midnight perambulations. I always wore a dark coloured habit; the rest of our party generally wrapped themselves in great coats to disguise them, excepting the Duke of York, who almost universally alarmed us by the display of a *buff* coat, the most conspicuous colour he could have selected for an adventure of this nature. The polished and fascinating ingenuousness of his Royal Highness's manners contributed not a little to enliven our *promenades*. He sung with exquisite taste; and the tones of his voice, breaking on the silence of the night, have often appeared to my entranced senses like more than mortal melody. Often have I lamented the distance which destiny had placed between us: how would my soul have idolized such a *husband!* Alas! how often, in the ardent enthusiasm of my soul, have I formed the wish that being were *mine alone!* to whom partial millions were to look up for protection.

The Duke of York was now on the eve of quitting the country for Hanover; the Prince was also on the point of receiving his first establishment; and the apprehension that his attachment to a married woman might injure his Royal Highness in the opinion of the world, rendered the caution which we invariably observed of the utmost importance. A considerable time elapsed in these delightful scenes of visionary happiness. The Prince's attachment seemed to increase daily, and I considered myself as the most blest of human beings. During some time we had enjoyed our meetings in the neighbourhood of Kew, and I now only looked forward to the adjusting of his Royal Highness's establishment for the public avowal of our mutual attachment.

I had relinquished my profession. The last night of my appearance on the stage, I represented the character of Sir Harry Revel, in the comedy of "The Miniature Picture," written by Lady Craven;[5] and the Irish Widow.[6] On entering the Green-room,[7] I informed Mr. Moody, who played in the farce, that I should appear no more after that night; and, endeavouring to smile while I sung, I repeated,

> "Oh joy to you all in full measure,
> So wishes and prays Widow Brady!"

which were the last lines of my song in "The Irish Widow." This effort to conceal the emotion I felt on quitting a profession I enthusiastically loved, was of short duration; and I burst into tears on my appearance. My regret at recollecting that I was treading for the last time the boards where I had so often received the most gratifying testimonies of public approbation; where mental exertion had been emboldened by private worth; that I was flying from a happy certainty, perhaps to pursue the phantom disappointment, nearly overwhelmed my faculties, and for some time deprived me of the power of articulation. Fortunately, the person on the stage with me had to begin the scene, which allowed me time to collect myself. I went, however, mechanically dull through the business of the evening, and, notwithstanding the cheering expressions and applause of the audience, I was several times near fainting.

The daily prints now indulged the malice of my enemies by the most scandalous paragraphs respecting the Prince of Wales and myself. I found it was now too late to stop the hourly augmenting torrent of abuse that was poured upon me from all quarters. Whenever I appeared in public, I was overwhelmed by the gazing of the multitude. I was frequently obliged to quit Ranelagh,[8] owing to the crowd which staring curiosity had assembled round my box; and, even in the streets of the metropolis, I scarcely ventured to enter a shop without experiencing the greatest inconvenience. Many hours have I waited till the crowd dispersed, which surrounded my carriage, in expectation of my quitting the shop. I cannot suppress a smile at the absurdity of such proceeding, when I remember that, during nearly three seasons, I was almost every night upon the stage, and that I had then been near five years with Mr. Robinson at every fashionable place of entertainment. You, my dear Sir,[9] in your quiet haunts of transatlantic simplicity, will find some difficulty in reconciling these things to your mind—these unaccountable instances of national absurdity. Yet, so it is. I am well assured, that were a being possessed of more than human endowments to visit this country, it would experience indifference, if not total neglect, while a less worthy mortal might be worshipped as the idol of its day, if whispered into notoriety by the comments of the multitude. But, thank Heaven! my heart was not formed in the mould of callous effrontery. I shuddered at the gulf before me, and felt small gratification in the knowledge of having taken a step, which many, who condemned, would have been no less willing to imitate, had they been placed in the same situation.

Previous to my first interview with his Royal Highness, in one of his letters I was astonished to find a bond of the most solemn and binding nature, containing a promise of the sum of twenty thousand pounds, to be paid at the period of his Royal Highness's coming of age.

This paper was signed by the Prince, and sealed with the royal arms. It was expressed in terms so liberal, so voluntary, so marked by true affection, that I had scarcely power to read it. My tears, excited by the most agonizing conflicts, obscured the letters, and nearly blotted out those sentiments, which will be impressed upon my mind till the latest period of my existence. Still, I felt shocked and mortified at the indelicate idea of entering into any pecuniary engagements with a Prince, on whose establishment I relied for the enjoyment of all that would render life desirable. I was surprised at receiving it; the idea of interest had never entered my mind: secure in the possession of his heart, I had in that delightful certainty counted all my future treasure. I had refused many splendid gifts which his Royal Highness had proposed ordering for me at Grey's and other jewellers. The Prince presented to me a few trifling ornaments, in the whole their value not exceeding one hundred guineas.[10] Even these, on our separation, I returned to his Royal Highness through the hands of General Lake.[11]

The period now approached that was to destroy all the fairy visions which had filled my mind with dreams of happiness. At the moment when every thing was preparing for his Royal Highness's establishment, when I looked impatiently for the arrival of that day, in which I might behold my adored friend gracefully receiving the acclamations of his future subjects; when I might enjoy the public protection of that being for whom I gave up all, I received a letter from his Royal Highness, a cold and unkind letter—briefly informing me, that *"we must meet no more!"*

And now, my friend, suffer me to call GOD to witness, that I was unconscious why this decision had taken place in his Royal Highness's mind; only two days previous to this letter being written I had seen the Prince at Kew, and his affection appeared to be boundless as it was undiminished.

Amazed, afflicted, beyond the power of utterance, I wrote immediately to his Royal Highness, requiring an explanation. He remained silent. Again I wrote, but received no elucidation of this most cruel and extraordinary mystery. The Prince was then at Windsor. I set out, in a small pony phaeton, wretched, and unaccompanied by any one except my postillion (a child of nine years of age). It was near dark when we quitted Hyde Park Corner. On my arrival at Hounslow, the inn-keeper informed me, that every carriage which had passed the heath for the last ten nights had been attacked and rifled. I confess the idea of personal danger had no terrors for my mind in the state it then was, and the possibility of annihilation, divested of the crime of suicide, encouraged rather than diminished my determination of proceeding. We had scarcely reached the middle of the heath, when my horses were startled by the sudden appearance of a man rushing from the side of the road. The boy on perceiving him instantly spurred his pony, and, by a sudden bound of our light vehicle, the ruffian missed his grasp at the front rein. We now proceeded at full speed, while the footpad[12] ran endeavouring to overtake us. At length, my horses fortunately outrunning the perseverance of the assailant, we reached the first Magpie, a small inn on the heath, in safety. The alarm which, in spite of my resolution, this adventure had created, was augmented on my recollecting, for the first time, that I had then in my black stock a brilliant stud of very considerable value, which could only have been possessed by the robber by strangling the wearer.

If my heart palpitated with joy at my escape from assassination, a circumstance soon after occurred that did not tend to quiet my emotion. This was the appearance of Mr. H. Meynel and Mrs. A.[13] My foreboding soul instantly beheld a rival, and, with jealous eagerness, interpreted the, hitherto, inexplicable conduct of the Prince, from his having frequently expressed his wish to know that lady.

On my arrival the Prince would not see me. My agonies were now undescribable. I consulted with Lord Malden and the Duke of Dorset, whose honourable mind and truly disinterested friendship had, on many occasions, been exemplified towards me. They were both at a loss to divine any cause of this sudden change in the Prince's feelings. The Prince of Wales had hitherto assiduously sought opportunities to distinguish me more publicly than was prudent, in his Royal Highness's situation. This was in the month of August [1780]. On the fourth of the preceding June, I went, by his desire, into the Chamberlain's box at the birth-night ball; the distressing observation of the circle was drawn towards the part of the box in which I sat by the marked and injudicious attentions of his Royal Highness. I had not been arrived many minutes before I witnessed a singular species of fashionable coquetry. Previous to his Highness's beginning his minuet, I perceived a woman of high rank select from the *bouquet* which she wore two rose buds, which she gave to the Prince, as he afterwards informed me, "emblematical of herself and him," I observed his Royal Highness immediately beckon to a nobleman[14] who has since formed a part of his establishment, and, looking most earnestly at me, whisper a few words, at the same time presenting to him his newly acquired trophy. In a few moments Lord C. entered the Chamberlain's box, and, giving the rosebuds into my hands, informed me that he was commissioned by the Prince to do so. I placed them in my bosom, and, I confess, felt proud of the power by which I thus publicly mortified an exalted rival. His Royal Highness now avowedly distinguished me at all public places of entertainment, at the King's hunt, near Windsor, at the reviews, and at the theatres. The Prince only seemed happy in evincing his affection towards me.

How terrible then was the change to my feelings! And I again most

SOLEMNLY REPEAT, that I was totally ignorant of any JUST CAUSE for so sudden an alteration.

My "good-natured friends" now carefully informed me of the multitude of secret enemies who were ever employed in estranging the Prince's mind from me. So fascinating, so illustrious a lover could not fail to excite the envy of my own sex. Women of all descriptions were emulous of attracting his Royal Highness's attention. Alas! I had neither *rank* nor power to oppose such adversaries. Every engine of female malice was set in motion to destroy my repose, and every petty calumny was repeated with tenfold embellishments. Tales of the most infamous and glaring falsehood were invented, and I was again assailed by pamphlets, by paragraphs, and caricatures, and all the artillery of slander, while the only being to whom I then looked up for protection, was so situated as to be unable to afford it.

Thus perplexed, I wrote to you, my friend, and implored your advice. But you were far away; your delighted soul was absorbed in cherishing the plant of human liberty, which has since blossomed with independent splendour over your happy provinces. Eagerly did I wait for the arrival of the packet [i.e., letter], but no answer was returned. In the anguish of my soul, I once more addressed the Prince of Wales; I complained, perhaps too vehemently, of his injustice; of the calumnies which had been by my enemies fabricated against me, of the falsehood of which he was but too sensible. I conjured him to render me justice. He did so; he wrote me a most eloquent letter, disclaiming the causes alleged by a calumniating world, and fully acquitting me of the charges which had been propagated to destroy me.

I resided now in Cork-street, Burlington-gardens. The house, which was neat, but by no means splendid, had recently been fitted up for the reception of the Countess of Derby, on her separation from her lord.[15] My situation now every hour became more irksome. The Prince still unkindly persisted in withdrawing himself from my society. I was now deeply involved in debt, which I despaired of ever having the power to discharge. I had quitted both my husband and my profession:—the retrospect was dreadful!

My estrangement from the Prince was now the theme of public animadversion, while the newly invigorated shafts of my old enemies, the daily prints, were again hurled upon my defenceless head with ten-fold fury.— The regrets of Mr. Robinson, now that he had *lost* me, became insupportable;—he constantly wrote to me in the language of unbounded affection; nor did he fail, when we met, to express his agony at our separation, and even a wish for our reunion.

I had, at one period, resolved on returning to my profession; but some friends whom I consulted, dreaded that the public would not suffer my reappearance on the stage. This idea intimidated me, and precluded my efforts for that independence of which my romantic credulity had robbed me. I was thus fatally induced to relinquish what would have proved an ample and honourable resource for myself and my child. My debts accumulated to near seven thousand pounds. My creditors, whose insulting illiberality could only be equalled by their unbounded impositions, hourly assailed me.

I was, in the mean time, wholly neglected by the Prince, while the assiduities of Lord Malden daily increased. I had no other friend on whom I could rely for assistance or protection. When I say protection, I would not be understood to mean *pecuniary* assistance, Lord Malden being, at the time alluded to, even poorer than myself: the death of his Lordship's grandmother, Lady Frances Coningsby, had not then placed him above the penury of his own small income.

Lord Malden's attentions to me again exposed him to all the humiliation of former periods. The Prince assured me once more of his wishes to renew our former friendship and affection, and urged me to meet him at the house of Lord Malden in Clarges-street. I was at this period little less than frantic, deeply involved in debt, persecuted by my enemies, and perpetually reproached by my relations. I would joyfully have resigned an existence now become to me an intolerable burthen; yet my pride was not less than my sorrow, and I resolved, whatever my heart might suffer, to wear a placid countenance when I met the inquiring glances of my triumphant enemies.

After much hesitation, by the advice of Lord Malden, I consented to meet his Royal Highness. He accosted me with every appearance of tender attachment, declaring that he had never for one moment ceased to love me—but, that I had many concealed enemies, who were exerting every effort to undermine me. We passed some hours in the most friendly and delightful conversation, and I began to flatter myself that all our differences were adjusted.—But what words can express my surprise and chagrin, when, on meeting his Royal Highness *the very next day* in Hyde Park, he turned his head to avoid seeing me, and even affected *not to know me!*

Overwhelmed by this blow, my distress knew no limits. Yet *Heaven* can witness the truth of my assertion, even, in this moment of complete despair, when oppression bowed me to the earth, I blamed not the Prince. I did then, and ever shall, consider his mind as nobly and honourably organized, nor could I teach myself to believe, that a heart the seat of so many virtues, could possibly become inhuman and unjust. I had been taught from my infancy to believe that elevated stations are surrounded by delusive visions, which glitter but to dazzle, like an unsubstantial meteor, and flatter to betray. With legions of these phantoms it has been my fate to encounter, I have been unceasingly marked by their persecutions, and shall at length become their victim.

Notes

1. George Capel, Viscount Malden (1759–1839); politician and companion of the Prince of Wales; one of Robinson's lovers, he paid her £500 per year after their separation.

2. Kew, in Surrey, England; home to the Royal Botanical Gardens and a royal residence until 1841.

3. Frederick (1763–1827), King George III's second son.

4. The attendance of the duke of York and Lord Malden kept suspicions away from the prince, who was just coming of age to be established as heir to the throne.

5. Now Margravine of Anspach [Robinson]; see pp. 239–251 of this volume.

6. Comic afterpiece by David Garrick, one of the first to encourage Robinson to consider a dramatic career.

7. Room where actors wait before going onstage.

8. A fashionable London pleasure resort; a rotunda built on the model on the Pantheon surrounded by gardens, it accommodated more than six thousand people.

9. The narrative of Robinson's affair with the Prince of Wales "is passed off as a letter written in 1783, though the style suggests it once formed part of Mary Robinson's narrative" (Levy ix). The "dear Sir" here addressed is the fictional recipient.

10. Worth no more than $200 today.

11. Gerard Lake (1744–1808), friend and advisor to the Prince of Wales.

12. A highway robber who travels on foot.

13. Elizabeth Armistead (1750–1842), mistress of the Prince of Wales and Robinson's rival; married Charles James Fox in 1795. Hugo Meynel (1727–1808) was her attendant.

14. The Earl of C. [Robinson]. George, earl of Cholmondeley (1749–1827); assigned the responsibility of paying Robinson her settlement from the prince; he had a brief a affair with her in 1781.

15. Lady Betty Hamilton (d. 1797); separated from her husband, the twelfth earl of Derby, after having an affair with the duke of Dorset.

Maria, Lady Nugent

1771?–1834

A Journal of a Voyage to, and Residence in, the Island of Jamaica, from 1801 to 1805, and of some subsequent events in England from 1805 to 1811. 2 vols. London: n.p., 1839.

Maria Skinner was born in 1771, probably in Perth Amboy, New Jersey, into a family with Irish, Scot, and Dutch antecedents. Her father, Courtlandt Skinner, held several high offices in the New Jersey government, and during the American War of Independence he was commissioned brigadier general of the state's loyalist troops. The Skinners returned to England after the war, and Maria was probably living on their Irish property when she met George Nugent. On 15 November 1797 they married. In 1801 Nugent was appointed lieutenant governor and military commander in chief of Jamaica, and the couple sailed for Jamaica in May, Lady Nugent thankful to have "my own little world with me, in my devoted husband and best of friends" (1:12). On their arrival in August, she took up her perceived duties: adjusting to a climate that produced "a sort of despondency" (1:39); Christianizing her Jamaican servants; and aiding her husband in ways that ranged from copying confidential dispatches, to storing up conversations "upon public matters" (1:391) that will be "useful to my dear N.," to lecturing the "worse than thoughtless young men" (2:105) of his staff for their tendency to father "unfortunate half-black progeny." The years of Nugent's lieutenant governorship were turbulent ones for the Caribbean colonies, and the *Journal* records the many causes for concern. On 18 March 1802 Lady Nugent described the "savage and frightful" (1:180) military maneuvers of the Maroons, the community of runaway slaves intermittently in rebellion throughout the eighteenth century, and a little more than a year later she recorded "alarming" accounts and prayed "God preserve us from the horrors of an insurrection!" (1:427).

As the Napoleonic Wars extended to the colonies and British power in Jamaica was destabilized, such fears intensified; during a walk with her children in April 1805, Lady Nugent was filled with "terror" by "a sort of fierce look" from a once "humble" black man (2:162). Interspersed with such reports of public events are her records of private life: the birth of her son, George, in October 1802, and of her daughter, Louisa, eleven months later; the day the general "gave up all business" (2:167) and had "a fine romp" with her and the children; both parents' misery at the death of their three-week-old son, Edmund, in 1807; their joy at the birth of a second daughter in 1809. The Nugents returned to England in 1805. By April 1806 Lady Nugent was no longer keeping a daily journal, but she continued to mark the children's progress "for their own future information" (2:391) and to note her own charitable and other activities. In 1811 the general was appointed commander in chief of the army in India, and the *Journal* concludes with their departure, Lady Nugent leaving it behind for her children along with other "relics of a father and mother, devoted to their interest and welfare" (2:515).

TEXT: Lady Nugent's *Journal* was first published in 1839. A modern edition appeared in 1907 and another in 1966. The excerpt (pp. 61–84 of volume one) is from the first edition; it covers one of Lady Nugent's early months in Jamaica, typical events in the Nugents' life at this time, and their affection for and reliance on each other.

⚭ ᎒Ꮅ

[SEPTEMBER] 29TH [1801]. At 4 o'clock, General N. &c. set off to review the troops at Stony Hill.[1]—I took a walk in the garden till the heat drove me in. Tête-à-tête with mine host[2] at breakfast. Had a learned conversation on the cultivation of sugar-canes, the population of the negroes, &c. Mr. C. told me he gave two dollars to every woman who produced a healthy child; but no marriages were thought of!! After I had got all the information I wished from Mr. C. I went to my own room and amused myself very well till dear N. returned; when we met with as much joy as if we had parted for months. He took some tamarind drink, and slept till dressing time.—An immense party, from Kingston and Up-Park Camp, at dinner, but no ladies, to my great joy;[3] so I did as I pleased, ordered tea in my own room, and went to bed at ten.

30th. General N. started at 4 this morning to review the troops at Up-Park Camp.—I had a nice early walk in the sweet garden, and conversed a great deal with Mr. Cuthbert, at our tête-à-tête breakfast, on the state of slaves in this country, &c. &c. He is a sensible man; but we are creatures of habit, his mind is prejudiced, and I fear his heart is hard.—My dear N. returned at 3, and, while he refreshed himself with a nap, I read and kept

Maria, Lady Nugent, by George Adcock. Frontispiece,
Journal of a Voyage.

off the Musquitoes from him. Several gentlemen at dinner, in addition to our party, whose names I don't recollect. No ladies; so I have had my tea, and now am enjoying the cool breeze from the mountains, until my dear N. comes from the dinner party. In the mean time I shall take a review of the week, as far as it has hitherto passed. It has been quiet and comfortable. I have heard much of slaves, plantations, and counting-houses, but these subjects are new, and I have curiosity. For the principal part of my comfort, I have seen my dear N. composed and cool. He has had what for him is moderate exercise, and he has had relaxation of mind; his countenance is quite changed, it is now placid, cheerful, and serene; he has no more that hurried heated manner, that has too often made me miserable. Oh, my God! grant to him health of mind as well as of body, and enable me, as far as may depend upon my conduct and ability, to contribute to his welfare and happiness. Grant that I may conquer every propensity that may occasion him the smallest uneasiness, or make me less worthy of the blessings thou has bestowed upon me. Teach me to repress all sinful repinings, and to become entirely resigned to thy Divine will. With this prayer I shall go happy to bed, though it has thundered and lightened [i.e., lightninged] dreadfully, and the rain is now pouring in torrents.

October 1st. Up at 4, and dress by candle-light. The fire-flies looked beautifully in the hall, as we passed through to our carriages. The walls were quite illuminated.

Drove to Mr. Hutchinson's place, called the Pepine estate. A large party of gentlemen, and a grand cavalcade of all descriptions. All sorts of meats and fruits at breakfast. See a fine bamboo walk afterwards, reaching from one end of the garden to the other. Every ten or twelve feet there is a cocoa-nut tree, as a pillar to support the feathering bamboo. Nothing could well be more beautiful. The bread-fruit tree is here in great perfection. The Jack-fruit tree is like an enormous pumpkin, growing on the trunk, as it is too heavy for the boughs. There is also an infinite number of beautiful flowers; in short, the garden is the best and most curious[4] I have yet seen.—The situation of the house is bad; it lies low, and it is shut out from the sea breeze, by what is called the Long mountain, and from the land breeze, by a range of mountains, under which the house is placed. Mr. Hutchinson is a quiet, awkward Scotchman, and so overcome by the honor we have done him, that it is quite distressing to see the poor man.

At 10 we drove to the Hope estate. We took a cross road, through a sugar plantation, or rather cane-piece, as it is called; a negro man running before the carriage, to open the gates. The Hope estate is very interesting for me, as belonging to dearest Lady Temple,[5] and I examined every thing very particularly. It is situated at the bottom of a mountain, and as the Hope river runs through it, the produce is more certain than on estates in general, which often suffer from the great droughts in this part of the world. A severe hurricane alone can affect it. It is said to be an old estate, and not further improveable than yielding, as it does now, 320 hogsheads of sugar.—They say that, though it is incapable of yielding more, it is better, as being a sure produce, than most estates in the island, which are liable to great vicissitudes.—As you enter the gates, there is a long range of negro houses, like thatched cottages, and a row of cocoa-nut trees and clumps of cotton trees. The sugar-house, and all the buildings, are thought to be more than usually good, and well taken care of. The overseer, a civil, vulgar, Scotch officer, on half-pay,[6] did the honours to us; but, when we got to the door of the distillery, the smell of the rum was so intolerable, that, after a little peep at the process, I left the gentlemen, and went to the overseer's house, about a hundred yards off. I talked to the black women, who told me all their histories. The overseer's chere amie,[7] and no man here is without one, is a tall black woman, well made, with a very flat nose, thick lips, and a skin of ebony, highly polished and shining. She shewed me her three yellow children, and said, with some ostentation, she should soon have another. The marked attention of the other women, plainly proved her to be the favourite Sultana of this vulgar, ugly, Scotch Sultan, who is about fifty, clumsy, ill made, and dirty. He has a dingy, sallow-brown complexion, and only two yellow discoloured tusks, by way of teeth. However, they say he is a good overseer; so at least his brother Scotchman told me, and there is no one here to contradict him, as almost all the agents, attornies, merchants and shop-keepers, are of that country, and really do deserve to thrive in this, they are so industrious. I should mention that there is an excellent hospital on this estate, which is called a hot-house, where the blackies[8] appear particularly comfortable, and well taken care of.

Return to Clifton to dinner; some dreadful peals of thunder this evening; for we are so near the mountains, it is quite terrific, and the house seems shaken to its very foundation; but, after our fright, we shall have a nice clear and cooler air to comfort us.

2nd. Dress by candle-light, and off at 4 o'clock.—The morning darker than usual, and the fire-flies more brilliant; all the walls seem covered with gold spangles. We drove first to Kingston, and I was left at Mr. Atkinson's,[9] while General N. reviewed the 69th regiment, quartered in the town. Mr. A. made grand efforts to amuse me during his absence. The mountain wind, the sea breeze, slaves, plantations, and the prices of different articles, were the edifying topics, till a little after 7, when breakfast made its appearance, and Mr. A.'s spirits were relieved by the appearance of Mrs. Pye,[10] who came to offer her services, hearing that I was in Kingston. Poor man, he seemed very happy, so was I. Some officers came soon after, and we sat down to the usually profuse breakfast. Afterwards, Mrs. Pye took her leave, Mr. A. and Mr. Bogle (his partner) went to their counting-house, and the officers to their camp. General N. brought General Churchill and some other officers with him. Admiral Smith and several officers of the Navy called.—At one, General N. and I drove about town, and then to General Churchill's Penn,[11] to see his monkey and other curiosities.—Back to Mr. Atkinson's; dress and dine with a large party, at 6. General C. Mr. Simon Taylor, Mr. Cuthbert, &c. &c. &c. officers of the Army and Navy, and, in short, half Kingston and Port-Royal, but no lady; so I did not meet the gentlemen after dinner, but went to bed at half-past nine, to be off early next morning for home.

3rd. Up at 4, and drive to the Admiral's Penn. Admiral Smith[12] and a party met us. See the house, grounds, and stables, and select what furniture we wish to have, as all was to be sold. Feel truly melancholy, in thinking of the sad fate of its late possessor,[13] and was glad to return to the carriage. Arrived at the King's House,[14] and breakfasted at 8, with the sun broiling over our heads, and the heat tremendous. Hear a great deal of gossip from some of our staff about favouritism; for I am such a great lady,[15] that all I say and do is remarked upon. Mrs. Pye, &c. are spoken of as in my confidence, and likely to guide me in my conduct towards others. What ninnies! But to avoid cabals, I determine not to go to Port Royal on Monday, and so I shall not have that lady in my train, and shall prevent at least some remarks. I mean, as much as possible, to live alone at my private hours, and so put an end to all these silly jealousies.—After breakfast, General N. held a Court of Ordinary[16] in the Egyptian Hall [of King's House], which lasted till 4 o'clock. We had only our usual staff dinner, and slept at dear little quiet Bellevue.[17]

4th. Breakfast at 7, read our prayers, then walk about the gallery, and have a snug conversation, which we enjoyed very much.—General N. made memorandums for the business of to-morrow, and I wrote French verses, and translated them for his amusement. They were very bad, but very affectionate, and he wishes me to keep them; but some future day they may make me blush for their want of merit; so I shall give them to the winds.—Drove to the King's House before 5; some clouds obscure the sun, and make the heat more supportable.—Dined at 6; the clergyman and his wife, Major and Mrs. Pye, Captain Taylor &c. &c. with our usual staff dinner.

5th. General N. &c. off to review the troops at Port Henderson.—As soon as I had breakfasted, made arrangements for his comfort, and mean to surprise him with a cool writing room, when he returns. Saw Monsieur Grandjean d'Aubancourt[18] in my dressing room,[19] and settle for his breakfasting here every morning, and reading French to me for an hour. He thinks my verses very good, but, query, does he speak the truth?—Read Mrs. Haverdon's papers[20] with real interest and attention; write and tell her, that all that can be done in her case shall be done.—General N. returned at 3, and was delighted with his new apartment, to my great joy.—Set off after dinner for Bellevue, much against the advice of Dr. Lind, as it was quite dark.[21]

6th. Have not suffered at all for our great imprudence, and, though the musquitoes were in myriads about our beds, we had a tolerable night, and went, at gun-fire [i.e., reveille] to see Mrs. Pennington's Mountain.[22]— Don't like it half as well as Bellevue, which I mean to try to persuade Mr. March to let to us.—After our breakfast, Captain Fraser &c. about barracks. A good deal of jobbing[23] going on, but General N. is determined not to countenance it.—Much rain, with thunder and lightning, the greatest part of to-day, but returned to town soon after 5.—Dined at 6. Monsieur Grandjean in addition to our party.

7th. General N. went off at 4 to Port Henderson again.—Read and write till breakfast; then read and conversed with Monsieur Grandjean, in my dressing room, till 12.—General N. returned at one, and gave audience to Monsieur Bunell, &c. from St. Domingo.[24]—Wrote to Mr. March, and sent him a present, of porter, hams, &c. all just arrived from England, and a great treat here.—General Bell, &c. dined with us.—Hear of the arrival of our carriages from England.—Drive with General N. in the curricle, as usual, to Bellevue, and enjoy sleeping once more in the fresher and purer air of that place.

8th. A sad [i.e., distressing] head-ache all this evening.—Some of the staff at breakfast, and some Kingston gentlemen on business with General N.—Rain, thunder and lightning, at intervals, all day.—Dine at the King's House, at 5; Colonel Maclean, Monsieur Grandjean, &c. at dinner. Carriages ordered for the navy officers to-morrow evening at Port Henderson.

9th. The carriages went at 4, but returned empty, as Admiral Montague's arrival at Port Royal has kept all our navy friends there. Am not very sorry, for I still have a head-ache, and am not very equal to any great gaiety.—Read and converse with Monsieur Grandjean, for an hour after breakfast, and have begun to write an Abridgement of French History.— At dinner, General Bell, Mr. Rose, Mr. Minot, Colonel Gillespie, Captain Macdonald, (just from England), Mr. H., Colonel MacMurdo, Mr. Matthews, Admiral Smith, and the eternal Major and Mrs. Pye, in addition to our staff.—In the evening an immense party, but not so many ladies as usual, on account of the torrents of rain.

10th. Was present at the review of the troops in this garrison, at 5 o'clock.—Colonel Gillespie &c. breakfasted with us afterwards.—Then General N. and I passed a most comfortable morning together, for as he could be with me, I denied myself[25] to Grandjean.—At 4, only our own family at dinner, and we slept at Bellevue.

11th. The early part of the day spent in reading, &c. General N. then wrote despatches, and I composed French epistles to Monsieur Grandjean, &c. for my amusement and improvement.—Several gentlemen called in the course of the day, but were not admitted.—Only Colonel Irvine and Captain Johnson, to dine with us, and they left us before nine.

12th. Drove into Spanish Town at 6, and spent the day quietly and comfortably.—Three of the staff at dinner, and we were left alone again at eight.

13th. Drive to the Government Penn at 6; the works there going on slowly, and Jones, the head workman, says, that, although Lord Balcarres[26] said he would lay out £700 in repairs, he had limited him to £55! As we called at the King's House, we did not get back to Bellevue till 9, when we found Mr. March, Captain Taylor, and two or three of our family, waiting breakfast for us.—Spent a very comfortable morning afterwards.— Only Colonel Irvine at dinner, and we were in bed before 9 o'clock.

14th. General N. surprised us by walking off at 6, to see a Penn, or rather a mountain, belonging to Mr. March, two miles off. He did not seem to be the worse for it, and I trust will not suffer; but such walks are very imprudent.—The Secretary, &c. with papers to sign, and, after breakfast, we were left to ourselves; when General N. wrote his speech.[27]—We had only two of the staff at dinner, who left us at 8. We actually now feel the cold quite uncomfortable. The heavy rains have so saturated the walls with damp, and the squalls of wind are so powerful, that they pervade every thing, and we live in almost a bath; so I fear we must soon leave this dear pretty quiet retreat.

15th. A pain in my head and shoulders from the damp air last night; but drive into town to breakfast. Find Lord Balcarres and a large party.— After breakfast, read and go through my usual avocations with Monsieur Grandjean. Dr. and Mrs. Ludford arrived at 10—Conversed with them till 2.—Very unwell; and I mean, as symptoms arise of any illness, always to mention it; because, if I should die in this country, it will be a satisfaction to those who are interested about me, to know the rise and progress of my illness, &c.

16th. Still unwell, but carriages are gone for the Navy, and I must do my best to be gay. At half-past seven, Captains Bayntun, Cathcart, and

Loring, Dr. and Mrs. Ludford, &c. &c. The morning as usual.—Then Lord Balcarres, Captain Woolley, Mr. Carthew, Mons. Le Vaillant, Major and Mrs. Pye at dinner.—A large evening party of ladies, and crowds of gentlemen, both civil and military. All in high spirits, and, in spite of my illness, I danced, and was as gay apparently as any of them; though the enquiries of my people shewed, that I did not disguise quite so well as I thought.

17th. Got our English letters.—All well, thank God! General N. all the morning reading his despatches. Dr. and Mrs. Ludford at Kingston all day, so we were left to ourselves.—Only our usual dinner party, with Monsieur Grandjean, our eternal guest now, poor man!

18th. Drive out with General N. at 6 o'clock, and go to church at 10.—Our English carriage and four horses for the first time.—A large party at dinner.—Still unwell, and glad to go to bed at nine.

19th. Drive out at 6.—The Marquis de la Jaille[28] in addition to our breakfast party. Then the Attorney-General, to consult with General N. about his speech, and some few alterations were made.—Read as usual with Monsieur Grandjean.—Mr. Warren, our chaplain, made his appearance for the first time.—All the morning interrupted by visitors, that I am obliged to receive.—General N. held a privy council at 5, to whom his speech was read.—At 6 a dinner in the Great Hall; about forty or fifty guests. I dined in my dressing-room, with Mrs. Pye and Mrs. Ludford.—Before 11 all dispersed.

20th. Too late to drive out to-day, as I did not rise till half-past six.—The early part of the day as usual.—Received several gentlemen visitors in my dressing-room.—At 4, the House of Assembly met, and came over to the King's House, in grand procession. General N. read his speech, and they departed to discuss it.—Dinner at 6; about the same number as yesterday, and I dined in the same way.—The two ladies left me at 10, and the gentlemen broke up at about half-past eleven, so we were not in bed till twelve.

21st. Too late again to drive out.—Mr.———, &c. at breakfast.—Send out cards for my balls, and distributed to the black women, gowns, petticoats, &c. and various presents for my wedding-day [i.e., anniversary]. Dr. and Mrs. Ludford took their leave at 3.—Messrs. Bogle, Atkinson, Forbes, B———, Donaldson, &c. at dinner, with Mr. Corbet, the St. Domingo agent.—After dinner had a great deal of conversation with Mr. Corbet, about General Toussaint l'Ouverture,[29] which was particularly interesting. He must be a wonderful man, and I really do believe intended for very good purposes.

22nd. The actual rainy season, they say, set in last night; and I believe it, for we were so uncommonly chilly, that we kept the counterpane on all night, and this morning it rains torrents.—We could not drive out, and I amused myself till 8, in translating General N.'s speech into French, for Monsieur Grandjean's edification.—At breakfast, Mr. Corbet, &c.—Drove, with some of the staff, to Lord Balcarres's auction.—Every article had its price put upon it, by Lord B. himself, who was present the whole time, and had his emissaries to bid for him, till all was sold at his own price, which was always more than their worth; consequently most of the things remain on his hands.—Returned and read French with Monsieur Grandjean, for a couple of hours; then gave audience to the old super-annuated President of the Council,[30] who wanted me to patronize a de-cayed milliner[31] of bad character. Altogether it was an unpleasant business, and I got rid of it civilly, but decidedly.—A very flattering answer to General N.'s speech came over from the House of Assembly,—The Members of the Council sent one equally so, and General N. replied to all at half-past four.—We went to dinner at 6.—Mr. Corbet, Colonel Skerrett, Mr. MacCluny of the 87th, &c. dined with us, and all departed at nine.

23rd. General N. rode out at 6; I had not had a good night, and did not accompany him.—Read and converse, after breakfast, with Monsieur D'Aubancourt, in my dressing-room, till 12.—Afterwards received a few visitors in my own room.—General N. and I then had a *tête-à-tête*, and conversed a good deal upon the subject of his situation, &c. and he sent several messages to the House of Assembly. He has strange people to deal with. The trade of this island has been for a long time much injured, and several merchants almost ruined, by the constant depredations of privateers and feluccas, which infest the coast; while the navy are engaged in distant pursuits. Admiral Montague, who succeeds to the naval command, *pro tempore*, has offered, at the representation of General N. of the necessity of keeping cruisers to guard the coast, that he will station his ships so, as to intercept these mischievous privateers; this offer was very handsomely made in a letter to General N., who shewed it to the gentlemen in Coun-cil, when it was drily received, as a matter of perfect indifference; although not many weeks since, the remissness of the navy, in this respect, was not only complained of by them, but was a cause of general complaint. Many very severe philippics appeared in the newspapers against poor Lord Hugh Seymour, on account of the cruisers not doing their duty in guarding the trade. But such are these people, and such is their littleness, that because they suppose that General N. has the orders of ministers to employ black corps in the island,[32] they seem determined to do every thing to make his situation uncomfortable, and to discourage every arrangement, though for their own good and advantage. He must, however, do his duty, and it is to be hoped that time will bring all things right.—Dined at 5—The two Mr. Cuthberts, Colonel de Charmilly, Mr. Warren, Captain Taylor, Mr. Matthews, Monsieur Grandjean, &c. in addition to the staff.—In the evening a very large party, and much dancing.—We had three hours to-day of the heaviest rain I ever saw: it came down like a torrent.

24th. Drive out.—Admiral Montague, and some of the navy, at breakfast, at 8.—At 10 received several visitors.—I forgot to say, that although Dr. and Mrs. Ludford did take their leave, they returned, and were still our guests.—Found time before dinner to translate one of Sappho's Odes from the French.[33] It is addressed to the Rose, and is very pretty.—Dined at 5. Mr. Herring, &c. &c. at dinner.—To bed at nine.

25th. Drove to the Penn at 6.—Went with Lord Balcarres to see the garden, or rather where the garden has been, for not a plant of any kind is there existing at present.—A party at breakfast, and go to church at 10.—After church, visit Mrs. Baily and Mrs. Romsey.—Find at the King's House all Lord B.'s poor negroes, to solicit favours. Make them all as happy as I can, by promising kindness.—At dinner, Monsieur and Madame Grandjean and Mademoiselle Roberts, Mr., Mrs. and the Misses Warren, Mr. and Mrs. Woodham, Major and Mrs. Pye, and some officers of the army and navy. A strange mixture of people altogether, and a most laughable party: but I was heartily tired by 9 o'clock, and was glad when they made their exit.

26th. After breakfast, drive to the Penn. The sun extremely oppressive. Lord B. very civil but, I am sure, very much annoyed. Dr. Ludford, who was of the party, taken ill of *the* fever,[34] in consequence of the heat; and, indeed, it is very unsafe to go out so late in the day. We all felt the heat very much.—Poor Mrs. Ludford was very uneasy, but the fever is not thought serious. Mr. Corbet, &c. at dinner.

27th. Dr. L. better this morning—General N. and I drove towards Kingston at 6.—Read, &c. with Monsieur G. after breakfast; then received a visit from the Attorney-General, with his niece, in my dressing-room.—Only Grandjean and our staff at dinner.—Dr. L. getting well.

28th. At 5, drive on a new road, by the river side, and enjoy it much.—After breakfast read with Grandjean, as usual.—The Attorney-General many hours in conference with General N. on the subject of black corps, &c. Employ myself and the maids in decorating the ball-room.—Send off Baptiste (our French cook) to Kingston, with orders for ornamental cakes,

&c.—A grand dinner given to-day to General N. by *King* Mitchell.[35]—Mrs. Pye and Mrs. Ludford with me.—To bed early.

29th. Drive out at half-past five.—The Attorney-General again at breakfast this morning—A long conference, and all about General N.'s message, respecting black corps, &c.—I feel very anxious myself for the issue, as it is all such a source of vexation to my dear N.—Read with Grandjean, write English letters, dine at 5, and the eternal Major and Mrs. Pye of our party.

30th. Up at gun-fire.—Did not drive out, but General N. rode. I was glad of the excuse to be quiet till breakfast time, as I was kept awake by the band of the 20th dragoons, that regiment having given a parting dinner to the 67th.—Dr. and Mrs. L. took leave, on account of their child's illness. Do all I can to comfort them before they left us, as we feel a particular interest for them, on account of Colonel and Mrs. M. Murray, and Sir J. and Lady M. Murray.[36]—Dress for dinner at 6.—My evening party full of ladies, but not so many gentlemen as usual; owing, I imagine, to the dinner and serenading last night. General N. did not make his appearance, but left me to do the honours, as he had so many letters to write, and so much business of various kinds on his hands. Poor fellow, he works hard, and I do indeed pity him!

Notes

1. The regimental barracks at Stony Hill.

2. The Nugents are visiting a Mr. Cuthbert, at his seat of Clifton.

3. After a formal dinner, the ladies and gentlemen separated for a time and then reunited; since Lady Nugent is the only lady present, this custom is not observed—hence her "great joy."

4. Worthy of interest or attention.

5. Anne Eliza, wife of Richard Grenville, Earl Temple; George Nugent was related to the Grenvilles, and the families were close.

6. Half wages; reduced allowance made to an officer not on active duty or after retirement.

7. Dear friend (Fr.); here a term for mistress.

8. A term frequently used by Lady Nugent; not intentionally racist, it is certainly condescending.

9. Matthew Atkinson, island secretary.

10. Wife of Hampden Pye, major of brigade in the Sixth West India Regiment and Nugent's aide.

11. A farm or property with livestock.

12. Admiral's Penn, official residence of the admiral on the Jamaica station; Admiral Smith, Rear Admiral Edward Tyrrel Smith.

13. Lord Hugh Seymour, naval commander in chief of Jamaica until his sudden death on 11 September 1801.

14. Residence of the lieutenant governor and commander in chief.

15. As always when she refers to herself in this way, Lady Nugent is speaking ironically.

16. For probating wills and granting letters of administration; one of the lieutenant governor's duties was to preside over such courts of law.

17. Penn that the Nugents later rented from attorney John March.

18. Louis Ambrose Grandjean d'Aubancourt, later attorney general at St. Marc in Sainte-Domingue (now Haiti) during the English occupation of that French colony.

19. Room opening off the bedroom, used for dressing and for receiving visitors.

20. Not further identified.

21. Night air was thought to be unhealthful, especially in a tropical climate.

22. A property or estate.

23. Secret (and often corrupt) maneuvering for employment, position, and so forth.

24. Joseph Bunel, French merchant and chief diplomatic representative of Toussaint l'Ouverture, ruler of Sainte-Domingue (see note 29). Saint Domingo is the English spelling.

25. Had a servant say that she was not at home.

26. Andrew Lindsay, sixth earl of Balcarres (1752–1825); George Nugent's predecessor as lieutenant governor, 1795–1801.

27. For delivery to the House of Assembly, the forty-three-member elected body responsible for Jamaica's civil administration.

28. André Charles, marquis de la Jaille (1747–ca. 1816); merchant and French administrator in Sainte-Domingue.

29. François-Dominique Toussaint (ca. 1743–1803); known as l'Ouverture (Fr. "the Opening") for his military prowess. A former slave, he led the rebellion against French rule that began in 1791 and concluded with Haiti's Declaration of Independence on 1 January 1804.

30. Thomas Wallen, age fifty-two; the Council is the twelve-member appointed body that served as the upper house of the legislature as well as advisory board to the lieutenant governor.

31. To give work to a hatmaker down on her luck.

32. Because of high mortality among European troops in the Caribbean, England had begun raising regiments of freed blacks as well as slaves. Over the objections of the planters, one such regiment had been quartered in Jamaica a few months before the Nugents arrived, and the House of Assembly was correspondingly truculent.

33. Sappho, Greek poet of the sixth century B.C. best known for her sensuous love poems, some addressed to women.

34. Yellow fever.

35. William Mitchell, member of the House of Assembly for many years and extremely influential—hence Lady Nugent's term "king."

36. The Murrays were related to the clan Macgregor, from which Lady Nugent was descended.

Mary R. Stockdale

1769–AFTER 1818

"To the Reader." The Mirror of the Mind. Poems by Miss Stockdale. 2 vols. London: John Stockdale, 1810.

Mary R. Stockdale was born in 1769 in London and lived there most of her life. Her father had been a porter but later became a bookseller and publisher. She was a sickly child and was thus educated at home rather than at boarding school. Her health later improved (on a diet of rich food), and she pursued her education assiduously, learning among other things that she was "a lost polluted creature, full of deadly sin by nature, and of actual transgression in life" (xxxii). Having recovered her own health, Stockdale was long occupied in nursing her mother and other members of the household, including a young maidservant, Elizabeth Haws, whose death inspired her first poem, "The Effusions of the Heart." Although her father wanted to publish it, she demurred until, expecting death from another illness, she reflected that granting his request "would probably be the last favour I might have the power to confer" (xli). This and other poems were published as *The Effusions of the Heart* in 1798. Over the next three years Stockdale wrote translations and poems between periods of recurrent illness. By the time *The Mirror of the Mind* was published in 1810, she had learned "the emptiness of sublunary things" (xlviii) and achieved "the most perfect indifference for every thing around me."

   "To the Reader," the autobiographical preface that opens *Mirror*, omits "many and various" (xci) incidents of her youth, "lest I might be thought by some to be tedious." It does, however, include a section of "observations" (xlix) on her poems, in particular her use of the sonnet form and her attraction to the subject of "sweet endearing, grief-alleviating friendship" (lv). In the hope of making one of her "fellow-creatures in love with virtue" (xcv), she also criticizes the "crying abomination" (lxxxv) of Sunday amusements. Although Stockdale planned two books of prose (*Meditations, or the Affectionate Monitor* for young people and a similar tome for older readers), she seems to have published only poetry. Between 1812 and 1818 she produced several long elegies, and her complete *Miscellaneous Poems* appeared in 1826. The date of her death is not known.

TEXT: Although Mary R. Stockdale's "To the Reader" was intended to make the readers of her poems "acquainted with the author," it reveals less about her life than about her views on such topics as education, Christianity, and prosody. The excerpt (pp. xiii–xxix) gives Stockdale's reasons for writing the essay, some information about her childhood, and reflections on various matters.

cᴥ ꝏ

TO THE READER

WHENEVER I have been gratified by the perusal of any work, I have uniformly felt a strong desire to become in some measure acquainted with the author: and I have not unfrequently employed the whole circle of my literary acquaintance, to obtain the desired knowledge; sometimes with success, but oftener without it. Judging of others by myself, I shall here make a few observations as concisely as I can, to satisfy in some degree a curiosity equally natural and innocent: for, although I have already repeatedly appeared before the public,[1] still there are undoubtedly many, into whose hands this book may fall, who have never heard of so humble an individual.

I was born in London, in the parish of St. James's, Westminster; on which spot I have spent the greatest part of my life. I was neither born to poverty nor riches, but in that happy medium which Solomon describes as the most desirable. Plenty crowned my paternal board; I had all the necessaries, and many of the luxuries, of life. The years of my childhood were so marked by ill health, which threatened at last to have ended in a decline, that any attempt at education was almost out of the question, till that period when others of my age thought of finishing what I had scarcely begun. I think I hear some feeling heart exclaim, "Poor thing! how unfortunate, what has she not lost!" Stay, gentle reader, withhold your pity till a time when it shall be more called for than it is at present: I need it not now: for, however the information may astonish you, it was at this very period, which you think so inauspicious, that I laid the foundation of all that is useful in my own sex; of all that is really estimable in either: for then I acquired domestic knowledge—then I learned to think, to reflect, to form my own judgment, and to imbibe that piety, which was intended, when ripened, to be my staff and stay, my rest and support, through succeeding years of trials; under which, without it, I should long since have sunk. But, if my sufferings in these early years were great, I had a support given me from above more than adequate to them: a patience which nothing could subdue; which nothing could weary; and on which I have since looked back with astonishment. In the course of my yet short life, trouble has wrung from my eyes many, very many tears: but never, no never, can I recollect one forced from me by any pain incident to sickness. The patient cheerfulness which I always shewed so won upon my parents, that I was indulged in every thing that could be thought of to alleviate the heavy dispensation: and, though I am sensible this with some would have produced unfavourable consequences, it had not that effect on me, but rather tended to inspire me with additional love and gratitude towards the respected authors of my being; and to make me only the more anxious to please those, to whom, young as I was, I was sensible I was indebted for a more than common portion of kind attention. But here let me observe, it is not indulgent kindness that will spoil a child, where the mind has already been properly informed: it is the child who has never had his passions restrained, who has never known any will but his own perverse one, who is spoiled by indulgence. The first thing a child ought to be taught is implicit obedience; for without this little good can be done: it is both a wholesome and easy restraint; and, whatever those may think who never learned it, I can say, from experience, that such children are far happier than those who are permitted to follow uncontrolled their own way in every thing. Not such however was my lot; I had so early, instinctively as it were, imbibed this quality, that I have heard my beloved mother frequently declare, that she used to think that I imagined it impossible to do otherwise than obey. It is true I had no bad examples before my eyes, and to that, in a considerable measure, may be attributed my ready acquiescence.

I was the only one of a large family brought up at home; the rest were all educated at boarding schools. Ever since I have been able to draw a comparison, I have congratulated myself that such was my destiny. There is much, certainly, to be said on both sides of this question, and on the other, more than on my sex, in defence of public education: many parents are forced from necessity, not choice, to adopt it: and, when this is the case, nothing more need be urged; it must be submitted to: but I am really surprized at seeing it so frequently embraced where there is no necessity. For boys, who are destined to fill public stations in various departments, much may be offered in its favour; for girls, whose sphere is certainly the domestic fireside, and whose rule, if any, will only be the management of a family; is it at boarding schools that they will learn to be good wives, good mothers, and good mistresses? Certainly not.—But while I speak of persons and things, I speak generally: I would not be understood to condemn all alike. I do know some schools whose superiors are pious people, and it may be easily imagined I feel for them a proportionate degree of respect: but this does not invalidate, or even weaken, my preference for females being brought up at home. There are, however, some observations in favour of private education equally applicable to both sexes; to which I would advert.

Private education is a great promoter of affection. A thousand nameless endearments bind the child to the parents, and the parents to the child. If parted, they find they are not indispensably necessary to each other's happiness; but, if together, their mutual love is so cemented that they cannot endure the idea of a separation.

This affection was implanted in our nature for wise and beneficial purposes; and O, how sad it is to see the beauteous structure destroyed in a moment by fashion, custom, neglect, indolence, &c.

This is one incontrovertible fact in favour of private education, and for the absence of which no advantage whatever, in my estimation, can possibly atone. Then again, where can that first of blessings, piety, be so advantageously inculcated as under the paternal roof? Can it be expected that a stranger should possess that anxiety for the welfare of a child which the parents are so ready to elude? Or even supposing, for the sake of argument, he should possess it, would it be in his power to act by a large number with the same affectionate solicitude that good parents would do with a few? Are not meekness and gentleness, modesty and humility, Christian graces? and are these generally found attendant on a boarding-school education? I believe not. Pride, vanity, haughtiness, and self-conceit, are generally allowed to supply their place: and many a naturally well disposed child has returned home from a public school with a temper totally spoiled; an open ingenuousness exchanged for sullenness, from the perpetual irritation occasioned by the continual opposition and petty broils incident to the uncontrolled humours of such a mixed, and various multitude. But I think I hear some exclaim, "This may do well enough for women, but would you have man, who is often called to defend his country, made so tame a creature?["] No, I would not have him tame at all: but, while the scriptures assure me that "A meek and quiet spirit is in the sight of God of great price,"[2] and while our Saviour himself, when on earth, declared that "The meek are blessed,"[3] I would not have man destitute of such a treasure: besides, a very little observation will prove that meekness is not incompatible with courage in men, or gentleness with fortitude in women: indeed medical men have always been ready to testify, that fortitude is more generally found in the weaker and more delicate sex, than in the other.

But where, as is very often the case, parents, from various reasons, are compelled to send their children from home, they ought undoubtedly to be careful to place them with pious people. I do not mean to say with either this sect, or that sect; I mean with real Christians, call them by what name you will: above all, let them beware of placing them with a bad clergyman: for by so doing they may imbibe a disrespect for religion, which may eventually prevent any good seed ever taking root in their hearts.

Perhaps a young parent is my reader: O, if so, let me entreat you in the most affectionate, the most earnest manner, as you value your own peace, as you value the ever-lasting welfare of your child, as you must answer it at the day of judgment, curb every rising evil passion in the bud! If you persevere, if your conduct be firm and judicious, if you commence with the infancy of your child, your task will be as easy as it will be profitable. Do not say to yourself, as I am persuaded too many parents but too often do, "He is but a babe, if he has done wrong: it would be a pity to grieve the little darling by correcting him: he will do better as he grows older." Mistaken idea! Delude not yourself with this flattering illusion: for you will never see it realised: sin not cropt in the bud, will soon blossom and ripen into poisonous fruit. While the plant is young and tender, you may with ease train it which way you will: but when it has attained its full growth, it has lost its pliancy, and will no longer bend to your hand. Just so is the human mind; take it early, and it will be what you wish; leave it to a later date, and it will be always very difficult, often impossible, to eradicate its evil passions: for by this time they have taken so deep a root, that they are sure to retain their influence, more or less, to the latest period of life: which many a good man who has afterwards been brought, by the grace of God, to see the error of his way, has been led to acknowledge, and most bitterly deplore.

But to return to my subject, for I have been led involuntarily to this digression, for which, I trust, the reader will pardon me, on account of the universal interest always taken in the topic of education.

The amusements of my childhood were different from those usually allotted to females. Having no companions of my own sex except occasional visitors, the usual plaything, a doll, was almost unknown to me, or, at least, quite unvalued. When my brothers were at home during the holiday intervals, I joined them in all their favourite sports; spinning tops, playing at marbles, &c. and to battledore and shuttlecock I was very partial, and somewhat of a proficient: but, as for the most part of my time I was alone, I was under the necessity of trusting only to my own resources for entertainment; and nothing that presented itself appeared to promise me so much pleasure as reading: it was in a measure also suitable to the state of my health, as it was a pleasure I could often enjoy when my feeble frame would have put it entirely out of my power to have taken any bodily exercise. My station in life also fostered my inclination, as, whether old or new, I could procure with facility any work I desired to peruse. Romances,[4] with a few exceptions, I never liked: they were out of nature, and therefore displeasing to me: but novels, which come nearer reality, quite fascinated my imagination for a considerable time. In short, I read uncontrolled, and indiscriminately, whatever came in my way, whether verse or prose; to the former of which I was excessively attached. But this mode of indiscriminate reading I am far from thinking advantageous to a young person; and as to works of imagination, generally speaking, I am sure, for I have witnessed their effects on others, to most young people their consequences are very pernicious: as they but too often give the mind a disrelish for more useful publications, and fill it with such romantic ideas as are totally unsuitable to real life: nay more, such as may ultimately occasion the most fatal events.

I am however only stating facts; happily for me they produced no ill effect; and as I grew older my ripening judgment taught me, with a very few exceptions of our best authors, to despise them as much as I had before admired them. I found they rather enervated than strengthened the mind, that the colours were too glowing for reality, and that to peruse them was folly and time lost, to say no worse of it: besides all which, when I had read a large number, I saw such a sameness in them, that if I had been disposed to give them up for no better reason, I should have done so because they ceased to amuse.

At this early period of my life my mother happened to have a very clever servant as cook, to whose unsought kindness I am indebted for all the little domestic knowledge I possess. Interested by my sufferings, when sickness confined me, as was not unfrequently the case, to my room, she devoted all the time she could spare from her daily avocations to my amusement: to effect which she would leave no effort in her power un-tried. At other times, when my health would permit, she delighted in having me with her, and teaching me various things useful in a family; and never appeared better pleased than when she heard my friends congratulate me on my success. If she was gratified with teaching, I was no less so with learning: I became her willing scholar because I found it afforded me a new source of enjoyment: and, alas! at this period my ill health would neither allow my resources to be many, nor various: I therefore found these domestic employments a very great relief to the monotony of life that I then experienced. Unfortunately for me, however, her residence in our family was not of any very long duration: I say unfortunately, because, had it been otherwise, I should have been the gainer of a larger portion of useful knowledge.

My ill health, my consequent retirement, and my much reading, altogether combined to stamp me with a degree of seriousness far beyond my years. I early learned to select all that was beneficial in every book I read, and to reject all that was the reverse. Blessed with a good mother, that first of earthly blessings that a child can know, I appeared to have imbibed piety, as it were, with the milk of her bosom: or else God in his mercy bestowed it upon me thus early, foreseeing, in infinite wisdom, how much I should stand in need of such a support. Be this as it may, I can never remember myself in a certain measure otherwise than as I am. I have, I trust, been advancing in the christian life, but I can never recollect being destitute of it. I hear others tell of their conversion at this or that time; under this or that minister: I have, no doubt, been very greatly benefited by different preachers, and by an intercourse with many Christian friends; but it is to God alone, both as principal and agent, I must ascribe my change of heart.

I cannot forbear relating one anecdote of my childhood, which I dare say would have passed by me entirely unnoticed had it not been impressed on my memory by the satisfaction which I saw, at the time, it had given the lady who taught me to read. At the period I am speaking of I was very young. Being one day in a room with a party of my playfellows, I took up a bible, and assembling them all around me, I read a chapter, explaining it as I went on verse by verse. What perhaps would not be very common on such an occasion, they were as attentive in hearing as I was ready in speaking. While standing thus busily employed, my instructress softly entered the room unperceived by me, for my back was to the door, and stood listening till I had finished; then advanced towards me with such manifestations of surprize and pleasure, and such greetings of approbation, as I had never before received from her. Another time, I remember, when very young indeed, weeping as my mother read some pathetic passage of scripture, and commented upon it.

But I think I hear some of my readers say, "I wonder of what religion our author calls herself? Whether Church of England, Dissenter, or Methodist? I suspect her to be the latter."[5] Indeed if you do, I shall neither be surprised nor offended by the suspicion: as that term appears to be the fashionable, but indiscriminate epithet applied to every really pious character. Being not unwilling however to answer this question, I shall inform you, I was christened, not in a room, as is the fashionable, but very improper practice, of the present day; confirmed by the ever to be respected Dr. Porteus, Bishop of London; and a partaker at the communion table in my parish church: and never shall I forget the heavenly satisfaction I enjoyed the day I first received that holy sacrament: a rite in which I have regularly joined from that time to this. "O!" you exclaim with somewhat of surprize, "She is then of the Church of England!" You may call me so if you please, and I undoubtedly am so: not because my forefathers were, for they were not; but because, after mature investigation and reflection, I am fully convinced of its excellency. I love the church, and I highly respect many of its ministers: would I could speak with the same approbation of the generality: but, as the twenty-sixth article of our church[6] justly observes, "though the evil be ever mingled with the good, yet the unworthiness of the ministers can never diminish the effects of Christ's ordinances to such as by faith and rightly do receive the same: which be effectual because of Christ's institution and promise, although they be ministered by evil men."

My readers, pray for the clergy; join your prayers with mine, that the Lord may increase the number of faithful ministers. "The harvest truly is great, but the labourers are few; pray ye therefore the Lord of the harvest, that he would send forth labourers into his harvest."[7]

But though the world may call me of the Church of England, I would rather, could I have my own choice, be called, as an excellent minister once observed to me, "A Christian at large:" I love all who love the Lord Jesus Christ in sincerity and truth: these are Christians, call them what you will, and none others are so.

> "Bound to no sect, to no one party tied,
> To sons of God in every clime allied;
> Like light's great orb to no one realm confined,
> My heaven-taught soul capacious grasps mankind."[8]

Notes

1. In 1798, with a translation and *The Effusions of the Heart*.
2. 1 Peter 3:4.

3. Matt. 5:5.

4. Here "romance" denotes not a love story but a nonrealistic fiction.

5. Methodism was a new reform movement within the Church of England, emphasizing methodical discipline in holy living and personal experience of salvation.

6. The 39 Articles constituted the Church of England's statement of its doctrine.

7. Matt. 9:37–38.

8. Source unidentified; perhaps written by Stockdale.

Bibliography

Adams, Timothy Dow. *Telling Lies in Modern American Autobiography*. Chapel Hill: University of North Carolina Press, 1990.

Adickes, Sandra. *The Social Quest: The Expanded Vision of Four Women Travelers in the Era of the French Revolution*. New York: Peter Lang, 1991.

Alden, John Richard. *General Gage in America, Being Principally a History of His Role in the American Revolution*. New York: Greenwood, 1948.

Alexander, John T. *Catherine the Great*. New York: Oxford University Press, 1989.

Applegate, Judith. " 'To Listen, to Struggle, and to Obey': Journals, Autobiographies, and Travel Narratives." In Garman et al., *Hidden in Plain Sight*, 151–170. Wallingford, Penn.: Pendle Hill, 1996.

Aravamudan, Srinivas. "Lady Mary Wortley Montagu in the Hammam: Masquerade, Womanliness, and Levantinization." *ELH* 62 (spring 1995): 69–104.

Arnold, Ralph. *The Unhappy Countess and Her Grandson John Bowes*. London: Constable, 1957.

Ashley, Kathleen, Leigh Gilmore, and Gerald Peters. *Autobiography and Postmodernism*. Amherst: University of Massachusetts Press, 1994.

Ashley, Leonard R. N. Introduction to *A Narrative of the Life of Mrs. Charlotte Charke*, vii–xxiv. Facsimile ed. Gainesville, Fla.: Scholars' Facsimiles and Reprints, 1969.

Augustine, Saint. *Confessions*. Trans. Rex Warner. New York: New American Library, 1963.

Bakhtin, Mikhail. *The Dialogic Imagination*. Ed. Michael Holquist. Trans. Caryl Emerson and Michael Holquist. Austin: University of Texas Press, 1981.

Balsamo, Anne. *Technologies of the Gendered Body: Reading Cyborg Women*. Durham, N.C.: Duke University Press, 1996.

Barlowe, Jamie. "Daring to Dialogue: Mary Wollstonecraft's Rhetoric of Feminist Dialogics." In *Reclaiming Rhetorica: Women in the Rhetorical Tradition*. Ed. Andrea Lunsford and James Murphy, 117–136. Pittsburgh: University of Pittsburgh Press, 1995.

Barros, Carolyn A. *Autobiography: Narrative of Transformation*. Ann Arbor: University of Michigan Press, 1998.

Barthes, Roland. *Roland Barthes by Roland Barthes*. Trans. Richard Howard. New York: Hill and Wang, 1977.

Bartlett, Roger, and Janet Hartley, eds. *Russia in the Age of the Enlightenment: Essays for Isabel de Madariaga*. New York: St. Martin's, 1990.

Baruth, Philip E., ed. *Introducing Charlotte Charke: Actress, Author, Enigma*. Urbana: University of Illinois Press, 1998.

Bell, Maureen. "Seditious Sisterhood: Women Publishers of Opposition Literature at the Restoration." In Chedgzoy et al., *Voicing Women*, 185–195. Pittsburgh: Duquesne University Press, 1997.

Benedict, Barbara M. "The 'Beauties' of Literature, 1750–1820: Tasteful Prose and Fine Rhyme for Private Consumption." In *1650–1850: Ideas, Aesthetics, and Inquiries in the Early Modern Era*. Vol. 1. Ed. Kevin L. Cope, 317–346. New York: AMS, 1994.

Benefiel, Margaret. " 'Weaving the Web of Community': Letters and Epistles." In Garman et al., *Hidden in Plain Sight*, 443–452. Wallingford, Penn.: Pendle Hill, 1996.

Benstock, Shari, ed. *The Private Self: Theory and Practice of Women's Autobiographical Writings*. Chapel Hill: University of North Carolina Press, 1988.

Benveniste, Emile. *Problems in General Linguistics*. Trans. Mary Elizabeth Meek. Coral Gables, Fla.: University of Miami Press, 1971.

Berg, Maxine. *The Age of Manufactures: Industry, Innovation and Work in Britain 1700–1820*. London: Fontana, 1985.

Bernstein, Susan David. "Confessing Feminist Theory: What's 'I' Got to Do with It?" *Hypatia* 7 (spring 1992): 120–147.

Bewell, Alan. " 'On the Banks of the South Sea': Botany and Sexual Controversy in the Late Eighteenth Century." In Miller and Reill, *Visions of Empire*, 173–193. Cambridge: Cambridge University Press, 1996.

Black, Clinton V. *The History of Jamaica*. San Juan, Trinidad: Longman Caribbean, 1983.

Blodgett, Harriet, ed. *Capacious Hold-All: An Anthology of English-women's Diary Writings*. Charlottesville: University Press of Virginia, 1991.

Bloom, Leslie Rebecca. *Under the Sign of Hope: Feminist Methodology and Narrative Interpretation*. Albany: State University of New York Press, 1998.

Boer, Inge E. "Despotism from under the Veil: Masculine and Feminine Readings of the Despot and the Harem." *Cultural Critique* 32 (winter 1995–1996): 43–73.

Bogel, Fredric B. "Crisis and Character in Autobiography." *Studies in English Literature 1500–1900* 21 (summer 1981): 499–512.

Bohls, Elizabeth. "Aesthetics and Orientalism in Lady Mary Wortley Montagu's Letters." *Studies in Eighteenth-Century Culture* 23 (1994): 179–205.

———. *Women Travel Writers and the Language of Aesthetics, 1716–1818*. Cambridge: Cambridge University Press, 1995.

Bolton, Betsy. "Romancing the Stone: 'Perdita' Robinson in Wordsworth's London." *ELH* 64 (fall 1997): 727–759.

Bordo, Susan. *Unbearable Weight: Feminism, Western Culture, and the Body*. Berkeley: University of California Press, 1993.

Braidwood, Stephen J. *Black Poor and White Philanthropists: London's Blacks and the Foundation of the Sierra Leone Settlement 1786–91.* Liverpool: Liverpool University Press, 1994.

Bree, Germaine. "Autogynography." In Olney, *Studies in Autobiography,* 171–179. New York: Oxford University Press, 1988.

Bridenthal, Renate, Susan Mosher Stuard, and Merry E. Wiesner, eds. *Becoming Visible: Women in European History.* Rev. ed. Boston: Houghton Mifflin, 1998.

Broadley, A. M., and Lewis Melville, eds. *The Beautiful Lady Craven. The Original Memoirs of Elizabeth Baroness Craven afterwards Margravine of Anspach and Bayreuth and Princess Berkeley of the Holy Roman Empire (1750–1828).* 2 vols. London: John Lane, 1913.

Brodzki, Bella, and Celeste Schenck, eds. *Life/Lines: Theorizing Women's Autobiography.* Ithaca, N.Y.: Cornell University Press, 1988.

Broughton, Trev Lynn, and Linda Anderson, eds. *Women's Lives/Women's Times: New Essays on Auto/Biography.* Albany: State University of New York Press, 1997.

Brown, Elisabeth Potts, and Susan Mosher Stuard, eds. *Witnesses for Change: Quaker Women over Three Centuries.* New Brunswick, N.J.: Rutgers University Press, 1989.

Browne, Janet. "Botany in the Boudoir and Garden: The Banksian Context." In Miller and Reill, *Visions of Empire,* 153–172. Cambridge: Cambridge University Press, 1996.

Brownfoot, Janice N. "Memsahibs in Colonial Malaya: A Study of European Wives in a British Colony and Protectorate." In Callan and Ardener, *The Incorporated Wife,* 186–210. London: Croom Helm, 1984.

Bruner, Jerome. "A Narrative Model of Self-Construction." *Annals of the New York Academy of the Sciences* 818 (1997): 145–161.

Bruss, Elizabeth. "Eye for I: Making and Unmaking Autobiography in Film." In Olney, ed., *Autobiography,* 296–320. Princeton: Princeton University Press, 1980.

Buck, Anne. *Clothes and the Child: A Handbook of Children's Dress in England 1500–1900.* New York: Holmes & Meier, 1996.

Bunkers, Suzanne L., and Cynthia A. Huff, eds. *Inscribing the Daily: Critical Essays on Women's Diaries.* Amherst: University of Massachusetts Press, 1996.

Bunyan, John. *"The Pilgrim's Progress" and "Grace Abounding to the Chief of Sinners."* Ed. James Thorpe. Boston: Houghton Mifflin, 1969.

Burke, Edmund. *A Philosophical Enquiry into the Origin of Our Ideas of the Sublime and the Beautiful.* 1756. Ed. James T. Boulton. Oxford: Basil Blackwell, 1987.

Burke, Kenneth. *A Grammar of Motives.* Berkeley: University of California Press, 1969.

——. *A Rhetoric of Motives.* Berkeley: University of California Press, 1950.

Bush, Barbara. *Slave Women in Caribbean Society 1650–1838.* Kingston, Jamaica: Heinemann Caribbean, 1990.

Buss, Helen M. "A Feminist Revision of New Historicism to Give Fuller Readings of Women's Private Writing." In Smith and Watson, *Women, Autobiog-*

raphy, *Theory: A Reader*, 222–231. Madison: University of Wisconsin Press, 1998.

Chaucer, Geoffrey. "The Tale of Melibee." In *The Riverside Chaucer*. Ed. Larry D. Benson, 217–239. 3d ed. New York: Houghton Mifflin, 1987.

Callan, Hilary. Introduction to Callan and Ardener, *The Incorporated Wife*, 1–26. London: Croom Helm, 1984.

Callan, Hilary, and Shirley Ardener, eds. *The Incorporated Wife*. London: Croom Helm, 1984.

Camden, Vera. Introduction. to Camden, ed., *The Narrative of the Persecutions of Agnes Beaumont*, 1–33. East Lansing, Mich.: Colleagues, 1992.

Carswell, John. *The South Sea Bubble*. Rev. ed. Dover, N.H.: Alan Sutton, 1993.

Chedgzoy, Kate, Melanie Hansen, and Suzanne Trill, eds. *Voicing Women: Gender and Sexuality in Early Modern Writing*. Pittsburgh: Duquesne University Press, 1997.

Churchill, Sue. " 'I Then Was What I Had Made Myself': Representation and Charlotte Charke." *Biography* 20 (winter 1997): 72–94.

Cixous, Hélène. *Rootprints: Memory and Life-Writing*. New York: Routledge, 1997.

Clark, Anna. *The Struggle for the Breeches: Gender and the Making of the British Working Class*. Berkeley: University of California Press, 1995.

Coleman, Deirdre. "Sierra Leone, Slavery, and Sexual Politics: Anna Maria Falconbridge and the 'Swarthy Daughter' of Late 18th Century Abolitionism." *Women's Writing* 2.1 (1995): 1–23.

———, ed. *Maiden Voyages and Infant Colonies: Two Women's Travel Narratives of the 1790s*. London: Leicester University Press, 1999.

Coleman, Linda S. "Gender, Sect, and Circumstance: Quaker Mary Penington's Many Voices." In Coleman, *Women's Life-Writing*, 93–107. Bowling Green, Ohio: Bowling Green State University Popular Press, 1997.

———, ed. *Women's Life-Writing: Finding Voice/Building Community*. Bowling Green, Ohio: Bowling Green State University Popular Press, 1997.

Colley, Linda. *Britons: Forging the Nation 1707–1837*. London: Vintage, 1992.

Conger, Syndy. "Three Unlikely Fellow Travellers: Mary Wollstonecraft, Yorick, Samuel Johnson." *Studies on Voltaire and the Eighteenth Century* 305 (1992): 1667–1668.

Conway, Jill Ker. *When Memory Speaks: Reflections on Autobiography*. New York: Knopf, 1998.

Craft-Fairchild, Catherine. *Masquerade and Gender: Disguise and Female Identity in Eighteenth-Century Fictions by Women*. University Park: Pennsylvania State University Press, 1993.

Craton, Michael. *Empire, Enslavement and Freedom in the Caribbean*. Kingston, Jamaica: Ian Randle, 1997.

Cullens, Chris. "Mrs. Robinson and the Masquerade of Womanliness." In *Body and Texts in the Eighteenth Century*. Ed. Veronica Kelley and Dorothea von Mucke, 266–289, 337–341. Stanford, Calif.: Stanford University Press, 1994.

Cundall, Frank, ed. *Lady Nugent's Journal. Jamaica One Hundred Years Ago*. London: Adam and Charles Black, 1907.

Dabydeen, David. *Hogarth, Walpole, and Commercial Britain*. London: Hansib, 1987.

Dailey, Barbara Ritter. "The Husbands of Margaret Fell: An Essay on Religious Metaphor and Social Change." *Seventeenth Century* 2 (January 1987): 55–71.

Davidoff, Leonore, and Catherine Hall. *Family Fortunes: Men and Women of the English Middle Class, 1780–1850*. Chicago: University of Chicago Press, 1987.

Davies, Gareth Alban. "Sir Richard Fanshawe, Hispanist Cavalier." *University of Leeds Review* 20 (1977): 87–119.

De la Cruz, Sor Juana Inés. *La Respuesta/A Woman of Genius*. Trans. Margaret Sayers Peden. Salisbury, Conn.: Lime Rock, 1982.

de Lauretis, Teresa. "The Essence of the Triangle or, Taking the Risk of Essentialism Seriously: Feminist Theory in Italy, the U.S., and Britain." In *The Essential Difference*. Ed. Naomi Schor and Elizabeth Weed, 1–39. Bloomington: Indiana University Press, 1994.

De Man, Paul. "Autobiography as De-facement." *Modern Language Notes* 94 (December 1979): 919–930.

DeJong, Mary. "Hymns as Autobiography." Paper presented at NEH Summer Seminar on Autobiography, Louisiana State University, June 1988.

DeRitter, Jones. " 'Not the Person She Conceived Me': The Public Identities of Charlotte Charke." In *Sexual Artifice*. Ed. Ann Kibbley et al., 3–25. New York: New York University Press, 1994.

Desai, Anita. Introduction to *Lady Mary Wortley Montagu. Turkish Embassy Letters*. Ed. Jack Malcolm, vii–xlii. Athens: University of Georgia Press, 1993.

Dobie, Madeleine. "Embodying Oriental Women: Representation and Voyeurism in Montesquieu, Montagu and Ingres." *Cincinnati Romance Review* 13 (1994): 51–60.

Donald, Diana. *The Age of Caricature: Satirical Prints in the Reign of George III*. New Haven, Conn.: Yale University Press, 1996.

Donaldson, Laura E. *Decolonizing Feminisms: Race, Gender, and Empire Building*. Chapel Hill: University of North Carolina Press, 1992.

Donoghue, Frank. *The Fame Machine: Book Reviewing and Eighteenth-Century Literary Careers*. Stanford, Calif.: Stanford University Press, 1996.

Doody, Margaret Anne. "The Law, the Page, and the Body of Women: Murder and Murderesses in the Age of Johnson." In *The Age of Johnson* 1. Ed. Paul J. Korshin, 127–160. New York: AMS, 1987.

Dronke, Peter. *Women Writers of the Middle Ages*. Cambridge: Cambridge University Press, 1984.

Dugaw, Dianne. *Warrior Women and Popular Balladry 1650–1850*. Cambridge: Cambridge University Press, 1989.

Dyson, Ketaki Kushari. *A Various Universe: A Study of the Journals and Memoirs of British Men and Women in the Indian Subcontinent, 1765–1856*. Delhi: Oxford University Press, 1978.

Eakin, Paul John. *Fictions in Autobiography: Studies in the Art of Self-Invention*. Princeton: Princeton University Press, 1985.

Edwards, Jonathan. *Personal Narrative*. Ed. Ola Elizabeth Winslow. New York: Signet, 1966.

Egan, Susanna. *Patterns of Experience in Autobiography*. Chapel Hill: University of North Carolina Press, 1984.

Elbaz, Robert. *The Changing Nature of the Self: A Critical Study of Autobiographical Discourse*. Iowa City: University of Iowa Press, 1987.

Ezell, Margaret J. M. *Writing Women's Literary History*. Baltimore: Johns Hopkins University Press, 1993.

Fantham, Elaine. *Women in the Classical World: Image and Text*. New York: Oxford University Press, 1994.

Ferguson, Moira. "Anna Maria Falconbridge and Sierra Leone: 'The Reality of a Coloniser.' " In *Cultural Readings of Imperialism: Edward Said and the Gravity of History*. Ed. Keith Ansell-Pearson, Benita Parry, and Judith Squires, 248–266. New York: St. Martin's, 1997.

Finn, Geraldine. *Why Althusser Killed His Wife: Essays on Discourse and Violence*. Atlantic Highlands, N.J.: Humanities, 1996.

Fitzgerald, Percy. *The Life of Mrs. Catherine Clive. With an Account of her Adventures on and off the Stage, a Round of her Characters, together with her correspondence*. London: A. Reader, 1888.

Fleckenstein, Kristie. "Writing Bodies: Somatic Mind in Composition Studies." *College English* 61 (January 1999): 281–306.

Folkenflik, Robert. "Charlotte Charke: Images and Afterimages." In Baruth, *Introducing Charlotte Chark*, 137–161. Urbana: University of Illinois Press, 1998.

———, ed. *The Culture of Autobiography: Constructions of Self-Representation*. Stanford, Calif.: Stanford University Press, 1993.

Friedl, Lynne. " 'Passing Women'—A Study of Gender Boundaries in the Eighteenth Century." In Rousseau and Porter, *Sexual Underworlds of the Enlightenment*, 234–260. Chapel Hill: University of North Carolina Press, 1988.

Friedman, Susan Stanford. "Women's Autobiographical Selves: Theory and Practice." In Benstock, *The Private Self*, 34–62. Chapel Hill: University of North Carolina Press, 1988.

Fyvie, John. *Tragedy Queens of the Georgian Era*. New York: E. P. Dutton, 1909.

Gagnier, Regenia. "The Literary Standard, Working-Class Lifewriting and Gender." *Textual Practice* 3 (spring 1996): 36–55.

Garman, Mary. "Introduction: 'Hidden in Plain Sight,' " In Garman et al., *Hidden in Plain Sight*, 1–16. Wallingford, Penn,.: Pendle Hill, 1996.

———. " 'Therefore I will prophesie': Tracts of Proclamation and Warning." In Garman et al., *Hidden in Plain Sight*, 19–34. Wallingford, Penn.: Pendle Hill, 1996.

Garman, Mary, Judith Applegate, Margaret Benefiel, and Dortha Meredith, eds. *Hidden in Plain Sight: Quaker Women's Writings 1650–1700*. Wallingford, Penn.: Pendle Hill, 1996.

Gazzanigam, Michael S. *The Mind's Past*. Berkeley: University of California Press, 1998.

Genette, Gerard. *Narrative Discourse*. Trans. Jane E. Lewin. Ithaca, N.Y.: Cornell University Press, 1980.

Gilbert, Sandra, and Susan Gubar. "Ceremonies of the Alphabet: Female Grandmatologies and the Female Authorgraph." In Stanton, *The Female Autograph*, 3–20. Chicago: University of Chicago Press, 1984.

Gilead, Sarah. "Emigrant Selves: Narrative Strategies in Three Women's Autobiographies." *Criticism* 30 (1988): 43–62.

Gilmore, Leigh. *Autobiographics: A Feminist Theory of Women's Self-representation*. Ithaca, N.Y.: Cornell University Press, 1994.

Goodman, Nelson. "Twisted Tales; or, Story, Study, and Symphony." In Mitchell, *On Narrative*, 99–115. Chicago: University of Chicago Press, 1981.

Graham, Elspeth, Hilary Hinds, Elaine Hobby, and Helen Wilcox, eds. *Her Own Life: Autobiographical Writings by Seventeenth-Century Englishwomen*. London: Routledge, 1989.

———. " 'Pondering All These Things in Her Heart': Aspects of Secrecy in the Autobiographical Writings of Seventeenth-Century Englishwomen." In Broughton and Anderson, *Women's Lives/Women's Times*, 51–72. Albany: State University of New York Press, 1997.

Granqvist, Raoul. "Her Imperial Eyes: A Reading of Mary Wollstonecraft's *Letters Written during a short Residence in Sweden, Norway and Denmark*." *Moderna Sprak* 91.1 (1997): 16–24.

Greene, Donald. "The Uses of Autobiography in the Eighteenth Century." In *Essays in Eighteenth Century Biography*. Ed. Philip B. Daghlian, 48–66. Bloomington: Indiana University Press, 1968.

Griffiths, David M. "Catherine II: The Republican Empress." In Hamburg, *Imperial Russian History I*, 35–56. New York: Garland, 1992.

Grundy, Isobel. "Editing Lady Mary Wortley Montagu." In *Editing Women*. Ed. Ann M. Hutchison and Margaret Anne Doody, 55–78. Toronto: University of Toronto Press, 1998.

———. "Rachel Hunter and the Victims of Slavery." *Women's Writing* 1.1 (1994): 25–34.

Gunn, Janet Varner. *Autobiography: Toward a Poetics of Experience*. Philadelphia: University of Pennsylvania Press, 1982.

Gusdorf, Georges. "Conditions and Limits of Autobiography." In Olney, *Autobiography*, 28–48. Princeton: Princeton University Press, 1980.

Hamburg, Gary M., ed. *Imperial Russian History I: 1700–1861*. Vol. 2 of *Russian and Soviet History 1550–1991*. New York: Garland, 1992.

Hammond, J. L., and Barbara Hammond. *The Skilled Labourer 1750–1832*. 1919. Reprint, Abingdon, U.K.: Fraser Stewart, 1995.

Harrow, Sharon. "Trading in the Blush: Domesticating the Colony in Anna Maria Falconbridge's Narrative." *Journal of African Travel-Writing* 5: 25–37.

Hassam, Andrew. " 'Farewell to old England, and now for a new Life and a new Journal': Emigration as Narrative." *Journal of Australian Studies* 36 (March 1993): 23–35.

Hattendorf, John B. *England in the War of the Spanish Succession: A Study of the English View and Conduct of Grand Strategy, 1702–1712.* New York: Garland, 1987.

Heilbrun, Carolyn. *Writing a Woman's Life.* London: Women's Press, 1989.

Heinzelman, Susan Sage. "Guilty in Law, Implausible in Fiction: Jurisprudential and Literary Narratives in the Case of Mary Blandy, Parricide, 1752." In *Representing Women: Law, Literature, and Feminism.* Ed. Susan Sage Heinzelman and Zypporah Batshaw Wiseman, 309–336. Durham, N.C.: Duke University Press, 1994.

Herrnstein Smith, Barbara. "Afterthoughts on Narrative III: Narrative Versions, Narrative Theories." In Mitchell, *On Narrative*, 209–232. Chicago: University of Chicago Press, 1981.

————. *On the Margins of Discourse.* Chicago: University of Chicago Press, 1978.

Hewitt, Leah. *Autobiographical Tightropes.* Lincoln: University of Nebraska Press, 1990.

Highfill, Philip H., Jr. "Performers and Performing." In Hume, *The London Theater World*, 143–180. Carbondale: Southern Illinois University Press, 1980.

Highfill, Philip H., Jr., Kalman A. Burnim, and Edward A. Langhans. *A Biographical Dictionary of Actors, Actresses, Musicians, Dancers, Managers and Other Stage Personnel in London, 1660–1800.* 16 vols. Carbondale: Southern Illinois University Press, 1973–1993.

Hill, Bridget. *Women, Work and Sexual Politics in Eighteenth-Century England.* London: University College London Press, 1994.

Hill, Christopher. *The Century of Revolution, 1603–1714.* Rev. ed. Walton on Thames, Eng.: Thomas Nelson, 1980.

————. *The World Turned Upside Down: Radical Ideas during the English Revolution.* Harmondsworth, Eng.: Penguin, 1978.

Hughes, Robert. *The Fatal Shore: A History of the Transportation of Convicts to Australia 1787–1868.* London: Pan, 1988.

Hume, Robert D., ed. *The London Theatre World, 1660–1800.* Carbondale: Southern Illinois University Press, 1980.

Innes, Joanna. "Prisons for the Poor: English Bridewells, 1555–1800." In *Labour, Law and Crime: An Historical Perspective.* Ed. Francis Snyder and Douglas Hay, 42–122. London: Tavistock, 1987.

Iser, Wolfgang. *The Act of Reading: A Theory of Aesthetic Response.* Baltimore: Johns Hopkins University Press, 1978.

Jacobs, H. P. *Sixty Years of Change, 1806–1866.* Kingston: Institute of Jamaica, 1973.

James, Lawrence. *Raj: The Making and Unmaking of British India.* New York: St. Martin's, 1997.

Janetta, A. E. "Anecdotal Humor in Maria Campbell's *Halfbreed*." *Journal of Canadian Studies* 31 (summer 1996): 62–75.

Jay, Paul. "What's the Use? Critical Theory and the Study of Autobiography." *Biography* 10 (winter 1987): 39–54.

Jelinek, Estelle, ed. *Women's Autobiography: Essays in Criticism*. Bloomington: Indiana University Press, 1980.

Jenkins, Carol. "The Major Silence: Autobiographies of Working Women in the Nineteenth Century." In *Writing and Victorianism*. Ed. J. B. Bullen, 38–53. London: Longman, 1997.

Joannou, Maroula. " 'She Who Would Be Politically Free Herself Must Strike the Blow': Suffragette Autobiography and Suffragette Militancy." In Swindells, *The Uses of Autobiography*, 31–44. London: Taylor and Francis, 1995.

Jones, Angela D. " 'When a Woman So Far Outsteps Her Proper Sphere': Counter-Romantic Tourism." In Coleman, *Women's Life-Writing*, 209–237. Bowling Green, Ohio: Bowling Green State University Popular Press, 1997.

Jones, D. W. *War and Economy in the Age of William III and Marlborough*. London: Basil Blackwell, 1988.

Kadar, Marlene. "Coming to Terms: Life Writing—from Genre to Critical Practice." In Kadar, *Essays on Life Writing*, 3–16. Toronto: University of Toronto Press, 1992.

———, ed. *Essays on Life Writing: From Genre to Critical Practice*. Toronto: University of Toronto Press, 1992.

Kanner, Barbara. *Women in Context: 200 Years of British Women Autobiographers, a Reference Guide and Reader*. New York: G. K. Hall, 1997.

Kenyon, J. P. *Revolution Principles: The Politics of Party 1689–1720*. Cambridge: Cambridge University Press, 1977.

Kirkwood, Deborah. "Settler Wives in Southern Rhodesia: A Case Study." In Callan and Ardener, *The Incorporated Wife*, 143–164. London: Croom Helm, 1984.

Kitchen, Martin. *The Cambridge Illustrated History of Germany*. Cambridge: Cambridge University Press, 1996.

Korshin, Paul J. "The Development of Intellectual Biography in the Eighteenth Century." *Journal of English and Germanic Philology* 73 (1974): 513–523.

Kramer, Lawrence. "Gender and Sexuality in *The Prelude*: The Question of Book Seven." *ELH* 54 (fall 1987): 619–637.

Langford, Paul, and Christopher Harvie. *The Eighteenth Century and the Age of Industry*. Vol. 4 of *The Oxford History of Britain*. Oxford: Oxford University Press, 1992.

Laurence, Anne. *Women in England 1500–1760: A Social History*. New York: St. Martin's, 1994.

Lejeune, Philippe. "Autobiography in the Third Person." *New Literary History* 9 (1977): 27–50.

———. *On Autobiography*. Trans. Katherine Leary. Minneapolis: University of Minnesota Press, 1989.

Levy, Martin J., ed. *Perdita*. Chester Springs, Penn.: Dufour, 1994.

Lew, Joseph W. "Lady Mary's Portable Seraglio." *Eighteenth-Century Studies* 24 (summer 1991): 432–450.

Loesberg, Jonathan. "Moving Beyond the Deconstructive Impasse in the Criticism of Autobiography." *Prose Studies* 20 (April 1997): 119–138.

Lowenthal, Cynthia. "The Veil of Romance: Lady Mary's Embassy Letters." *Eighteenth-Century Life* 14 (February 1990): 66–82.

Lupton, L. F. *Behind Mr. Bunyan*. London: Fauconberg, 1962.

Lury, Celia. "Reading the Self: Autobiography, Gender and the Institution of the Literary." In *Off-Centre: Feminism and Cultural Studies*. Ed. Sarah Franklin, Celia Lury, and Jackie Stacey, 97–108. London: HarperCollins Academic, 1991.

Luther, Susan. "A Stranger Minstrel: Coleridge's Mrs. Robinson." *Studies in Romanticism* 33 (fall 1994): 391–409.

Mack, Maynard. *Alexander Pope: A Life*. New York: Norton, 1985.

Mack, Phyllis. "Gender and Spirituality in Early English Quakerism, 1650–1665." In Brown and Stuard, *Witnesses for Change*, 31–63. New Brunswick, N.J.: Rutgers University Press, 1989.

———. *Visionary Women: Ecstatic Prophecy in Seventeenth-Century England*. Berkeley: University of California Press, 1992.

Mackenzie-Grieve, Averil. *The Great Accomplishment*. London: Geoffrey Bles, 1953.

Mackie, Erin. "Desperate Measures: The Narratives of the Life of Mrs. Charlotte Charke." *ELH* 58 (winter 1991): 841–865.

Marcus, Laura. *Auto/biographical Discourses: Theory, Criticism, Practice*. Manchester: Manchester University Press, 1994.

———. "The Face of Autobiography." In Swindells, *The Uses of Autobiography*, 13–23. London: Taylor and Francis, 1995.

Mascuch, Michael. *Origins of the Individualist Self: Autobiography and Self-Identity in England, 1591–1791*. Stanford, Calif.: Stanford University Press, 1997.

McCooey, David. *Artful Histories: Modern Australian Autobiographies*. Cambridge: Cambridge University Press, 1996.

McGann, Jerome. "Mary Robinson and the Myth of Sappho." *Modern Language Quarterly* 56 (March 1995): 55–76.

Melman, Billie. *Women's Orients: English Women and the Middle East, 1718–1918: Sexuality, Religion and Work*. Ann Arbor: University of Michigan Press, 1992.

Michaels, Walter Benn. "The Interpreter's Self: Peirce on the Cartesian 'Subject.' " In *Reader-Response Criticism: From Formalism to Post-Structuralism*. Ed. Jane Tompkins, 185–200. Baltimore: Johns Hopkins University Press, 1980.

Midgley, Clare. *Women against Slavery: The British Compaigns, 1780–1870*. London: Routledge, 1992.

Milhous, Judith. "Company Management." In Hume, *The London Theatre World*, 1–34. Carbondale: Southern Illinois University Press, 1980.

Miller, David Philip, and Peter Hanns Reill, eds. *Visions of Empire: Voyages, Botany, and Representations of Nature*. Cambridge: Cambridge University Press, 1996.

Miller, Nancy K. *Getting Personal: Feminist Occasions and Other Autobiographical Acts.* New York: Routledge, 1991.

Mills, Sara. *Discourses of Difference: An Analysis of Women's Travel Writing and Colonialism.* London: Routledge, 1993.

Mingay, G. E. *The Gentry: The Rise and Fall of a Ruling Class.* New York: Longman, 1976.

Minter Strange, Sallie. "Charlotte Charke: Transvestite or Conjuror?" *Restoration and Eighteenth-Century Theatre Research* 15.2 (1976): 54–59.

Misch, Georg. *A History of Autobiography in Antiquity.* Trans. E. W. Dickes. 2 vols. Cambridge: Harvard University Press, 1951.

Mitchell, C. J. "Women in the Eighteenth-Century Book Trade." In *Writers, Books, and Trade: An Eighteenth-Century Miscellany for William B. Todd.* Ed. O. M. Brack, 25–75. New York: AMS Press, 1990.

Mitchell, L. G. *Charles James Fox.* Oxford: Oxford University Press, 1992.

Mitchell, W. J. T., ed. *On Narrative.* Chicago: University of Chicago Press, 1981.

Moore, Jane. "Plagiarism with a Difference: Subjectivity in 'Kubla Khan' and *Letters Written during a Short Residence in Sweden, Norway and Denmark.*" In *Beyond Romanticism: New Approaches to Texts and Contexts, 1780–1832.* Ed. Stephen Copley and John Whale, 140–159. Syracuse, N.Y.: Syracuse University Press, 1991.

Moore, Lisa. " 'She Was Too Fond of Her Mistaken Bargain': The Scandalous Relations of Gender and Sexuality in Feminist Theory." *Diacritics* 21 (summer–fall 1991): 89–101.

Morgan, Fidelis, with Charlotte Charke. *The Well-Known Troublemaker: A Life of Charlotte Charke.* London: Faber and Faber, 1988.

Moskal, Jeanne. "The Picturesque and the Affectionate in Wollstonecraft's *Letters from Norway.*" *Modern Language Quarterly* 52 (September 1991): 263–294.

Myers, Mitzi. "Mary Wollstonecraft's *Letters . . . in Sweden:* Toward Romantic Autobiography." *Studies in Eighteenth-Century Culture* 8 (1979): 165–185.

———. "Pedagogy as Self-Expression in Mary Wollstonecraft: Exorcising the Past, Finding a Voice." In Benstock, *The Private Self,* 192–210. Chapel Hill: University of North Carolina Press, 1988.

Neuman, Shirley, ed. *Autobiography and Questions of Gender.* London: Frank Cass, 1991.

Newton, Judith Lowder. *Women, Power, and Subversion: Social Strategies in British Fiction, 1778–1860.* Athens: University of Georgia Press, 1981.

Nilsen, Ann. "Stories of Life—Stories of Living: Women's Narratives and Feminist Biography." *Nordic Journal of Women's Studies* 4 (1996): 16–30.

Nussbaum, Felicity A. *The Autobiographical Subject: Gender and Ideology in Eighteenth-Century England.* Baltimore: Johns Hopkins University Press, 1989.

———. "Heteroclites: The Gender of Character in the Scandalous Memoirs." In *The New Eighteenth Century: Theory, Politics, English Literature.* Ed. Felicity Nussbaum and Laura Brown, 144–167. New York: Methuen, 1987.

————. *Torrid Zones: Maternity, Sexuality, and Empire in Eighteenth-Century English Narratives*. Baltimore: Johns Hopkins University Press, 1995.

Okenfuss, Max J. "Education and Empire: School Reform in Enlightened Russia." In Hamburg, *Imperial Russian History I*, 107–134. New York: Garland, 1992.

Olney, James, ed. *Autobiography: Essays Theoretical and Critical*. Princeton: Princeton University Press, 1980.

————. *Studies in Autobiography*. New York: Oxford University Press, 1988.

O'Loughlin, Katrina. " 'Our Floating Prison': Anna Maria Falconbridge and Travel to the River Sierra Leone." *Journal of African Travel-Writing* 5: 38–52.

Ormsby-Lennon, Hugh. "From Shibboleth to Apocalypse: Quaker Speechways during the Puritan Revolution." In *Language, Self, and Society: A Social History of Language*. Ed. Peter Burke and Roy Porter, 72–112. London: Polity, 1988.

O'Toole, Fintan. *A Traitor's Kiss: The Life of Richard Brinsley Sheridan 1751–1816*. New York: Farrar, Straus and Giroux, 1997.

Parry, J. H. *Trade and Dominion: The European Overseas Empires in the Eighteenth Century*. London: Sphere, 1974.

Pascoe, Judith. "Mary Robinson and the Literary Marketplace." In *Romantic Women Writers: Voices and Countervoices*. Ed. Paula R. Feldman and Theresa M. Kelley, 252–268. Hanover, N.H.: University Press of New England, 1995.

————. "The Spectacular *Flâneuse*: Mary Robinson and the City of London." *Wordsworth Circle* 23 (summer 1992): 165–171.

Pearson, Jacqueline. *The Prostituted Muse: Images of Women & Women Dramatists 1642–1737*. New York: St. Martin's, 1988.

Peavy, Charles D. "The Chimerical Career of Charlotte Charke." *Restoration and Eighteenth-Century Theatre Research* 8.1 (1969): 1–12.

Perreault, Jeanne. *Writing Selves: Contemporary Feminist Autobiography*. Minneapolis: University of Minnesota Press, 1995.

Perry, Gill, and Michael Rossington, eds. *Femininity and Masculinity in Eighteenth-Century Art and Culture*. Manchester: Manchester University Press, 1994.

Peterson, Linda H. "Becoming an Author: Mary Robinson's *Memoirs* and the Origins of the Woman Artist's Autobiography." In *Revisioning Romanticism: British Women Writers, 1776–1837*. Ed. Carol Wilson Shiner and Joel Haefner, 36–50. Philadelphia: University of Pennsylvania Press, 1994.

————. "Female Autobiographer, Narrative Duplicity." *Studies in the Literary Imagination* 23 (fall 1990): 165–176.

————. "Institutionalizing Women's Autobiography: Nineteenth-Century Editors and the Shaping of an Autobiographical Tradition." In Folkenflik, *Culture of Autobiography*, 80–103. Stanford, Calif.: Stanford University Press, 1993.

Pinchbeck, Ivy. *Women Workers and the Industrial Revolution 1750–1850*. 3d ed. London: Virago, 1985.

Porter, Roy. *English Society in the Eighteenth Century*. Rev. ed. London: Penguin, 1990.

————. "A Touch of Danger: The Man-Midwife as Sexual Predator." In Rousseau and Porter, *Sexual Underworlds of the Enlightenment,* 206–232. Chapel Hill: University of North Carolina Press, 1988.

Poston, Carol H. Introduction to *Letters Written during a Short Residence in Sweden, Norway, and Denmark,* by Mary Wollstonecraft, vi–xxiv. Lincoln: University of Nebraska Press, 1976.

Prior, Mary. "Women and the Urban Economy: Oxford 1550–1800." In Prior, *Women in English Society,* 93–117. London: Methuen, 1985.

———, ed. *Women in English Society 1500–1800.* London: Methuen, 1985.

Ramdin, Ron. *The Making of the Black Working Class in Britain.* Aldershot, Eng.: Wildwood, 1987.

Rediker, Marcus. "Liberty beneath the Jolly Roger: The Lives of Anne Bonny and Mary Read, Pirates." In *Iron Men, Wooden Women: Gender and Seafaring in the Atlantic World, 1700–1920.* Ed. Margaret S. Creighton and Lisa Norling, 2–33. Baltimore: Johns Hopkins University Press, 1996.

Reiman, Donald H. "The Beauty of Buttermere as Fact and Romantic Symbol." *Criticism* 26 (spring 1984): 139–170.

Relke, Diana M. A. "In Search of Mrs. Pilkington." In *Gender at Work: Four Women Writers of the Eighteenth Century.* Ed. Ann Messenger, 114–149. Detroit: Wayne State University Press, 1990.

Rendall, Jane. " 'A Short Account of My Unprofitable Life': Autobiographies of Working Class Women in Britain 1775–1845." In Broughton and Anderson, *Women's Lives/Women's Times,* 31–50. Albany: State University of New York Press, 1997.

Renza, Louis. "The Veto of the Imagination." In Mitchell, *On Narrative,* 268–295. Chicago: University of Chicago Press, 1981.

Ricouer, Paul. "Narrative Time." In Mitchell, *On Narrative,* 165–186. Chicago: University of Chicago Press, 1981.

Roberts, P. E. *History of British India under the Company and the Crown.* 3d ed. London: Oxford University Press, 1952.

Robinson, Jane, ed. *Unsuitable for Ladies: An Anthology of Women Travellers.* Oxford: Oxford University Press, 1994.

Rogers, Deborah D. *Ann Radcliffe: A Bio-Bibliography.* Westport, Conn.: Greenwood, 1996.

Rogers, Pat. "The Breeches Part." In *Sexuality in Eighteenth-Century Britain.* Ed. Paul-Gabriel Bouce, 244–258. Manchester: Manchester University Press, 1982.

Rose, Mary Beth. "Gender, Genre, and History: Seventeenth-Century English Women and the Art of Autobiography." In Rose, ed. *Women in the Middle Ages and the Renaissance: Literary and Historical Perspectives,* 245–278. Syracuse, N.Y.: Syracuse University Press, 1986.

Rosenberg, Seymour. "Multiplicity of Selves." In *Self and Identity: Fundamental Issues.* Ed. Richard D. Ashmore et al., 23–45. New York: Oxford University Press, 1997.

Roughead, William. *The Trial of Mary Blandy.* Edinburgh: William Hodge, 1914.

Rousseau, G. S., and Roy Porter, eds. *Sexual Underworlds of the Enlightenment.* Chapel Hill: University of North Carolina Press, 1988.

Rousseau, Jean-Jacques. *The Confessions.* Trans. J. M. Cohen. New York: Penguin, 1952.

Schweitzer, David. "Biographical Essay." In *Charles James Fox 1749–1806: A Bibliography*, ix–xxviii. New York: Greenwood, 1991.

Setzer, Sharon M. "Mary Robinson's Sylphid Self: The End of Feminine Self-Fashioning." *Philological Quarterly* 75 (fall 1996): 501–520.

———. "Romancing the Reign of Terror: Sexual Politics in Mary Robinson's *Natural Daughter.*" *Criticism* 39 (fall 1997): 531–555.

Sherlock, Philip, and Hazel Bennett. *The Story of the Jamaican People.* Kingston, Jamaica: Ian Randle, 1998.

Smith, Sidonie. *A Poetics of Women's Autobiography: Marginality and the Fictions of Self-Representation.* Bloomington: Indiana University Press, 1987.

Smith, Sidonie, and Julia Watson, eds. *De/colonizing the Subject: The Politics of Gender in Women's Autobiography.* Minneapolis: University of Minnesota Press, 1992.

———. *Women, Autobiography, Theory: A Reader.* Madison: University of Wisconsin Press, 1998.

Spacks, Patricia Meyer. *The Female Imagination.* New York: Knopf, 1975.

———. "Female Rhetorics." In Benstock, *The Private Self*, 177–191. Chapel Hill: University of North Carolina Press, 1988.

———. *Imagining a Self: Autobiography and Novel in Eighteenth-Century England.* Cambridge: Harvard University Press, 1976.

Spargo, Tamsin. "Contra-dictions: Women as Figures of Exclusion and Resistance in John Bunyan and Agnes Beaumont's Narratives." In Chedgzoy et al., *Voicing Women*, 173–184. Pittsburgh: Duquesne University Press, 1997.

Spencer, Jane. "Not Being an Historian: Women Telling Tales in Restoration and Eighteenth-Century England." In *Contexts of Pre-Novel Narrative: The European Tradition.* Ed. Roy Eriksen, 319–340. Berlin: Mouton de Gruyter, 1994.

Spengemann, William C. *The Forms of Autobiography: Episodes in the History of a Literary Genre.* New Haven, Conn.: Yale University Press, 1980.

Spivak, Gayatri. "Can the Subaltern Speak?" In *Marxism and the Interpretation of Culture.* Ed. Cary Nelson and Lawrence Grossberg, 271–315. Urbana: University of Illinois Press, 1988.

Sprinker, Michael. "Fictions of the Self: The End of Autobiography." In Olney, *Autobiography*, 321–342. Princeton: Princeton University Press, 1980.

Stallybrass, Peter, and Allon White. *The Politics and Poetics of Transgression.* Ithaca, N.Y.: Cornell University Press, 1986.

Stanley, Liz. *The Auto-biographical I: The Theory and Practice of Feminist Auto/Biography.* Manchester: Manchester University Press, 1992.

Stanton, Domna C. "Autogynography: Is the Subject Different?" In Stanton, ed., *The Female Autograph: Theory and Practice of Autobiography from the Tenth to the Twentieth Century*, 3–20. Chicago: University of Chicago Press, 1984.

Staves, Susan. *Married Women's Separate Property in England, 1660–1833.* Cambridge: Harvard University Press, 1990.

Stimpson, Catharine R. "The Female Sociograph: The Theater of Virginia Woolf's Letters." *New York Literary Forum* 12–13 (1984): 193–203.

Stone, George Winchester, Jr. "The Making of the Repertory." In Hume, *The London Theatre World,* 181–209. Carbondale: Southern Illinois University Press, 1980.

Stone, Lawrence. *Uncertain Unions and Broken Lives: Marriage and Divorce in England 1660–1857.* Oxford: Oxford University Press, 1995.

Straub, Kristina. *Sexual Suspects: Eighteenth-Century Players and Sexual Ideology.* Princeton: Princeton University Press, 1992.

Stuard, Susan Mosher. "Women's Witnessing: A New Departure." In Brown and Stuard, *Witnesses for Change,* 3–25. New Brunswick, N.J.: Rutgers University Press, 1989.

Suedfeld, Peter, and Susan Bluck. "Cognitive Concomitants of Life Events: Finding a Balance Between Generalizability and Contextualization." *Journal of Personality and Social Psychology* 71 (October 1996): 781–784.

Swaab, Peter. "Romantic Self-Representation: The Example of Mary Wollstonecraft's Letters in Sweden." In *Mortal Pages, Literary Lives: Studies in Nineteenth-Century Autobiography.* Ed. Vincent Newey and Philip Shaw, 13–30. Hants, Eng.: Scolar Press, 1996.

Swindells, Julia, ed. *The Uses of Autobiography.* London: Taylor and Francis, 1995.

Todd, Barbara J. "The Remarrying Widow: A Stereotype Reconsidered." In Prior, *Women in English Society,* 54–92. London: Methuen, 1985.

Todd, Janet. "Marketing the Self: Mary Carleton, Miss F and Susannah Gunning." *Studies on Voltaire and the Eighteenth Century* 217 (1983): 95–106.

———. *Sensibility: An Introduction.* London: Methuen, 1986.

———. *The Sign of Angelica: Women, Writing, and Fiction 1660–1800.* New York: Columbia University Press, 1989.

———, ed. *British Women Writers: A Critical Reference Guide.* New York: Continuum, 1989.

———, ed. *A Dictionary of British and American Women Writers 1660–1800.* London: Methuen, 1987.

Todorov, Tzvetan. *The Poetics of Prose.* Ithaca, N.Y.: Cornell University Press, 1977.

Trevett, Christine. "The Quaker Margaret Fell: Religion and Gender in a Seventeenth-Century Dissenting Group." Paper presented at the British Association for the Study of Religions conference, 1989.

Tuana, Nancy. *The Less Noble Sex: Scientific, Religious, and Philosophical Conceptions of Women's Nature.* Bloomington: Indiana University Press, 1993.

Turley, Hans. "'A Masculine Turn of Mind': Charlotte Charke and the Periodical Press." In Baruth, *Introducing Charlotte Charke,* 180–199. Urbana: University of Illinois Press, 1998.

Ty, Eleanor. "Engendering a Female Subject: Mary Robinson's (Re)Presentations of the Self." *English Studies in Canada* 21 (December 1995): 407–431.

———. "Writing as a Daughter: Autobiography in Wollstonecraft's Travelogue." In Kadar, *Essays on Life Writing*, 61–77. Toronto: University of Toronto Press, 1992.

Vickery, Amanda. *The Gentleman's Daughter: Women's Lives in Georgian England*. New Haven, Conn.: Yale University Press, 1998.

Walker, James W. St. G. *The Black Loyalists: The Search for a Promised Land in Nova Scotia and Sierra Leone 1783–1870*. New York: Africana–Holmes & Meier, 1976.

Walker, Nancy. *A Disobedient Writer: Women and Narrative Tradition*. Austin: University of Texas Press, 1995.

Walker, Roger M. "A Rediscovered Seventeenth-Century Literary Friendship: Sir Richard Fanshawe and Dom Francisco Manuel de Melo." *Seventeenth Century* 7 (spring 1992): 15–26.

Wall, Cynthia. "Editing Desire: Pope's Correspondence with (and without) Lady Mary." *Philological Quarterly* 71 (spring 1992): 221–237.

Wanko, Cheryl. "The Eighteenth-Century Actress and the Construction of Gender: Lavinia Fenton and Charlotte Charke." *Eighteenth-Century Life* 18 (May 1994): 75–90.

Welsh, Alexander. *Strong Representations: Narrative and Circumstantial Evidence in England*. Baltimore: Johns Hopkins University Press, 1994.

White, Hayden. "The Value of Narrativity in the Representation of Reality." In Mitchell, *On Narrative*, 1–23. Chicago: University of Chicago Press, 1981.

Wilcox, Catherine M. *Theology and Women's Ministry in Seventeenth-Century English Quakerism: Handmaids of the Lord*. Lewiston, N.Y.: Edwin Mellen, 1995.

Wills, Margaret. *Gibside and the Bowes Family*. Newcastle, Eng.: Society of Antiquaries of Newcastle upon Tyne, 1995.

Winston, Elizabeth. "The Autobiographer and Her Readers." In Jelinek, *Women's Autobiography*, 91–111. Bloomington: Indiana University Press, 1980.

Wiseman, Susan. "Read Within: Gender, Cultural Difference and Quaker Women's Travel Narratives." In Chedgzoy et al., *Voicing Women*, 153–172. Pittsburgh: Duquesne University Press, 1997.

———. "Unsilent Instruments and the Devil's Cushions: Authority in Seventeenth-Century Women's Prophetic Discourse." In *New Feminist Discourses: Critical Essays on Theories and Texts*. Ed. Isobel Armstrong, 176–196. London: Routledge, 1992.

Wright, Philip, ed. *Lady Nugent's Journal of Her Residence in Jamaica from 1801 to 1805*. Kingston: Institute of Jamaica, 1966.

Yaeger, Patricia. *Honey-mad Women: Emancipatory Strategies in Women's Writing*. New York: Columbia University Press, 1988.

Yeazell, Ruth Bernard. "Public Baths and Private Harems: Lady Mary Wortley Montagu and the Origins of Ingres's *Bain Turc*." *Yale Journal of Criticism* 7 (spring 1994): 111–138.